**Hilde F. Johnson** was the Specia̶...
General and Head of the United N̶...
South Sudan (2011–14). She has si̶...
Secretary General's High-Level Indep̶........ ̶...̶. ̶... Peace Operations
and as Senior Visiting Fellow at the Norwegian Institute for International
Affairs (NUPI). From 2007–11 Hilde F. Johnson was Deputy Executive
Director of UNICEF, where she was in charge of the organization's
humanitarian operations and crisis response. As Minister for International
Development of Norway during the period 1997–2005 Hilde F. Johnson
was a key player in brokering the Comprehensive Peace Agreement
(CPA) for Sudan in 2005. She is the author of *Waging Peace in Sudan:
The Inside Story of the Negotiations That Ended Africa's Longest Civil War.*

'This devastating insider account by the former UN Special Representative in South Sudan of the corruption and bad governance that have
brought the world's newest state to its knees provides a vital service not
only to the truth, but to the people of South Sudan.' – **Christopher
Clapham, Centre of African Studies, University of Cambridge**

'From the West, we observe countries of civil war, famine, and institutional degradation with a bewildered, hopeless eye. Hilde F. Johnson
takes us inside one of the world's sketchiest countries. South Sudan. Its
challenges, collapses, proxy interventions, and the courage of its hope.
She's been at the centre of it, and has candidly written an eye-opening
exploration of its history, political manoeuvring, and its brave people's
journey forward.' – **Sean Penn**

'In 2011 South Sudan became the world's newest nation. I was among
those who celebrated with the people who had endured and lost so
much. It was a jubilant time. But instead of the longed for peace and
justice, there came mayhem; massacres and atrocities of the worst kind.
How could the leaders, liberators of South Sudan betray themselves and
their people? Hilde F. Johnson was there. In *South Sudan: The Untold
Story*, she gives us an inside account. With insight and uncommon
objectivity, she details the corruption and greed for power that brought
this hope-filled, newborn nation into catastrophe. This is an invaluable,
outstanding book.' – **Mia Farrow**

'Those engaged with Sudan and South Sudan for decades are all asking fundamental questions about how the world's youngest nation went from celebrating its freedom in 2011 to plunging into the abyss three years later. Hilde F. Johnson's in-depth analysis leaves no stone unturned in her search for answers in this excellent and well-researched book. *South Sudan: The Untold Story* tells it all – with sharp observation, honesty and uncompromising objectivity. It is a must read for anyone interested in Africa and the fate of South Sudan, as it stands on the brink of state implosion.' – **John Prendergast**

'Hilde F. Johnson was appointed head of the United Nations Mission to South Sudan following that country's independence in 2011. She brought more experience in Sudanese and South Sundanese affairs to that job than most diplomats and NGOs who came to the country following the signing of the Comprehensive Peace Agreement that ended Sudan's second civil war in 2005. An academic, a humanitarian, a former Norwegian government minister, and a diplomat involved in the CPA negotiations, she was well acquainted with the outstanding issues of the peace agreement and the Sudanese and South Sundanese personalities involved. Her tenure as head of UNMISS was not without controversy, as she records here. But this is more than an autobiographical memoir. It is a sharp analysis of South Sudan's launch into nationhood, based on her insider's knowledge as an active participant, and buttressed by extensive independent reporting by academics, journalists and NGOs. She got to know well many of the prominent personalities in South Sudan's on-going political crisis, and she has left perceptive descriptions of the competent and incompetent, the well intentioned who lacked the will to bring about necessary reforms, and the totally self-serving chancers whose main goal in independence was self-enrichment. The challenges she faced as head of mission were not all generated by South Sudanese. She also had to contend with a remote UN bureaucracy, slow to respond to new emergencies, as well as self-publishing and uncooperative NGOs. For anyone involved in South Sudan now who wants to learn lessons from the past failures in order to avoid them, this book is essential reading.' – **Douglas H. Johnson, Fellow of the Rift Valley Institute and author of *South Sudan: A New History for a New Nation***

# SOUTH SUDAN
## THE UNTOLD STORY
### From Independence to Civil War

## HILDE F. JOHNSON

I.B. TAURIS

LONDON·NEW YORK

*To the suffering South Sudanese people, for your resilience,
endurance and perseverance, against all odds.*

*You did not deserve this.*

New paperback edition published in 2018 by
I.B.Tauris & Co. Ltd
London • New York
www.ibtauris.com

First published in hardback in 2016 by I.B.Tauris & Co. Ltd

ISBN:    978 1 78831 378 0
eISBN:   978 1 78672 005 4
ePDF:    978 1 78673 005 3

A full CIP record for this book is available from the British Library
A full CIP record is available from the Library of Congress

Library of Congress Catalog Card Number: available

Typeset by Fakenham Prepress Solutions, Fakenham, Norfolk NR21 8NN
Printed and bound in Sweden by ScandBook AB

# CONTENTS

MAPS     vi

FOREWORD by Desmond Tutu, Archbishop Emeritus     xi

PREFACE     xiii

ABBREVIATIONS     xix

PROLOGUE     xxi

1     A Dream Comes True     1

2     A Country without a State     16

3     An Incomplete Divorce     57

4     Jonglei: The UN – Between a Rock and a Hard Place     97

5     The Leadership     145

6     The Nightmare     179

7     The Heart of the Matter: Security     224

8     Waging Peace in South Sudan     263

EPILOGUE     287

APPENDIX 1     304

NOTES     306

BIBLIOGRAPHY     362

INDEX     368

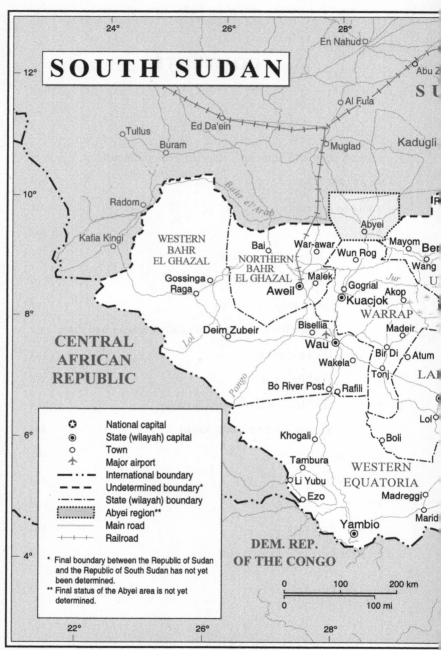

The boundaries and names shown and the designations used on this map do not imply official endorsement or acceptance by the United Nations.

Department of Field Support
Cartographic Section

# JONGLEI STATE

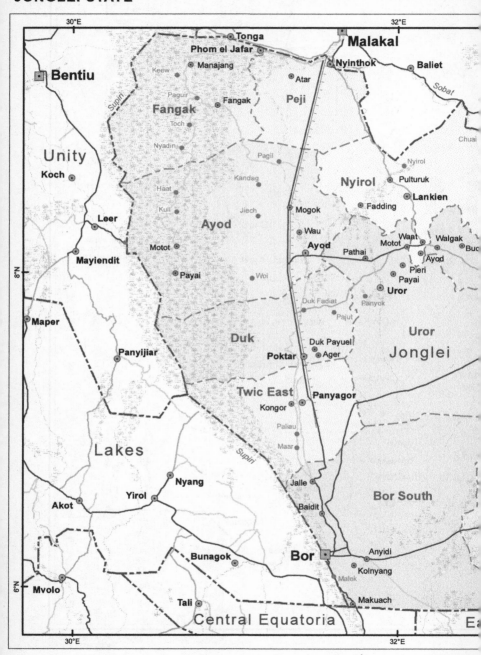

# Sudan–South Sudan

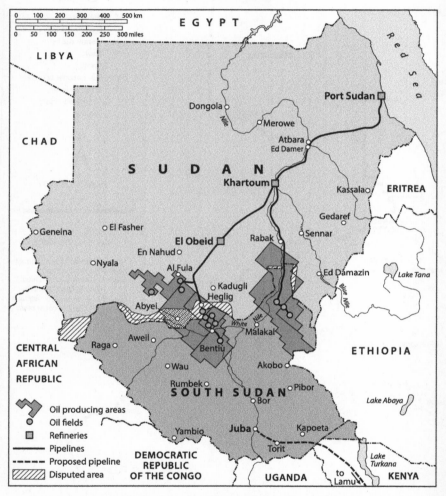

The final boundary between the Republic of Sudan and the Republic of South Sudan and the final status of Abyei have not yet been determined. The illustrated disputed areas are only reflected *indicatively* and not precisely.

# FOREWORD

Our South Sudanese brothers and sisters spent decades fighting for freedom. In South Africa, we joined hands with them. Our apartheid was not very different from theirs. They were exploited, subjected to slavery, abuse and discrimination, not only on racial, but also on religious grounds. Their oppression was systematic and institutionalized. Their struggle lasted almost 50 years. Indeed, for the South Sudanese – as for us in South Africa – the biblical stories of Moses, who spent 40 years in the wilderness before reaching the promised land, gave hope.

And in 2005, with the signing of the Comprehensive Peace Agreement, peace was achieved; the promised land was in sight. God had heard the suffering of his people. Chairman John Garang was their Moses; Salva Kiir their Joshua, taking over after his brother and leader was killed in a helicopter crash in July the same year.

The next six years were difficult, but in the end – the referendum took place, and almost every South Sudanese voted for independence. They wanted liberation, running their own country themselves. With independence in July 2011, it was time for delivery. All South Sudanese thought they would finally enjoy the fruits of freedom. Expectations were sky high.

We expected a lot, too. I went to Juba myself to see what could be done to support the world's youngest nation, born out of freedom from oppression. Already at this time, we were concerned about the way the country's affairs were managed, the lack of delivery of services to the people, and the high levels of corruption. I reminded the leadership of what was expected of them.

Indeed, our own Nelson Mandela once said: '*For to be free is not merely to cast off one's chains, but to live in a way that respects and enhances the freedom of others.*' Instead, we watched with horror how the political crisis escalated, leading to violence which spun out of control and took an ethnic turn, ending up in an atrocious and senseless civil war. The atrocities that were committed were beyond comprehension, this time not by their oppressors, but committed by South Sudanese against their own people. All of us wondered how this could happen?

In this book Hilde F. Johnson provides many of the answers. She had long-standing relations with the SPLM and the Southern Sudanese struggle. With her leading role in South Sudan as the United Nations Secretary-General's Special Representative, she also had first-hand knowledge of the developments in the country during the period 2011–14. This book provides her inside account of what happened, with unique insights – both into some of the root causes of the conflict, the dynamics in the leadership and the implosion of key South Sudanese institutions. She also makes it clear that the international community could have done more to prevent the latter.

As Hilde points out, South Sudan now needs to be saved, not only from fighting, but also from failing. While structural factors are important, leadership will remain most critical. The South Sudanese leaders finally signed a peace agreement and agreed on a way forward. They also agreed to create a Commission for Truth, Reconciliation and Healing. It is vital that a genuine reconciliation process now is taken forward, both between victims and perpetrators, collectively and individually, and even more importantly, within the South Sudanese leadership itself. This book confirms what I always have been advocating: without confronting the truth about the past, openly and honestly, without reconciliation, healing and accountability, it will not be possible to build a new future. This is more true for the South Sudanese leadership than almost anywhere else. They now have to change their ways.

A new beginning is what the world's youngest country really needs. For all South Sudanese finally to taste the fruits of freedom, this is imperative. In the midst of all the darkness, believing in this change is now our hope.

God Bless You.

**Archbishop Emeritus Desmond Tutu**
Cape Town, South Africa

# PREFACE

South Sudan, the world's youngest country, has been at war since December 2013. As the UN Secretary-General's Special Representative in South Sudan from its inception in 2011 to 2014, I had the privilege of leading the UN's support for the country during its first years of independence. I witnessed firsthand how the seeds of conflict were sown and how legacies of liberation inhibited the many attempts to prevent it.

I had engaged with Sudan and Southern Sudan for almost 15 years when I left for my new position in Juba. As Minister of International Development of Norway, I had been a key player in the negotiations that resulted in the signing of the Comprehensive Peace Agreement (CPA) for Sudan between the Sudan People's Liberation Movement and Army (SPLM/A) and the Government of Sudan in 2005. The CPA ended the almost 50-year-long civil war.

During the following six-year interim period, in leading positions in the African Development Bank and UNICEF, I was regularly in Sudan, including Darfur and Southern Sudan, and engaged with the country's various leaders. The UN's peacekeeping mission in Sudan, UNMIS, supported the country's first general elections in 2010 and the referendum in January 2011. At this time, I released my book on the CPA, *Waging Peace in Sudan: the Inside Story of the Negotiations that Ended Africa's Longest Civil War*.[1] Almost every Southern Sudanese voted in favour of secession. Half a year later, South Sudan's independence was a fact. At the same time, I took up the position as Special Representative of the new and independent country.

Those of us who knew the SPLM and Southern Sudan well were aware that it would not be smooth sailing; we would be in for tough times. But it ended up being much worse than anyone expected. The nightmare that started in December 2013 engulfed the world's youngest country in a civil war and shattered the dreams of millions of South Sudanese. The speed, scale and gravity of the violence shocked everyone, including the South Sudanese leaders themselves. Atrocities on a massive scale were committed by both sides, driving a brutal civil war. This book tries to answer a simple, but complicated question: Why?

It was incumbent upon me to understand how the country's liberators could let this happen. After leaving South Sudan, having lived through the period of most intense fighting, I spent a year trying to understand more of the reasons. My mission would not be completed until I had written this untold story.

This book covers the period from my arrival in South Sudan as Special Representative of the Secretary General (SRSG) in July 2011, until the end of my three-year tenure in July 2014. By the time the first edition was published, a peace agreement had been signed[2] and a transitional government was about to be formed. The two antagonists, President Salva Kiir and First Vice President Riek Machar would be at the helm.

Only 100 days after the formation of the new government,[3] South Sudan was plunged into another devastating crisis. On its fifth birthday, the world's youngest country was again embroiled in conflict. Soon stories of targeted ethnic violence flourished; dead bodies were once more being buried in mass graves in the country's capital, Juba. In the civil war that ensued, thousands more were killed.

Since July 2016, the conflict has escalated, with the emergence of more armed groups and militia, covering almost the whole country. The impact on innocent civilians has been even more calamitous, forcing record numbers to flee their homes. More than 2 million South Sudanese are now refugees in other countries and close to 2 million are internally displaced. The UN estimates that there are 7 million people in need of humanitarian assistance.[4] Hence, the vast majority of the population are severely impacted by the war and in need, their social fabric torn apart.

At the same time, the country's economy has hit rock bottom. Soldiers and public servants have not received salaries in months. Several international reports have revealed more details of massive corruption by the elites of the country. But now there is nothing more to loot and no patronage money to retain loyalty of neither military nor civilian leaders.

The ensuing fragmentation witnessed on the battlefield is also happening on the political side, where ethnic politics have proliferated, amplified by a President whose survival now relies entirely on his own narrow ethnic base and loyalists in the army. However, support is eroding – with once strong allies having turned against the head of state. Former Chief of General Staff of the SPLA, Paul Malong is among them, an indication of the growing dissent within the President's own constituency and security apparatus. At the same time, the position of Salva Kiir's arch enemy, Riek Machar, is also weakened, having been held in confinement in a house in South Africa for almost two years. Another complicating factor is the increasing divisions in the region and beyond, making a unified voice on South Sudan more difficult.

The warring parties are once again convening, under the region's auspices, at the negotiating table in Addis Ababa.[5] The aim is to revitalize the 2015 agreement and at the same time adapt its terms to new circumstances, including all the new armed groups and political opposition fora. The term of Salva Kiir Mayardit's presidency ends on 17 August 2018.[6] By that time agreement on the way forward for South Sudan has to be reached. Time is short.

With recent events, the SPLM has been compromised, the aspirations from 2005 and 2011 destroyed. However, the movement may still be able to reinvent itself and once again become a unifying force in an increasingly fragmented country. At the end of this book I indicate that the current leadership across all factions of the SPLM is facing its greatest ever test. From the events of the past two years, it is clear that they failed the test, failed the struggle, failed their people, and failed their country. Now a revitalized peace agreement may be on the way. This time the liberators *must* pass the test. It will be the very last chance they have to prevent their country not only from fighting, but from failing, and much worse – and ever more likely – from falling apart.

## Methodology

In the research for this book, I have made use of much information gathered prior to – and during – the December 2013 crisis, mostly in the form of personal notes. Other sources include eyewitness accounts and conversations in South Sudan and the region during the same period. I also conducted some 50 interviews, mostly with SPLM leaders on all sides of the conflict, as well as regional leaders and other stakeholders. Only information I have corroborated independently was used in this book. In the few instances where I refer to inadequately verified accounts, I refer to them as 'allegations', 'claimed' or 'reported', or specify that the information has not been verified.

This book could not have been written without the help of many people in South Sudan and elsewhere. Particular gratitude is extended to SPLM-leaders, including members of the SPLM Political Bureau, representing all factions, the government, the SPLM/A-In Opposition and the Former Detainees (FDs) or the G10. They all gave generously of their time to be interviewed and helped me understand more. Other regional leaders and international experts and interlocutors also provided valuable advice and assistance, and in some cases vital information.

The vast majority of both South Sudanese and foreign interlocutors preferred not to be named. The conflict was raging in South Sudan at the time of research, and they did not want to be exposed. Following the leakage of the draft report of the African Union Commission of Inquiry in 2014, quoting a number of individuals without their consent, concerns related to anonymity increased further. Exposure of this nature can put people's lives at risk. For security reasons, therefore, I have not been able to provide a list of names of those interviewed for this book. Reference is therefore made to the interview number and date. I have, nevertheless, provided a list of SPLM-leaders during the period 2011 to 2014, whether in the SPLM Political Bureau or in ministerial positions during the period (Appendix 1). Many of those interviewed, but not all, are among the leaders listed. All interviews are on the files of the author. In cases that can imply possible criminal responsibility, I have retained anonymity.

As this account tells the story of South Sudan, the terms Southern Sudan and Southern Sudanese are used for the period prior to independence. In 2011, the Republic of South Sudan was born, and hence, the terms South Sudan and South Sudanese are applied for the independent country and its people. As regards the maps, the border between Sudan and South Sudan is still disputed and has not yet been demarcated. The maps in this book have been included without prejudice to the final border demarcation, reflected in a disclaimer on maps covering the border area.

It is often said that the first casualty of war is truth. There will always be different versions and interpretations of what unfolded. This book is not the authoritative history of this period in South Sudan, and the views and assessments expressed in this book do not necessarily reflect those of the UN. This version of the story of South Sudan's first three years of independence is therefore fully and solely my own.

## Acknowledgements

There are many people who deserve special thanks for helping me making this book a reality and whose assistance were invaluable during my tenure. I have already mentioned my South Sudanese interlocutors in the SPLM, across all factions, as appreciated above. I would also like to put on record my personal appreciation for the dedication and commitment of UN military, police and civilian personnel in the United Nations Mission to South Sudan (UNMISS) and UN Agencies, Funds and Programmes, NGOs, faith leaders and civil society organizations that I had the honour to work with from 2011 to 2014, and especially those who served in the most remote and hardship duty stations in the country. I take this opportunity to acknowledge those UN peacekeepers and civilian personnel who died in the line of duty and to reiterate my most profound gratitude for their commitment to the cause of peace in South Sudan.

Particular thanks are owed to my two Deputy SRSGs, Rai Zenenga and Toby Lanzer, and all the members of my Senior Management in UNMISS, with whom I worked so closely during trying times. My immediate team deserve special thanks for their patience, competence and tenacity, and for putting up with me at all times. Very special appreciation goes to Peter Mutua, who provided invaluable counsel at critical junctures throughout my time in South Sudan. The list of others is too long, but Jane Kebambazi, Dawn Peebles, Ignacio Saez-Benito and Sandi Arnold in Juba, and Naresh Perinpanayagam at headquarters in New York deserve heartfelt thanks. In the Executive Office of the Secretary General, the dedication and support of Political Director Andrew Gilmour has been indispensable throughout my tenure and beyond.

In trying to get to the bottom of what happened, collaboration with Øystein Rolandsen, Senior Researcher at PRIO, the Norwegian Peace Research Institute, has been valuable, both concerning interviews with key interlocutors and analysis. While writing this book, I have also benefited from the advice of, inter-alia, Luka Biong Deng, Jok Madut Jok, Richard Burton Rands, Brian da Silva, Eirin Mobekk, Petter Lindquist, and others who preferred not to be named. In the last phase, Dr Martin Daly provided editorial assistance.

Both in the research phase as well as the development of the manuscript, I have benefited from the hospitality of friends in East Africa who provided the best possible working environment. Particular thanks to Stephan Meves, Stein Erik Horjen and Victor Rønneberg and families, Hanne Marie Kaarstad and Tony Kuijlen.

I owe my special thanks to the Secretary General of the UN, Ban Ki Moon, who appointed me as his Special Representative, and who also backed me throughout my tenure. His support during the crisis of December 2013 to July 2014 was particularly valuable. My most sincere appreciation also to the United Nations who gave permission to publish this book. Finally, without financial assistance from Fritt Ord, this book would not have been possible.

While I sincerely thank all of these friends, advisers and institutions for their unstinting advice and help, I must of course take full responsibility for any slips or errors that remain.

# ABBREVIATIONS

| | |
|---|---|
| ANC | African National Congress |
| AU | African Union |
| AUHIP | African Union High Level Panel |
| CBTF | Capacity Building Trust Fund |
| CCM | Chama Cha Mapinduzi-Tanzania |
| CMC | Crisis Management Committee |
| CPA | Comprehensive Peace Agreement |
| DDR | Disarmament, Demobilization and Reintegration |
| DYY | David Yau Yau |
| ECHO | European Commission Humanitarian Aid Office |
| FTA | Financial Transfer Arrangements |
| GoSS | Government of Southern Sudan |
| GRSS | Government of the Republic of South Sudan |
| IDP | Internally Displaced People |
| IFI | International Financial Institution |
| IGAD | Intergovernmental Authority on Development |
| IMF | International Monetary Fund |
| JEM | Justice and Equality Movement |
| JIF | Joint Integrated Forces |
| JIU | Joint Integrated Units |
| JMEC | Joint Monitoring Evaluation Commission |
| JMM/JMC | Joint Monitoring Mission/Joint Military Commission |
| JPSC | Joint Political and Security Committee |
| MDTF | Multilateral Donor Trust Fund |
| MOFEP | Ministry of Finance and Economic Planning |
| MSF | Doctors Without Borders (Médecins Sans Frontières) |
| NCP | National Congress Party |
| NDI | National Democratic Institute |
| NGO | non-governmental organization |
| NISS | National Intelligence Security Services |

| | |
|---|---|
| NLC | National Liberation Council |
| ODI | Overseas Development Institute |
| RPG | rocket-propelled grenade |
| SAF | Sudanese Armed Forces |
| SDBZ | Safe Demilitarized Border Zone |
| SDG | Sudanese pound(s) |
| SOFA | Status of Forces Agreement |
| SPDF | Sudan People's Defense Forces/Democratic Front |
| SPLM/A | Sudan People's Liberation Movement/Army |
| SPLM/DC | Sudan People's Liberation Movement/Democratic Change |
| SPLM/A (IO); SPLM/A I-O | Sudan People's Liberation Movement/Army Opposition |
| SPLM/North | Sudan People's Liberation Movement/North |
| SPLM/N (SRF) | Sudan People's Liberation Movement/North (Sudan Front) |
| SRSG | Special Representative of the Secretary General |
| SSDF | South Sudan Defence Forces |
| SSDM/A | South Sudan Democratic Movement/Army |
| SSDM/A Cobra Faction | South Sudan Democratic Movement/Army (Cobra Faction) |
| SSLM/A | South Sudan Liberation Movement/Army |
| SSNPS | South Sudan National Police Service |
| SSPS | Southern Sudan Police Service |
| UK | United Kingdom |
| UN | United Nations |
| UNDP | United Nations Development Programme |
| UNICEF | United Nations Children's Fund |
| UNISFA | United Nations Interim Security Force for Abyei |
| UNMIS | United Nations Mission in Sudan |
| UNMISS | United Nations Mission in South Sudan |
| UNODC | United Nations Office on Drugs and Crime |
| UNPOL | United Nations Police |
| UPDF | Ugandan People's Defense Force |
| US/USA | United States of America |
| USD | United States Dollar(s) |
| UNHCR | Office of the United Nations High Commissioner for Refugees |

# PROLOGUE

[O]ur detractors have already written us off, even before the proclamation of our independence. They say we will slip in to civil war as soon as our flag is hoisted. They justify that by arguing that we are incapable of resolving our problems through dialogue. They charge that we are quick to revert to violence. They claim that our concept of democracy and freedom is faulty. It is incumbent upon us to prove them all wrong!

This was Salva Kiir Mayardit, president of South Sudan, on Independence Day, 9 July 2011.

Two years later the detractors were proven right. Competition for political power had turned violent, and would eventually shake the foundations of the new Republic of South Sudan. Before its third birthday, the dream of independence and freedom had turned into a nightmare. The liberators risked destroying the very country they had spent decades fighting for.

How could this happen?

South Sudan's journey to nationhood had been characterized not only by decades of liberation war, colonial and Sudanese violence against Southern communities, and local conflict, but also by the resilience of its people. They had faced destruction of their livelihood and societies, famine, displacement, and resort to foreign countries. But they had also sustained the hope that this suffering in the end would be rewarded with independence.

As minister of international development for Norway, I was deeply involved in the negotiations that led to the Comprehensive Peace Agreement (CPA) in 2005 between the Government of Sudan and the Sudan People's Liberation Movement/Army (SPLM/A). After almost five decades Africa's longest civil war had ended. The CPA did not grant the Southerners independence; it guaranteed self-determination. The parties were giving unity a chance, over an interim period of six years, after which Southern Sudan would have the right to hold a referendum on its own future. In January 2011, an overwhelming majority chose independence.

After the CPA was signed in 2005, the United Nations was tasked with supporting its implementation. Southern Sudan, for its part, had to go through at least three internal changes, each extremely demanding. Transition from war to peace, for people who had known little but war, was a major shift. Transition from liberation struggle to government was another. Third was the complex transition to independence. All three transitions were still under way on Independence Day 2011, when I took the helm as Special Representative of the UN Secretary-General (SRSG) and head of its mission in South Sudan (UNMISS).

South Sudan separated from Sudan in 2011 before all the terms of the 'divorce' had been reached. Relations between the neighbours were expected to be difficult, but few foretold bombing raids hitting refugee camps, occupation of oil fields and a complete shutdown of oil production in South Sudan, which in turn affected all efforts of state-building and peace-building.

At the same time, South Sudan had major internal security problems. The country's largest state, Jonglei, was mired in a cycle of communal violence in which thousands of civilians had been killed. The country's hallmark ethnic diversity posed a challenge to building national identity. Jonglei was a microcosm testing the country's leadership and us in the UN.

The transition from liberation struggle to government was predictably difficult. The country was awash with weapons, mostly in civilian hands. Lack of commitment prevented necessary reform. Separating the liberation movement from the SPLA and turning the Movement into a political party and the liberation force into a national army – stalled.

The liberators failed to use the interim CPA period to strengthen the foundations on which the country could be built, and ignored warnings against corruption and mismanagement. Following this 'liberation curse', South Sudan was soon afflicted by the 'oil curse'. Oil revenue became an irresistible temptation for cadres who had spent most of their lives in the bush. Resources lubricated patronage networks, while significant amounts were simply syphoned to foreign bank accounts.

State institutions, including the Army, were insufficiently developed to sustain the pressure of an escalating political crisis.

That violence could occur was clear to many of us, and serious efforts were made to prevent it. The international community, myself included, could still have done more. But the speed, scale and gravity of the December 2013 violence shocked everyone, including South Sudanese leaders themselves. They played with fire, and allowed a power struggle to put everything they had fought for at risk. That tensions bursting to the surface had deeper roots and were influenced by other factors is clear, but responsibility for what happened rests with the leaders, across factions.

The civil war that followed had devastating consequences. Millions were affected. The atrocities committed were beyond comprehension, the intransigence of the leaders appalling. It was as if people no longer mattered. The social fabric of South Sudan was tearing apart. The nation-building project, which was extremely hard to begin with, would now be more difficult than ever. It was set back decades.

This book covers the period from my arrival until the end of my tenure in July 2014. The Epilogue captures recent developments and reflections on the way forward for South Sudan; it shows that there is not much reason for optimism. But there is still a glimmer of hope.

Prior to my departure I paid a farewell visit to Malakal and met tens of thousands of displaced who had sought refuge in the UNMISS compound after December 2013. A small group of prayer women came forward to greet me, a life of pain and suffering written over their faces. The oldest of them offered the most precious gift, her own hymn book, torn at the seams and with her own personal notes. As we embraced I felt an immense gratitude. It was I who needed to thank them for allowing me to serve. It was the South Sudanese people who now gave reason for hope, with their resilience and ability to persevere against all odds.

This book is the story of the betrayal of trust of the liberators against them and themselves. It is dedicated to the South Sudanese people. I hope it will provide some answers to their questions. I hope it will also help pave the way for change, for a new start for South Sudan, to finally become a nation where their dreams can be fulfilled.

# 1

◆

# A DREAM COMES TRUE

'We have waited for 56 years for this day. It is a dream that has come true!'[1] On 9 July 2011, six months after Southern Sudanese had voted overwhelmingly for independence, Salva Kiir Mayardit, chairman of the SPLM and president of the new Republic, proclaimed that freedom had come. Amid the cheering and dancing of at least 100,000 people at the John Garang Mausoleum and in the presence of heads of state and government from around the world, freedom songs brought tears to the eyes of almost everyone present. 'SPLM Woyee', a famous cheer of the struggle,[2] resounded from the masses.

One celebrant was an old Shilluk chief from a village in Upper Nile State. He wore traditional pink shawl, long bead necklaces and ankle chimes; his sandals seemed to have been marching in the bush for decades. Beneath his wide brimmed straw hat he wore something more striking: huge pink Dolly Parton-style sunglasses. He looked at me and said:

> I never thought this day would ever come. I have been active in the struggle ever since the British left. We have been fighting ever since. And now this! I have to pinch my arm.

Salva Kiir was likewise moved:

> From today on, we shall have no excuses or scapegoats to blame. It is our responsibility to protect ourselves, our land and our resources [...] While the pillars of a house are important,

its foundation is even more critical. We must build a strong foundation for our new nation.

This was also the first day on the job for me as SRSG and Head of UNMISS, which came into existence that day, a sign of the international community's commitment to the new country. South Sudan was welcomed into the United Nations as its 193rd member in record time, and other regional organizations followed suit.

South Sudanese had fought for decades for independence.

## The struggle[3]

Many dated the struggle back to developments in the nineteenth century, when Sudanese merchants (including officials of the Egyptian regime) were prominent among those involved in the slave trade that devastated the South. The rule of the Mahdiyya (1881–98) made conditions worse, as it raided and conquered. Under the ensuing Anglo-Egyptian regime the South was 'pacified' and neglected, with minimal investment in infrastructure and services. Christian missionaries helped, but their work was not on a scale that reached the population at large.

A conference in Juba in 1947 is often referred to as sealing the South's fate; London's imperial interests in Egypt and elsewhere trumped local British officials' concern for Southern Sudanese. Although not documented, Southerners insist that a promise of self-determination was made after World War II by the departing colonial rulers, Britain and Egypt, a commitment they claim was later broken by the Northern Sudanese in connivance with Egypt:

> The roots of the war run deep. After imperial conquests in the nineteenth century, the peripheries of Sudan were ruled by means of administrative and militarized tribalism, and were grossly underdeveloped; the people of the southern periphery, in particular, were regarded as second-class citizens, and at worst as commodities.[4]

A mutiny by Southern soldiers in August 1955, and the widespread killing of Northerners that ensued in the South, is often regarded as the beginning of open hostilities. With the coming of Sudan's independence in 1956, the reins of power passed to a tiny Arab Muslim elite in Khartoum. During the period 1956–62, fighting in the South was sporadic; Southern politicians had failed to win the federal constitution that many thought was the only way to protect Southern rights. After a military coup in 1958, efforts to propagate Islam and spread the use of Arabic were intensified, further alienating the small Southern educated elite, many of whom were Christians. By the early 1960s armed resistance had escalated to the level of civil war.

From the early 1950s 'federalism' had already become a core demand for many educated Southerners and a main point of contention between North and South.[5] After the 1964 overthrow of the military regime in Khartoum, a 'round-table' conference was convened. It failed to bring about a rapprochement because representatives of Northern parties would consider only limited self-rule in the South. A split was now revealed between Southerners calling for federalism and those demanding self-determination. During the period 1966–9 the war was fought with increasing intensity.

Another military junta, under Col Jafar Mohamed Nimeiri, took power in Khartoum in 1969. At about the same time leadership of the resistance movement, the Anya-Nya, consolidated under the ex-army officer Joseph Lagu. Secret contacts eventually led to formal negotiations and in 1971 peace talks took place under the auspices of the All Africa Council of Churches and Ethiopia. A Southern lawyer, Abel Alier, represented Nimeiri in negotiations in Addis Ababa. The demand for secession was shelved; a limited form of self-rule was accepted. Splits within the Anya-Nya were papered over to establish the autonomous Regional Government. Competition within it was fierce, however, with Abel Alier and Joseph Lagu soon becoming bitter rivals.

Important terms of the Agreement were never honoured. Nimeiri could not resist the temptation to interfere, helped by internal tensions among Southern politicians. Promised economic development did not take place. Advantage was eventually taken of rivalries within the South to 're-divide' the region into the old provincial units, the better to control them all from Khartoum. These divisions continue to play into heated discussions about federalism today.

Although successive regimes in Khartoum differed in degree, the common denominator was the exclusion of Southern Sudanese from most influential roles in the civil service, the private sector and in public life overall. The lack of investment in South Sudan remained systematic, whether in infrastructure or services to the people.

Khartoum governments also, with varying intensity, used religion to discriminate. While most Southern Sudanese were either Christians or practised their traditional religion, the Northern part of the country was Muslim. Islam was the country's official religion, and several prominent movements aimed to Islamize the whole country and Arabicize the South. The balance was finally tipped when Nimeiri, as a sop to growing opposition from the Northern religious right, declared *Sharia* the law of the land – including in the South.

This happened despite Southern Sudan's rich religious and ethnic diversity. The region had multiple ethnicities, dominated by pastoralist and semi-pastoralist communities in its northern, eastern and western regions, and more traditional subsistence farming communities in the south. The largest ethnic community was by far the Dinka, divided by sub-groups, with the Nuer ranking second. Other communities, such as the Zande, the Bari and the Shilluk were much smaller. In total, there were 64 ethnic groups in Southern Sudan.

## The freedom fighters – the SPLM/A

The Addis Ababa Peace Agreement of 1972 was, in many Southerners' opinion, too weak, granting self-government but not self-determination. Furthermore, it was a sketchy document with no international guarantors or mechanisms to ensure implementation. These flaws led to its collapse, and contributed to resumption of civil war. When Commander John Garang de Mabior was sent to suppress the so-called Bor Mutiny in 1983, little did the authorities know he had been engaged in planning it. With other defectors he headed for Ethiopia. Together they formed the Sudan People's Liberation Movement and Army (SPLM/A).

Deliberations on its Manifesto revealed difficulty in uniting the Movement's leadership. Two power centres emerged, which eventually resorted to armed conflict, first primarily in the Upper Nile region. One comprised veterans of the first civil war who had been absorbed into the Sudanese Army and became members of an underground military syndicate; the most prominent were John Garang and Salva Kiir, Kerubino Kuanyin and William Nyuon. The second centre comprised veterans who had become politicians after 1972. After two prominent commanders died, this group negotiated a deal with Khartoum, making it easier for the regime to exploit divisions.

Within the SPLM/A, John Garang pursued his vision of justice and equality for all Sudanese. Although often accused of separatism, 'Dr John', as he was popularly known, advocated a 'New Sudan', in which marginalized peoples would have a rightful share in governing a multi-religious and multi-ethnic country, respecting diversity rather than privileging an elite.

At the same time, Southerners' right to self-determination became a cornerstone in his thinking. The South should, through a referendum, decide whether to remain part of a united Sudan or be independent. Areas under SPLM/A control were therefore experimentally a nucleus of the 'New Sudan'. In this way, Garang aimed to reconcile those demanding independence immediately and those advocating justice for all marginalized Sudanese.

The second civil war differed from the first. It was much deadlier, had a greater impact on civilians, and engulfed a larger territory. Neighbouring countries were more actively involved. After Nimeiri was overthrown in 1985, Khartoum relied on local militias to attack the SPLA and harass civilians. In 1988, sections of the rebel Anya-Nya II, largely Nuer from Upper Nile, were absorbed into the SPLA, whose main factions thereafter consisted of Dinka from the Bahr el Ghazal, Dinka on the east bank of the Nile and a constellation of Nuer groups. Backed into a corner by military failure and a collapsing national economy, the Khartoum government was on the verge of signing a preliminary peace deal with the SPLM/A when it was overthrown by a military coup in 1989.

The new regime under Omar Hasan Ahmad al-Bashir and the spiritual guidance of Hasan al-Turabi adopted a radical Islamist policy. Terrorizing domestic opponents and associating with the world's most notorious regimes and non-state groups, the government acquired pariah status. From a struggle for pre-eminence the more 'pragmatic' President Bashir eventually emerged victorious, but skirmishing with Turabi became a permanent feature.

For more than 20 years, the SPLM/A fought the Sudanese Armed Forces (SAF). There was no 'front': the SAF usually held most of the towns, while the SPLM/A held most of the countryside. Neither side was able to deliver a decisive blow. The consequences for civilians were devastating. Estimates of the number killed reach as high as 2 million.[6]

Throughout this period, Garang was the most prominent leader of the liberation movement. In 1991 he was challenged by Riek Machar and Lam Akol, commanders from Unity and Upper Nile states respectively. They justified rebellion on political grounds, openly favouring secession from Sudan and confronting what they saw as dictatorial tendencies within the Movement. Machar's followers carried out a wave of massacres in Twic East, Garang's home area, and around Bor, killing an estimated 2,000 people in November 1991. A period of fierce factional fighting ensued. In 1997 Machar, under increasing pressure, signed a separate peace with Khartoum.

Regarding both the first split of the SPLM/A in 1983, and the second, in 1991, differences have been depicted in political and ideological terms. Some analysts contend that initial infighting was misrepresented as between unionists and separatists, and that differences masked a power struggle. In fact, many other factors contributed to the split, including the capacity to mobilize along ethnic lines, shifting external relations, and the Anya-Nya II merger. In any case, Khartoum exploited the differences, divided and ruled – and used the factions in counter-insurgency tactics.

Efforts were made during the 1990s to reunite the SPLM/A and end the war, but it was only with the 2001 terrorist attacks in the USA that change became possible. The US Government confronted 'rogue regimes' assumed to be harbouring or supporting terrorists, leading Khartoum to show willingness to cooperate against terrorism and to engage with the South. The SPLM/A was stronger and better positioned than in the 1990s, and had every interest in serious talks under the auspices of the Inter-Governmental Authority on Development (IGAD) and with the support of the US, UK, Norway and the IGAD Partners Forum.

Meanwhile Garang worked to consolidate Southern factions. In January 2002 Riek Machar and other Nuer political and military leaders ended their long and damaging split with the SPLM/A and strengthened the call for Southern self-determination. Further agreements followed with other disaffected commanders.

## Peace from within

These developments were important precursors to negotiation of the CPA of 2005. Local peace processes also played a role. Traditional systems of arbitration, formalized and structured under British rule, had survived and successfully applied customary law. In 1999 the New Sudan Council of Churches initiated the Wunlit conference, which resolved differences in the border region, with what proved to be lasting effect.[7]

Efforts related to local, regional and even cross-border migration also exemplified sub-national peace and reconciliation processes. Along the border between the South and Kordofan this was particularly important, involving agreements between the Malual Dinka and Misseriya and Rizigat, and between the Misseriya and Ngok Dinka.

Other 'people-to-people' initiatives took place among cattle-herding communities in Greater Bahr al-Ghazal, Greater Upper Nile and in Eastern Equatoria. These attempts at reconciliation were sometimes mediated by outsiders or through homegrown local practices. They tended to be more successful when supported by civil society, religious leaders and other stakeholders, and when government authorities facilitated implementation of agreements.

The SPLM/A's leaders knew that negotiating peace without a united South would be impossible. Unity involved agreement and integration of militia groups, and peace between communities affected by the war. The churches had continuously tried to reconcile communities, often creating tension between church leaders and the SPLM/A. It was widely acknowledged, however, that these efforts provided an important basis for negotiation of the CPA.

## The Comprehensive Peace Agreement of 2005

The peace negotiations would not have succeeded without support from the IGAD Partners' Forum (the 'Friends' group, renamed), with the US, UK and Norway (the 'Troika') as the driving force. This involved funding the negotiation secretariat, the team of experts assisting the talks, and the chief negotiator, the IGAD Special Envoy, General Lazarus Sumbeiywo. Politically, senior officials and ministers of the Troika countries played a significant role, as did their envoys at the talks. As Norway's minister of international development, I chaired the support group at the centre of these efforts. Having engaged with the Sudanese parties early on and been party to the peace efforts in 1997–9, I knew both sides quite well.

Most observers did not give the talks much of a chance until the break-through Machakos Protocol of July 2002. This granted Southern Sudan the right to exercise self-determination while Sudan was guaranteed an Islamist character under *Sharia* law. The deal implied that the SPLM/A's goal of a secular and reformed Sudanese state was less important than a Southern Sudanese option of secession.

The agreement surprised the international community; only a few Troika officials had been aware of developments. While Sudanese negotiators thought peace was near, leaders of the SPLM/A faced internal criticism. The Movement's national agenda had attracted marginalized peoples and movements outside the South; in the Nuba Mountains, Blue Nile, and eastern Sudan, armed opposition had become an integral part of the SPLM/A. Now the Machakos Protocol was widely interpreted as abandoning the vision of a New Sudan, leading to difficulties within the Movement and the negotiations. The SPLM/A demanded separate protocols for the Nuba Mountains, Blue Nile and Abyei. Khartoum charged bad faith.

On 1 September 2002 the SPLA stormed Torit, taking control of this most important town in Eastern Equatoria. Pretending that Khartoum attacked first, the SPLM leadership shocked friends, allies and international stakeholders. It was only through an agreement on cessation of hostilities, brokered by the Troika in cooperation with Abel Alier and General Sumbeiywo, and signed on 15 October, that the parties were brought back to the table.

Negotiations almost collapsed in July 2003. Then, Khartoum walked out over a proposed solution to all remaining issues, the so-called Nakuru draft, and started 'forum shopping' to avoid the IGAD process. This was unsuccessful, however, and in September the Sudanese first vice president, Ali Osman Taha, took charge of the negotiations. On 31 August he had asked me to persuade Chairman Garang to come to Nairobi and negotiate directly. Several of us intervened, and a reluctant

Garang finally agreed. Thus began almost 18 months of intense negotiation, mainly between the two leaders, alone and behind closed doors.

Uniquely during the long period of peace talks, this crucial stage was conducted mostly without mediation; the importance of personal commitment can hardly be exaggerated. General Sumbeiywo provided strong leadership in coordinating the process; the Troika and individuals including myself contributed significantly on the phone and by numerous visits to Naivasha, where the talks took place. Without international pressure, and the clear timeline set by the Security Council, the negotiations might still have foundered.

The highly detailed Comprehensive Peace Agreement was signed on 9 January 2005 in Nairobi, in the presence of a number of heads of state and government. The SPLM/A had insisted on negotiating every single element, including an implementation matrix with timelines. Southerners' experience of 'too many agreements dishonoured' proved that implementation would be fraught.[8] International guarantees and strong security arrangements were intended to make it difficult for Khartoum, as they saw it, to renege.

The CPA incorporated the Machakos Protocol, protocols on security arrangements, wealth sharing and power sharing, and the so-called Protocol for the Three Areas (the Nuba Mountains, Blue Nile and Abyei). An Implementation Protocol contained timelines for the agreements. The document provided for a reformed national government and the exercise of Southern self-determination through a referendum.

There has been criticism that the CPA negotiations were monopolized by the Sudanese ruling party, the NCP, and the SPLM/A, and that they should have addressed also internal tensions in the North and South.[9] The parties themselves took full ownership of the talks, however, both format and content, rejecting proposals for more inclusive arrangements. The negotiations were extremely complex. Attempts by external actors to dictate a different arrangement would probably have led to their collapse.

As the agreement was signed, a dark cloud on the horizon was the burgeoning catastrophe in Darfur. This had already drawn worldwide attention, but hardly deflected the joy of the Southern Sudanese, for whom a half-century of struggle was over. They celebrated in their millions, locally and abroad, young and old, from all walks of life.

But for many Southerners, and particularly SPLA officers whose objective had always been independence, the CPA was little more than a ceasefire: final victory – and peace – would come only with independence. An interim period of six years was stipulated before a referendum, so there was much room for doubt.

## Orphaned

On 9 July 2005 John Garang flew to Khartoum to become first vice president of Sudan. That he was greeted by enormous crowds, and that, the next day, when he was inaugurated, millions of people celebrated all over the country seemed to shock senior Sudanese officials who had belittled his support outside the South. Garang took seriously the embryonic Government of National Unity, the reforms needed in Khartoum, and his role in making sure the CPA was fully implemented. This evident determination, combined with popular support he now seemed to command, led the political elite to wonder whether he had ambitions to take on the top job in the country, the presidency.

That question is unlikely ever to be answered. Only three weeks later, on 30 July Garang was killed when his helicopter crashed in the Imatong Mountains. The circumstances have never been fully clarified; foul play has inevitably been suspected. Theories abound.

In the wake of Garang's death, a much-feared power struggle did not take place. Through what seemed a premonition, Dr John had in early July clarified the issue of succession, reaffirming the pre-eminence of his deputy, Salva Kiir. Upon learning of Garang's death, the Leadership Council of the SPLM/A gathered at New Site and by consensus elected Kiir the new chairman.[10]

Garang's death had significant political implications for Khartoum and the SPLM/A. At the funeral in Juba on 7 August, President Bashir praised Garang as the peacemaker. As we proceeded to the gravesite, the arrangements were in the hands of both armies, the SAF and SPLA – which just days before had been at war with each other. Powerfully symbolic of the New Sudan, their soldiers lined the streets of Juba as the coffin was transported to its final destination, and a team of young soldiers drawn from each army carried it, wrapped in the SPLA and Sudanese flags, to the grave.

## The road to independence

After John Garang's death, ominous political developments took place in Khartoum. Ali Osman Taha, his partner in peace, was sidelined. The CPA was subjected to renewed criticism. And although the government – or Bashir himself – had approved every detail in the CPA, Taha was scapegoated for giving too much away. Compromises are difficult to defend in contexts such as this; hardliners always have the easy way. In Khartoum, they soon had the upper hand. Many who had negotiated the CPA and knew its provisions were sidelined, too. And on the Southern side the centre of gravity also shifted from the negotiating team to others preferred by Salva Kiir. As first vice president of Sudan and, now, president of the Government of South Sudan (GoSS), he would appoint ministers in Khartoum and the South, selections influenced by tensions within the SPLM/A. Hence the Government of National Unity consisted largely of ministers less committed to the CPA. This had an impact on implementation.

The next five years would test Salva Kiir's authority. On 12 August, less than two weeks after assuming the chairmanship, he met for the first time in years the disaffected Nuer militia leader Paulino Matip. While Garang had reached out to several militia bosses, Salva Kiir's 'Big Tent' approach went much further, resulting in the Juba Conference of January 2006, representing most Southern Sudanese factions. The Agreement reached then became the basis for Southern unity throughout the CPA period, consolidated Salva Kiir's and the SPLM's leading position, and prevented destabilizing competition for power.

In implementing the CPA the challenges were immense. A first crisis occurred on 9 January 2006, when President Bashir visited Juba for the anniversary of the Agreement. A heated argument with Kiir occurred at the stadium, and violence was only with difficulty averted. The ceasefire largely held thereafter, until midway through the interim period. But the CPA's security arrangements were never implemented as intended. For the GoSS a separate army meant insurance for the referendum; defence would account for 40 per cent of the autonomous Southern Government's budget.

In October 2007 dissatisfaction with implementation of the CPA led to the SPLM's suspending participation in the Government

11

of National Unity. Tensions ran so high that both sides deployed additional troops to border areas. The crisis was defused, however, and the forces pulled back. After new commitments, the SPLM returned to government.

A serious violation of the ceasefire occurred in May 2008 near the town of Abyei. Within hours tanks were involved; within days, fighting had intensified: SAF forces burnt the whole town to the ground, sparing only the mosques. Ninety thousand people fled. Abyei had long been one of the most contentious North–South issues, and the area would suffer similar incidents twice again, with the Sudanese Army moving in. In all of the 'Three Areas' there were severe tensions.

## Broken promises

Predictably, the political process in Sudan proved challenging. Implementation of the CPA lagged. In some cases, delays were caused by lack of capacity, in others an apparent lack of commitment. There was continuous tension surrounding transfer of oil revenue and the transparency of oil-production data; payments were late, and sometimes in local currency, contravening the CPA. The Petroleum Commission and Joint Defence Board never functioned properly; decisions related to the referendum were deferred. These included border demarcation and the Referendum Act itself. Even in 2009 important national security legislation was still pending.

On 19 October 2009 the SPLM withdrew its legislators from the national parliament to protest against the lack of progress. They returned only when the delayed laws were enacted at the end of the year. The key to change at the centre, however, was control over the levers of power. This remained the main challenge in Khartoum.

Meanwhile the international community turned its attention to Darfur and other crises. Despite the presence of a UN mission, high-level leadership in monitoring implementation of the CPA was missing, and there was little pressure to 'make unity attractive' to the South. This had serious consequences; inattention to the CPA allowed the two parties to resume a cycle of tension and conflict. But as long as they kept the peace, most stakeholders seemed unconcerned. Even the Troika went dormant. As detailed in my book on this period,[11] intense shuttle diplomacy started in late 2009, just a few months before scheduled elections.

Despite apparent good intentions, those elections, in 2010, were tarnished by many irregularities. The result was not a broadening of the two governments, but clean sweeps by the ruling parties – which won almost every governorship and 422 of 446 seats in the National Assembly.[12] Worse, almost all timelines in the CPA had been violated and the six-year interim period would soon be over. It was clear that the parties were looking toward the bottom line: the referendum on unity versus separation.

There had always been a strong bipartisan constituency for South Sudan in the US. Salva Kiir had a good relationship with President George W. Bush.[13] President Obama's administration also included several top officials of long-standing engagement with South Sudan, most prominently Susan Rice, Permanent Representative to the UN and later National Security Advisor. The US had a strong interest in the success of the CPA and ultimately of South Sudan, as did the UK, the former colonial power, and Norway – a country with decades-long engagement with the South. The three governments knew that any attempt to delay the referendum and independence would lead to a resumption of civil war.

## Second thoughts

Among other stakeholders there had long been resistance to secession. This continued during the CPA negotiations and interim period. Among some members of the UN Security Council and the African Union, independence for South Sudan was seen to threaten stability and security on a continent replete with movements that could be tempted to do the same.

Regarding the current (2013–15) conflict in independent South Sudan, many observers make incorrect assumptions: the CPA was intended to give unity a chance. (For most international observers, the slogan was 'making unity attractive'.) Khartoum was given six years to prove seriousness about the CPA and a better future for all marginalized peoples. The referendum would test that seriousness. Stakeholders were aware of the overwhelming popular sentiment for independence, but with John Garang at the helm, a number of observers had thought a unified Sudan was still possible. It was his death that made this entirely unrealistic.

The interim period failed to 'make unity attractive'. Southerners would never be convinced by words, only deeds, and there was not much of the latter. While all relevant international bodies had signed the CPA as witnesses, or supported it through resolutions or statements, there was continuing strong resistance to the referendum and possible secession. Many argued for delay, saying the South was unready. A few African leaders quietly advised more time. Others made public pronouncements and proposals; many were looking for a way out. Elements in Khartoum similarly argued for longer timelines, hoping that the referendum – one likely result of which would be loss of significant oil income – could be avoided altogether. This only added to the SPLM's conviction that any delay would threaten the whole CPA and their right to self-determination.

Through intense diplomatic efforts, Southern Sudanese leaders managed to change the international atmosphere. The critical turning point was the roundtable held in the margins of the UN General Assembly on 24 September 2010. President Barack Obama and other world leaders participated; Salva Kiir and Ali Osman Taha represented the two parties. (President Bashir, subject to arrest for war crimes, crimes against humanity and genocide under warrants issued by the International Criminal Court, did not travel to the US.) The American President set the tone: the referenda must take place on time.[14] Significant work behind the scenes prior to the meeting, resulted in unanimous public commitment to full implementation of the CPA, including the timelines for the referendum.

There was no going back.

From a Southern Sudanese perspective, the referendum was the 'red line'. Private conversations with SPLM leaders confirmed this. Some observers later forgot that the alternative to Southern independence was not the status quo, or peace, but resumption of the civil war.

Indeed, even when it became clear that they had overwhelming international support for the referendum, many SPLM leaders thought Khartoum would prevent it. Only when President Bashir visited Juba on 4 January 2011, less than a week before the referendum, did they believe the vote would go ahead. His statement that day surprised not only Southern Sudanese, but the world: he promised he would 'congratulate and celebrate with you' should they choose secession, and help to build a secure, stable and 'brotherly' state.[15]

On 9 January 2011 Southern Sudanese went to the polls; 98.8 per cent of the population voted in favour of secession and independence.

Time was short. During the next six months, to 9 July 2011, former President Thabo Mbeki of South Africa, his colleagues in the AU High Level Panel; UNMIS; the Special Representative of the Secretary-General, Haile Menkerios; the Troika; and others worked closely with the two parties, but progress was slow. Fundamental interests were at stake: border demarcation, oil and the tariffs for use of the Sudanese pipeline, transitional financial arrangements, citizenship, currency and other issues.

Some observers mooted delaying the date of independence. But again the Southern Sudanese were firm: the date was enshrined in the CPA. Terms of separation would have to be negotiated between the two countries afterwards.

Nothing could stop the dream from coming true. Salva Kiir, now as president, stood on the podium and declared:

> Today is the most important day for the people of South Sudan,
> the proclamation of whose birth and emergence as a member on
> the community of world nations you have just witnessed. It is
> a day which will be forever engraved in our hearts and minds.

But dreams can turn into nightmares.

# 2

◆

# A COUNTRY WITHOUT
# A STATE

South Sudan is larger than Kenya, Rwanda and Burundi together, but with a population density one-tenth that of Uganda.[1] It has enormous natural resources, but is one of the most underdeveloped areas in Africa, with virtually no infrastructure. The country comprises some 64 ethnic communities, and more than 80 languages.[2] Its ethnic diversity is a source of great pride.

Different from many other African countries, whose history often have included large kingdoms and experiences of traditional statehood, the majority of Southern Sudanese are clan-based pastoralist or semi-pastoralist communities, posing special challenges to state- and nation-building. In other countries on the continent, liberation movements entered government offices of functional post-colonial institutions. This was not the case with Southern Sudan.

As one could expect, freedom fighters who had spent most of their lives in the struggle were not necessarily the ones best prepared for the task of taking over the semi-autonomous government of Southern Sudan in 2005. Although many had been governing liberated areas, these were still military administrations and not political governments based on at least some principles of the rule of law. In addition, corruption and nepotism soon prevented the building of stronger and more effective institutions.

Furthermore, assistance from the international community to support Southern Sudan in the right way, building the core functions of the state, proved to be partly patchy and uncoordinated, and partly non-existent. The latter was related to the CPA and the importance of not pre-judging the outcome of the referendum. Signals from Khartoum and the caution of donors and international stakeholders prevented institution building which could be interpreted as preparation for independence prior to the referendum in 2011. Although capacity building was happening, it was not done in the comprehensive and systematic way needed to build a functioning state.

Finally, and not least important, the CPA-scheduled time from the referendum in January 2011 to the declaration of independence in July was only six months, far too limited to make much progress in institution building at par with running an independent state. The timelines in the CPA were non-negotiable for the SPLM, out of fear of losing the referendum and independence altogether.

As we shall see in this chapter, all these challenges implied that South Sudan, come independence, in reality was a country without a state. Two years later its weak institutions were unable to provide a buffer against the implosion that followed the political crisis. It is against this background it is important to analyse what unfolded during the interim period.

## The liberation curse: When the 'rebels' become the state

Juba, the capital in the South, had always been under government control. During the second civil war (1983–2005) it had deteriorated completely. When I visited the town in 1998 and later it was like a ghost town. The country's only stretch of tarmac was so potholed that it was difficult to know where the road ended and the ditch began.

On 5 August 2005, only two days before John Garang's funeral but after 21 years of struggle in the bush, Juba received the liberation hero and chairman of the SPLM/A in a way none had expected, in a coffin. The funeral brought thousands onto the dusty streets, but the atmosphere was tense. Dinka do not traditionally wail over the death of a hero or chief, so awesome silence prevailed.

Akol Maror, an elderly Apuk Dinka, expressed the general feeling: a rope had been pulling them across the river from *loony* (slavery), Arab domination and massacres. Garang had been holding the rope on the other side. Now he was gone.[3] Without him, most thought that peace would not hold.

Immediately after the funeral, the guerrilla army – or liberation movement, as Southern Sudanese preferred to call the SPLM/A – took over Juba. While there had been discussions about a capital elsewhere,[4] the leadership had decided to stick with the status quo. After Dr John's death, and his burial in Juba, that decision became institutionalized.

Unlike elsewhere in Africa, at the onset of the interim period, the liberators inherited a host of problems with few functional institutions. Government entities were mere shells, with dilapidated buildings and a few people shuffling papers inside. Yet there were still thousands on the payroll, another legacy. Regular pay for doing little or nothing had kept some people from joining the 'rebels'.

During the years of colonial rule and subsequent Khartoum regimes, services hardly existed. Development indicators were among the worst in the world, whether of health, infant mortality, maternal mortality, drinking water and sanitation, or food security. This construction of underdevelopment, to quote Edward Thomas,[5] had a serious impact on Southern Sudanese. Such education, as the World Bank reported, had been a tool to coercively assimilate Southerners into Arab and Muslim culture.[6]

The SPLA quickly swapped their uniforms for dark suits, whether for government offices or the Legislative Assembly. Having spent most of their adult lives in the bush, fighting, however, many had become accustomed to one way of thinking and operating; Southern Sudan was a deeply militarized society. But it was now time for change. At least, that was what we all thought.

## Liberation rule

Although the CPA was a result of painfully crafted compromises, not military victory, the SPLA won the credit. They were, in their own eyes, and in the eyes of many people, victors, liberators, heroes.

Unifying the country was a major challenge, as many communities had been isolated from each other and the outside world, uprooted and displaced, often multiple times, during decades of war. Traditional institutions and coping mechanisms had been weakened.

The transition of the SPLM/A from liberation movement to government of Southern Sudan would never be easy. Civilian administration would be merged with government structures of the past, whether in Khartoum or in areas already under SPLM/A control. The SPLA itself was supposed to become a conventional army, while the Movement (the SPLM) should evolve into a political party with a democratic role.

Christopher Clapham's outline of legacies of liberation in African countries where liberators subsequently attained political power provides a useful template for analysis of South Sudan.[7]

Victorious movements inherit a powerful sense of legitimacy. As Clapham says,[8] they comprise people prepared to sacrifice their lives for a cause, and who come to power with an abiding memory of martyrs. They believe that with independence they have earned the right to run the government. They find it hard to recognize others' right to govern, instead imbuing their own sacrifices with a virtually permanent and exclusive claim on state power. With this sense of legitimacy, actual performance in government becomes less important, and might even be irrelevant. In some cases, when the hegemony of the liberators is threatened, repression as a means of maintaining power may even be legitimized, relying on state power.

Liberation movements are seldom monolithic. A common feature is the contest for 'movement hegemony', frequently with fighting between rivals or factions. This has been the case also during the SPLM's history, as we have seen. These splits may affect governance after the liberators take over the state, since they may reflect differences, for example on the basis of ethnicity, that could be interpreted as bringing one group to power over others. What from the viewpoint of the winners is presented as 'national' liberation may not look that way from the viewpoint of other elements in the population.[9] Also here there are parallels to the SPLM, with a competition for power and hegemony which would prove so disastrous in later years.

Furthermore, to be able to manage the difficult transition to government, Clapham points out that self-transformation is necessary. A liberation war has a single clear goal that calls for unity, commitment, discipline and a hierarchal structure of command; running a government is a complicated exercise with multiple and competing goals and requires consensus-building in setting agendas and identifying priorities. Indeed, demolishing a bridge is a lot easier than building one. In this regard, an effective bureaucracy is critical. In addition, differences among pragmatists, power seekers and ideologues, as well as rivalries between the 'ins', who have gained important positions, and the 'outs', who have not, greatly complicate necessary transformation.[10] This was the case also for Southern Sudan.

Finally, liberators seldom recognize internal splits and domestic opposition as signals that they have outstayed their welcome, treating them instead as challenges to the rightful order. Yet credit for liberation is finite, and the moment inevitably arrives when a regime is judged not by its promises but by its performance. Luka Biong Deng, a senior SPLM politician and former minister in the GoSS, has applied these characteristics of the 'curse' of liberation.[11] Many of them can be seen in successive governments controlled or dominated by the SPLM since the signing of the CPA. Old tensions were fuelling new divisions in the leadership, eventually leading to the crisis in 2013.

## Guerrilla Government

Edward Thomas and Cherri Leonardi use the term 'state capture' when referring to the SPLM's sense of entitlement to govern.[12] The SPLM's policy reforms of the late 1990s, described in Øystein Rolandsen's book *Guerrilla Government*,[13] and converging in the agenda for 'Peace through Development',[14] were a start. But it was only with the *SPLM Strategic Framework: For War-to-Peace Transition*, published in August 2004, that the SPLM outlined this complex transition process.[15] The document, clearly bearing the hallmark of Chairman John Garang, was particularly detailed on the governance arrangements of the transition and in outlining decentralized and community-oriented development plans, setting a different course from the legacies of liberation. But it was less specific on the transformation of the SPLA into a professional army.

The SPLM/A's transformation programme committed to a 'social contract' defining relations between the people and their government as based on justice, accountability, inclusiveness, responsibility and openness.[16] Government would have 'working rules of collective action, where the institutions of Southern Sudan were seen as a summation of positive elements of social values, traditions and beliefs of all its peoples.'[17] The SPLM/A thus departed from the notion that state-building starts 'from scratch'. It envisioned a decentralized system:

> The aim is a community-driven development paradigm that emphasizes and promotes the concept of taking towns and services to people in rural areas, where 98% of our people live, instead of the conventional development paradigm that results in attracting rural people to towns and trapping them in slums with consequent reduced quality of life. This will be an SPLM contribution to development economics.[18]

The SPLM/A did not want to replicate Khartoum's marginalizing of peripheries. Righting the wrongs of the past would necessarily involve social transformation. At the same time, the experience of administering liberated areas during the civil war was not the same as running an inclusive government. Governance structures were entirely different; strong institutions, transparency and accountability, central to effective civilian government, were beyond the scope of a liberation movement.

While progress was uneven in institutional development, it was almost non-existent in healing a society broken from decades of civil war and underdevelopment. Southern Sudan's would-be liberators were unable, in the course of their long struggle, to re-think relations between state and society. Military credentials and rank would often be more decisive than political competence and technical skills when allocating ministerial positions. Influence in decision making was often more determined by the prominence of the past than the competence of the present. And in the absence of alternatives, they ended up structuring relations between the state and the citizens more around traditional roles from the liberation struggle and ethnic representation.[19]

There is always a danger that former liberators will become complacent beneficiaries of state power.[20] The clearest sign of this is the tendency to resort to ethnicity and patronage as the primary governing framework. This can sow the seeds of ethnic divisions going forward. In the Southern Sudanese case the sense of entitlement also led to monopolization of economic benefits through corruption. A decade after the CPA we note that the SPLM's ambitious transformation programmes were never implemented. It was not easy to shed the uniform. In what follows we will provide some of the reasons.

Tangible benefits and services for the people, particularly in the first year or so after a conflict, are among the most important factors for sustaining peace.[21] In 2005 I repeatedly reminded Dr John himself, other SPLM/A leaders, and donors about this. It was important to get it right from the outset. Aware of the challenges, I had proposed establishment – several months *before* the signing of the CPA – of a trust fund. The Capacity Building Trust Fund (CBTF) was meant to assist in transforming the SPLM/A into a civilian administration, establishing the nascent government of Southern Sudan, assisting with some recurrent costs in the 'pre-interim' period, and funding early peace dividends. The CBTF would thus be an interim financing mechanism until the Multi-Donor Trust Fund (MDTF) administered by the World Bank started to disburse funds.

UNICEF had been in charge of the main aid operation, Operation Lifeline Sudan, during the civil war, and was the organization best positioned to host the trust fund during the transition. A few donors put money in, but not much, and certainly not enough. The Trust Fund was therefore not used as intended to help address critical start-up problems. That it became essential in dealing with payroll and other problems in service-delivery ministries later showed that it could have been used in a much better way from the outset.

The World Bank's MDTF, which received a major part of donor funds in the absence of governmental financial-management capacity, did not help matters. The World Bank's rules and regulations are not adapted to fragile states, leading to apparent paralysis of the MDTF. Between 2005 and 2008, the MDTF spent only $264 million, mostly towards the end of this period. In other words, it failed to function for several years.[22] This made even more critical the assistance of bilateral donors and the UN, which, however, were also dilatory. Bilateral donors came late, and with programmes operated largely by contractors or inexperienced short-term contracted staff. UN agencies' programmes were inadequately funded and skewed towards humanitarian assistance. Donors' priorities were now in Darfur and elsewhere.

In April 2005 I had hosted an international donors' conference in Oslo, at which $4.6 billion was committed. The international community did not deliver as promised. The consequence of the delay was that basic services the population had received in the past – food, health services, education – were cut back rather than increased with the advent of peace.[23] As late as 2009, in Juba, when one mentioned 'the road', everyone knew what was meant because only one was paved. Observers, me included, who witnessed the missed opportunity of providing early peace dividends, feared that this failure would contribute to rapid destabilization. Two or three years was too long to wait for visible progress.

## 'It is our turn to eat'[24]

At first, there were delays in transferring oil income, and disputes between the Government of National Unity in Khartoum and the Southerners. Disagreements over amounts and transfer arrangements were sorted out over time, and eventually payments came regularly, in the correct amounts and in US dollars.

But the Juba Government had no financial institutions to speak of. During the 'pre-interim' period of early 2005, cash was shipped in boxes, and not to the government, which had not been established yet, but to the SPLM offices in Juba. I visited party headquarters at this time, a dilapidated building with no sign that anyone was in charge. This was the SPLM Secretariat of Finance. When oil transfers began there was only a nominal Ministry of Finance there.

The Central Bank, a national institution headquartered in Khartoum, had only a small office in Juba. There were no credible commercial banks beyond those operating in dinars and Islamic banks under Khartoum's auspices. The first bank branches were established with the help of UNMIS.[25] With credit cards unusable, most of the economy was cash-driven throughout the interim period and even after independence.

It was this situation that the CBTF had been established to address. But a transfer from Khartoum, reportedly of $60 million, intended to help the SPLM/A to establish a government, went missing. No investigation was ever conducted.[26]

The World Bank reported two years later that the:

> former SPLM Secretariat of Finance, which managed resources of around $100,000, has transformed itself into a Ministry

responsible for managing over one and a half billion dollars annually, including significant external financing.[27]

The report went on to aver that the government had committed to establishing sound and transparent financial management systems and to combating corruption; some progress had been made, but government finances were still characterized by weak management and lack of accountability. It is surprising that the World Bank, the IMF – and bilateral donors for that matter – raised no alarms. There was no way the former liberators could be capable of managing such amounts at this juncture. And there were other options, as we shall see later.[28]

But capacity gaps proved to be secondary constraints. The more important factor, it appeared, was absence of political will.[29] The oil money was seen not only as a blessing but also as an entitlement. The liberators had been cheated by Khartoum of what they regarded as Southern oil resources for all these years. It was time to be rewarded.

Norway had experienced SPLM/A cadres' lack of fiscal discipline, having witnessed mismanagement and corruption in a project supposedly supervised by the Movement. Interestingly, characters charged with the accounts and books of the SPLM/A, operating in secrecy, and with little disclosure about what went where and to whom, would later become finance ministers. As one senior SPLM member put it: 'When leopards are assigned the responsibilities of shepherds, the flock stands no chance.'[30]

In mid February 2005, I raised this issue with John Garang. I had just come from Rumbek having met the deputy chairman, Salva Kiir, and the rest of the SPLM/A leadership, and I now proceeded to see the boss, who was at the location New Site, where the SPLM/A had one of their headquarters, on other business. I pointed to other African countries where petroleum had become a curse rather than a blessing, and where corruption had become a cancer undermining development and destroying fragile institutions. The SPLM/A and its leaders were at great risk of developing the same habits, I told the chairman, unless the process was checked at the outset. It was critical to establish mechanisms of control and oversight, making corruption more difficult; otherwise it would destroy everything they had fought for.

I had sensitive information to share with Dr John. Norway, an important oil producer, always followed developments in the petroleum business, and we knew that individuals in the SPLM/A had done deals with oil companies without the chairman's knowledge. How significant these were we did not know, but the documentary evidence we had contained licences in blocks that were meant for new Southern Sudanese companies. Later it appeared that still others had engaged in telecom deals, and other contracts, pending the signing of the CPA.

The chairman expressed no surprise. He said he knew something was going on. Though concerned, he said that deals undertaken during the pre-interim period, prior to establishment of the government of Southern Sudan, would be illegal the minute legislation was passed. In the event, however, it took many years to enact the necessary laws, probably because the very cadres who had made the underhanded deals did their utmost to procrastinate.

## Bad habits die hard

This was hardly the chairman's first encounter with corruption. Peter Adwok Nyaba, an SPLM minister in the Government of National Unity and in South Sudan, had in 1996 published an account of how food rations during the early days of the struggle were misappropriated and sold in Ethiopia, contributing to deaths by disease and starvation.[31]

During the civil war, unpaid soldiers had to rely on help from local people, scrounging food in the bush, looting, and when in trouble, stealing and finding other ways to support operations and feed their families. Looting food aid was an aspect of military strategy during the 1990s, when SPLM/A factions were fighting each other.[32] SPLA bases were sited near refugee camps or where humanitarian operations distributed food.[33] Some cadres managed to get their hands on other resources. Bad habits had thus already developed among the liberators.[34]

Corruption was a hot topic at the famous commanders' meeting at Rumbek in late November 2004, when Salva Kiir opposed Garang:

> Corruption, as a result of the lack of structures, has created a lack of accountability which has reached a proportion that will be difficult to eradicate.[35]

Reverting to this issue later in the discussion, he said:

> I would also like to say something about rampant corruption
> in the Movement. At the moment some members of the
> Movement have formed private companies, bought houses and
> have huge bank accounts in foreign countries. I wonder what
> kind of system are we going to establish in South Sudan consid-
> ering ourselves indulged in this respect?[36]

Dr John did not comment on these allegations directly, and others
present criticized complacency in this regard. And corruption was but
one of 13 problems Cdr James Wani Igga listed:

> Problem 8: Corruption which remains rampant in the
> Movement. Corruption must be fought [...] some years back
> the Chairman in a meeting informed us that Cdr. Deng Alor
> brought some money from Nigeria, but how that money was
> spent had never been explained to us again. I ask the question
> where is the transparency and accountability we talked about?[37]

And interestingly, he added: 'Let's avoid "Kitchen Cabinets" and combat
corruption.'[38]

Dr John did not dispute some of these charges in his conversations
with me. He agreed that it was very important to establish robust systems
of financial control, particularly for the petroleum sector, contracts and
financial transfers. I proposed a series of measures, based on best practice
internationally, to combat the problem.

One creative idea was to establish a mechanism to hold back some
oil income until adequate financial institutions and controls were in
place. Access to funds would happen with special permission and
through periodic transfers, with transparency and necessary controls.
International accounting companies could host such funds ad interim.
Dr John was open to such ideas. We agreed to explore them further,
when he would be in Khartoum in July for his inauguration. But before
it was possible to get any further, he died.

That the CPA did not address this explicitly was the responsibility
of the parties. Early on the SPLM/A raised the issue of an 'offshore

account' under the custody of international experts to ensure that both parties got their fair shares of the oil income. Sudan rejected the idea outright on the basis of national sovereignty. Bilateral offers to the SPLM/A on revenue management in 2002 were not taken up. While there was pressure in the wealth-sharing talks to ensure best practice in financial management, the World Bank was slow in establishing advisory capacity in Juba. Although constrained by the fact that Southern Sudan was not yet a shareholder, the IMF and World Bank could have done more. Donors could also have put more pressure on the Southerners to establish a transitional financial mechanism in 2005. Whether there would ever have been political will was a question never answered.

After my political party in Norway lost elections in September 2005, I left office as minister for international development. Before my departure, I mentioned the importance of pursuing this issue with SPLM/A leaders. While several countries and institutions funded advisers to the ministries of finance and petroleum during this period, management of the oil revenues itself needed a stronger and separate mechanism.

The Southern Sudanese inherited mismanagement and corruption from the pre-CPA system – Khartoum's and the SPLM/A's. That system had resulted from the war and its political economy, and from the tendency to use access to state resources to accumulate private wealth, a habit in Sudan that carried over into the Southern Government. With no institutions, financial management in Southern Sudan relied on personal honesty, clearly an unsustainable basis in a post-conflict situation. The international community therefore shares responsibility for the problems that ensued.

Many in the Movement regarded the CPA as only a ceasefire. They believed that Khartoum would never allow self-determination, and that they would be going back to the bush to continue the fight. The death of the chairman probably strengthened this expectation. Meanwhile they might as well take what they could get before fighting resumed.

A story that President Museveni told me about the mentality of liberation movements illustrates the point. When you go hunting, he said, and make a catch, you skin the animal, gather around the fire, and wait for the meat. One cannot tell the hunter to go home hungry. Expecting them to leave office before eating the meal was naive.

In a number of languages, including Swahili and Arabic, the term for stealing or corruption is 'eating', not only in relation to money, but also in reference to land and other resources. Alfred Lokuji of Juba University puts it this way: 'only the SPLM/A leaders appear to have full rights to the dividends of peace.'[39]

Salva Kiir, taking over after the death of Garang, soon discovered that running a government was different from administering SPLM/A-controlled areas in 'New Sudan'. Southern Sudanese had often joked about the corruption in Khartoum, claiming that they would not make the same mistakes. However, once in office they soon found their fingers deep in the same coffers. Salva Kiir now had to address the corruption he had long complained about.

## Nascent state-building

At the same time, the interim-period Government of Southern Sudan started off with a significant financial burden. Khartoum had paid for salaries, but not for much else. Many people on the government payroll sat around doing nothing, constituting a financial burden and political 'hot potato'. Payroll clean-up was thus controversial, not only from the perspective of old beneficiaries, but soon also for government officials quickly recruiting their own people, whose salaries lubricated patronage networks.[40] The Government's budget in 2005 was $14.5 million; in 2006 it budgeted $1.34 billion and spent $1.56 billion.

Southern Sudan during the interim period had more income than most post-conflict countries, owing to its oil revenue. Its share was 50 per cent of net revenue from oil wells located in Southern Sudan. A significant shortfall was recorded – according to audits, about $430 million between 2005 and 2008[41] – but subsequently the GoSS regularly received its share. Southern Sudan was entirely oil-dependent, however, with some 98 per cent of its income from oil, and little effort was made to develop non-oil revenue. What was missing was a functioning government.

Donors supported capacity-development programmes and some did well in selected sectors. Despite elaborate plans in some ministries, however, such assistance was not provided in the systematic and coherent way needed to establish a strong foundation of the state. Aid continued to be dominated by humanitarian assistance even until the onset of the crisis of 2013, when 43 per cent went for emergency assistance. Even for countries such as Afghanistan, the Central African Republic and Iraq, much more aid was for longer-term development assistance.[42] Whether this was related to the long history of humanitarian operations in Southern Sudan or a matter of donor priorities is not easy to tell.

Another challenge was that some important capacity-building programmes had to wait, because of the CPA requirement to 'make unity attractive'. The outcome of the referendum could not be taken for granted. Government institutions in such fields as the Central Bank, immigration, customs and border control, civil aviation and intelligence could not be established before it was clear that Southern Sudan would become independent.

Between 2005 and the referendum in January 2011, United Nations agencies, funds and programmes, and its peacekeeping mission, UNMIS, as well as bilateral donors worried about seeming to pre-judge the outcome. Khartoum, and especially the ruling party, the NCP, deplored anything resembling support for sovereign institutions, and would immediately react when programmes could be interpreted as providing it. They were cautious.

Most donors supported capacity building programmes with consultants, either embedded in ministries or flying in and out, in public financial management, decentralization and the like. But there was no comprehensive programme covering the core functions of the state. Many countries in the region provided courses in foreign affairs, security and other areas, mostly focusing on individual training. We knew this would not add up to what was needed. Courses seldom teach the 'trade' of running a government and a civil service, which is best done on site and through embedded experts. Institution-building requires a different approach and it takes a long time.

Without a bureaucracy to translate policies and plans into action, massive investment was needed to build government capacity. Early on, when in the African Development Bank, I tried to convince the Southern Sudanese to take on a large-scale secondment programme on the model of post-conflict Mozambique. That country had benefited from a large number of foreign experts from Lusophone countries imbedded in ministries under national leadership. The successful programme had lasted for more than ten years and seemed a possible way forward now.[43] But scepticism about 'foreigners' working alongside Southern Sudanese counterparts precluded such a step. Some members of the GoSS and SPLM leadership seemed to think they could manage on their own, traits we would see more of after independence. More importantly, foreigners could see too much and interfere with dubious practices.

Neighbouring countries did offer to send experts, and second teams of experts,[44] and to assist with reforms. Delegations were sent to Juba again and again, and agreements were reached during visits to the respective countries. But little happened. I met frustrated heads of governments and ministers of a number of countries in Africa who had had several meetings with Southern Sudanese counterparts about this, and such contacts continued after independence. They told me that the Southern Sudanese leaders always agreed, but hardly ever followed up. In the end, they gave up.

An IGAD programme that did move forward, however, with experts seconded to various government offices, was an exception proving the rule. Administered by the UNDP, not the government, and externally funded, by Norway, even this won cabinet approval only with difficulty, as sceptical ministers did not want foreigners in their offices: they would handle capacity-building themselves. The President had to intervene before the programme could go forward.[45]

One does not know what one does not know, and particularly if one has never been part of a functional government. If one has not worked in institutions with well-established legal and regulatory frameworks and civil servants implementing policies according to instructions, rules and regulations, budgets, mandates, and in a transparent way, one cannot know how big the gaps are in one's own institutions. And if the only point of comparison was Khartoum, or liberated areas administered through the SPLM/A's Civil Authority of New Sudan during the war, there were big gaps indeed.[46] But as one senior SPLM official said with a big grin, some people do not want to be shown what they do not know.[47]

## Liberators are not peace-builders

Christopher Clapham points out tensions that often build up between an old bureaucracy and the liberators, when the latter want to run the show. In Southern Sudan, this pitted Southerners who had been civil servants in the North, some of them very competent, against cadres from the SPLM/A. But that alone does not account for lack of follow-through with African countries' or donors' offers of help. There were other reasons. Pride was a trait outsiders often interpreted as arrogance. This was even more prominent after independence. I suspected also that an international presence within ministries, even during the interim period, would have made nepotism, patronage and corruption more difficult to conceal.

After three or four years, in any case, some physical and organizational infrastructure was finally in place at the GoSS level and, to a lesser degree, at the state level. The central Government at Juba worked somehow, with planning and budgeting systems facilitating decision making processes, but without essential legislation and policy frameworks in key areas. Bureaucratic systems and processes were set up, but were ineffective and faulty; management of financial resources was the worst. The Ministry of Finance and Economic Planning (MOFEP) was characterized by very weak capacity and undeveloped structures, with directors formally appointed only in July 2006. As in most ministries, there were no appointments below the Assistant Director level: staff were paid but not formally appointed.[48]

Five years into the interim period, in 2010, half of the statutory positions in the ministries of the GoSS remained unfilled. Whether this was related to lack of qualified personnel or lack of recruitment capacity, is not clear. Only 5 per cent of employees had a graduate degree. Fifty per cent had only primary education, with a significant number literate primarily in Arabic, and not English – even though the latter for political reasons had been chosen as the national language of the South and the official language of the government.[49]

Lack of infrastructure, information systems and equipment made matters worse. Government structures were largely absent outside Juba, and despite rhetoric about decentralization, not much was done to empower the second and third tiers. As in Khartoum, resources and decision making were concentrated in the capital, with limited powers delegated below, little capacity built, and few services delivered.

As James Copnall points out,[50] the weakness of the ten states' governments today is structural, replicating that of the national government:

just as the latter's revenue comes almost entirely from oil, the states' is from Juba. Such transfers were unreliable.

Lessons learned by other liberation movements were not applied. John Garang's vision of 'bringing the towns to the people' (in ideological opposition to Khartoum's centralization) was never realized. Nor was his other vision to invest massively in agriculture in a country where 90 per cent of the land is arable, benefiting the largely rural population.[51]

Although capacity was built in a number of areas, much more would have been achieved if a strategic, systematic approach had been adopted and resources had been controlled and wisely spent. Both donors and liberators must account for the absence of comprehensive development of the core functions of the state during the interim period. Once the referendum was held and independence was only six months away, there was too little time to complete the job. In hindsight, more should probably have been done to convince Southern Sudanese of the need for time for preparations during that phase. It could have prepared them better.

In key areas, legislation was not passed and institutions were kept weak for political reasons, making transparency and accountability more difficult. One area was financial management, where institutional gaps, legislation and regulatory frameworks remained unaddressed. Almost any attempt at tightening financial controls was delayed or shelved. While foreign donors and international financial institutions could have made a decisive coordinated effort to establish robust management, the complacency and delays of the Southern Sudanese seemed quite deliberate. Financial institutions and contractual arrangements that were weak and opaque made it easier to misappropriate funds.

Throughout the interim period the GoSS operated without statutory guidelines in public financial management, revenue management, including management of oil income, audit, procurement and the public service. Without legislation and basic regulations, there was basically a free-for-all. Even adherence to the Appropriations Act of 2007 was problematic; there was no multi-year expenditure framework. Before independence, there was not even a functioning auditor-general's office: audits for the interim period were issued only after independence.

The only experience any minister had of government institutions and their financial operations was in Khartoum. While in bureaucratic procedures and government decision making those systems were not bad, institutions were weak and operations questionable.[52] In Khartoum a tiny elite made political decisions behind closed doors.[53] This experience and the SPLM/A tradition of administration in liberated areas were not a basis for good governance.

With no credible institutions and systems of governance, and when productive systems failed to provide sustainable livelihoods, what remained were handouts, at multiple levels. Ethnicity became the organizing principle. To cater for patronage responsibilities, transparency and accountability were not priorities. And in Southern Sudan there was money to grab from the oil revenue, which to uninformed comrades, seemed likely to last forever.

## The oil curse: Entitlement in dollars

The oil curse has afflicted most oil-producing countries, creating both a culture of corruption and a culture of overspending, often leading to the so-called Dutch disease (an overheated economy with major macro-economic imbalances). However, one important point must be made at the outset; without oil production and the income expected from it, South Sudan would not have been seen as a viable state. Prospects of international support for self-determination (and subsequently independence) might have been dim. A viable economy is generally considered a precondition for self-government. For the SPLM/A and Southern Sudanese, therefore, oil was initially a real blessing. When analysing the 'curse', this needs to be acknowledged.

Corruption manifested itself in several ways. We have already seen how the SPLM's Secretariat of Finance was handling an exponential increase in revenue.[54] It is no wonder that there were problems; the liberators could happily reap the fruits of their struggle, without any controls or accountability. Secondly, in a heavily militarized society the lion's share of the budget went to security. Salaries and contracts were most corruption-prone. Under the radar, SPLA commanders influenced the economy through an informal network of closely held companies and contracts. The flawed procurement system was never fixed; legislation and regulatory procedures were stalled, allowing massive corruption in connection with contracts. Suppliers associated with the liberators and elites won contracts without any competition. Some contracts involved leasing large areas of land to foreign companies.[55]

Infrastructure is prone to corrupt practices worldwide, not only in airports, but also roads, electricity, water and other construction projects. The same goes for the defence and petroleum sectors. Kickbacks and 'cuts' are often easy to arrange when contracts are negotiated. Southern Sudan was no exception.

President Kiir knew what was going on, and soon encountered major problems. Overspending was rampant during the first years, with a total lack of fiscal discipline. Planned investments in roads, schools, clinics and so on were squeezed out by the burgeoning payroll.[56] There was already an exponential increase in organized forces (SPLA, police, prison guards, wildlife wardens and war veterans), constituting about 80 per cent of government personnel.[57] Kiir dismissed his first minister of finance and a number of officials on corruption charges after only a year, disciplined several ministers, and tried with international help to establish a more robust financial system. It soon became clear that most in the leadership of the government in Juba, the army, and the SPLM itself expected to 'eat', one way or another. Kiir seemed to fear that rocking the boat would threaten the unity of Southerners before the all-important referendum.

For Southern Sudanese appointed to the Government of National Unity in Khartoum it was more difficult to engage in corruption because they were under scrutiny by Northern counterparts. But some there, notably in the Ministry of Petroleum or in positions related to national security had easy access to substantial amounts of cash[58] and to money-making opportunities connected to state contracts.[59]

One area involved telecom companies. Some cadres got involved very early in mobile-phone licensing, and some acquired significant holdings in companies. The first mobile phone company in the South was Gemtel, which registered in 2004 and began operations (without Khartoum's approval) in 2005. The main reason for its establishment was to avoid Khartoum's monitoring of Southerners' communications. The shareholders included leading commanders in the SPLM/A and a Ugandan investor, who put up most of the capital. Gemtel soon became profitable, and was sold, controversially, to Libyan interests in 2006. Speculation about the sale price, the beneficial shareholders (one of whom, a prominent SPLM politician, was rumoured to have got the biggest share of the massive profits) and kickbacks has continued with deleterious effect until today.[60]

Vivacell, another Southern Sudanese mobile-phone company, resulted from an agreement between a Lebanese investor, with a 75 per cent share, and SPLM cadres (with a 25 per cent share paid from unknown sources) through a party-owned company called Wawad Ltd. The party was also rumoured to be involved, presumably to generate profits. But Wawad also had shares in Imatong Gas, which operated in the oil industry, New Insurance Company, and other enterprises.[61] Both Gemtel and Vivacell were granted tax exemptions not extended to competitors.[62]

If, as rumoured, the SPLM put up some of the Vivacell's initial capital, shareholder dividends should have appeared in the party accounts. The company is reported to have generated monthly revenue of $90–180 million;[63] even the lower figure translating to more than $200 million in profits in a year. Sources with access to the books state that nothing of the kind appeared in the government's or SPLM's accounts. This issue was included in investigations into the party coffers in 2013.[64] Some money from Vivacell allegedly still continues to go to a senior party official.[65]

Such practices were hardly alien to the national Sudanese scene, where corruption was a significant long-term problem. Institutions still functioned somehow in Khartoum; economic mismanagement and total lack of financial controls, as evidenced in numerous audits, had a much more serious impact in the south.[66] Building state institutions while their financial basis is being eaten away and their staff are involved in illicit activities is extremely difficult. As late as 2010, observers waiting for a meeting with a senior official at the President's Office in Juba saw big cardboard boxes, stacked with bundles of US dollars, being delivered.[67] Even making allowances for a cash-based economy, the absence of a paper trail make it very likely that this money was never properly booked.

Doling out large amounts of cash was a practice in Khartoum, too, where high-level government officials regularly did so from their offices.[68] Stories circulated widely of money changing hands between staff at the presidency and visitors. Well-wishers' leaving cash at the President's Office in Juba was likewise not uncommon.[69]

During the interim period, one minister of finance, on his last day in office, was observed in the VIP lounge of Juba airport with seven black brief cases as hand luggage, waiting for a flight.[70] One could only guess the contents.

## From the horse's mouth: South Sudan's audits

During the period 2005–11, some $12 billion in oil revenue was reportedly transferred to Southern Sudan.[71] Detailed monthly oil reports indicated some level of transparency. A similar picture of expenditure has not been available. As we shall see, President Kiir estimated the gap between income and expenditure at $4 billion, a figure Copnall considers possibly too low.[72] Clearly a huge amount of money was unaccounted for. This does not mean it was all stolen. There is no doubt, however, that vast sums were misappropriated one way or another.

The best source for studying this development is the Audit Chamber. Under the professional and courageous leadership of Auditor General Stephen Wondu the chamber produced impressive, transparent and straightforward reports. In statements for the fiscal years 2005–8,[73] procedural mishaps, massive overspending, gaping holes in accounting and amazing misappropriation were revealed. Hundreds of millions of dollars were unaccounted for. For 2005–6, for example, oil revenue transfers were reported as over $580 million, while the financial statement recognized receipt of $704 million.[74]

What many regard as the first major case of GoSS corruption involved the Aweil-Miriam road project in Northern Bahr el Ghazal. Some $12 million was paid out for construction, while another $68 million was 'earmarked for road construction' and loans of $288 million were reportedly guaranteed for road works in the same state.[75] The Legislative Assembly authorized no such extra-budgetary appropriation, and the Minister of Roads and Transport denies all knowledge of the project.[76] Whatever the case may be, to date no one has seen the road.

In the same fiscal year 2005–6, more than $120 million was spent on purchases of vehicles, with absolutely no records. Fifteen government institutions, accounting for more than 80 per cent (or $440 million) of total payroll, could not present any records of their staff.[77]

The Auditor General actually dared to suggest what such sums meant to his poor country. More than $114 million missing from the GoSS financial statements for 2007 would have been enough to import 3,800 heavy tractors, significantly reducing or even eliminating dependence on imported food, alleviating rural poverty and generating additional revenue for local and state governments.[78] The Ministry of Education, for its part, granted itself a novel 'weekend allowance' that could have paid the salaries of 855 teachers.[79]

Even the detailed monthly oil reports were subject, in the Audit Chamber's terms, to 'creative' accounting.[80] The chamber complained that accounts and records on oil production and revenue were inaccessible, making it impossible to report on the credibility of records upstream, or the sales downstream, including invoicing and payment details.[81] In what was to be a repetitive complaint, the Audit found no evidence that the Ministry of Finance and Economic Planning based its release of funds on approved budget lines. There was indeed no way to affirm that the financial affairs of the country were conducted in accordance with the Appropriations Act of 2007, one of the few pieces of legislation passed during the interim period.[82]

The Ministry of Finance received particular attention from the Audit Chamber. In 2006–7 that Ministry could provide documentation for only one-third of its (alleged) employees. Not to be outdone, in 2007–8 the Ministry of Legal Affairs tripled its payroll expenditure *every month for four months in a row*.[83] No explanation was given to auditors. The same thing happened in other ministries, as I later ascertained from relevant documents.[84]

Accountants elsewhere might be surprised that the Ministry of Finance and Economic Planning was one of the GoSS's biggest spenders, in 2008 exceeding almost all of its own budget by as much as 400 per cent.[85] The Ministry's purchase of 400 Land Cruisers, without tender,[86] was one of the first corruption scandals of the era, and led eventually to the Finance Minister's demise. As the Audit Chamber points out in numerous damning reports, single sourcing was systematically used in public contracts throughout the interim period.

It was also in 2008 that the so-called Dura Scandal erupted. The Audit of 2008 notes contracts to purchase some $2.3 billion worth of dura (sorghum). Companies unregistered or incapable of delivering the grain were nonetheless awarded contracts.[87] Several investigation committees were set up, but not much happened. When international investigations were launched several years later, it became clear that although contracts had been signed, in the majority of cases money had not been transferred. In the end some $250 million had been subject to fraudulent transactions.[88]

As in 2005/6 and 2007, every report for 2008 issued by the Audit Chamber ends with a telling sentence:

> Without the benefit of the review of oil revenue documents (97.5%) of total revenue, without review of substantial records of SPLA pay roll expenditure for the year, and in light of the discrepancies found in the sample tests in my opinion, the financial statements of the Government of Southern Sudan for the year ended 31st December 2008 do not present a true and fair financial position.

It is worth noting that an Anti-Corruption Commission had been toothless from its inception. Attempts to strengthen itself during the interim period, or after independence, whether legislatively or through greater capacity, proved unsuccessful. Whatever the Commission tried, others prevented. Its independent prosecuting authority was actually set out in the Transitional Constitution.[89] The Ministry of Justice nevertheless hobbled it, for what reasons we can only speculate. Despite the President's strong rhetoric, the Commission clearly did not get the teeth necessary to do its job.[90]

## Broken social contract

In 2009 the drop in the world price of oil had serious repercussions in Southern Sudan. When the government tried to mobilize emergency financial assistance from donors, they held back. Most aid was in the form of projects or funds administered by others, and not the Southern Sudanese;[91] now the government wanted assistance directly. A so-called Compact between the government and donors was eventually reached, based on mutual accountability, and covering a range of issues.[92] By this time, June 2009, as the Dura Scandal hit the headlines, no donors would help without a strong commitment to accountability.

The Government failed to fulfil its promises.[93] Several years passed before the necessary legislation was enacted, and even the Dura saga was not dealt with until 2012, when Kosti Manibe Ngai was minister of finance and won the help of the World Bank and UN Office on Drugs and Crime. They investigated, clarified financial implications, and identified the fraud. To date (2015), however, none of the individuals involved have been charged or taken to court.

From the donors' point of view there were still grave problems within the financial institutions themselves. The sub-office, not a proper Central Bank, managed billions of dollars of oil revenue. With a weak institution and limited transparency, there was a danger that millions could get 'lost'. Stories circulated privately about Central Bank officials engaging in dubious practices.

Networks within the Ministry of Finance were corrupt, and linked up with accounts sections or payments units in other ministries. People knew whom to approach to get a signature to release funds, or for approval of contracts that were inflated or included kickbacks.[94] The security ministries lacked normal accounting procedures and record keeping, avoided transparent registration of personnel ('the parade'), and had massively inflated payrolls, as we shall see. Some ministers, trying to clean things up, showed me documents indicating the enormity of what was going on.[95] Copnall tells us that:

> A foreign consultant witnessed a senior official at a ministry receive a brown envelope, count the wedge of cash around three inches thick, and then tell the person who had handed him the envelope 'That's fine, you will get the contract on Monday.'[96]

More recently, in 2014, the South Sudanese presidency threatened punitive action against finance ministry officials who extorted bribes from companies seeking contracts. The media reported alarm at the extent of bribery at the ministry, allegations of widespread delays in payments, kickbacks, and nepotism.[97] I had received the same information from confidential sources.

Some suggest that Kosti Manibe's attempt to break these networks – through switching people in or out of key positions, and moving payment officers from one department to another, led to his suspension as minister of finance in April 2013 on charges of corruption. Others deny this, highlighting his failure to stop a dubious transfer of money by a ministerial colleague as the reason.[98]

Corruption behind closed doors is one thing. What people observe in town is another. One could see cars worth $150,000 or more – one SPLM leader has at least five. There were watches on display that cost $25,000 or more – one liberator had a $75,000 watch. They showed off smartphones costing hundreds of dollars, and were drinking the most expensive whisky and finest champagne. During the interim period, citizens could not fail to note construction of multi-storey buildings, and residential areas populated by SPLA generals and government officials with their own houses or even with two or three. Some ministers stayed in hotels, at government expense, while renting out their houses.[99] Houses rented for outrageous amounts, often as much as $25,000 a month.

Despite Juba's terrible roads at this time, it probably had more expensive four-wheel or luxury cars than almost anywhere else in East Africa. Flashy cars lined up at the airport, row upon row, including Hummers and the like. The old freedom fighter, Edward Lino, has published a recent example of the South Sudanese elite's new habits:

> I encountered a teenager [...] who appeared to belong to one of the newly 'privileged classes' driving an elegant leather seated 2012 V8 Balloon (i.e: a Porsche racing car). I heard him asking some of his colleagues about the availability of a 2013 Model to change his 'outdated' wind-dropped Balloon.[100]

Beyond the parking lot the airport itself was a different story. Its rundown buildings were scheduled years ago for replacement by a new international terminal that stands half-finished next to it. Contracts worth some $30–50 million (at conservative estimates) were awarded by the first minister of roads and transport, with successors funding first South African, then Ugandan contractors. But the work was never completed.[101] A $158 million loan from a Chinese bank is now supposedly intended to complete the terminal, incurring even more debt for the government.[102] A parliamentary enquiry has been launched.

The ring road around Juba is another example. When finally completed, it cost three or four times more per kilometre than the advanced tarmac road constructed by USAID from Uganda to Juba.[103] The same company got a number of infrastructure contracts around the capital, reportedly in the order of around $160 million.[104] Considering all the money spent across the country over the years, and such meagre results, I used to call the senior official in charge the 'Minister of No Roads and No Bridges'. As a very senior SPLM member from the early days put it: 'They built a system like a buffet. Anybody could come and take their dish and go.'[105]

Patronage expected from people in office should not be underestimated. Transparency International has observed this phenomenon in South Sudan.[106] It is true that a 'big man' in a 'big office' is expected to deliver a lot for his (or – much less often – her) community. Ethnic and clan affiliation leads to expectations of handouts, favours, jobs, contracts, and the rest. Several ministers told me about the pressures. They could set up 'camp' outside their office. Also at home 20–30 people would be living in their house at any point in time, expecting cash in hand. There was 'inflation' in expectations related to contributions of cattle for bride-wealth and communal events.

While it is expected that a leader should have more than others, and should assist, excessive wealth on display goes way beyond popular imagination. A 'big man' does not need $27,000,000 to subsidize his relatives and wider patronage network, but that is how much one SPLM leader held in his Kampala accounts; others reportedly have much more.[107] Indeed, credible sources also report that liberators have individual bank accounts or holdings abroad of over $10 million and some up to $100 million or more.[108] These fortunes are kept mostly in Kenya and Uganda, but a lot also in London, the US, South Africa, Australia and Switzerland. In Nairobi and Kampala there are many houses owned by South Sudanese in rich neighbourhoods; some look like palaces.[109]

Unless all of these characters were planning to run for president, and needed to fund election campaigns, they have stolen and salted away much more than any 'big men' would need. Alex de Waal has summarized the situation succinctly:

South Sudan obtained independence in July 2011 as a kleptocracy – a militarized, corrupt neo-patrimonial system of governance. By the time of independence, the South Sudanese 'political marketplace' was so expensive that the country's comparatively copious revenue was consumed by the military-political patronage system, with almost nothing left for public services, development and institution building.[110]

## From liberators to big spenders

So while some became fabulously rich, and did nothing to hide it, the results were meagre for ordinary citizens. Peace did not give them food on the table, clinics for their sick, or schools for their children.

As they awaited the 'peace dividend', the GoSS budget surged, almost doubling between 2006 and the end of the interim period. At independence, South Sudan had become the biggest spender in the African neighbourhood, close to $350 per capita – three times what Kenya spent, and more than four times as much as Uganda. In 2011 South Sudan overspent its budget by 50 per cent.[111]

By the time of independence in 2011 the appalling state of budgetary management revealed by the Auditor General should have improved. As the price of oil rebounded after the 2008–9 financial crisis, and despite increased capacity and support, actual budgetary management remained very poor. The World Bank, for example, characterized payroll management and personal accounts as being 'grossly mismanaged'.[112]

A major part of the budget was still allocated to the security sector, and most of the expenditure in the ministries went to salaries rather than services. Programmes for the suffering people, whether in education, health or rural livelihood support, were few and largely implemented by external donors, faith-based organizations, or NGOs. By independence not a single inter-state trunk road had been completed. Only 5,000 km of dirt roads had been constructed, and a lot of that by the World Food Programme.[113]

For the more than 80 per cent of Southern Sudanese who lived in rural areas, what mattered most was security, food, schools, clinics and roads. In numerous speeches, President Kiir claimed that these were among his highest priorities. But numbers alone show the opposite. The budget for the entire education sector was constant throughout the interim period, at about five per cent of the total, with around half going to primary education. This was among the lowest allocations in the world; the average for East Africa was 20 per cent.[114] While the number of children enrolled in primary school almost doubled during the first years, this was mostly owed to international support, and from 2009 transfers to education declined and most indicators deteriorated.[115] More than half of the children in South Sudan were still out of school, and illiteracy rates were still astoundingly high. Only one-third of the adult population could read and write; in Kenya the number is over 85 per cent.[116]

In the health sector the situation was worse. After 2006 the amount budgeted actually declined, and since 2010, at 2.1 per cent of the budget, has been among the lowest in the world.[117] Donors have funded 70 per cent of the services in the health sector, which was probably the main factor in reducing infant mortality between 2006 and 2010.[118] But only one person in ten had access to health services, and the maternal mortality rate was the highest in the world.[119] *Even now, it is more likely that a teenage girl will die in childbirth than that she will enter grade eight at school, 13–15 years old.*[120] At independence, almost half the population had no access to clean water and one in five to sanitation.[121] Hardly any investment was made in agriculture and livestock, key areas of livelihood and economic development in Southern Sudan.

It seemed clear that SPLM leaders had not delivered on their many promises. Rather than bringing towns and services to the people, ever-more resources were concentrated at the centre.

Illustrative of the challenges was a comment from an ordinary citizen, a driver. I asked how Juba had changed since the CPA. His response was surprising:

> Actually, it was better under the Arabs. At least they left us alone – unless we got ourselves into trouble. But the Dinkas, they don't respect us, they abuse us, use rude language, and take our land.

To him the Dinka appeared foreigners too, not Southern Sudanese brothers. He was not alone. Similar language would be used against Equatorians; Juba was alien territory even for many SPLM and SPLA cadres and government officials of Nilotic origin, many of whom never felt welcome in their own capital. Such feelings, on both sides, would later fuel ethnic tensions.

The Sudanese state had been a disturbing element extracting resources from the peripheries rather than providing services. A Nuer description of government is 'a group of people who have decided to come together to eat on behalf of the people'.[122] But the liberators appeared to continue in the footsteps of Khartoum. Instead of changing the political order, the new centre, Juba, monopolized financial resources and the towns got most of the services.[123] Figures from the interim period suggest that South Sudan compared unfavourably even with Sudan when it came to concentration of national wealth.[124]

South Sudan became a highly centralized state, an unintended consequence of greed, short-sightedness, inexperience in government, and lack of commitment to build the capacity necessary to do better. According to Thomas, under SPLM's leadership:

> the national capital [in many respects] relates to rural South Sudan in a manner that many ordinary people compare to Khartoum.[125]

The new contract between state and citizen reflected in the SPLM's transition strategy[126] was never implemented.

## Independence: Time for delivery

Frustrated SPLM cadres counted on independence to set a new course. To prepare for independence, in 2010 the government started the GOSS Priority Core Functions programme focusing on the main areas of state responsibility regardless of the referendum's outcome. After consultations across ministries, and coordinated by a competent team at the undersecretary level, 6 priority areas and 19 core functions were identified as most urgent. The priority areas were executive leadership, the security sector, rule of law and rule enforcement, fiduciary management, public administration and management of natural resources.

An Action Plan was launched in September 2010 and presented to donors at a high-level meeting in Brussels.[127] Together with the UN, World Bank and other donors, bilateral and multilateral, support programmes were identified and committed to. Some were already under way, others commenced, to build institutional capacity prior to independence.

The plan was intended to make sure that the process was completed in a timely manner. After the result of the referendum was clear, there would be only six months left before independence. The GoSS would have to focus on the most urgent short-term priorities, which were identified as 'executive peer learning', legislation (linked to independence), police training, customs, currency, the oil sector and oil revenue. Work had started in these areas, but time was short.

The whole process was managed by the Southern Sudan 2011 Task Force chaired by Vice President Riek Machar, which would oversee the building of institutions for state 'take-off' and preparations for Independence Day celebrations, as well as supervise negotiations over secession. It met weekly and almost became a parallel cabinet, and in doing so epitomized the widening rift between the two most senior SPLM figures Salva Kiir and Riek Machar.

The Core Functions programme was to be followed by a grandiose South Sudan Development Plan (2011–13), supported by a revised GoSS Aid Strategy. These were intended to address medium-term needs in the post-independence period, and involved elaborate programmes developed by the different 'pillars' (clusters of sectors) of the Government of South Sudan, with consultations in all ten states as well as with the Legislative Assembly.

The South Sudan Development Plan was a massive 400 pages.[128] Main priorities were identified as improving governance, achieving rapid rural transformation, improving and expanding education and health services, and deepening peace-building and improving security. The plan had baselines, targets, indicators per sector, and a monitoring framework. It would involve a herculean effort. But with the limited capacity of the Southern Sudanese administration and no cost estimates or public expenditure framework, a major question was whether the plan was at all realistic.

Observers might be surprised that the GoSS decided to conduct a self-assessment during the interim period. This was a SPLM initiative, entirely homegrown, funded from government coffers, conducted by Southern Sudanese researchers, and led by a ministerial committee collaborating with relevant local networks, think tanks and academics. Substantial resources were devoted to this effort, and the results were impressive.

The in-depth evaluation highlighted gaps that most of us long-term observers had noted, and identified dysfunction and deficiencies critically in need of correction. It addressed weaknesses in the executive, including the presidency, the ministries and directorates. It highlighted problems at the national, state and county levels, and the National Legislature. It provided a number of bold recommendations, even including restructuring the cabinet and presidency.

This truly unique product, completed only in the first quarter of 2012 (with the help of Priscilla Nyandeng Kuch, a deputy minister), was duly circulated, with strict confidentiality, to key SPLM leaders. As SRSG I was briefed, and I repeatedly pushed for the report to be deliberated at the highest levels in the cabinet and the SPLM, suggesting that a retreat discuss the findings. The report was eventually ignored, in part because of increasing tensions within the leadership.

What were the perceptions of the people? More than 2,000 were interviewed in all parts of the country in 2011, prior to independence.[129] Their responses were unsurprising. The top concern was hunger. Insecurity and health were seen as major problems, followed by education. Corruption was listed as a problem, but not in relation to mere survival. Stories of corruption had been rife on the streets of Juba, but people had given the SPLM the benefit of the doubt. They blamed Khartoum. And they still had hope that independence would change things.

## Independence

When President Bashir visited Juba on 4 January 2011, five days before the referendum, and said he would respect the result, whatever the outcome, the Southern Sudanese finally believed that their dream would come true; 3,930,816 had been registered eligible to partake in the referendum, 51 per cent of them women.[130] On 9 January, the long queues started at dawn and continued until dusk. Waiting was not a problem; it seldom is in Southern Sudan. Women lined up as much as men. Many places people were dancing in the queue, playing drums, singing and cheering. It was a blessing to wait for something so precious. More than anything, the referendum was a celebration; they would now take the final decision on where they belonged.

The referendum was conducted without incident. All international observers noted that it had been free and fair; the result was credible and legitimate. As we have seen, the outcome was an overwhelming majority for secession and an independent South Sudan. When the result of the vote was announced, with all members of the SPLM leadership and government seated in anticipation, even the toughest freedom fighters could not hold their tears back. Several SPLM leaders later told me that this moment was the most emotional of all. The vote was even more overwhelming than expected. The celebration that followed lasted for days.

With independence, people really expected change. Otherwise, there was a high risk that the credibility of the liberators would be at risk. After secession they could no longer blame Sudan. As one leading member of the SPLM says, 'The scapegoat had escaped.'[131]

It appeared that a country had been born, largely without a state. While the former peacekeeping mission for obvious reasons had a limited mandate in relation to building capacity, and was focused on monitoring implementation of the CPA, this role changed with establishment of the United Nations Mission in South Sudan the day before independence. UNMISS had a more ambitious state-building and peace-building mandate than was normal in similar missions elsewhere, with capacity development a priority.

In addition to the mandated tasks of building capacity in areas such as rule of law, police and law enforcement, extension of state authority, and support for democratic governance, the Mission was tasked with developing and coordinating one of the first Peace Building Support Plans in the UN's history. Peace consolidation, peace- and nation-building were thus at the heart of the mission's mandate.

Political capital had all been invested in getting the referendum and independence; underneath the euphoria of newly won freedom was a lingering question: what now? The SPLM had not developed a vision for building their new nation, a strategy to heal broken relationships and weld diverse pieces into one. At the same time, the leadership was swamped in crisis management, unable to focus attention on the long term. This in itself might have contributed to exacerbating the impending crisis.

A major problem for all state-building efforts, a concern of donors, national and international stakeholders alike, was entrenched corruption. South Sudan entered Transparency International's index as an independent country in 2011 with the following description:

> Corruption permeates all sectors of the economy and all levels of the state apparatus and manifests itself through various forms, including grand corruption and clientelistic [sic] networks along tribal lines.[132]

Kiir's steps to curb corruption were timid, too little and too late. In his independence speech the President recognized as much:

> Official corruption has been one of our major challenges during the interim period. In order to develop our country, and deliver on the important goals of our National Development Plan, it is critical that we fight corruption with dedication, rigour, and commitment. As president, I pledge to you to do all I can to remove this cancer. We will work closely with our development partners as we move forward.

But the Independence Day celebrations themselves had ludicrously been another opportunity for kickbacks, 'cuts' and backroom deals. At least several million dollars was reportedly misappropriated by companies and officials.[133]

Mismanagement was also illustrated by another scandal related to independence. Only after passports for the new Republic of South Sudan were produced in huge numbers and at a cost of millions was it realized that a printing mistake rendered them invalid. Yet, I hoped this was not an omen.

## New country – new currency

Only two days after independence, the Government of South Sudan sent waves through the international community. It intended to adopt a new currency within a matter of days. Normally such a process takes a year, and at the very least six months. Less than that would entail significant macro-economic risk; the IMF's advice was crystal clear. The reason for haste was a rumour that Khartoum was about to change its own currency, the Sudanese pound, and revert to the old dinar, presumably to render worthless the pounds held by the public and the Central Bank in South Sudan.

The leadership claimed solid evidence of Khartoum's plans, and crisis meetings were held. The IMF and World Bank communicated their concern to the Ministry of Finance and the Central Bank. No country had ever done what the government contemplated.

When a new currency is launched it must either be pegged to another currency or floated on the open market to determine its exchange value. Pegging could be dangerous because it would commit the government to supporting an official rate of exchange without the reserves needed to do so. And even a 'managed float' entailed the risk of immediate collapse when done in such a short time.

Although the cabinet before independence had agreed on a transition period of nine months during which South Sudan would continue to use the Sudanese pound,[134] they now seemed to reject advice on the issue. Apparently, no IMF missions were granted meetings with senior government officials. When I met the President on 11 July about this and other issues, with technical advice in hand, he said that they had not reached a decision. He promised to contact the Minister of Finance and discuss the issue further.

During this same week Sudan and South Sudan were meeting in Addis Ababa. There had been no indication that Khartoum would change its currency. On Sunday 17 July, at about noon, my phone rang. My colleague Haile Menkerios, Special Envoy to the Sudan–South Sudan process, was calling from the Ethiopian capital. The talks had just finished. Sudan and South Sudan had disagreed on interim financial-transfer arrangements, and no solution seemed in sight.

That evening I met informally the cabinet's Crisis Management committee to discuss the currency issue. They were all sure that Khartoum planned to withdraw the Sudanese pound, with almost immediate effect. I argued the opposing case. But when Kosti Manibe, normally the most pragmatic and least emotional of SPLM leaders, also advocated quick action, I knew I had lost. 'We are in a currency war with Khartoum', he said. 'They will try to use this issue to create havoc in our economy.'[135]

The Government went ahead. The South Sudanese pound was launched on 19 July, ten days after independence. It was a popular move. The initial exchange value was set at 2.96 to the dollar. Instead of letting the market determine its value over a longer period the government chose a managed float, requiring support should the currency come under pressure.[136] All Sudanese pounds on the Southern side of the border now had to be exchanged for South Sudanese pounds in one go. The fear was that their Sudanese pounds would otherwise be rendered worthless. That exchange rate was 1:1.[137] The Central Bank needed hard currency and gold equivalent in value to all currency brought into circulation. This was estimated at $432.5 million.

On 24 July, a week later, we got another surprise. While Khartoum kept the same currency in name, they launched new banknotes.[138] People in Sudan could exchange their notes, but Khartoum would not redeem old notes in circulation in South Sudan (i.e. exchange it for USD or gold). This violated the agreement allowing use of Sudanese pound for nine months. So although there was no change of currency as such, in the end the South Sudanese Government was right, and I – among others – had been wrong. Fortunately they had gone to Switzerland in time to design a new currency of their own. In the 'currency race' South Sudan had been quicker.

## New country – new reform opportunities

The Government's decision to introduce a new currency so soon after independence met with resounding applause at the Opening of the National Legislative Assembly a month later. On that occasion the President also launched a 100-day plan for early peace dividends, of which some 85 per cent was implemented on time, despite criticism.[139] The President also went much further in detailing concrete plans to root out corruption. Using the rhetoric of the liberation wars, Kiir defined the corrupt as enemies of the people, and launched several initiatives that included long-awaited legislation on financial management and audit, and strengthening of the Anti-Corruption Commission and the Audit Chamber. He warned senior officials present:

We will take action on their findings [...] and there will be no loopholes for people who are addicted to mishandling public resources. There will be no sacred cows this time around.[140]

This made some people nervous. Maybe this time the President really meant business. Would there be a crackdown on corruption? The President told me privately that he had had enough. He had tolerated the corruption of comrades and ministers up to independence. But now it had to stop.

As combating corruption was also very important for state-building, I discussed with Salva Kiir what we in the international community could do to help. As early as in August 2011 high-level foreign experts were identified for secondment to key financial institutions. They were lined up, awaiting word from the President's Office to move forward. The Central Bank was a particular subject of concern. It would now be responsible for receiving all oil income through the Treasury Account.[141] South Sudan produced 350,000 barrels of oil per day, which would return billions of dollars in annual income. After independence this would no longer be shared with Khartoum, except for any special provisions the parties agreed on. The sheer scale implied higher risk of corruption.

Getting high level foreign experts for the Central Bank, Ministry of Finance, Anti-Corruption Commission and Audit Chamber was a top priority. The intention was to help reform the systems, build stronger institutions, and provide mentorship from experienced practitioners from other African countries. UNMISS was also in a position to assist the presidency with expertise in coordinating this effort.[142] Progress seemed possible; the political cost of taking action would only increase with time.

The new cabinet was appointed on 26 August 2011, after a long delay. Ironically the signatories on the new currency notes, the Minister of Finance and Governor of the Central Bank, were no longer in office. Many other ministers remained, however, and some new faces and a number of deputy ministers catered for ethnic and gender balances.

A few weeks later the new government created consternation among international stakeholders. On the very day that the Bank of South Sudan was established, in September, the newly appointed Governor, Kornelio Koryom, announced a decision to fix the exchange rate of the

South Sudanese pound against the dollar.[143] Under terms of the Central Bank Law the authorities had been expected to operate a managed float for a period of up to six months, beginning in July 2011, and subsequently to peg it at a sustainable level vis-à-vis the US dollar.[144] The Bank argued that a fixed exchange rate was necessary to drive down the black market for the pound, which in mid October was at about 4 to the dollar. But the rate fixed by the Bank overvalued the pound.[145] To maintain it the Bank would need more dollars to buy pounds. Since it lacked sufficient dollars to do so, parallel exchange rates were born, one official, the other on the black market.

In acting in the way it did, the government had adopted a policy very lucrative for dealers in foreign exchange, who included a number of well-connected members of the SPLM/A and the government. Although the Bank of South Sudan was legally independent, it still had no board of governors. The Governor and staff operated without oversight. In practice, moreover, the government continued to intervene.

For international players – donors, businesses, the IMF and World Bank – the currency decision became another corruption scandal. Donors and commercial enterprises operating at the official rate of exchange all lost, as indeed did the government eventually. Donors calculated a loss in development aid of as much as $145 million and from international investors as several times more.[146] Calculating losses was difficult, however, as the true (if imperfect) value of the currency could be ascertained only on the black market.

The decision of September 2011 was also politically costly. It made many stakeholders question South Sudan's capacity for macro-economic decision making. And it added to suspicions that the entrenched culture of corruption had found in South Sudan's independence new ways to serve the elite.

Following the appointment of the new cabinet, and these discussions, there was therefore a real sense of stasis. But on 21 September, as he departed for the UN General Assembly, Salva Kiir released another strong statement listing far-reaching steps he would take to fight corruption.[147] This time there were concrete measures. His legislative programme centred on five bills related to public financial management and accountability, procurement, internal auditing, and petroleum and oil revenue management. He also launched processes for investigating and prosecuting corruption cases; public declaration of officials' income and assets;[148] review of land sales during the transitional period; and facilitating the return, anonymously or through the intervention of foreign governments, of illegally diverted funds.[149] Would he now act on his promise that 'those who had eaten stolen food would vomit it'?[150]

It was my clear impression that we would finally see action, a view which was buttressed by the President's statement to the General Assembly and his comments in bilateral meetings in New York.

## South Sudan loses its innocence

In New York, however, we got a first hint of problems that would arise in relations between South Sudan and the international community. (A meeting with President Obama will be discussed in the next chapter.) The Troika countries' elaborate dinner in collaboration with Secretary-General Ban Ki-moon in tribute to South Sudan's independence, with President Salva Kiir as guest of honour, descended into farce. The President sent word that he was 'not well', leaving the Secretary-General and some 70 heads of government, ministers and ambassadors waiting for a long time, before his ministers finally turned up, oblivious to the gravity of their diplomatic faux-pas. The SPLM's sense of entitlement seemed to include the international community.

Interestingly, a similar charade occurred in the margins of the General Assembly in 2014. Illustrative of the change that had taken place in South Sudan in only three years, this time the event was not a celebratory dinner but a fundraising event to alleviate the humanitarian crisis caused by the current civil war. Despite the great personal efforts of the UN Secretary-General to make the event a success, Kiir did not attend. Similar inexplicable absences from summits and bilateral meetings gave rise to questions about the South Sudanese President's commitment and health.

Protocol was one thing; war was another. Rumours were rife that elements within the South Sudan security apparatus were supporting the newly established SPLM-North in the Nuba Mountains of Southern Kordofan, as well as in Sudan's Southern Blue Nile region. When the CPA protocols for both areas went largely unimplemented, and tensions rose, South Kordofan and Blue Nile, just as Abyei before them, were soon engulfed in open warfare with Khartoum.

Just prior to independence, Abyei was again engulfed in violence.[151] In May the Sudanese Armed Forces occupied the town, which was burnt to the ground, and 100,000 people were displaced,[152] prompting the UN Security Council to establish a protective force.[153]

But now the focus was on the other two areas. I had warned the President, before his departure for New York, that alleged military support for the SPLM-N would be raised in New York. Several countries reportedly had evidence through their own sources; he needed to be prepared to respond in a way that inspired trust. To me he denied that any lethal support was being provided. As expected, the issue dominated discussions in the margins of the General Assembly, and it would continue to torment Sudan–South Sudan relations and the latter's engagement with the international community for a long time. Severing links between comrades would never be easy, but the issue could have been managed better by the South Sudanese Government in diplomatic circles, thus retaining at least some credibility.

The handling of other issues was also puzzling. After the currency issue, the first act of the new cabinet was the decision to move the capital from Juba to a place called Ramciel, which few people had even heard of. I had to find it on a map – and with some difficulty, for it was a tiny village. The rationale for this decision appeared to be tensions between the central Government and Equatorian communities and authorities in Juba.[154] I later learned that a ministerial committee had been engaged at the President's request: consultants had been hired and some sketchy reports made. No one had done a proper feasibility study or any calculations of cost. It seemed clear that the new government had a long way to go.

Within two months of independence South Sudan's Government had made several decisions that surprised most observers. But most international interlocutors continued to give the government the benefit of the doubt. They still thought that independence had given the South Sudanese a new opportunity to get things on the right track.

More worrying was the concern that such decisions might prove the norm rather than the exception, as the cabinet settled into a disappointing and ineffective modus operandi. We saw no plans for reforms or commitment to clean up the existing system. We saw no evidence that the Core Functions process was under way, or any desire to wage war against poverty. Ministers appeared more interested in protecting their positions than in moving the country forward. In discussions with me the President expressed serious concern, and a desire for change. But would he now deliver?

One of the experts we helped to recruit was John Githongo, the anti-corruption tsar from Kenya, whom I had known for many years. He met the President, and was convinced of a willingness to fight corruption. We organized a preliminary consultancy contract, pending other arrangements. Several top-notch foreign experts, all from the region, met the President, and a plan was adopted to deploy them to key sectors of financial management and monetary policy.[155] But despite these commitments, nothing happened.

The political cost of moving on these issues should have been lower now than at almost any other time. Independence had been achieved. Elections need not be held for almost five years. It was time, one assumed, to fight corruption, clean up payrolls, be bolder in reforming the security sector, pass legislation that had been delayed for ages, and so forth. Yet there seemed to be little political will. The key was the President; would he show strong leadership on these issues? Without it not much would move.

The Security Council had requested UNMISS to develop the Peace-building Support Plan within four months, by 9 November 2011.[156] The plan was meant to strengthen assistance and coordination in key peace-building areas such as conflict prevention and resolution, rule of law, security sector reform and socio-economic interventions. The process was delayed, however, as the cabinet first discussed the issue around this time.[157] During the next quarter, there were consultations with all stakeholders and donors. While this could have been an opportunity to move critical reforms forward, the government had neither the appetite for this, nor the capacity for yet another plan, and the outcome was based on already agreed objectives.[158]

In any case, the new cabinet was engulfed in disputes with Khartoum over the terms of the secession, whether border demarcation, the status of Abyei, or the use of the oil pipeline. Indeed, an important reason for the delays and lack of attention to important issues was the tension with Sudan. Despite all the efforts and pressure exerted on both sides, independence had been declared against the backdrop of numerous unresolved issues, of which some were linked to fundamental national interests. The divorce from Sudan was incomplete. Most fundamentally, there was no agreement on the international boundary.

I had always thought that the two parties would 'muddle through', usually after all deadlines had passed and when they had peered over the edge of the abyss. This had been the case throughout the CPA negotiations, and was a traditionally Sudanese way of doing things.[159] As Daly mentions in his book on Darfur, a word for delay in Arabic, *tajil*, had led to an Anglo-Sudanese coinage of 'tajility' as a method of getting one's way by stalling.[160] But now things had been delayed to the point of inanition.

Unresolved issues included the border; border security and trade; use of the oil pipeline to Port Sudan, including interim financial arrangements; management of water resources, including the Nile; division of assets and liabilities; citizenship and citizens' rights; and cross-border migration.[161]

Opinion polls now showed mounting concern. That as many as 42 per cent thought the country was heading in the wrong direction in September 2011, just after independence, said a lot.[162] In a representative focus-group study conducted across all ten states by the National Democratic Institute (NDI) in November 2011 found the same. A large majority said that South Sudan was headed in the wrong direction, a result ascribed to poor management, lack of development and services, and insecurity.[163] The new 'liberation war', against poverty, ignorance and disease had not been waged; people were beginning to see that their leaders were responsible.

The 'liberation curse' prevailed. The leadership did not make the necessary transitions or implement essential reforms. It also allowed the 'oil curse' to skew priorities, delaying critical state-building and peace-building interventions. While some progress had been made in the transition from war to peace and from liberation movement to government, there was a very long way to go.

The transition from being part of a united Sudan to completing the secession as an independent country had reached its most difficult stage. The South Sudanese were consumed by numerous crises. But relations with Sudan trumped everything else, whether the country's reform agenda, or growing tensions internally in the leadership. And as the tensions with Khartoum increased, the liberators were soon back in the trenches, united against Sudan.

The liberation struggle was not over.

# 3

◆

# AN INCOMPLETE DIVORCE

With independence, South Sudanese thought that peace had finally come. They were now masters in their own house. However, the greatest challenge for the new country remained relations with Khartoum. Agreements for a border-monitoring mission had been signed in July and August 2011,[1] but many issues, including border demarcation, the fate of Abyei, oil resources and use of the oil pipeline remained. As SRSG in Juba I had no role in these talks, which were conducted by the African Union High Level Panel (AUHIP), supported by my UN colleague, Special Envoy Haile Menkerios.

Tensions had increased following the take-over of Abyei by the Sudanese Armed Forces (SAF) on 19 May 2011, and Khartoum's subsequent unilateral dissolution of the Abyei Administration.[2] The situation in Southern Kordofan and Blue Nile, although not directly related to secession of the South, impacted relations between the two countries. On 5 June fighting broke out in Southern Kordofan between the SAF and remaining elements of the SPLA, followed by massive SAF aerial bombardment.[3]

Prior to independence, a meeting of the SPLM Leadership Council had adopted resolutions transforming their all-Sudanese movement into a South Sudan political party. Comrades in the Nuba Mountains/ South Kordofan and Blue Nile had been integral to the SPLM/A from the mid 1980s, and in its leadership. They now vacated their seats in the SPLM's highest organ, and created their own Northern party, SPLM-N.

A few days after Independence I attended a farewell dinner for Malik Agar, governor of Blue Nile State and Yasir Arman, secretary-general of SPLM/N. Both had hoped for a political solution to the problems of the border regions, in accordance with the Protocols of the CPA. But nothing had happened. Khartoum had rejected proposals to integrate former SPLA fighters from the North into the SAF, and instead ordered them to disarm without further dialogue. It seemed that the political avenue was closing.

They were now establishing SPLM-North to fight for a New Sudan and for justice in the marginalized areas. The third Northern leader, Abdel Aziz Adam El-Hilu, had already departed for Kordofan and the Nuba Mountains, following the fighting. A pragmatist at heart, Malik Agar wanted to avoid war in Blue Nile and give the political process another try. On 31 August 2011 he travelled to Khartoum with the Ethiopian Prime Minister, Meles Zenawi, to meet President Bashir and propose a process for negotiating issues related to the future of Blue Nile. According to Malik, Bashir showed no willingness to find a solution.[4] And sure enough, on 1 September, the SAF launched a major offensive. The surprise attack started in Damazin, the capital of Blue Nile, and Malik himself had to flee his compound in his slippers.[5] The SPLM-North was banned.

## Comrades in arms

With an escalation to civil war in Kordofan and Blue Nile, relations between those regions, and between the rebel forces and South Sudan, became complicated.

Increased intelligence from several sources indicated that South Sudan, despite promises to the contrary, was providing old comrades with military support which, if confirmed, threatened to undermine relations between the two countries and fuel a continuing proxy war. President Obama raised this issue at his first meeting with Salva Kiir in September 2011. George W. Bush had met the South Sudanese leader eight times, but Obama had not engaged in the same way,[6] and Kiir needed to establish good personal relations with the American President.

But in New York Kiir denied that his government was supplying the SPLM-N. The Americans knew this was not true, and despite an apologetic letter he wrote later,[7] Kiir continued his denials. Other members of the Security Council, with their own sources of information, likewise criticized South Sudan in bilateral meetings.

On 8 October 2011 Salva Kiir paid his first visit to Khartoum as President of South Sudan. He was for the first time received at the airport by President Bashir. Their discussions centred on remaining issues related to the secession. Kiir tabled financial proposals. To compensate for Sudan's loss of oil revenue and to assist with the transition of the battered Sudanese economy, South Sudan would offer $2.04 billion as an interim financial package.[8] In return, however, South Sudan would expect concessions on the final status of Abyei, border demarcation, trade relations, settlement of debts and division of assets.[9]

As late Ethiopian Prime Minister Zenawi would remind me when we discussed these issues, on almost all of them Bashir was expected to give way. He would need something substantive in return. The only 'hook' South Sudan now had in relation to Sudan and President Bashir, he said, was oil. With a net loss of 20 per cent of its oil revenue, Sudan faced an economic crisis. But Bashir did not accept the offer.

The issue of South Sudanese support to the SPLM-N was looming. In Khartoum Kiir, with a straight face, continued to deny that his government was providing such assistance. President Bashir would later tell me how betrayed he felt: 'I accepted the referendum and independence of South Sudan to finally get peace in Sudan, at great cost to my country and my people. But what I got instead was war.'[10] But the conflicts in Southern Kordofan and Blue Nile were not of South Sudan's making. They were a result of Khartoum's own policies; the CPA had addressed them; the conflicts were a consequence of non-implementation. Sudan, moreover, had long denied its own support for numerous Southern rebels. This rendered such frustrations limited credibility, despite feelings of betrayal.

The parties made no progress on Abyei. Sudan had promised to withdraw its forces by 30 September 2011, only to renege when it made withdrawal conditional on full deployment of the United Nations Interim Security Force for Abyei (UNISFA). Other measures in relation to Abyei were therefore stalled. Only on 1 November were 3200 UNISFA troops deployed, even as some 800 SAF soldiers remained.

Even after their withdrawal, Khartoum maintained a military presence under the rubric of 'oil police'.

On 9 November I received reports that SAF Antonov planes had made bombing raids across the border into South Sudan, first on Guffa and then on the refugee camp at Yida. Observers were shocked, and the Security Council was urgently convened. The Permanent Representative of the US, Susan Rice, and most other members condemned Sudan, but failed to agree on a statement. It was generally assumed that the incidents were linked to fighting between the SAF and SPLM-North in Southern Kordofan, the camps in South Sudan being seen by Khartoum as 'harbouring rebels'. Crossing the border and hitting a refugee camp was an entirely different story, however. UNHCR had photos of the bomb craters, and UNMISS representatives sent to both locations returned with evidence, pictures and eyewitness accounts.[11] Similar incidents took place during the next few months, escalating tensions between the two countries.

In a meeting of the African Union High Level Panel at the end of November, South Sudan presented its proposal for transitional financial arrangements.[12] Observers were pleasantly surprised by their approach: accepting to pay $2.6 billion over a period of four years, an increase over their original proposal.[13] Khartoum did not grasp the opportunity. Instead, Sudan asked for pipeline user-fees, demanding $10 billion, which most observers found unreasonable. The South Sudanese delegation understandably rejected this out of hand.

Worse was soon to come. In late November Sudan's parliament passed a resolution that implied a pipeline user fee for South Sudanese oil of $35 per barrel. (Standard fees elsewhere were between 10 cents and $3.50 per barrel.) Khartoum's position was so extravagant that observers hardly knew what to make of it.

In December, a border incident occurred, near Jau, north of Pariang, in the vicinity of the north-eastern corner of Unity State. South Sudan accused Khartoum of violating its sovereignty, and Sudan returned the favour. Both sent letters to the Security Council.

## Oil – the sharpest sword

In December, Sudan announced that if South Sudan refused to pay the pipeline user-fees demanded, Khartoum would confiscate the oil as payment.[14] At a meeting prior to Christmas, Sudan promised it would not execute this threat; negotiations would resume on 17 January. Juba meanwhile awaited agreement on user fees before paying anything. In the absence of an agreement they declined to recognize the unilaterally stipulated fees set by the Sudanese parliament.

Most external stakeholders in Juba were now focusing on the International Donor and Investment Conference in Washington in mid December, and had not closely monitored the pipeline dispute. At UNMISS, however, all eyes were on Jonglei, where a major crisis was developing.[15] On Christmas Day Sudan broke its promise, started confiscating oil from the pipeline and, according to our information, was selling it on the international market. Messages were sent to Khartoum, insisting on resumption of normal transfers, and urging Sudan to stop what was perceived as literally stealing the oil. These appeals were not heeded.

In early January 2012 it appeared that something was about to happen. I understood there were disagreements about the transfers, with government officials being upset with Khartoum. There was a lot of secrecy surrounding the deliberations in Juba, however. On 6 January the South Sudanese cabinet discussed six options provided by technical experts in the Ministry of Finance. Two were discarded at the outset as unrealistic, of which one was a shutdown of oil production.[16] An alternative oil pipeline circumventing Sudan might take five years to build and become operational.[17] There were no conclusions from this discussion, other than that another attempt would be made to address the situation with Khartoum before the cabinet's next meeting.

Meanwhile the Juba Government asked neighbouring countries to intervene with Khartoum. According to South Sudan, their northern neighbour had by now 'stolen' oil worth more than $800 million.[18] (Experts I consulted in Juba calculated that a more likely figure was about $685m, but that was bad enough.) If Khartoum did not relent, the South Sudanese said that they would be forced to shut down oil production. Vice President Stephen Kalonzo Musyoka of Kenya went to see President Bashir to make a personal appeal. Kalonzo told me about the interview: Bashir's response was that South Sudan had not paid its transit fees, and confiscation of oil was Khartoum's way of getting payment; they would not change their position.[19] Ethiopian contacts, which reportedly included a telephone call from Prime Minister Meles, likewise failed to move President Bashir.[20]

On 13 January the Government of South Sudan signed a so-called Transitional Agreement with oil companies from China, Malaysia and India, by which, among other things, the companies were partially responsible for the safe transit of crude from the field to vessels of the designated buyers at Port Sudan. Senior representatives of the Chinese Government then proceeded directly to Khartoum for further discussions. The visit was unsuccessful; Khartoum was unwilling to change its approach.

At this point a South Sudanese delegation travelled secretly to Addis Ababa to meet Sudanese counterparts to resolve the impasse, but this meeting too was to no avail. The South Sudanese Government made no attempt to inform other foreign stakeholders. The Norwegians, who had played an important role in supporting the development of the petroleum administration in South Sudan, knew nothing. Even the Americans had no idea. None of us had been asked for advice, or to explore other strategies, including the possibility of linking measures to the talks sequentially, increasing the pressure.

At about noon on 21 January I learned that the South Sudanese cabinet had decided to shut down oil production the evening before. I could not believe it. I immediately called Kosti Manibe, the minister of finance, to inquire whether this was a negotiating tactic, but no, Kosti told me, the decision had been made. The complicated process of halting production would be completed within two weeks.

I still thought that the government could be convinced to delay implementation and use this decision as a card in the negotiations. But the South Sudanese argued that since Khartoum was stealing all the oil, the result of a shutdown would be effectively the same. It would also at least deprive Sudan of revenue and force it to negotiate. South Sudan's oil crisis had become a game of chicken on a grand scale.[21]

I started working the phones, followed by meetings at the highest levels. Closing down production was not only senseless, I argued, it also implied throwing away an important negotiating card. I pointed out that a phased shutdown in conjunction with pressure from the international community had a better chance of success and with less risk to the South Sudanese economy. I had long discussions with Vice President

Riek Machar, the petroleum minister, Stephen Dau Dhieu, the minister of cabinet affairs, Deng Alor, and Kosti Manibe. But they were intransigent. South Sudan could not accept more stealing by Sudan. It was a matter of national pride; it was better that the oil remain underground for later use. What they wanted was 'economic independence' from Khartoum. They would rather suffer in the meantime.

Listening to the President's statement to an emergency meeting of the National Legislative Assembly, and to members' euphoric responses – shouts of 'SPLM Woyee' after every verbal attack on Khartoum – I realized that the liberators were now back in the trenches. The parliament seemed totally oblivious to the implications of the decision, as were the crowds shouting slogans against Khartoum outside the parliament. It was distressing, knowing that these poor people would soon enough realize that this was one of the least thought-through decisions that the leadership would ever make. And they would be the ones to suffer from it.

As a former MP from the oil capital of Norway, I knew quite a lot about pipelines in the petroleum industry, how long they could take to build, and how much they might cost. So it was astounding to hear Riek Machar, an engineer by training, claim that they would have an alternative pipeline operational to ports in Kenya or Djibouti (through Ethiopia) within ten months, and referring offhandedly to experience with the pipeline to Port Sudan. I told him that there was no comparison, since no preparatory analysis or feasibility studies had been done, a new pipeline would have to cross international borders, and the terrain presented many practical difficulties. It would also be very expensive. Unless deals had already been negotiated with oil companies, studies already completed, and funding lined up, a new pipeline could possibly see the light of day in years, not months. And it was unlikely to compete in economic terms with the existing route through Sudan.

Even more astonishing was that the advice of technical experts in the ministries of petroleum and finance also appeared to have been ignored. Whatever my arguments, nothing helped. Not even Dinka wisdom seemed to apply – 'If you have only one cow giving milk, you don't slaughter it.' It seemed obvious that the government's decision had been political, or even merely emotional, another phase in the South

Sudanese liberation struggle. The oil had become the sharpest sword, for both sides.

After further persuasion, both the President and Vice President agreed to hold off irreversible steps until after the African Union summit in Addis Ababa in a week's time. I had warned that a shutdown of oil production – in addition to all the other strikes against it – could be suicidal in relation to the AUHIP talks, which we hoped would be nearing a final deal on finance in the margins of this meeting.

On 21 January the AUHIP put forward a roadmap to resolve the impasse and reach final agreement on all oil issues within 90 days. The impact of moving ahead without giving the talks a chance was devastating, and it seemed that my appeals, and those of others, helped. Prime Minister Meles called an IGAD summit for 27 January, to help negotiate a solution in cooperation with the AUHIP. However, to the dismay of the South Sudanese delegation, the AUHIP abandoned its own compromise proposal. Following the shutdown of oil, at the summit the AUHIP tabled yet another proposal calling upon South Sudan to provide more than double the wealth transfer to Sudan for the same four-year period: from $2.6 billion to $6.5 billion. Indeed, this was more than a 150 per cent *increase* from the AUHIP's original proposal. The South Sudanese believed the AUHIP had abandoned them. Prior to the summit, South Sudan had rejected the new proposal.[22]

The IGAD summit ended in disarray. From multiple sources we were told that President Kiir had accepted the AUHIP's proposal for financial transitional arrangements at a meeting chaired by Prime Minister Meles Zenawi in the margins of the IGAD Summit.[23] When Zenawi, the Chair of IGAD at the time, announced the good news to the plenary meeting of IGAD heads of state, however, Kiir declared that his delegation was still discussing the matter and might not be able to sign.[24] Meles told me: 'Salva clearly could not carry "the traffic"', meaning that other members of the leadership had put up too much resistance.[25] De Waal and other observers were certain that the 'real reason' for the South Sudanese decision was regime change in Khartoum,[26] giving Pagan Amum the blame.[27] This analysis was in my view far too simplistic. While the liberators would not regret negative consequences in Khartoum, South Sudan was much more dependent on the oil income than Sudan. People with knowledge about the internal discussions in the South Sudanese delegation also say that the opposition to the AUHIP proposal was strong, given the substantive reasons mentioned above.[28]

Not only were the AUHIP members and its chairman Thabo Mbeki upset, but as stories whirled about at the AU summit the following day, these events also damaged the reputation of the South Sudanese leadership.[29] Observers and mediators alike now expected the talks to be stalled for quite a while.

Pagan Amum, the chief negotiator and secretary-general of the SPLM, whom I met during the AU summit, maintained that the South Sudanese delegation had made the right decision, but admitted that the situation was serious; they had lost the public-relations battle, and steps were now necessary to recapture lost ground, not least with friends in the region and internationally.

The South Sudanese had shot themselves in both feet, with the shutdown of oil, and the debacle of the AUHIP talks did not help matters. I went to Brussels immediately after the Addis Ababa meetings, and the message from the High Level Representative of the European Union at the time, Catherine Ashton, was clear: there would be no help from the Europeans in managing this self-inflicted economic crisis. The same message echoed in most donor capitals. The decision to shut down oil production also had ripple effects as far as the Chinese, Indian and Malaysian governments, whose companies had major stakes in South Sudanese oil fields.

The South Sudanese, for their part, were offended that their 'shut down' was not understood by the international community, and they questioned why people were not angry at Khartoum, who had stolen their oil. By the beginning of February, all production wells had been closed in cooperation with the oil companies.

The South Sudanese followed up with legal proceedings against anyone trying to purchase or ship the 'stolen' oil.[30] World-class advisers from Skadden Arps were contracted, and Sudan was unable to monetize the oil. (For its work, Skadden Arps was named 'Litigation and Dispute Resolution Team of the Year' at the African Legal Awards 2013, and was also commended by the *Financial Times* in its 2013 'Innovative Lawyers' report for Europe.)[31]

## Oil shutdown – Doomsday?

The decision to stop producing oil would soon have an impact on the economic situation in South Sudan. The Government established an Austerity Committee, and a separate sub-committee was tasked with preparing a revised budget on the basis of worst-case predictions. At the time of the shutdown, South Sudan had reportedly only $1 billion in reserves in foreign accounts. Analysis by the World Bank and IMF showed the danger of a total collapse of the South Sudanese economy. They had never seen a situation as dramatic as this; it appeared that the leadership of the country had not fully absorbed the implications of their decision, or did not care.[32] A strictly confidential World Bank presentation, including worst-case scenarios and meant only for the President and ministers of economic departments, leaked to the media and made headlines around the globe. The presentation estimated an 82 per cent decline in GDP, and depletion of foreign reserves within eight months.[33]

Now the South Sudanese Government finally realized that the timelines for an alternative pipeline were unrealistic, and that they needed a revenue stream to fund both short-term and medium-term needs. Appeals to traditional donor countries got nowhere,[34] and international financial institutions turned down their informal requests for assistance.[35] The leadership found it difficult to understand that a decision to stop Khartoum from 'stealing their oil' should lead to their being 'punished'. Ministers went on a flurry of foreign trips, hunting for loans, primarily against future oil income.

First on the itinerary were the home countries of the oil companies, China, India and Malaysia. Visits were paid also to South Africa, Angola and the Gulf countries. Delegations came and went. South Sudanese officials were inquiring, not only about loans, but – when they approached Japan and Russia – also about investment in alternative pipelines, construction of refineries and the like. Half the cabinet seemed to be on the road at the time, hunting for money in one form or the other, while the other half travelled back and forth between Juba and Addis Ababa for negotiations with Khartoum. Hardly anyone remained to concentrate on running the government. South Sudan was back in crisis-management mode.

The results of this flurry of activity were not at expected levels. In the end, the three oil companies with operations in South Sudan provided some advances against the future sale of oil, reportedly some $450–500 million. Limited emergency loans were also forthcoming from the United Arabic Emirates in the order of $200 million. Later, a commercial loan was obtained from Qatar National Bank.[36] In total these amounts were far from what the government needed to keep itself afloat.

As tensions increased with Sudan, and the shutdown starved government budgets (except those in the security sector), ordinary people were largely dependent on the subsistence economy. They got by as always with animal husbandry, cultivation and fishing. Since oil income primarily had gone to fund public administration and some public services, it was here that the impact was worst. As prices rose, however, the oil shutdown started to affect daily lives. The states bordering Sudan suffered most, because the frontier was closed; prices skyrocketed to three or four times normal levels. For a while the countrywide inflation rate was estimated at 80 per cent, and there was a further significant depreciation of the South Sudanese pound.

But the crisis hardly affected the lifestyle of some government ministers. The budget still paid for their continuous accommodation in hotels in Juba, travels on business and first class and stays in five-star hotels during their desperate trips to request loans and investments. Some still had champagne with their lunches at favourite Juba restaurants.

Some of us tried to argue that the crisis could provide an opportunity to show people that the government could change its ways and implement reforms that had previously been too costly politically. If there was a time when corruption and waste could not be tolerated, it was now. I made specific proposals to the President and relevant ministers, including belt-tightening among senior officials. But it soon became clear that even now there was no political will to take bold steps.

Meanwhile, Khartoum also felt the pinch from the loss of its oil-pipeline revenue and South Sudan's transitional compensation. When by the end of the year South Sudan's coffers were said to be almost empty, the situation was also very serious in Sudan. I visited at the end of February 2013, as part of a tour of all South Sudan's neighbours to discuss issues related to the mandate of UNMISS. I used the opportunity to meet old friends and colleagues from the time of the CPA negotiations, including at the highest levels of government. Many were furious. They had never expected South Sudan to shut down its oil production, and they saw the decision as a strategy for regime change in Khartoum. Sudan was in serious economic problems, and losing the income from the user fees from transport of South Sudanese oil had consequences. They predicted that the Sudan economy had only two–three months before the situation became really critical. This could impact on their political survival. Many felt betrayed by their South Sudanese 'brothers', in the same way that the South Sudanese had felt betrayed by Khartoum. Unless they changed their approach, both sides would fall into an economic abyss.

Key players in Khartoum conveyed an important message to me: they were willing to make a deal with South Sudan. It was no longer important whether funds came as lump sums or in the form of user fees for the pipeline. Thus, they were open to reconsider previously rejected proposals, and asked me to convey this discreetly to Juba. From Kampala I telephoned Haile Menkerios; he and Thabo Mbeki were in touch with the parties and preparing the next round of talks. Haile said he had picked up some signals through his own sources. I also called Pagan Amum, South Sudan's chief negotiator, and cabinet ministers. They received my information with great relief.

The leadership met President Kiir on Sunday evening, 4 March, the day before the negotiation team's departure for Addis Ababa. In Khartoum the following day, Foreign Minister Ali Karti proposed that the two presidents should meet, and said that Bashir was ready to come to Juba.

Despite some initial grumbling,[37] things soon changed. Pagan Amum arrived in Addis Ababa with a strong commitment to change the dynamic of the talks, and found fertile ground with his opposite number. On 6 March a breakthrough was achieved and agreements were initialled in the Ethiopian capital on the process for demarcating the international border and for a framework for the status of each country's citizens in the other.[38] The latter included full acceptance of 'the four freedoms' in a similar agreement between Sudan and Egypt, thus granting citizens of both countries freedom of residence, freedom of movement, freedom of economic activity and freedom to acquire and dispose of property.

For two countries so closely knit, with interdependent economies and hundreds of thousands of citizens living in each other's territory, this was the only logical thing to do.

A decision was also made to hold a summit meeting of the two presidents. The two chief negotiators, Pagan Amum and Idris Mohammed Abdul Gadir, were now in frequent contact, and I witnessed the change in atmosphere myself. A South Sudanese ministerial delegation visited Khartoum the same week, from 8 to 10 March, and President Bashir was invited to visit Juba on 3 April, when it was expected that the two agreements would be signed.

But soon another turn of events sent things spinning in the opposite direction. Hardliners in Khartoum had started mobilizing. It was 'the four freedoms' that fired them up the most. They were worried that this loss of control would imply an entry point for the SPLM to unduly influence developments in Sudan. Afraid that the freedoms would lead to SPLM infiltration of Khartoum, and totally oblivious to the benefits of the agreements for Sudan's businesses and people, Bashir's powerful uncle, al-Tayeb Mustafa made sure that dire warnings were repeatedly proclaimed at Friday prayers in the mosques, and used his influence with the government's military and intelligence network to try to stop Bashir from signing.[39]

This reminded me of the talks on the CPA: whenever we had been close to a breakthrough, or to concluding a serious deal, hardliners took action and the whole process would be undermined. In this case it was a border incident that set the ball rolling, and it rolled very quickly downhill. Key players on the South Sudanese side believe that al-Tayyeb Mustafa and the hardliners deliberately sparked the events which happened next.[40] We will probably never know.

## The Sudans – on the brink of war

On 26 March 2012 we sat in the hall of the Legislative Assembly in Juba, awaiting remarks by Salva Kiir opening the National Liberation Council of the SPLM. Just before he reached the podium someone handed him a piece of paper and whispered in his ear. In the middle of his speech, Kiir deviated from his text to disclose that the SAF was attacking positions at Tishwin, on what South Sudan considered its side of the border. We had heard from our personnel in the area that there had been SAF troop movements, but these had not yet been confirmed.

The attacks were backed up by Khartoum-supported South Sudanese rebels from Unity State, the South Sudan Liberation Movement/Army (SSLM/A) and their commander Bapiny Monytuil. This had prompted a response from the SPLA, which, Kiir said, had chased the SAF back across the border, pursued them and then 'taken' Heglig.[41] There was wild cheering and applause as the cadres rose to their feet; many raised their fists, and the slogan 'SPLM Woyee' could be heard throughout the audience. The majority of the comrades were old freedom fighters, or had participated in the struggle in one way or another. I felt we were back in the bush, celebrating a military victory, and not in a newly independent country trying to find its feet – and in peace with its neighbours.

At a press conference in Khartoum, the Sudanese Government claimed that the SPLA had started the fighting. This led to the immediate cancellation of President Bashir's visit to Juba; he had already ordered mobilization of all paramilitary forces and announced a committee to undertake preparation of 'jihadists'.[42] Both sides now claimed to hold parts of oil-rich Heglig. Emotions were running high. The next day, Tuesday, 27 March, the SAF took control and launched aerial bombing raids on South Sudanese territory.[43] Now both armies regrouped and faced each other in the disputed border area, only a few hundred metres apart.

On Wednesday the 28 March Haile Menkerios telephoned me from Khartoum. He had the chief of staff of the SAF, Ismat Abdel Rahman on the line, while on another line I had the South Sudan's deputy defence minister, Majak D'Agoot who, in turn, was in direct contact with the SPLA command and those leading the SPLA operations in the border area. Through 'telephone diplomacy' we negotiated between the two and managed to prevent further escalation. Both sides agreed to disengage and redeploy to their original positions. We all sighed with relief.

President Salva Kiir, at the end of the National Liberation Council meeting, reported the decision, then ordered a full mobilization to prepare for the defence of South Sudan. He instructed all ten state governors to mobilize 5,000 soldiers each to protect their own people and country. The apparent complacency of the international community was a factor in South Sudanese thinking. In November 2011 and

February 2012 a number of bombing raids by the Sudanese Armed Forces had taken place over South Sudanese territory, one of which had resulted in ten deaths.[44] But no one had said anything. Now the raids had resumed.[45] If they could not count on the Security Council or UNMISS to protect them, they would have to take matters into their own hands. (UNMISS did in fact issue statements when verified incidents impacted civilians.)

The respite did not last long. On Sunday morning, 1 April, I learned that another aerial bombing raid had taken place, this time at Manga in Unity State. This was the home area of Governor Taban Deng Gai, and the SPLA saw it as a clear provocation. At 2.30 p.m., Deputy Defence Minister Majak D'Agoot called me and reported that SPLA troops had come under attack by Khartoum's ground forces. Worried about another escalation, I called Haile Menkerios. He said that the Sudanese defence minister, Abdul Rahman Hussein would be going to Addis Ababa for the next round of talks in the Joint Political and Security Committee (JPSC), after significant pressure from the mediators. The Khartoum delegation arrived on the 2nd, while attacks were still under way.

In Addis Ababa there was agreement that only one issue should be on the agenda, which was to reduce tension on the border. The Khartoum delegation had decided to take a 'tell all' approach with regard to support for proxy militias and insurgents in South Sudan. Dr Ghazi Salahuddin Atabani, the then influential parliamentary leader of the National Congress Party, had hinted at this during my visit to Khartoum in early March. He said that a similar approach had been successful with Chad, when both sides had 'confessed' what they had been up to and relations had improved significantly. This gambit should be tried in relation to South Sudan, he said. By now he had taken over the Sudanese government's committee in charge of relations with South Sudan, and I recognized his influence in the new approach.

But when, despite Khartoum's admissions, South Sudan refused to confirm its support for the SPLM-N, Sudan's delegation walked out of the talks. Left unsigned, therefore, was a draft calling for cessation of hostilities and withdrawal of armed forces. I asked South Sudanese officials what prevented them from openly admitting something everyone knew. I was told that Juba had been aware of Khartoum's support for South Sudanese militias for a long time and these posed no significant military threat. On the other hand, if South Sudan were to admit all it knew about the SPLM-N, Khartoum would reap a great military advantage.

After both President Obama and the Secretary-General of the UN called Salva Kiir, South Sudan remained non-committal. In our own meetings he either denied his government's support for the SPLM-N or remained silent. At the negotiating table in Addis Ababa, Abdul Rahman Hussein was upset. He fumed as he left the room and headed back to Khartoum for 'consultations'. We knew that relations were now likely to deteriorate.

## The occupation of Heglig/Panthou

During the first week of April SAF aerial attacks in the border areas had continued. Given the risks involved, we at UNMISS had already decided to start relocating our staff from Unity State to Juba and abroad. And sure enough, on the 8th we received reports that ground forces were moving 'across the border' (a loaded term, of course). SPLA sources claimed that the attacks originated from Heglig/Panthou.[46] These were followed by further bombing raids on several locations in Unity State, verified by UNMISS, which were far into internationally recognized South Sudanese territory. At the same time, the mobilization launched by President Kiir had led to thousands of new recruits for the SPLA, who were now advancing towards the border.

On 10 April yet another attack by SAF land and air forces was reported, and it was clear that Heglig/Panthou was a springboard. At this juncture the SAF were allegedly employing both the usual Antonovs and Mig 26s. The SPLA pursued SAF ground troops to Heglig/Panthou, not spontaneously but, this time, according to my sources, with the full blessing of the President and military leaders. The SPLA advance was reportedly supported by forces of the Darfurian rebel group, the Justice and Equality Movement (JEM). This was likely an opportunistic move to get back at their enemy, SAF. JEM had been observed by UNMISS in Rubkona, and close to the border, for several months.[47] The SPLA did not stop until it had seized full control over Panthou/Heglig, including its oil fields. Khartoum's forces put up very limited resistance, and suffered a truly humiliating defeat. South Sudan now proclaimed that it had occupied Heglig. This, Haile Menkerios said on the phone, was a trigger for full-scale war. He was right.

While Heglig, or Panthou was virtually unknown to most foreign observers until this point, it was a place of symbolic importance to South Sudanese. For this was the ancient homeland of the Rueng Dinka of Panaru, which in colonial times had been part of Upper Nile Province, at the time seen as part of Southern Sudan. But after the discovery of oil in the late 1970s Khartoum had (in 1980) attempted to change regional boundaries so that the oil fields were in Kordofan.[48] The subsequent civil war prevented exploration, which could anyway take place only after Panaru had been cleared of its inhabitants, a process undertaken in the late 1990s in what the historian Douglas Johnson has called 'ethnic cleansing'.[49]

When I first set foot in Southern Sudan in 1998, it was actually Panthou that I went to. Operation Lifeline Sudan, which ran a major humanitarian operation there, certainly considered it part of the South. A famine was under way as a consequence of population-clearing operations of Kerubino Kuanyin Bol, the renegade militia leader. Until 2003 it was generally understood that Panthou or Heglig was under the administration of Southern Sudan's Unity State. In mid 2004, however, as the CPA talks were drawing to a close, Nafie al-Nafie, Khartoum's minister in the Office of the Presidency sent a letter to the Governor of Unity State, stating that Heglig belonged to the (northern) state of Western Kordofan, and with an accompanying map approved by the National Survey Corporation.[50] If left unchallenged, this move would have obviated the need to share revenue from this very significant oil field under terms of the CPA.

The Permanent Court of Arbitration's ruling on Abyei determined that Heglig did not belong to Abyei (or 'the box', as it is often called).[51] Khartoum interpreted this decision as applying to Heglig, and that therefore the territory belonged to them, but the court had not been mandated to rule on Heglig's status; the court had ruled only on whether Heglig belonged to Abyei or not, a position that South Sudan took in the Technical Committee for North-South Borders, a body provided for in the CPA.

Heglig had been administered by Khartoum during the CPA period and indeed after South Sudan achieved independence in July 2011

– without much protest from Juba. But while Heglig or Panthou to many observers appeared to be a 'new' issue, it was not. The status of the area had immediately been raised by South Sudan after the Permanent Court of Arbitration's ruling and consistently in the Technical Committee for North-South Borders. South Sudan later insisted on adding another category of 'claimed areas', including Heglig or Panthou, since this area was not otherwise to be included among the five priority disputed areas. Whatever the case may be, the area accounted for roughly half of Sudan's oil production of 115,000 barrels per day.[52]

On 12 April 2012, as the SAF conducted aerial bombardment near Bentiu, President Kiir made a triumphal speech in the National Legislature.[53] Although he stressed that his government wanted negotiations and peace, his language on the subject of Heglig was that of a liberation leader. Referring to phone calls throughout the prior evening from world leaders, he stated: 'The UN Secretary-General gave me an order' to withdraw immediately from Heglig. 'I said I am not under your command', Kiir said to resounding applause, and to the tune of 'Never Surrender' from the military band. 'This time I will not order the forces to withdraw,' he concluded, as members rose to their feet amid cheers of 'SPLM Woyee'.[54]

I had been briefed about Kiir's conversation with the Secretary-General, and what I had been told did not tally with what Kiir was saying now. He used the occasion to attack UNMISS, too, charging that I wanted to be 'co-president' of South Sudan.[55] The expression 'co-president' had never been used in the public domain, and certainly not by the head of state. Kiir's comments were seen as unacceptable, and immediately reverberated at UN headquarters in New York.

Through third parties I made the President aware of the need to retract, and his office soon issued a statement differing in tone and content.[56] This behaviour was characteristic. Kiir would make strident, and at times rude, off-the-cuff remarks, and subordinates would follow up with soothing explanations of what he had intended to say. But this time the explanation did not mince words over the most important issue, the military occupation of Heglig/Panthou. Observers, including me, knew that Kiir would soon have to eat his words on this one, too.

By using military means to claim territory, South Sudan had shocked the world. As expected, in the days after the President's 'declaration', condemnation came from almost every quarter, Security Council-members, 'friends' such as the US and Norway, and the African Union.[57] Regional leaders worried. As I repeatedly explained to senior cabinet ministers, whatever the merits of their position with regard to Heglig/ Panthou, any reaction from the international community short of condemnation would set a precedent for territorial disputes around the world. The only acceptable way to resolve border disputes was through a political process and peaceful means. Anything else was out of the question.

At a meeting of the Security Council on 12 April a strong presidential statement was unanimously adopted, calling for complete and immediate withdrawal of SPLA from Heglig.[58] 'Further steps' were threatened if this did not happen. As a small consolation, for the first time the Security Council also called for cessation of the SAF's aerial bombardments. South Sudanese officials were shocked: Khartoum was the aggressor, and South Sudan had a right to defend itself, they said. But the days when Sudan would always be blamed, while they, the Southerners, were the 'good guys', whatever happened – had passed. After only eight months of independence, playing the victim had very limited credibility.

I worked hard to get senior officials to realize the urgent need for the government to withdraw, despite comprehensive security-and-border preconditions set by its National Security Council on 13 April and Kiir's public statements.[59] Telephone calls from world leaders were almost continuous. In a letter to the Security Council on the 14th the South Sudanese undertook to withdraw from Heglig if an international monitoring mechanism were put in place, and it urged a 'neutral' force there until final status could be settled.[60] But this was not going to happen, and I told them so. They had no choice but to renounce the occupation of territory through military means.

## Antagonizing the AU and the UN

Meanwhile, tensions were mounting in the country against the UN. I worked quietly behind the scenes, and through personal contacts, avoiding any public visibility.[61] The moderating statement from the President had not been given any play in the local media. Instead, public opinion was being ignited. There were demonstrations in almost all state capitals, with slogans denouncing the UN and the African Union, as well as the Chairman of the AUHIP, Thabo Mbeki. Petitions were handed in to UNMISS bases all over the country.

In South Sudan there is, as yet, no strong democratic tradition. Protests or demonstrations are usually staged through networks of the SPLM and the government. One could often discern when this was not the case. If security forces are not warned through appropriate channels that demonstrations have been organized, and have been permitted, they are not sure how to handle the situation. They usually intervene, and often move from shouting to shooting in split seconds. In this case, however, the security forces remained calm – which indicated support from government circles.

These demonstrations did, however, reflect popular sentiment. They were fuelled by further air raids on South Sudanese territory, now also in Warrap state.[62] We got reports from our people all over the country and sounded out various contacts. No one, whether academics, intellectuals, parliamentarians, civil society leaders, bishops or other religious figures seemed to understand why the world was criticizing South Sudan. Knowing that Dinka had always lived in Panthou, they regarded it as undeniably South Sudanese; they were all familiar with the history. But they did not seem familiar with international law, and responded to the international reactions with anger. I got a sense of the depth of feeling when I addressed the All-Bishops conference in South Sudan. The bishops were quite emotional, and it took me a long time to explain the reasons behind the international reactions.

There was also serious fall-out in Sudan from the Heglig crisis. Abdul Rahman Hussein was under serious pressure to resign. Rumours circulated that he had indeed done so, but that President Bashir wanted him to stay. The SAF intensified its bombing, now on a daily basis. More civilians were killed and wounded.[63] On 16 April the small UNMISS County Support Base at Mayom was hit, another violation of international law.[64] Because the base was under refurbishment and only temporarily manned, no staff were present, and there were no casualties.

On the same day, Sudan's parliament declared South Sudan an enemy state.[65] Relations between the two countries hit rock bottom. Bashir followed up and – with a talent for off-the-cuff remarks surpassing that of Salva Kiir – fired off new insults. In a speech on the 18th, he declared that the people of South Sudan needed to be 'liberated' from the 'insects'.[66] Bashir appeared to have meant the SPLA,[67] but in South Sudan his aspersion was taken to refer to Southerners in general and was reminiscent of past incitements of ethnic cleansing.

As expected, South Sudan announced on 20 April that it would withdraw its forces from Heglig. According to informed and very credible sources, withdrawal had actually commenced two days before that announcement, in order to allow the SPLA to pull out heavy equipment. When Sudan subsequently bombed the area, expecting to take out SPLA military hardware, the South Sudanese had already evacuated. It is still contested whether they, Khartoum's forces, or the JEM militia hit some of the oil facilities in Heglig, damaging them in a way that would make it more complicated to resume production.

While South Sudan maintains that the SAF bombed the oil fields, Mohammed Atta al-Moula Abbas, the head of Sudan's National Intelligence and Security Services (NISS), claimed to have intercepted phone calls in which Taban Deng, the Governor of Unity State, had ordered JEM commanders to attack the fields. Attah was still fuming when I met him in June 2014. Stories were also rife in Juba at the time that Taban had been careless on the phone, and that some information had come out about collaboration with JEM. Whatever the case may be, it is an open question whether Taban's phone calls were related to coordinating the move to take Heglig, or involved orders to attack the oil fields.

The two countries had been on the brink of full-scale war. But as usual they managed to pull back from the brink at the last minute. It would take several months before temperatures cooled, and another six before oil production could resume. The decision to withdraw from Heglig/Panthou was not popular in South Sudan.

Fighting continued in the border areas after the withdrawal. According to Mac Paul Kuol Awar, South Sudan's chief of military intelligence, air raids on 22 April were the heaviest experienced in South Sudan since 1995.[68] The following day, the bridge between Bentiu and Rubkona was hit. These continuing aerial bombardments, affecting also civilians, prompted statements by the UN Secretary-General and the Mission, calling on Sudan to cease and desist.[69] So far, we had registered more than 16 killed and more than twice as many wounded, but the number was likely higher on both accounts, as UNMISS did not have access to all border areas. The bombing was dangerously close to the UNMISS base in Bentiu. I went there a few days later. It was almost surreal to visit the Governor's office. With the exception of Taban, everyone was in military uniform. Local SPLA commanders had been joined by high-ranking officers from Juba. It was clear that the border operations had been directed from here. I got a real sense that the liberators were back in the trenches, their comfort zone.

## The new 'bad' guys

Based on events during the first nine months of South Sudan's independence – support for the SPLM-N, collaboration with JEM, the oil shutdown, and then the Heglig occupation – there was a widespread assumption that the government's goal was regime change in Khartoum.[70] This was also Khartoum's interpretation, and most certainly that of the AUHIP chairman, Thabo Mbeki, and it influenced perceptions in the Security Council. Not everyone shared this opinion, however, and certainly not most neighbouring countries. The South Sudanese claimed that each decision they had taken was based on the circumstances at the time, in response to what they saw as aggression from Khartoum. But it was a new experience not to be regarded as victims.

On 24 April the African Union's Peace and Security Council met and adopted a strong statement[71] which, coupled with its roadmap for normalization of relations, comprised its most comprehensive statement of policy regarding the two states since South Sudan's independence. The Council called for cessation of hostilities, including aerial bombardment, within 48 hours; unconditional withdrawal of all armed forces from the border; activation of border security mechanisms and the so-called Secure Demilitarized Border Zone[72]; cessation of the harbouring or support of rebel forces; an end to hostile propaganda; and redeployment of both sides' forces from the Abyei area.

The Council also urged the parties to resume negotiations within two weeks. Should they fail to reach agreement on outstanding issues within three months, AUHIP would be empowered to present final and binding solutions for all outstanding post-secession issues. The AU called upon the UN Security Council to endorse its action with a similar resolution. This was unprecedented. The AU had never adopted such a concrete time-bound resolution, and had certainly never called on the Security Council to give the process teeth.

African leaders had seen enough, and so, it seemed, had the wider international community. The United States duly circulated a draft resolution to the Security Council, building on the AU demarche. Security Council Resolution 2046, adopted on 2 May, copied most of the language of the AU and threatened both Sudan and South Sudan with sanctions should they fail to meet its terms.[73] It was passed unanimously. China and Russia did not normally support threats of sanctions against member states. Active lobbying against the text by the Sudanese Foreign Minister Ali Karti had failed.

In a short time, South Sudan had the dubious distinction of achieving what very few countries have ever done, the threat of sanctions by the Security Council. While there was some grumbling about the resolution among hardline characters in the government, its negotiating team regarded SCR 2046 as a major asset. Finally, pressure had been put on the parties and, in their view, Khartoum, with appropriate carrots and sticks. They were particularly pleased with the support provided for a solution of Abyei.

The American ambassador at the UN, Susan Rice, would soon be the driving force behind efforts in the Security Council to hold both sides accountable. Every fortnight the UN Secretariat had to report on progress made in implementing the resolution according to the AU roadmap.

## A new beginning?

During the period 2–6 May the SAF resumed aerial bombardment on South Sudanese territory. Later in the same week, claims of SAF ground incursions were made. It was not possible for UNMISS to verify these, as the alleged location was beyond our Area of Operations.[74] Disagreement on where the border was made it difficult anyway to assess such claims. What seemed clear was that the deadline of 48 hours had not been honoured.

This time, South Sudan did not retaliate. Vice President Riek Machar sent a letter to the President of the Security Council and chairman of the AU reiterating the government's commitment to implement the resolution in full and listing steps already taken.[75] South Sudan also announced a decision to start withdrawing its police forces from Abyei in the following week. These steps were well received internationally.

In my meetings with President Kiir he likewise expressed determination to implement the resolution. He also committed to push his old comrades, the SPLM-N, to the negotiating table, and made it clear that he understood what the relevant language in the resolutions really meant. Thabo Mbeki met both presidents, Kiir and Bashir, preparing for a resumption of talks. The focus now was on establishing a buffer zone of 10 kilometres on each side of the border. Both sides committed to a joint mechanism for monitoring the border and demilitarized zone.

At this point Pagan Amum noted that Mbeki's panel itself had violated the roadmap of the AU and Security Council by not calling the two countries together before the deadline of 17 May. South Sudan could now not be accused of non-compliance.[76] Salva Kiir told me that his delegation would go to Addis Ababa early, and would stay there until Khartoum's delegation turned up. The threat of sanctions by the Security Council appeared to be working.

While the parties made some progress in Addis Ababa on border security, emotions were too raw for agreement to be reached. Sudan rejected the map for the Safe Demilitarized Border Zone (SDBZ), and aerial bombardment continued. The South Sudanese filed a complaint with the Security Council. Together with other Sudanese rebel groups the SPLM-N had formed an alliance now controlling almost 40 per cent of the border, complicating matters further. In late June, despite misgivings on several fronts, Juba announced unconditional acceptance of the AUHIP map. By this time, things had also calmed down on the border.

On 14 July, in the margins of the African Union summit in Addis Ababa, Presidents Kiir and Bashir discussed a wide range of issues. These included the SPLM-N, border demarcation, opening of the border for trade, transitional financial arrangements, and Abyei. Kiir pressed for solutions, but Bashir focused mostly on the SPLM-N and South Sudan's alleged support for rebels in Darfur; he was unwilling to address other issues until the most important – for him and the Sudan, namely security – was addressed. Kiir told me that he had repeated his offer to help Bashir negotiate a settlement with the SPLM-N. Despite the lack of progress there was agreement on a timeframe for further talks in August.

Eager to recapture lost ground internationally, South Sudan tabled a comprehensive proposal in Addis Ababa on 22 July. The idea was to get agreement on a 'strategic framework' for talks, based on 'a partnership commitment' and simultaneous negotiations on all remaining issues, with no sequencing. The presumed point was to return to the status quo ante Heglig and achieve 'normalization' on a number of matters, possibly in August. Border issues and Abyei, however, were likely to slide.

On 20 August Ethiopian Prime Minister Meles Zenawi died after a period of illness and was succeeded by Hailemariam Desalegn. This had a significant impact also abroad, and notably on Sudan-South/Sudan relations. Zenawi had been active in all the talks, and was very familiar with the leaders on both sides. It is not unlikely that events could have taken a different course had he lived.

On 4 August, following expiry of the three-month deadline, the parties reported to the AU Peace and Security Council that they had reached a deal in principle on oil transit, processing and transportation fees. To the eagerly waiting press, however, both sides sold the skeleton agreement differently, leading to conflicting reports. Only later would the full agreement be thrashed out and signed.

## The September Agreements

Serious progress was finally made in September. On the 21st, Presidents Bashir and Kiir held what had been intended as a one-day meeting in Addis Ababa.[77] As usual, however, things took much longer than expected. In the end, the two remained in the Ethiopian capital for almost a week before they could sign anything. I got a detailed account of those days, and of the dynamics. They hardly met, preferring to give directions to their chief negotiators. Unlike Taha and Garang, who had seemed to enjoy the intellectual challenge of personally hammering out the difficult compromises of the CPA, Kiir and Bashir remained in their hotel suites, as their delegates ran back and forth between them and the mediators.

On the 22nd, the Government of South Sudan provided a letter claiming that they had severed all ties with the SPLM-North prior to independence. Bashir purported to accept this at face value, and within a few days nine agreements had been hammered out. On the 27th the two presidents signed what became known as 'The September 2012 Cooperation Agreements',[78] providing a basis for resolving most remaining issues related to secession. The impetus for agreement was probably economic necessity more than anything else.

Most importantly, the Cooperation Agreements provided security arrangements including a safe demilitarized zone, and agreement on cross-border trade, citizenship, pensions for pre-secession retirees, and banking arrangements. The two parties also finalized an agreement facilitating resumption of oil production and its transport through pipelines to Port Sudan.

Despite the appearance of a comprehensive settlement, and true to their tendency towards 'taijility'[79] on the most difficult issues, Khartoum and Juba had chosen agreement on process rather than substance. Border demarcation and Abyei remained unresolved. Where did Sudan end and South Sudan begin? And AUHIP's compromise proposal on Abyei had been accepted by Juba, but rejected by Khartoum.

Regarding the vexed issue of border demarcation Sudan refused to comply with the Security Council's demand regarding a demilitarized zone, and introduced instead a new condition, the demilitarization of – and thereby SPLA withdrawal from – a resource-rich 14-mile (22 km) area south of the Bahr al-Arab (Kiir river). Mediators pressured South Sudan to concede this. But Southerners in general (and particularly the SPLA) had always claimed the territory up to and even beyond the Kiir river. Under the SDBZ agreement both armies were to withdraw 10 kilometres from the centreline that ran along the Kiir. Now they had been requested to pull back an additional 12 kilometres south to demilitarize the full 14-mile area. Despite significant political risk and his own misgivings, the President agreed. The SPLA was furious, as was one of Kiir's closest allies, Governor Paul Malong of Northern Bahr el Gahzal.

Malong even went to Addis Ababa to protest against 'giving up' the so-called 'Fourteen Mile' area, and he publicly criticized the President. SPLA generals who arrived were also very angry about having been kept in the dark by the negotiating team. Kiir held his ground, stating that the issue was not demarcation of the border but only determination of the median line for the buffer zone. But protest demonstrations were staged even in the Bahr el Ghazal region, his homeland. In an unusual show of collective support, and through several meetings, Riek Machar, Deng Alor and members of the negotiating team talked to community leaders of the Bahr el Ghazal region and won them over.[80] The Government's decision was upheld. The AUHIP was informed, just in time to brief the Security Council.[81]

Demarcation would now be subject to a process by which an independent panel of experts of the African Union would provide a non-binding opinion. The parties could agree to adopt this, but failing that would extend the period of discussion, and refer the decision to international arbitration, or any other binding settlement process, for a final ruling.[82]

A complicating factor was how the demilitarized zone could work with fighting raging in South Kordofan and Blue Nile. Khartoum had no control over vast areas of the two states, and establishing a demilitarized zone without talking to the forces that were in control there, notably the SPLM-N, would be problematic. This issue had yet to be addressed, sensitive as it was to Sudan, where multiple rebellions threatened the state.

Relations slowly improved. For both, the biggest problem was now economic. The August skeleton agreement on oil had been fleshed out and signed, with South Sudan paying transportation fees of $11 per barrel from Unity, and $9.10 per barrel from Upper Nile.[83] The transitional financial payments were now also to be added automatically on a per-barrel basis to the transit fees. This arrangement served two purposes. It would provide an incentive for Sudan to allow the oil to be piped to Port Sudan without interference, and South Sudan's contribution need not be subject to further debate in Juba, with a high risk of interruption. Providing Khartoum with money when Southern territory had been recently subject to aerial bombardment was not popular.

## Oil starts flowing

Despite the desperate economic situation – the government having been without revenue for almost a year – none of the September

Agreements were implemented for several months. Oil production had been scheduled to resume on 16 November; President Kiir would go to Upper Nile and personally 'turn the key'. But Sudan delayed, and he ended up only laying the foundation for a refinery. The message from Khartoum was that the pipeline would not be re-opened until South Sudan cooperated in providing 'security', which meant ending support for the SPLM-N in Southern Kordofan and Blue Nile. This new condition had not been negotiated, and was widely criticized – by the mediators, the Troika and members of the Security Council.

Implementation is always the toughest challenge. This had been the case with the CPA, as it was now with the September Agreements. Mediators had to introduce implementation matrixes, denoting specific actions and deadlines, pushing the parties to move forward and enabling international pressure at successive points.

Only on 12 March 2013,[84] after months of further negotiation, did Sudan and South Sudan finally agree on an implementation matrix, with timetables for the most difficult issue, security arrangements and the withdrawal of forces from the 10 km buffer zone.[85] It was, once again, most likely economic necessity that impelled both sides.

The agreement stipulated that South Sudan would order resumption of production 14 days after 'D-Day', which was set at 10 March. Prior to the order becoming effective the oil companies had to check if the oil pipelines were fully functional. I recall how the South Sudanese delegation returned from Addis and Khartoum with smiles on their faces. Khartoum confirmed on 22 March that the pipelines were fit to receive oil, and South Sudan declared the opening of production on 8 April.[86]

A few days later, signalling a new start, President Bashir visited Juba for the first time since independence. As he drove from the airport and passed the multi-story buildings and all the construction along the road, he was impressed. Paradoxically, Juba had been experiencing a boom, even during the oil shutdown. We could all guess where the money was coming from; it was certainly not from ordinary salaries, but more likely pocketed money from government coffers or contracts. Bashir reportedly laughed and exclaimed: 'So now I see what our brothers have been up to; they have learnt the trade quicker than I thought.'[87]

Another sign of the thaw in relations came on 26 April. The South Sudan Liberation Movement/Army (SSLM/A), a Khartoum-supported rebel group dominated by former commanders of the pre-independence Southern Sudan Defense Force from western Unity State, accepted President Kiir's offer of amnesty and began moving across the border from Sudan to Mayom county in South Sudan. I had been alerted to this a few days earlier. The SSLA was the last major militia group at large, and the only one with any destabilizing potential.

For Khartoum to make this happen, Kiir must have promised something in relation to the SPLM-N or remaining negotiation issues. Some reject this, however, and maintain that the decision to come in was the militia's alone after solicitations from the SPLA.[88]

In any case, soon after this, Commander James Gatduel Gatluak, in Unity, who was very close to Governor Taban Deng, was replaced. This foreshadowed removal of the Governor himself later in July, and was a sign of rising tensions within the SPLM. The new Governor was Joseph Nguen Monytuiel, a brother of the militia leader Bapiny Monytuiel. President Kiir's faction suddenly had full control over Unity, the home state of his perpetual rival, Vice President Riek Machar.

While relations with Sudan had been at their worst, the leadership stood united against the common foe, as usual throughout Southern Sudanese history. They knew that splits could easily be exploited by Khartoum, as they had been so often before. As a saying from the struggle goes: 'If we split like groundnuts, the chicken will eat us all.' Now, with Sudan apparently appeased, oil flowing, and revenue again accruing to the government, people started to relax. Soon after Bashir's visit to Juba, tensions within the SPLM started coming out into the open. It would take only a few weeks before the 'lid' blew off.

## Threat of a new shutdown

Appeasement of Sudan did not last long. On 27 April, the Sudan Revolutionary Front (an umbrella group including the SPLM-N and JEM) took Abu Kershola, an important oil-producing town in the centre of the country. This was unprecedented and shocking to the Khartoum military and security establishment. These rebels had never operated so successfully that far from their bases. A month later, on 27

May, the Sudanese Army claimed to have retaken the town.[89] Whether or not South Sudan was directly involved in what happened, Khartoum's subsequent threats indicated where blame had been placed. President Bashir, appearing in military uniform and flanked by top officials, angrily waved his stick in front of the large crowd and said:

> I now give our brothers in South Sudan a last, last warning that we will shut down the oil pipeline forever if they give any support to the traitors in Darfur, South Kordofan and Blue Nile.[90]

A deadline of 6 September was set. Copnall quotes a source close to Bashir as saying that the President was making up policy as he went along; Bashir's threat came as a surprise even to his close advisers.[91] South Sudan now reiterated that it did not support the rebels. But it is hard to prove a negative.

Whenever Sudanese, Northerners and Southerners, meet, the capacity for jovial pretence is impressive. This had been on display throughout the CPA negotiations; those engaged in the secession talks experienced the same thing. One observes in astonishment how they hug, trade school-day reminiscences, and crack jokes. But the capacity for bitterness reasserts itself proportionally with distance in time and space. And as Copnall observes, the harshest statements usually start with 'my brother'.[92]

Other events contributed to the souring of relations. On 4 May, the Ngok Dinka Paramount Chief, Kuol Deng Kuol, was brutally killed in Abyei when his convoy, under protection of the UN force in Abyei (UNISFA), was ambushed by Misseriya Arabs.[93] South Sudanese were convinced that Khartoum had 'organized' the ambush. The Paramount Chief was a critical participant in consultations to end the deadlock on Abyei. A moderate among his own people, he had the credibility to pursue compromises and generate support. The killing provoked fury all over South Sudan, not only among those from Abyei. It also worsened the UN's reputation.

In late June, Vice President Riek Machar went to Khartoum to calm the waters, and was welcomed with fanfare.[94] Rumours in Juba had it that he was up to his old machinations of suggesting himself as a better horse to bet on than President Kiir. My sources at the highest levels in Khartoum rejected these as calumnies, but the rumours themselves signalled that the rivalry was re-heating. Sure enough, only days later, the Vice President told international media that it was time for Kiir to go; he made no secret of his intention of seeking the chairmanship of the SPLM.[95] On 23 July President Kiir dismissed the entire cabinet, including Machar. A cabinet reshuffle had been expected for a long time, but the scale of the shake-up shocked observers.

Sudanese I met at this time could hardly hide their pleasure at the list of ministers named on 31 July. Although some were reappointments, most 'Garang Boys' and hard-core SPLM leaders were out, while some were 'old hands' who had been cabinet members under Khartoum's National Congress Party or regarded as close to it.

Sudan was monitoring the turmoil with great interest. The 'Garang Boys' were regarded as hardliners, and people such as Pagan Amum, South Sudan's chief negotiator, among the worst. On the Abyei issue Deng Alor, now gone, was seen as most intransigent. Khartoum saw more room for maneuver with close associates of Salva Kiir.

It should be noted that intra-party tensions were not the only rationale for a reshuffle. Given the parlous state of relations with Sudan since independence, there was sense in appointing ministers supportive of rapprochement. That this was a risky strategy, increasing tensions within the SPLM, was obvious, however. Both results – a friendlier yet divided South Sudan – served Khartoum's interests.

Only a couple of days after appointment of the new cabinet, on 2 August, President Kiir is said to have promised to suspend all aid to the SPLM-North, aid which had anyway always been denied.[96] This has not been verified. We do know that the new government provided a fresh dynamic between the two countries.[97] On 3 September Kiir went to Khartoum, marking the first time in almost two years that he had set foot on Sudanese soil. According to reports I received from both sides, this proved to be the most successful meeting that he and President Bashir had ever had. It is likely that Kiir gave assurances of disassociation from the SPLM-N and JEM; there were strong indications thereafter that no further support was provided to them.[98] Gone too were threats to shut down the oil pipeline.

Bashir would pay a return visit to Juba as soon as 22 October, during which he supposedly offered full support for Kiir's new government.[99]

The intention was to cement implementation of the September 2012 oil agreement.[100] The thawing of relations at this particular time was notable, and probably also prompted the government to avoid upsetting Khartoum over Abyei. When on 27 October the Ngok Dinka went ahead with a unilateral, self-organized referendum to determine whether Abyei would be part of Sudan or join South Sudan, without any legal basis or international facilitation or presence,[101]Kiir made it clear that the government would not recognize the vote. But Ngok Dinka in the civil service and security forces who wanted to vote were permitted to go to Abyei and do so.

Former ministers and senior officials from Abyei, including Deng Alor, Luka Biong Deng and Edward Lino were all there to support the referendum; Kiir sent Deng Alor. Majak D'Agoot went later, while Riek Machar, now only a member of parliament, made statements advocating recognition of the Abyei vote.[102] Security concerns prompted Kiir to dispatch the inspector-general of Police, Pieng Deng, himself a Ngok, to the contested area to monitor the situation. In the end the referendum took place without incident; an overwhelming majority voted for Abyei to join South Sudan. Khartoum duly expressed unhappiness with the return to Abyei of many members of the security forces, and about their continued presence.

## When liberators become kleptocrats

Many of the interim period's problems of mismanagement outlined in the previous chapter continued after independence. These included graft in contracts and procurement, overspending of public funds, and massive corruption in the security sector, which we will revert to in more detail later. While some lubrication of the machinery of government probably had to be accepted for reasons of politics and patronage, the scale was stupendous. Even basic functions of the state were put at risk.

Ministers operated in a mode of constant crisis management during the first two years of independence, literally a 'state in emergency', diverting attention from state-building. To us in Juba, the absence of political will to tackle corruption was clear. Still there were a few important differences between the corruption issues of the interim period and those since independence.

With the oil shutdown there were fewer opportunities to misappropriate funds from the budget, but more at the Central Bank and in the currency market and security sector. Furthermore, while during the interim period economic mismanagement was attributable to institutional weaknesses and lack of political will, the latter prevented state-building processes from succeeding after independence. Legislation on public financial management had been passed, but implementation was a problem. As ordinary citizens had suffered the impact of economic crisis, the contrast between the affluent (and often corrupt) elites and those struggling to get by was even starker.

In 'When kleptocracy becomes insolvent: Brute causes of the civil war in South Sudan',[103] Alex de Waal notes that the shutdown of oil production made it more difficult to sustain cash-based patronage networks and bargaining arrangements that could keep internal peace. He claims that corruption and patronage are not distortions of the system in South Sudan: they *are* the system. When the shutdown stalled loyalty payments to keep the system running, it fell apart, he claims, and he seems to regard this as the main cause of the subsequent crisis.[104] While his analysis of the scale of corruption to a large extent appears accurate, blaming kleptocracy for the conflict in South Sudan is too simplistic.

As we have seen, President Kiir had launched his five ambitious steps against corruption.[105] Two Presidential Orders followed, one on operationalization and implementation, including the repatriation of funds in foreign accounts,[106] and the other on declaration of officials' assets by 30 January 2012.[107] Five thousand government officials handed in their forms.[108] But most of the liberators in office continued to shrug their shoulders. Some refused cooperation, although this was meant to lead to dismissal.[109]

This did not happen, however. No action was taken. Attempts to repatriate funds also faced difficulties.[110] Although the Anti-Corruption Commission pursued a number of investigations, and information declared would warrant further investigations, no cases led to prosecution.[111]

When belated audits for the interim period were published in 2011 and 2012, shock was expressed but there was little immediate effect. Instead, more and more politicians made fiery speeches about rooting out corruption, probably to immunize themselves. The President now had to choose between criminal investigations and prosecution, and an alternative course. He was also increasingly vulnerable to accusations related to the conduct of his own office.

## The politics of corruption

Salva Kiir chose an unorthodox approach. In June 2012 he sent letters to 75 senior officials, giving them the opportunity to 'come clean', pay back part of what they had misappropriated, and make a new start.[112] The letter was harsh in tone.[113] Those who did not cooperate would face accountability processes.

The letter referred to a total of $4 billion unaccounted for during the interim period. This figure appeared to be calculated simply on the basis of oil revenue since 2005 (against expenditures that were unaccounted for) and large-scale contracts that the government had entered into. For 2005–6 alone $1 billion could not be traced.[114] For those who returned a significant part of the misappropriated funds, there would be no legal action. While not everyone was suspected, each got a letter – again to avoid the impression of targeting individuals.[115] And the letter was made public. It set off a firestorm of enormous proportions in the Assembly and within the SPLM leadership.[116] Personal relations that were already strained deteriorated further.

At the same time, this made the President himself vulnerable to similar accusations. The dubious practices at the President's Office had continued. Significant amounts of cash were stolen from the President's Office as late as March 2013, and staff were suspended; following inconclusive investigations most were reinstated. Only in June 2015 was action taken against the main culprits, who were dismissed and detained.[117] That the South Sudan presidency later appeared to want to resolve the corruption case out of court may, however, be an indication that larger interests are at stake.[118] When this book went to print, however, senior officials were eventually charged.[119]

In a way, the SPLM leaders kept each other in check, since most of them knew about others' malfeasance. This made progress difficult. Rumours circulated, not only about ministers, but now also the President's office. Only after the 2013 crisis did the cadres begin to go public with what they knew, primarily to undermine other factions. Corruption became an instrument in internal political battles.

The effectiveness of Kiir's approach may be judged by the fact that not much happened. The corruption problem in the financial sector actually worsened. It was public knowledge that even more government officials now had shares in banks and foreign exchange bureaus, many in silent partnerships, despite such ownership's illegality. Learning the identity of actual shareholders is difficult; although the business registry and other relevant documents are ostensibly public, access usually requires ministerial approvals. This opaqueness includes the ownership of foreign exchange bureaus. These were highly lucrative, since the black market in currency had driven down the value of the South Sudanese pound, allowing companies to pocket even more of the windfall from the dual exchange rate.[120]

The IMF continued to criticize the dual exchange rate, which distorted the economy and reinforced perceptions of poor economic management by fostering corruption and rent-seeking.[121] In surprisingly plain language, the IMF wrote of 'a hidden transfer of resources from the government to those with privileged access to foreign exchange at the official rate'.[122] The diversion of dollars to the black market was estimated at three times the amount going to South Sudanese banks.[123] Differences in exchange rates made it possible to make up to a 400 per cent profit on every transaction. The number of foreign exchange houses multiplied as a consequence.[124] Indeed, stories were rife of top officials in the government and the Central Bank owning or having shares in forex bureaus, characterized by economic experts as an oligopolistic cartel.[125] The significant rents totalled around 12–15 per cent of government expenditure or an estimated 3 per cent of GDP.[126] Media outlets listed a number of such companies.[127] The collective refusal to address this large-scale scam was one of the worst aspects of South Sudan's corruption problem.

The Central Bank's custody of national resources was hardly water-tight. In late 2012 a senior official of the bank ran off with several million dollars in a suitcase. He evaded a team of security officials and managed to board a flight to Nairobi. They contacted the airport tower to order the plane to return, but it was too late.[128] The farce continued in Nairobi, where a pre-arranged reception with allies prevented an arrest. A year later, in a similar incident, the son of a top official at the Central Bank reportedly fled with $2 million. In both cases, no further action was taken against the known individuals.

While the people of South Sudan suffered from the oil shutdown, some liberators tried to gain financial advantage from it (on projects related to refineries, alternate pipeline projects through Kenya to Lamu and through Ethiopia to Djibouti, and the like).[129] In 2013 the great majority of the population were unable even to meet the basic needs of their families.[130]

The President knew how the public perceived the corruption problem, and this was one motive for his long-standing plans for a cabinet reshuffle. We will analyse later the political impact of the sacking of two ministers on corruption grounds in April 2013, the removal of the whole cabinet and the Vice President the following July, and the composition of the new cabinet a week later.

Despite all this, some progress was made in legislative matters. Although there had been question marks about hidden reserves on foreign accounts and dubious loans, probably against future oil income,[131] it was also widely acknowledged internationally that South Sudan did in fact pass the test of macro-economic survival posed by the period of austerity.[132] The 'Core Functions under Austerity' programme helped. With the re-start of oil production, preparations for a New Deal Compact between the government and the donors on delivery across five key peace-building and state-building goals also gained pace.[133]

The main goal was to protect spending on education and health so that ordinary citizens did not suffer from the austerity measures. An international investment conference was to take place in early December 2013. But progress hinged on South Sudan's abandoning the policy of parallel exchange rates and approving critical measures such as the Petroleum Revenue Management Act. Regarding the latter, the President hesitated, reportedly over the audit clause.[134] This in turn was a prerequisite for IMF support for a staff-monitored programme, and its approval again was a precondition for funds from the World Bank and several other donors. The Minister of Finance and the Governor of the Central Bank decided, with the blessing of the President, to devalue the currency on 11 November, and align it with the black market rate.[135] This was done in time for the meeting of the IMF board and the agreed date for launching the New Deal at the beginning of December.

While unification of the currency rate raised genuine problems in the market place and for salaries, it also hit vested interests.[136] In parliament Riek Machar denounced the measure and, to international observers' surprise, held that the legislature's authority had been usurped. The Finance Minister was out of the country, so the Governor had to turn up in parliament – and caved in. The Government reversed its decision, and formally retained the dual exchange rate policy. With this, the process stopped. The planned financial facility was shelved, and the New Deal Compact was never signed.

According to de Waal, South Sudan's insolvency because of the oil shutdown made it impossible to buy – and keep – the peace; corruption itself was therefore the underlying 'brute cause' of the crisis that erupted in December 2013.[137] But owing to domestic security concerns, payments to the security sector and salaries were largely maintained; the austerity budgets did not significantly affect the leaders of the SPLM or SPLA.[138] The elites also appear to have misappropriated enough to keep them and their patronage networks going, as the construction boom in Juba during the shutdown indicated. De Waal's assumption therefore appears misguided.[139]

The incomplete divorce from Sudan, however, does seem to have mattered. De Waal appears to monetize that relationship too, by averring that Bashir could have cut a deal, buying the Southern elite's acceptance of a united Sudan.[140] On this fundamental issue, however, almost no one in the SPLM leadership was for sale. Even those who at times had entertained links to Khartoum were clear that they would never sacrifice independence. Relations with Sudan remained controversial, however. The SPLM leadership appeared 'united in war – divided in peace'. And with oil production switched on, tensions escalated.

## Drivers of division

Other undercurrents increased tensions and exacerbated South Sudan's fragility. The elite, whether political or military, depended on ethnic identity as a main avenue to public office. In the absence of functioning public institutions which could provide services, the government's principal means of redistribution of wealth and mitigating inequalities continued to be the state payroll.[141] Ethnicity became one of the main qualifications for receiving a salary, making patronage all-important for access to public finances.

The communities knew this, and agitated for new counties or payams (sub-counties), preferably along ethnic or sectional boundaries. New counties would give more people income through salaries. And if borders followed ethnic lines, they could ensure that their own community would benefit. This was a recipe for division and fragmentation.

### Ethnic politics

In March 2012 Riek Machar argued for establishment of no fewer than 400 new counties, five times the current number.[142] He contended that this would be a way to distribute state resources more widely. There was a misguided view that such proliferation would create peace: after all, people would be administered by their own communities. But in fact the more counties you have, the more competition you get for resources; and the scarcer the resources, the worse the fight.

As vice president, Machar later sent a letter to all governors requesting the establishment of new counties.[143] The CPA and Local Government Act of 2009 did not encourage this; policy generally was to ensure that many counties had mixed ethnic identities.[144] Both in the Upper Nile and Equatoria regions, for example, authorities deliberately tried to avoid drawing county boundaries along ethnic lines. Was the vice president now trying to change the law and national policy through the back door?

Some governors followed up on the instructions. And sure enough, UNMISS State Coordinators reported that this was fuelling conflict in several rural areas. Violence was breaking out over land, boundary demarcation and the siting of county headquarters.

The real reasons for this initiative appeared rather obvious: state patronage and competition for political power and resources. Establishing more counties, and along ethnic lines, would provide benefits for any ambitious politician. The number of loyal county officials would be increased, as would influence within the SPLM, the structure of which was based on counties rather than local chapters: the more counties there were, the more representatives the patron would have in party organs. For a perennial candidate for chairmanship of the SPLM, the potential of such a development was clear.

And for other politicians and community leaders down the line, the temptation to expand their own client base was significant. Where would particularism end? Ethnic groups are divided up into clans and sub-clans, and extended families.

President Salva Kiir put an end to this initiative. In his Independence Day speech on 9 July 2012 he said the time was not right to create new counties, and that further assessments were needed. This was received with a sigh of relief by several governors, but it hardly brought an end to patronage politics.

Contrary to the Local Government Act, whereby county commissioners are to be elected by the people and accountable to them, the liberators appointed local authorities, making county commissioners accountable to the Governor and thus to the centre.[145] The Transitional Constitution already provided the President with very significant powers, with limited checks and balances. Now, constitutional provisions for electing governors were also increasingly violated.[146] President Kiir's dismissal of three governors and reappointment of two to other positions (in 2012 and 2013), implied that governors were answerable to him. It did not help that Kiir was perceived to progressively give more power to his own Dinka community, in particular in relation to key government institutions such as the Central Bank and the judiciary. This increased tensions.

Centralization of power and fragmentation of the periphery ethnically was politics on the cheap. It implied that rural people and ordinary citizens did not have a collective platform to challenge leaders, no outlet for complaints or grievances. This in turn reduced whatever checks and balances there were on the elite in political office at all levels. But in the end, not everyone could be 'salaried' to contentment.

## Tightening controls

Another worrying undercurrent surfaced. The first bad omen was the killing of the South Sudanese journalist and blogger Diing Chan Awuol, often called Isaiah Abraham, on 5 December 2012. This was seen as an assassination and sent shock waves through both government circles and the public.[147] Rumours were rife that elements in the government's security apparatus were behind it, but this was never confirmed. Investigations were conducted, but not conclusive. In the end, no one was held to account. In Juba, threatening text messages had been sent to a number of dissenting voices, in particular among civil society activists, young journalists and bloggers. Some fled the country. South Sudan dropped 12 places in the 2012 press ranking published by Reporters without Borders due, in part, to the 'heavy handedness by security forces in dealing with journalists'.[148]

Soon after, nine people were killed in peaceful demonstrations in Wau in Western Bahr el Ghazal by government security, and more than 100 arbitrarily detained.[149] UNMISS protested publicly, but to no avail.[150] We were also unable to complete our investigation, which was impeded by state authorities. When I raised such incidents with the President and higher echelons of government, they usually responded with a commitment to correct things. Yet no one was held to account.

While tensions between Salva Kiir and Riek Machar increased, there was a clear impact on the political climate in the country. There had been relative tolerance for voicing discontent, but government officials now began to warn journalists against publishing criticism of the President.[151] By 2013, fewer felt it safe to speak about their ideas in public.[152] Threats against the media were frequent, and there were increased arrests and abusive behaviour, including use of torture, by security forces.[153]

Although the cabinet passed to parliament a package of eight human-rights instruments for accession and ratification,[154] three bills tabled towards the end of 2013 showed an opposite trend. One was a media law criticized for being too restrictive. Another was the NGO bill that would seriously impact organizations' ability to operate.[155] A third bill gave the National Security Service expanded powers in several areas, including arrest, monitoring of communications, conduct of searches, and seizure of property,[156] despite significant resistance in the National Legislature.[157]

The tightening of controls made it more difficult for ordinary citizens to voice their concerns. A climate of fear took hold. UNMISS was also affected. Suspicion and mistrust increasingly dominated relations. What had started off as a close collaboration between the newly independent country and the UN Mission mandated to support it was about to go sour. What had happened?

**4**

◆

# JONGLEI: THE UN – BETWEEN A ROCK AND A HARD PLACE

At the inaugural meeting of the South Sudanese National Legislative Assembly on 8 August 2011, the Speaker, James Wani Igga, noted:

> Without the full commitment of the two UN Secretary Generals [...] Independence of South Sudan would not have seen the light of day [...] I think we are duty bound to give the esteemed UN and its Secretary General a standing ovation in this noble hall.[1]

Members rose to their feet, in a round of applause that could have lifted the roof.[2] Indeed, without the support of the UN the exercise of self-determination would never have happened in accordance with the Comprehensive Peace Agreement of 2005. After independence the UN was given the arguably more difficult job of helping its 193rd member state stand on its own feet. As we shall see, relations with the UN would soon become vexed.

The UN Mission in South Sudan faced an almost unprecedented state-building and peace-building challenge. In recent cases, newly independent countries such as of Kosovo and Timor Leste were much smaller, and more 'manageable' from the demographic, ethnic and geographic perspectives and had benefited from a transitional UN administration. In the case of South Sudan, however, the interim period was seen as preparatory, and although supported by the UN, the CPA did not provide for additional transitional administrative arrangements. Even as UN missions in the Democratic Republic of Congo, Ivory Coast, Liberia and Sierra Leone had faced very difficult circumstances, they were not tasked with literally building a country, almost from scratch, in the same way. Beyond the scale of the task, the UN's relations with the liberators and the Government of South Sudan would soon prove to be equally difficult.

Resource constraints and the scale of protection required, particularly in the largest state, Jonglei, soon beset the Mission. Mobility problems meant that the Mission could do little to protect civilians under imminent threat in difficult, swampy terrain, particularly during the rainy season. Criticism came from observers and local communities alike. The Mission also came under fire over human rights: while NGOs and others blamed the Mission for not holding the government accountable for abuses, South Sudanese from all segments of society repeatedly accused the UN, and me personally, of being too hard on the SPLA. Some human-rights staff were expelled from the country. UNMISS was squeezed between a rock and a hard place.

When the crisis broke out in December 2013, confidence had thus already been eroded. The UN became a handy punching bag, not least for government hardliners.

With independence, South Sudanese leaders expected the UN to deploy peacekeepers primarily on the border with Sudan, to protect the new country's sovereignty and territorial integrity. A secondary task was to help build capacity and state institutions. When the Security Council gave UNMISS a different mandate – to protect civilians within the country, and not explicitly to protect South Sudan from external aggression – the new Government immediately took umbrage. They interpreted the so-called Chapter VII mandate, authorizing the UN to intervene with force if the government failed to protect civilians under imminent threat, as an insulting infringement of sovereignty. In their view, such a mandate had been needed *before* independence, when Southern Sudan was part of Sudan and violent incidents, perpetrated by

Khartoum, were frequent, not now, when their own security forces were sufficient.

The UNMISS mandate also encompassed peace-building and state-building, including supporting core functions of the state such as the rule of law, police, the justice sector, conflict mitigation and resolution, strategic support to reforms in the security sector, military justice and special protection of women and children.[3] The number of troops at our disposal was limited, however, and with regard to infantry very small compared to missions of a similar nature.[4] Given the thorough planning process that preceded establishment of the mission, this surprised me. No one could explain how the force level had been calculated.

While some SPLM-leaders fully understood the comprehensive role of the UN and the rationale for its mandate, many others felt that they had got rid of one 'colonial' power, after decades of struggle, only to face another. They did not like the idea of foreign babysitters.

The rather poor reputation of the former Mission in Sudan, UNMIS, particularly among Southerners, did not improve matters. That Khartoum-based mission had been perceived as leaning towards Northern Sudanese positions on most issues. Its emphasis on unity, and the slogan of 'making unity attractive', did not go down well, although this was indeed its mandate after the CPA. The former mission was also perceived as having stood idly by when Khartoum's forces killed civilians, and, for that matter, when civilians were under threat from inter-communal violence.

When the vast majority of the population was not literate, and one Mission's name sounded the same as another's, the communications challenge for UNMISS was even greater. Even well-informed people thought the two Missions were the same, and that our headquarters were in Khartoum. Many complaints we faced at the outset were found upon examination to be linked to the former mission. As with most peacekeeping missions, ordinary people also questioned the impact of our investment, the number of white Land Cruisers roaming about, the helicopters, all the staff, and so forth. The perception of being 'invaded' prevailed in Juba, despite the UN's efforts to leave a lighter footprint and improve its image.

It might have been a consolation that I, as Head of Mission, was no stranger to South Sudan, but was familiar with the struggle, the CPA negotiations and many of the personalities involved. But there would soon be a list of complaints specifically related to UNMISS, as well.

Although I briefed many leaders early on, we did not meet the full cabinet until September, when we gave a comprehensive briefing that included our proposed plan of implementation. Some ministers were familiar with the mandate and the UN's modus operandi; others were open and positive despite their earlier misgivings; several ministers complained about not having been consulted about the mandate, including its Chapter VII. A handful were negative and complained that the sovereignty of their newly independent country was threatened. One highly educated minister asked whether I would be co-president of the Republic, or even governor general of South Sudan.[5] He was not joking. This was my first encounter with government hardliners who would later make ample use of such terminology in their campaigns against the UN.

South Sudan had in fact been consulted informally about the establishment of UNMISS at an early stage in the process, when the assessment team was preparing the mission, and subsequently by the country in charge of drafting the resolution in the Security Council, the United States. A Working group of ministers had studied the draft mandate and commented. Riek Machar, the vice president, had seen at least two drafts of the resolution, including the final one, and given the green light on behalf of his government. Clearly more consultations could have taken place, and with more ministers, but the mandate had hardly come out of the blue. In the cabinet discussion with the Mission, however, those who had been involved remained silent.

While some politicians were sceptical, I frequently heard from South Sudanese citizens, church leaders and community leaders that they felt reassured by our presence. Indeed, many had unrealistically high expectations of what UNMISS could do. They seemed to think that UN peacekeepers were so many and had such powerful assets that we could protect not only their new country, but also their communities and individual families – whatever the threat was – anywhere. Although campaigns were launched to explain the mandate and its implications, managing expectations was a consistent challenge.

An early test in this regard was the build-up of tensions with Sudan. As we have seen in Chapter 3, the first bombs fell on the Yida refugee camp already in November 2011, followed by other incursions across the border. People wondered why the UN did not prevent the raids or stop them once they began. But the Mission had neither a mandate to protect the borders nor ability to do so. Both would warrant discussion in the Security Council, but the greater the tensions, and the more incidents in which civilians were killed, the heavier the criticism; the more silence the South Sudanese detected internationally, the louder were their own complaints. To the people, the UN and the international community were one and the same.

Constant communication with South Sudanese through radio and directly was one of the Mission's, and my, main roles. Our teams met leaders all over the country. Bishops and other clergy were important opinion leaders; they could help explain things to congregations in their own languages. I launched a consultative forum of elders, representatives of civil society, religious leaders from Muslim and Christian denominations, and of women's and youth organizations.

This outreach would be needed especially in relation to the perpetual Jonglei crisis. It was here that the UN would face its greatest challenge in protecting civilians, at least before the events of December 2013. Throughout 2011–13, UNMISS would be severely tested in this largest and most volatile state of South Sudan. As one observer has put it, 'Jonglei is a place where wars are more likely to start than to finish.'[6]

## Jonglei: Mission impossible?

The first attacks against civilians after UNMISS's establishment happened only five weeks into our deployment, on 18 August. Several hundred were killed or wounded in Pieri in Jonglei State in a vicious revenge attack.[7] This was only the latest spike in a cycle of large-scale communal violence that had tormented the state for a long time.

Jonglei is the largest of South Sudan's ten states. With approximately 1.3 million inhabitants, it was also the most populous, but the least developed in terms of infrastructure, virtually without functional roads, and none of them tarmac. During the rainy season the plains turned into wetlands and flood zones. While more than 60 per cent of South Sudan was very difficult to access during the lengthy rainy season, Jonglei was the site of the famous Sudd, the world's biggest swamp, when flooded, the size of England. For almost eight months of the year some places were hardly reachable except by air or boat. And parts of the state's vast hinterland, where it meets Ethiopia and Kenya, had barely been touched by the outside world. Decades of marginalization by central authorities and civil war had also left Jonglei State the most underdeveloped in South Sudan, with its remotest periphery areas suffering some of the worst development indicators in the world.

Most of the population of Jonglei were young and unemployed, and without access to the dividends of peace and oil revenue. The lives of the state's proud, fiercely independent and primarily pastoral communities revolved around cattle. Cattle-raiding linked to competition for scarce resources had been a main trigger of conflict between ethnic groups. The cycle of violence had continued throughout the CPA period, complicated by (at times violent) disarmament campaigns. Tit-for-tat attacks escalated in 2009 when several conflicts erupted at once, eventually turning into sustained confrontation between the Lou Nuer and Murle.

Such attacks had a long history, motivated partly by ethnic tension and partly by traditional competition over cattle and grazing areas. This latest violence, however, at times involving also the Bor or Twic Dinka, showed an increase in scale and gravity. There were three conflict zones, Greater Akobo, Greater Pibor, and Greater Bor. A cycle of retaliatory attacks in 2009 seemed to mark a change in strategy, whereby cattle rustling was accompanied by direct attacks on civilians, communities as a whole, and state institutions. Devastating attacks on Lou Nuer communities early in the year, and subsequent attacks and counter-attacks in Akobo and Pibor constituted a major escalation. These resulted, according to unconfirmed reports, in more than 1,000 casualties – with more than 700 killed in one week-long attack on Pibor. Violent conflict killed or displaced twice as many people in South Sudan that year as in the year before.[8]

Like much of South Sudan, Jonglei was awash with weapons, and civilian disarmament became a priority during the interim period.[9] Among the Lou Nuer and Murle in 2009/10 disarmament failed: both communities managed to hide weapons, and the voluntary aspect of the process was short-lived. The proliferation of weapons thereafter fuelled civilian violence, with a series of smaller raids, particularly in the absence of an adequate state security apparatus.[10] And the nomination processes for the 2010 elections – and elections themselves – led to new violence.

The killing of three Lou Nuer chiefs by Murle assailants in Thiam Payam in February 2011 provoked one of the largest armed mobilizations in South Sudan since the CPA. Revenge came two months later, when the Lou Nuer launched a coordinated attack on Murle cattle camps in the eastern part of Pibor County. Smaller attacks by both communities ensued, before a major Lou Nuer attack was launched against the Murle in June, lasting almost ten days, reportedly killing hundreds, and with many women and children abducted.[11]

There were two main modes of violence, the opportunistic raid and the massive attack, primarily along two front lines; opportunist raids predominantly against the Dinka of Greater Bor, and reciprocal massive attacks between the Murle and Lou Nuer.[12] In both Murle and Nuer society, there had been a militarization of the youth, and the generational balance of power appears to have shifted youthwards.[13] This development would have serious implications for any peace process. As Edward Thomas puts it:

> The White Army [Nuer Youth] and armed youth groups are not traditional structures – they are examples of how traditional structures are transformed by violent experiences of modernity [...] [T]hese groups operate within a semi-autonomous youth sphere, not entirely under the control of, or accountable to, traditional leaders.[14]

What happened in Pieri soon after independence was thus only the most recent manifestation of conflict between the Lou and Murle. We had an inkling that something could happen. Our aircraft had been overflying the Pibor and Akobo areas for deterrence and monitoring, and we had deployed personnel on overnight patrols into the two most critical locations. But in August 2011 UNMISS was still in start-up mode on all fronts, which limited our capacity, the territory involved was vast, and it was the middle of the rainy season, which made things worse. While attacks were more usual during the dry season, armed youths could march long distances even during the rains. The Murle were particularly hard to track and could move at night, often in small units, at times very well coordinated, and then attack.[15] The assault on Pieri came without warning and with lightning speed in a remote location. Preventing inter-communal violence, deterring it, and protecting civilians from it was at the heart of our mandate. But I soon discovered that our military capabilities were wholly inadequate.

In late July I went to Pibor town, site of the April attack, taking place before UNMISS had been formally established in July. The wife and children of the local SPLA commander, a Murle, had been abducted during the attack. Local leaders told me they felt both victimized and ignored by central and state authorities, and accused all of us of siding with the Lou Nuer. (There was not a word about the Murle's own previous assaults.) I was not afraid of anger and emotional outbursts, but this was my first confrontation with such despair. I urged them not to avenge the attack, and to give us a chance to work on a peace process that could yield positive results.

But only a month later came the attack on Pieri in the Lou Nuer area, presumably perpetrated by the Murle. We did not get information early enough to prevent the attack, and we would anyway have had major problems deploying into such a remote area on time. After some humanitarian assistance had been provided, I went to Pieri to meet the community. We sat under a tree, with all the chiefs and youths and women in large numbers. I expressed my deepest regrets and apologized that we had not been in a position to prevent the attacks or deploy forces to protect them.

Their story was the mirror image of the one in Pibor, and just as emotional. And there were no references to their own assaults on the Murle. They were clear that this attack would be avenged unless the government proved it could provide protection. I told them I would see the Murle in Pibor and would convey their outrage, but I also emphasized that this cycle of violence and revenge had to stop. In the end they would all be losers. This was my message to the Murle too, in Pibor immediately afterwards.

At this time, neither the two communities nor their local authorities were in contact. When I told each community that the other felt just as angry, abandoned and betrayed they were surprised. They saw themselves as victims and the other side as aggressors. By definition, the aggressor was the stronger, had the full support of powerful allies (the government, the UN), and was able to kill more people and steal more cattle. As far as each side was concerned, they had not done anything but respond to the terrible attacks of the other.

These assumptions were based on entrenched perceptions. Reconciling the communities was going to take a long time, maybe a decade or more. We had to try to take the first steps, contain the violence and halt the major attacks. But this was made even more difficult by politicians stoking the fires and the government's failure to provide security. The communities had to rely on themselves. Armed youths appeared to be their protection.

## Protect yourselves

Security is the most basic need for everyone, often underestimated as the prime driver of the actions individuals and communities take to protect themselves. If government does not provide protection, and the risk of attacks that can kill one's family and destroy one's livelihood escalates, measures must be taken. Communities then bind together to do what they can.

When the government itself is the main perpetrator of violence, danger reaches an entirely different order of magnitude. The record of the civil war is replete with examples of Sudanese forces, and at times also SPLA, attacking civilians. Militia were predators rather than protectors of civilians. The problem did not end with independence. The SPLA never warmed to the idea that protection of civilians was central to its role: this was a job for police. Besides, protecting civilians could be seen as the favouring of one community against another; they preferred to stay away. But the police had not yet been developed as an institution, and where they had been deployed, unarmed, they had no chance of handling ferocious inter-communal violence.

Hence, the government's tacit message was: protect yourselves. While people hoped that inter-communal violence would decline after independence, it only increased. Communities had little choice but to organize their own youths. In some cases they formed police, in other cases groups of armed youths were tasked with protection. One example was the 'Arrow Boys' which was a local armed group formed to protect the community along the south-western border against the attacks of the Lord's Resistance Army. Several state governors even backed local initiatives during 2012 and 2013, in the absence of protection from government security forces. However, as recruitment tended to be based on ethnic or clan identity, there was a risk that the raising of local forces could exacerbate, rather than reduce, ethnic violence. This appeared to have happened in Jonglei.

The majority of the population of Jonglei were so-called Nilotes, predominantly cattle herders, with strong traditions of cattle rustling against neighbouring communities. Among these ethnic groups the traditional age-class systems implied that warriors were expected to provide protection for their community, whether Nuer or Dinka. The Murle, although not seen as Nilotic, still regarded themselves as cattle-people and had similar age-set systems.[16] In all three communities, young warriors are supposed to engage both in traditional cattle raiding, as well as in protecting their own people.[17] The definition of 'youth' varies widely, and has in many cases lately expanded to include most able-bodied men with weapons.[18]

These traditions had taken on several other new dimensions. Many elders and chiefs told me that abhorrent acts of violence had not been seen in the old days, or not so widely. While rustling in the past was conducted with simple and less lethal weapons, we were now seeing civilians targeted in vicious and large-scale inter-communal attacks conducted with modern weapons. While raiding in the old days had strong principles and norms of protection of women and children, where warriors took pains not to harm them, now women, children and vulnerable people were targets. The anthropologist Jonathan E. Arensen has observed this development among the Murle, whose ethics of war have changed; many women, children and old men are now being killed in the attacks, and houses and crops burned.[19]

Sharon Hutchinson, an anthropologist and expert on the Nuer has observed the same changes among them and the Dinka. Until 1991, she says, the norms against slaying a child, woman or elderly person were very strong, such actions being seen as a reprehensible affront against God.[20] Following decades of civil war, the availability of modern weapons and the fragmentation of traditional practices, this has changed. The killing of unarmed women and children has become standard practice.[21] Combined with the mobilization of many thousand armed youths, often in uniform, and the use of RPGs, attacking neighbouring communities, we were no longer talking about 'cattle raids' in the traditional sense. Now the aim appeared not only to steal cattle, but also to kill civilians, to hurt the other community in a way that would make a decisive impact.

The Lou Nuer had, for example, organized large-scale, military structures with a clear chain of command. Traditional structures had been transformed by violent experiences of modernity.[22] An additional layer of complexity was related to the supply of arms. During 2011–12 there were strong suspicions that the conflict was fuelled by arms supplied by George Athor, an ex-SPLA commander turned militia leader in Jonglei, allegedly supported by Khartoum. He was later killed in suspicious circumstances, and rumours of external involvement in the state subsided.

Widespread stereotyping, creation and use of 'enemy' images, and hate speech amounting to incitement to violence exacerbated conflicts. This included messaging about wiping out entire communities or forced removal from their lands. After the Pieri attack, the diaspora in Canada issued several press releases with this type of content. On 25 December 2011 another press release, originating in Nebraska, stated that the Nuer youth army had decided to 'wipe out the entire Murle tribe on [sic] the face of the earth'.[23] Not surprisingly, my public statements against hate speech a few weeks earlier had not had any impact. We could not ascertain, however, whether the fundraising of the radicalized diaspora and their messages of incitement had a direct influence on Lou Nuer youths and their operations.

Nowhere was the cycle of violence greater and more entrenched than in Jonglei. One minister had reminded me early on: 'If Jonglei succeeds, South Sudan is more likely to succeed. If Jonglei fails, South Sudan is likely to fail.' We later learned that other factors were to become even more decisive for peace in South Sudan, but Jonglei and the whole Upper Nile region were a constant, volatile reminder of the fragility of the new, independent country. Virtually all components of UNMISS were mobilized to try to prevent and deter attacks. The violence in Jonglei would continue to torment the government and UNMISS throughout the first three years of independence.

Immediately following the Pieri attacks we consulted widely, and a multi-pronged strategy was adopted in order to advance a reconciliation process and deter further attacks. The Anglican Archbishop Daniel Bul Deng was asked by the government to lead the process. A four-step approach involved delegations from both communities going to their respective communities and discussing how to address their grievances and prevent new attacks. Then joint delegations of both communities would go together, involving chiefs, women and youths, to show that this was a collective responsibility. They would also consult on how a negotiation process could be taken forward, which would be the third step. Finally, the plan was to organize a peace conference that would include agreement on return of abducted children and women just before the dry season commenced in mid December 2011.

UNMISS assisted the reconciliation process through logistical support and advice, calling for restraint through advocacy by key leaders with authority in the communities, and through sending integrated mission teams to the field to meet the communities. From 21 August, the Mission made significant efforts to prevent a major counter-attack, deterring violence through the effective use of our forces and air reconnaissance. Teams with civilian and military components and patrols were deployed to vulnerable communities for deterrence, early warning and heightened situational awareness. They ranged far and wide over the affected areas. During this period UNMISS conducted 600 ground patrols or air sorties[24] and maintained a permanent presence in the four locations of highest risk.[25]

When threats of new counter-attacks were picked up in October 2011, we sent more delegations into the field to try to dissuade the armed youths. Throughout the next three months there was intense activity, with daily overflights of the most high-risk areas, and engagement with the communities. Revenge attacks by the Lou Nuer were stalled, at least for a while. The Nuer prophet, Dak Kueth Deng, was a prime mobilizer of the Lou (and at times of the so-called White Army), and would play a key role in determining when and how they attacked. Government officials, politicians and church leaders later made several attempts to reach out to him.[26] At this juncture, he seemed to be holding back. Stories were even told that the prophet was afraid of the UN helicopters, believing they were evil forces that could attack him: this itself might have deterred revenge. Leaders of the armed youths said that they would give the peace process until mid December (2011). If no agreement had been reached by then they would go on the attack.

Up to December we had used our aviation assets massively to deter attacks, for information gathering, and facilitating the peace process through transporting leaders to remote locations to meet with the communities. On several occasions our helicopters were held by security forces or even shot at with small arms. Suddenly we got word that the military aviation unit from Russia was withdrawing from the Mission; their four helicopters left UNMISS in early November. Their unit was a 'carry-over' from former UNMIS, and although they had hinted that they might not stay in the new mission, we had hoped they would. It might also be that the many security incidents contributed. It was a great loss. This slowed down our operations and affected the peace process. Fourteen months would pass before we would again have military helicopters at our disposal.

By the end of November, the peace process had completed three of the four steps, but now our efforts were delayed. I had urged Vice President Riek Machar, a Nuer, to get involved, and in mid November he started calling youth leaders on their satellite phones. They did not pick up. The date for the peace conference was repeatedly pushed back, and the two sides' commitment appeared to be faltering. We called on the government to fulfil its responsibility to protect civilians by deploying its own forces.

The SPLA dragged its feet. Senior officers said that the cycle of violence was part of life in South Sudan, and it would be impossible to stop it. Such responses frustrated me, and I continued to push, including at the highest levels, for the military to deploy. The President promised to send in forces, but there were no visible signs of SPLA deployments.

At the end of the rainy season, with roads still impassable in Jonglei, the Mission was entirely dependent on aircraft. Helicopters were the only realistic means of transport for most of our operations, but even they had trouble landing, since according to UN rules every landing site had to be tested regularly. And our helicopters could usually carry only 20 soldiers at a time.

## Baptism by fire[27]

On 5 December 2011 we got bad news. Another attack had taken place, now at Jalle, in the area of the Bor Dinka. Forty-one people had been killed, many wounded, and more than 1,000 cattle reported stolen.[28] Murle youths were allegedly behind the attack.

This seemed to be the last straw for the peace process. It was the trigger for the Lou Nuer (and Dinka) to take revenge, both for this last attack and the one in August.[29] We alerted the government that we needed to prepare for a major conflict and deploy larger forces to protect the population. We continued our daily flights to deter attacks, despite the loss of the Russian military helicopters. The Prophet Dak Kueth called for a full mobilization of the Lou Nuer, and they started moving in huge numbers from three different places. It would take time before they had all gathered, but it was now very urgent to try to stop the movement towards Murle territory.

At the highest levels and through public statements I urged the SPLA to deploy additional forces to Pibor and surrounding areas.[30] On our side, we strengthened our military presence in the area to almost one battalion[31] within a short time. Through air reconnaissance we monitored the movement of the Lou youths, who were making steady progress towards the Murle area; in mid December an estimated 6,000–8,000 were observed marching towards Pibor. I called on the President, the Vice President, and SPLA Chief of the General Staff to speed up deployment to protect civilians. I also gave orders to increase the deployment of UNMISS forces, although the numbers we had at our disposal were very small.

UNMISS deployed to the main population centres. As of 25 December, more than 50 per cent of our infantry, amounting to eight of 15 companies, were committed or had been mobilized to protect civilians in Jonglei. I had given specific instructions to the Force Commander to protect civilians, and he conveyed these in writing to field commanders. These instructions included the use of lethal force.

Despite his unsuccessful effort to reach White Army leaders, I now urged the Vice President to try again. Riek Machar cancelled a visit to Dubai and returned from Nairobi to handle the situation, held long meetings with leaders of the Lou Nuer in Juba, and tried to contact the

White Army leaders. UNMISS facilitated his travel to Likuongole, deep in Murle territory, which the White Army leadership was approaching, on 28 December.

But Riek was unable to convince the thousands of youths to go home. They ignored his pleas, and proceeded with the attack. Local authorities had already advised civilians to leave Likuongole for surrounding areas where they would be safer. We helped evacuate quite a number by helicopter; only about 100 were left. Now I instructed our forces not to leave a single vulnerable civilian behind.[32] After confirming that they had searched the town and completed the mission, they pulled out to reinforce Pibor. It was here that most civilians would be at risk and where we now expected the biggest attack. After a second unsuccessful attempt to dissuade the armed youths, the Vice President was flown back to Juba.

The White Army then burnt down Likuongole. Among the messages daubed in the ruins were: 'We come to kill all of the Murle' and 'We [will] come again [so] don't [come] sit [here] again.'[33] The number of killed in town was considered low, given the early warning and the evacuation efforts; 100 civilians had taken shelter in the SPLA barracks outside the town, while human-rights investigators found 8 people dead in town.[34]

By this time the SPLA had finally managed to get reinforcements to Pibor, and we had moved all our nearby forces there. This was necessary, as none of the forces alone was adequate to face an attack of the expected size. At the same time, our armoured personnel carriers had finally reached Pibor, late in the evening on 31 December. As heavy-lift aircraft could not land at Pibor's airstrip, the trip from Juba had taken days owing to nearly impassable roads. All forces were now positioned.

The White Army, in massive numbers, camped across the river and on 2 January marched on the town. When some 150–200 of them tried to cross the river to attack, the SPLA opened fire. Simultaneously UNMISS forces had moved two armoured personnel carriers to the eastern side of town and deterred the Lou Nuer youths from advancing there. After seeing several killed, the Lou pulled back. And on 3–4 January the attackers were observed retreating northwards to their home areas. This marked the first time in history that the SPLA had opened fire to stop inter-communal violence. Thousands of civilian lives had been saved by these defensive actions.

But our sigh of relief was premature. Two groups had broken away from the main Lau column and unexpectedly circled around Pibor and headed south into regions, I was told, where they had never before ventured. They were heading deep into Murle land, where there were no roads, very few helicopter landing sites, and thus no way our forces could pursue them through the bush.

Our later investigations indicated that the Lou Nuer attacks had begun as early as 23 December. When the White Army passed along the Nanaam river; many civilians were killed and cattle taken. There were similar attacks on settlements while advancing on Likuongole and in villages south of Pibor.

We learned that the objective of the attacks appeared to go beyond retaliatory reprisals, to destroy the livelihood of the Murle, depopulate and displace, and to undermine the credibility of the state. The scale of the three Lou Nuer raids within a nine-month period in 2011 indeed suggested these were part of a wider strategy; by targeting not only vulnerable civilians but also social and economic infrastructure, this was designed to neutralize the Murle capacity to retaliate. If our conclusion was correct, the strategy failed: the Murle would later retaliate in kind.

This was my first encounter with all the difficulties a mission like ours, in vast and extremely difficult and hostile terrain, was facing. In many ways, it was baptism by fire. And it showed with stark clarity that the Mission lacked the resources needed to implement its mandate to protect civilians. To defend territory against an attack, the normal military calculation is a requirement of two to three times as many troops as the enemy. Protecting civilians is different. Still, being outnumbered in the way UNMISS was, made it close to impossible to succeed.

The Lou Nuer were no motley crew of rampaging teenagers. They were as many as 8,000 young men, most of them in uniform, well organized and in formations, under a unified command, with small arms and RPGs. The total number of UNMISS infantry in the whole of South Sudan was no more than 3,500, deployed all over the country. During this crisis, more than half of our infantry were in the Pibor area, far too few in relation to a much larger threat.[35] We seemed to be set up for failure. And I knew that I would be the one accused before the Security Council if we failed.

A few days after the Lou Nuer attack in the Pibor area, a frustrated county commissioner of Pibor stated publicly that more than 3,000 people had been killed. This set off a firestorm in the media.[36] UNMISS was accused of not protecting civilians. We knew that consolidated figures of casualties could not have been gathered by this time, and we were pretty sure the commissioner's figure was highly inflated. When our own investigations were completed, the number of killed was estimated at 612.[37] Most civilians killed had been in the settlements and villages along the Nanaam, when the Lou were advancing between Likuongole and Pibor, and by the break-out flanks venturing farther into the bush south of Pibor. Few were killed during the attack on the town. Some 90,000 people had fled into the bush, and it was impossible to protect them all in such remote areas and difficult terrain. In the aftermath, they were now dependent on humanitarian aid, and we had to launch a massive operation to avoid severe and acute malnutrition.

A few days later, the media frenzy resumed. We had become front-page news globally. The UN was accused of standing idly by as Pibor was attacked. There was no mention that the attackers had been repulsed.[38] A reporter had joined a visit organized for the Juba ambassadors of Security Council members to Pibor.[39] Extensive patrols by UNMISS over the following three weeks did not find the 'trail of corpses' stretching 'miles into the bush' that had been alleged.[40] I knew that it was almost impossible to refute this account without appearing defensive; an impression of a failing Mission festered. I had learnt another lesson.

But the picture was even more complex. On 27 December, four days after the first Lou Nuer groups started attacking Murle communities, UNMISS had begun receiving reports of attacks the other way, by Murle on Lou Nuer and Dinka communities. There were credible accounts that many were killed. At the same time, I realized that communities were playing politics with the numbers. Thorough investigations were needed to prevent such hype from taking hold and making reconciliation even more difficult. Numbers of killed and cattle taken could in themselves be mobilization tools, not least in the hands of politicians regarded as community leaders.

## A small victory turns sour

The scale of the Pibor incident sent shock waves through the government. They had rarely seen such a large inter-communal attack, and regarded it as an affront to the state. The President and security ministers were all clear: the armed youths had to be disarmed, if need be by force, all over Jonglei, whether Lou Nuer, Murle or Dinka. The President conveyed this commitment to the UN and counterparts at the AU summit in Addis Ababa at the end of January. Even if people were killed in the process of forceful disarmament, that would be better than allowing these attacks, risking the lives of thousands, to continue.

I worked hard through numerous informal meetings to convince the ministers and President that this was not the way to go. As long as the government was not providing security, people would arm themselves and would not willingly hand over their weapons. It was critical to avoid violent confrontations. I reminded them that such disarmament campaigns had had devastating effects in the past, with hundreds of people killed. Initially, hardly anyone agreed. By the end of February, however, following intense engagement, we had managed to make progress.

The Government decided instead to conduct the campaign in two phases. First there would be a voluntary disarmament led by community leaders and local authorities. Security forces would stand by in case of trouble. The process would be simultaneous in all three communities to avoid concern about vulnerability to attack if one disarmed before the other. The second phase would then involve the police, and as necessary the SPLA, and be conducted in areas of resistance. Only as a last resort would the government permit the use of force by the SPLA.

The change of approach was positive. Before the disarmament campaign started, a high-level sensitization campaign in the whole of Jonglei State, among all affected communities, was conducted to prepare them and engage their leaders. Before the process started, I urged respect for international humanitarian law and the Geneva Conventions on human rights in the disarmament process, and that instructions to this effect be sent to all security forces. I was reassured by the President that such instructions had been given.[41]

UNMISS also tried to prevent further revenge attacks, this time by the Murle. There were many rumours; concern focused on the Lou Nuer area of Akobo. We sent additional forces there, but logistical constraints prevented any sizable deployment. Integrated teams moved in to talk to the communities. Up to 4 February, a total of 44 incidents took place, involving killings and other casualties, abductions and looting or destruction of private property and public facilities in Lou Nuer and Dinka settlements. All were attributed to Murle groups. In these attacks some 276 people were killed.

Without reconciliation, the cycle of violence would be perpetual. Our main focus was therefore the peace process. It was re-launched by Archbishop Daniel Deng Bul, who in February was appointed by the President to chair the Committee for Community Peace, Reconciliation and Tolerance. This, a second try at a peace process, included all the ethnic groups of Jonglei. Through visits to all communities and every county in the state, through meetings with youths, women, chiefs and other leaders, the process culminated in early May in an All-Jonglei Peace Conference. UNMISS facilitated the whole process, through transport and logistical support, and with our Civil Affairs officers. At the same time, we engaged actively with political leaders of the different communities, both in Juba and in Jonglei.[42]

On 5 May the Paramount Chiefs of all three communities signed a detailed Framework Agreement for peace, in the presence of the President, a number of ministers, and the UNMISS leadership. Everyone praised this, not least owing to the commitment to return abducted women and children, and to the detailed implementation plan.[43] Some politicians from the Jonglei communities had misgivings, however,[44] and another warning signal came from some of the young people: 'This is a peace conference for people in towns,' said Gok Nahek Kok, a youth leader representing the Lou Nuer.[45]

After the signing in Bor, the paramount chiefs were flown together to various parts of Jonglei to sensitize the people. Some of them had never been outside their own areas. For pastoralist communities, grazing land is all-important. If other communities are seen to be encroaching on their land, their livelihood is threatened, and they feel obliged to defend themselves, their cattle and their territory. It was therefore important for us to give the chiefs a 'bird's-eye view', literally – of their land in relation to the territory of others. When the Murle Paramount Chief flew over Lou Nuer land in the helicopter, for the first time in his life, and came to their 'capital', Akobo, he exclaimed: 'I never knew that the Nuer-land was so big. Now I understand that we have nothing to fear. The Nuer will not try to take over the Murle land.' Similar realizations dawned on the other chiefs and were important for any reconciliation process to have a chance of succeeding. By this time UNMISS had assisted with a total of almost 1,000 flights to support peace efforts in Jonglei. It was a massive investment.

The disarmament process had started at this time.[46] All three communities had recommended this at the peace conference, as long as the process was conducted peacefully and simultaneously. UNMISS had supported the sensitization campaign to make sure local chiefs and communities were informed. On the day the President had launched the campaign, 12 March,[47] UNMISS issued a statement of clear expectations of a peaceful and voluntary disarmament campaign. The Mission established a monitoring process with an extensive field presence, deterring abuse. This would also enable the SPLA to take action if human-rights violations were reported. We had decided to share all the reports from our monitoring missions to make it possible for the SPLA to deal with any commanders mismanaging the process. More than 110 Integrated Monitoring Teams and Integrated Protection Teams were deployed to various locations in Jonglei State. All of them included human-rights officers.

Initially, they found that the process was conducted in a largely voluntary and peaceful manner, with few human-rights violations in Lou Nuer and Dinka areas. Community leaders appeared to have convinced the youths to cooperate, and to hand over at least some of their weapons. The process brought at least a lull in inter-communal attacks. Human-rights violations, registered and verified, were raised with the SPLA directly. Some incidents happened; in another press statement we urged restraint and respect for human rights.[48] Disarmament was not implemented in a simultaneous manner as planned, however. There were capacity problems, leading to a sequential approach by default. Those disarmed early feared attacks from the others, which also complicated implementation.[49]

When the campaign moved to Pibor County, the Murle area, serious concerns arose.[50] From late May onwards a number of human-rights violations were reported there, perpetrated by the SPLA. There was limited cooperation with community leaders, and a voluntary approach seemed to have given way to force. The SPLA was in the forefront of the process, and its contingents were Nuers. This raised concern that ethnicity was a motivating factor behind their rougher and at times violent behaviour.

We reported our findings of verified human-rights violations to the SPLA, urging them to change strategy and deal with perpetrators. From June onwards we shared the reports on a weekly basis, showing increasing numbers of violations. We requested the government to take urgent action, and to hold commanders to account. On several occasions, the SPLA acknowledged abuse, and this led to some arrests and courts martial.[51] The Government also decided to establish a joint investigation committee including state and central authorities. While this was a positive step, the negative trend continued. Rapes, abductions and other abuses were reported, as well as six killings.[52] In late June we issued a critical press statement and reported the incidents to the Security Council.[53] Nevertheless, from mid July there was a sharp increase in violations.

A number of rapes were reported to us from Pibor on 23 July, and in early August several cases of abduction, rape and abuse were also registered elsewhere. Our human-rights teams were sent to verify the incidents. Simulated drowning had reportedly been used to make people cooperate.[54] On 6 August, the Pibor County commissioner asked for civilian disarmament to be temporarily suspended, as he feared that the abuses would lead Murle youths to join a burgeoning rebellion. His call went unheeded.[55]

We had raised our concerns many times, seemingly to no avail. We now had to go public. On 24 August, following additional verification, we issued a statement criticizing the SPLA for the most recent spike in serious violations, and called for immediate action to halt abuse and bring perpetrators to account.[56] *Before issuing the statement* I called the relevant security ministers, the Minister of Information, SPLA Chief of General Staff and local division commander, informing them about the contents and asking them to inform the President.

At the same time it was reported to us that on the 23rd the SPLA had lost 24 soldiers killed and 14 wounded in clashes with the Murle-dominated militia of David Yau Yau close to Likuongole.[57] We later learned that there had been three separate battles, and that the SPLA had been ambushed and suffered losses on the 22nd also. Including soldiers missing, the total number of casualties could rise to around a hundred; the number was never confirmed to us. The timing of UNMISS's statement was clearly very unfortunate.

Worse, and typical in an environment where people hardly ever check facts, our statement became confused with an open letter to President Kiir from Human Rights Watch made public on 23 August,[58] and indeed with our own human-rights report on Jonglei that had been released some two months earlier but gone unnoticed by people who should have read it.

## Under fire

The whole SPLA, security apparatus and government, even at the highest levels, seemed to think we had issued a report without advance warning. Even church leaders averred that I had been too tough on the human-rights issue, and that we would have to tone down the public criticism in order to make progress in the Jonglei peace process. The President accused the UN, in a speech that was widely broadcast, of spreading false information; Human Rights Watch and the UN had 'a hidden agenda against us', he said, 'but one day, we will deal with these individuals that are trying to confuse the whole world.'[59] Little did I know that this was a warning of what was to come. I had earlier requested a meeting with the President, and now I insisted. It was delayed. At a presentation I gave at the SPLA commanders meeting,[60] criticism was severe.

I had already been under fire from some NGOs in Juba for not taking the Mission's human-rights mandate seriously. They accused us of avoiding public reporting on violations and even of being in the 'pocket' of the government. They criticized the Mission for supporting the SPLA's disarmament campaign with logistical support, which was not true. In fact, UNMISS had followed exactly the same procedures as the former Mission. We did not support the SPLA in any way, except by providing fuel on a cost-recovery basis when they were running out. And we screened any activity against human rights provisions.[61]

The President's public criticism was obviously a message to me and the Mission. And while his staff were friendly, for two months I had not been able to secure a meeting with him. On 22 October I was called to the Ministry of Foreign Affairs for what I thought might be a formal complaint or protest about our human-rights reporting. But I was not prepared for this: our Director of Human Rights, Richard Bennett, and Senior Advisor in the Human Rights Division, Sandra Beidas, were required to leave the country within 48 hours. As the formal statement was read to me I was reminded of Khartoum, where the government had made a habit of declaring UN officials *personae non gratae*; it seemed that independent South Sudan was following suit. The order had come from the President's Office. I was informed that my two officers had been:

> engaging in clandestine misinformation to the international community about events in South Sudan by producing false information on issues of human rights and other reports from non-existing crimes or victimization. Their activities construed a national security threat to the Country, as well as being incompatible with the impartial nature of their duties under Article (VI) Section (5) of the SOFA-agreement [...] Due to the above, the two officials have been ordered to leave the Country within 48 hrs upon receipt of this letter.[62]

I knew that the President must have approved this. I went straight back to the office and called the Vice President, the relevant ministers, and the President's closest advisers, asking for a reversal of the decision, of which, I found, none of them had been aware. I worked the phones until 11.00 p.m., and continued the next morning. Oyay Deng Ajak, the minister of national security, went to the President and appealed that Richard Bennett at least should to stay.[63] But the minister of presidential affairs, Emmanuel Lowilla, advised Kiir to stick to his decision and expel both officials. In the end, the President let Bennett stay,[64] but unfortunately, we did not succeed with Sandra Beidas, who had to leave the country.

I had still not seen President Kiir. Within the diplomatic community, and among NGOs and my own staff there was understandable impatience that we had not issued a statement condemning the action against the two staff members. But with tensions that had been building between the UN and the government, I had to see the President before going public. Finally, another week later, I managed to meet him at his house. It was made clear that a reversal about Beidas was out of the question; I conveyed that a statement protesting against this decision would now be issued. I also used the opportunity to go over the Jonglei issues in detail, and the reasons for my earlier statement. Kiir had obviously not been properly briefed about how the human-rights monitoring was conducted, the regular sharing of information with all relevant SPLA commanders, and the thrust of the findings. We cleared the air. UNMISS's statement was immediately released.[65] Subsequent condemnation by the international community – including some of South Sudan's closest supporters – was, as expected, very strong.

The clash with the militia leader David Yau Yau (DYY), who was allegedly Khartoum-sponsored, sent shockwaves through the SPLA. While his was originally a small armed group, not taken seriously, fears were growing that he could mobilize armed Murle youths against the government. Most towns in the Pibor area had by this time been emptied of men, and not least youths, who it seemed had all ventured into the bush to avoid disarmament, as had happened during previous campaigns, where a common strategy was to evade the state altogether. The Murle youths were never among the 'lost boys'; rather than fleeing the country they simply went into hiding in remote parts of their own territory.[66]

The disarmament process had in fact been put on hold, although not publicly, in the hope that an understanding might be reached with David Yau Yau. A number of youths now appeared to have joined his group, beyond the large number of child soldiers already recruited.[67] Abuse and harassment against civilians were reported, as well as abductions of women and children. These allegations could not be verified, however, owing to lack of access. UNMISS contingents deployed to protect civilians were threatened by DYY several times, including the unit in Likuongole.[68] Murle leaders wanted to avoid a convergence between their armed youths and the militia leader that would lead to a confrontation with the state. As early as in late September 2012 a meeting of all Murle chiefs was convened.

I travelled to Pibor and listened carefully. The most prominent Paramount Chief, a so-called 'Red Chief', spoke last as custom dictated. Usually, as I knew from having heard him previously, he conveyed his thoughts through analogies and stories from Murle tradition. This time, the message was clear:

> For so many years we have been 'urinated upon by dogs' [he said, alluding to the treatment they had been given by Khartoum]. Independence helped us be separated from these people. But we are now in a situation where differences between us are being exploited. People have become tribalists. Now that we have got our independence, we are turning against each other. This has to stop.[69]

The chiefs had already sent people to talk to David Yau Yau several times, and now agreed to send a letter, carried by more prominent chiefs, in an attempt to persuade him to negotiate. The militia leader rebuffed them.

More and more armed Murle youths joined David Yau Yau, angered by the atrocities against their people and in protest against the disarmament campaign. Skirmishes with the SPLA took place in Pibor County in November and December, as did incidents involving SPLA human-rights abuses of civilians, including killings, although disarmament had stopped.[70] By that time thousands of armed youths had joined, including the two most important age sets among the Murle, the Botonya and the Lango.[71] Airdrops of boxes had also been observed by UNMISS in the vicinity of David Yau Yau's base, and although we could not confirm their contents, it was thought that they held weapons and ammunition from Sudan. Several of his lieutenants were still in Khartoum, and presumably in regular contact with Sudan military intelligence.

The situation in Pibor town was deteriorating. In late December SPLA soldiers went on a rampage, burnt houses and caused many civilians to flee to the bush. Some 1,100 civilians came to our base for protection. A government investigating committee condemned the military's behaviour.[72] But similar incidents took place on 27 January, when parts of the town were burnt and infighting between SPLA elements led to the killing also of innocent civilians. By then most of the population had left, with only the old, sick, and pregnant or nursing women and children remaining. They sought refuge in our base when things got rough – from fighting in the vicinity, SPLA abuse, looting or vandalism. In Pibor such rampages happened at least ten times. In Boma there was a similar episode in late December, with reports of dead or wounded civilians. If these bad practices were allowed to continue, many civilians would be caught in the middle between misbehaving SPLA forces and militia attacking SPLA positions.

The first time we had opened our gates to fleeing civilians was during the crisis in Wau on 19 December 2012, after nine civilians had been killed by security forces, and many wounded in ensuing ethnic violence.[73] That episode too had involved smaller ethnic groups such as the Fertit and the Balanda, who had been at odds with the SPLA establishment.[74] We protested the incident, as we received more than 5,000 civilians in our base within a few hours. The Mission developed a Standard Operating Procedure for such incidents, negotiated and agreed within the whole UN family, including humanitarian partners. Civilians would later be protected a number of times, including in Pibor and Gumuruk.

## Peacekeeping illusions

UNMISS's mandate to protect civilians was strong and wide-ranging. But we faced major difficulties in Pibor. We needed early warning, the ability to deploy quickly, adequate numbers of troops, and the ability to deter attacks or protect against them. UNMISS had deficits in all these areas. Without river transport or all-terrain vehicles we were entirely dependent on our helicopters. In Jonglei there had been a mission for six years prior to UNMISS's establishment, but few lessons appeared to have been learnt.

Our troop strength was much lower than that of similar missions – one soldier per 100 km, about a third fewer than the least-manned comparable UN Mission.[75] Since, admittedly, no amount of troops realistically available would be enough for a country like South Sudan, force multipliers were needed, and particularly a much more diverse set of mobility assets. But we had none, and we appeared to be talking to deaf ears. As late as April 2013, during a review of UNMISS, we had trouble convincing visiting colleagues of the urgent need for strengthening the capabilities of the Mission.

When the Mission lost its military helicopters, the situation became worse. Civilian aviation companies volunteered to compensate for the loss.[76] On 21 December 2012, however, the SPLA shot down one of the civilian-contracted Russian helicopters of the NVA company, killing the four personnel aboard.[77] They had been testing helicopter landing sites in the vicinity of our base in Likuongole. This was regarded as a priority in the event of an evacuation of our troops or the need to deploy additional forces to protect civilians.[78] This was also close to an area where David Yau Yau's militia was active. White helicopters were allegedly used by Khartoum to supply him,[79] and the SPLA claimed to have mistaken the UN craft for one of those. But the UN markings on the helicopter could not have been mistaken, and were visible from all angles. A high-level Board of Inquiry convened by UN headquarters completed a thorough investigation into the downing; it verified that UNMISS had communicated the flight plan to the SPLA, whose officer confirmed receipt. The shoot-down was the responsibility of the SPLA. It was a war crime, and condemnation came from all over world, including the Security Council.

From both the personal and professional perspectives, the loss of personnel in service is one of the toughest things one can go through. The way the incident was managed by the South Sudanese made things worse. Unwillingness to take responsibility, carry out credible investigations, and hold commanders to account was embarrassing and had repercussions for relations with the Russian Federation and the UN. It took a lot of effort from me and from key staff to get a minimum of cooperation and transparency in the process. To date, however, no one has been held criminally responsible.

The shooting down of the helicopter had an enormous impact on the Mission and its operations. A number of security incidents had occurred earlier, including helicopters shot at by small arms, and these had led to additional safety measures. But now procedures were taken to a whole new level. As an immediate reaction, we put all reconnaissance flights on hold. Pilots would not fly unless there were new procedures in place to strengthen aviation safety and security. They included written safety guarantees from three levels of the SPLA, the local commander, the sector command and general headquarters, prior to departure to high-risk areas. This could take days, of course, and paperwork was often stuck somewhere, stalling the whole operation. The best we could hope for was two days between request and flight assurance, but usually it took three or four or even longer.

The Mission had been without military helicopters for a total of 14 months when finally a unit of six military helicopters from Rwanda arrived in January 2013. The new safety procedures were made applicable both to civilian and military helicopters. Insecurity in Jonglei meant that most of the state was categorized as high risk. For such areas, additional safety procedures applied, and had to be verified before take-off. For example, helicopters had to follow certain routes that were regarded as safe, and were not permitted to fly below 5,000 feet, which was the expected range of anti-aircraft missiles. The days when we could fly low to deter and monitor columns of armed youths were over. The prospects for air reconnaissance, both as early warning and as a safety measure, were much reduced.

The UN's aviation safety procedures[80] were a particular challenge. First, helicopters could not land except at a site that had been recognized and tested every third month, usually with two flights each time. In a country as vast as South Sudan, it was almost impossible that there would be a recently tested landing site exactly where civilians were under threat.[81] Secondly, before UN helicopters could test new landing sites, these needed to be secured by UNMISS troops or other friendly forces. But when the reason for reconnoitring was that helicopters were unable to land, how could friendly forces or peacekeepers on location secure the site? There were no other means of transport. Thirdly, if a landing site was, against all odds, near civilians under threat, helicopters were still not allowed to land if there was fighting, or an immediate risk of fire. 'Nearby' in this context meant within about 5 kms or 3.1 miles, both for testing flights and normal ones. And it was this rule that had determined the flight plan for the fatal flight that was shot down in December. Protecting civilians or evacuating soldiers was a problem if one was not permitted to land anywhere near them. Another was that this could actually increase the risk that something could happen, rather than reducing it. But this, I was told, was a non-negotiable rule. And the same rules applied to military aircraft, an issue a UN High Level Panel on Peace operations recently addressed.[82]

In UNMISS, additional, elaborate safety procedures now applied. In my position I had no choice but to follow them, especially after a helicopter was shot down and numerous other safety and security incidents against our helicopters had been traced to the government's security forces. It was UN headquarters, however, that had decided that military helicopters should be subject to the same safety rules as civilian choppers.[83] On the other hand, the Rwandans had infrared cameras on one of their military aircraft, which permitted effective reconnaissance from higher altitudes. Even then, however, we soon discovered that the cameras had been placed on the aircraft with the smallest fuel tanks, and it could not get to the most important monitoring areas at this time, such as large parts of Pibor County. It did not help much.

The beginning of the dry season made mobility by land easier, however. We decided to reinforce our presence across Jonglei with the use of the best vehicles we had. With these we could prepare for a worst-case scenario. But there were no roads, and the vehicles were not all-terrain. This limited our reach. The Mission was in a perpetual mobility crisis.

Keeping large forces in remote locations for a long time is a huge logistical challenge. While trucks had some reach in the dry season, a lot of our bulk supplies had to be flown in, several times a week. Unless an established base had a recognized airstrip for fixed wing aircraft, we were usually limited to between 150 and 300 troops at a time at any remote location. This meant that in the event of a surprise attack on civilians, without prior warning, our forces would be few, in the wrong place or easily circumvented. It felt as if we were searching for a needle in a haystack.

## Mobility crisis becomes credibility crisis

In our regular meetings with the government and SPLA leaders, we encouraged stronger action to protect civilians. This was, after all, first and foremost the obligation of the state. We mapped hotspots where major efforts were needed to prevent communal violence, and not only in Jonglei. The other main trouble areas were Lakes State, where inter-clan fighting regularly took place, as well as communal violence across the boundaries in the Tri-State area, the triangle in the vast border zone of Lakes, Unity and Warrap. The numbers at risk did not reach those usually affected in the Jonglei violence, however.

We advocated early engagement by the government in cooperation with communities at all levels. In some cases we succeeded in getting processes under way to prevent the worst outcomes. The Tri-State area was particularly volatile, with cattle raiding and fighting regularly taking place between armed youths of the Dinka and the Nuer across state borders. As this was also an area of less risk to our aviation assets, we could deploy more rapidly and flexibly. The Mission engaged actively in prevention efforts, as well as deterrence through flights and military presence, in some cases successfully even against columns of thousands.[84] Successful UN actions often went unnoticed.

But the situation in Jonglei continued to be our greatest headache. On 8 February 2013 there was another incident, this time at Walgak in north-west Jonglei. This appeared to be a revenge attack by the Murle. The county commissioner of Akobo, Goi Yol, had heard rumours of an impending attack, and warned people a few days in advance not to use the normal migration route.[85] He guessed that civilians taking their cattle for grazing would be targeted. But where the attack would come was impossible to know. One of our patrols went to Walgak but could not get more information from the local people. We could not deploy without knowing more. Then suddenly, a couple of days later, we learned that an attack had indeed taken place.

Two groups had already successfully migrated to the Sobat river, and now a population of about 1,000, mainly of women and children, were reportedly on their way with their cattle, some 6,000 or 7,000 in number. Despite warnings, they were taking the normal route, escorted by 40 SPLA soldiers. This was the first time I had heard of such an escort. They were proceeding through the Mantor area towards the river when they were attacked. The SPLA engaged the attackers in fighting that lasted several hours. UNMISS later counted 85 bodies at that site alone; the total figure of 118 mentioned by local authorities might have been correct. The operation appeared to have been very well planned. The majority of those killed were women and children. Surviving witnesses wept while telling how the attackers had danced triumphantly after-wards, and had celebrated their revenge as they made off with the cattle.[86]

The Walgak attack took place during the dry season. But the area was very remote, and had no helicopter landing site. Even investigating this terrible incident proved farcical. There were no roads. Our brave and dedicated human-rights team walked 55 kms in 48 hours through the bush from the sub-county centre to the location of the attack, with

UN military and local scouts leading the way. They were able to secure a landing site, which later enabled reinforcements and supplies to arrive by helicopter.

In all of this, one thing bothered me most of all: UN procedures for medical evacuations differed from other operations.[87] It was a paradox for me that flying in to save one or two UN staff could be done without further ado, while lifesaving missions to protect civilians at risk of being killed were subject to the same aviation rules as those transporting water and fuel to our bases. I felt that lifesaving missions should be subject to the same rules, whoever was at risk.

I flew up to Walgak and met the community. Visiting the hospital set up by Doctors Without Borders to treat the wounded, I heard the horror stories of survivors. Under a tree outside the hospital, community leaders, women and youths were gathered. I braced myself for another tough encounter with people who had lost so many. The message from all of them was clear: 'The UN is protecting the Murle, not us.'

While international NGOs, and at times also diplomats, blamed us for not protecting the Murle, or not being concerned about their fate, the situation was the exact opposite among South Sudanese in general. We were accused by all the other communities in Jonglei, and by the government, of favouring the Murle. This was becoming a credibility problem for the Mission, which could endanger our ability to contribute to and support a peace process.

Upon returning to Juba I met even sharper attacks from leaders of the Lou Nuer. They had lost faith in the Misson; they had had enough. I should just leave the country and go home. Of course the Murle had used the same sort of language on several similar occasions.

These were very difficult and painful conversations. If I referred to the government's primary responsibility for the protection of civilians on its own territory, with security forces almost 20 times the number of our peacekeepers, this was seen as scapegoating. After hours of conversation, these community meetings, often including legislators and ministers from the relevant communities at the state and national levels, usually ended on a different note, as the leaders understood better the constraints on the Mission and were able to continue working with us.

I held a press conference on 15 February in order to convey a strong but balanced message on the protection of civilians, whatever their ethnic background, to express concern about human rights violations generally and in Jonglei, and to reiterate again the urgent need for accountability there and in Wau. We were worried that there might be another big retaliatory attack by the Lou Nuer, and in late March we saw the first signs of mobilization. The clock was ticking for the government in Jonglei. Unless an understanding was reached with David Yau Yau and his forces, the SPLA would resume operations in the state. Knowing the likely impact on civilians, I hoped that such a counter-insurgency campaign could be forestalled.

## Protection in peril

The Government had made an effort to reach out to David Yau Yau and to avoid a military campaign. At its request, UNMISS had facilitated delegations of community leaders to meet the Murle traditional leaders and agree on a strategy; Murle chiefs would go to Yau Yau in January with the President's offer of an amnesty. But he remained evasive. The Government held off a full-scale military operation to curb this new and growing militia.

The Government's security team asked discreetly whether the UN would be willing to engage as a third-party mediator. It was assumed that DYY needed to feel secure before he would come forward, and that the UN would be best placed to provide such guarantees. We preferred to facilitate the efforts of another third-party mediator, but the UN was willing to guarantee DYY's security. James Ellery, a retired British colonel with experience in South Sudan, both as a UN official and in other capacities, went to meet him in mid February 2013.

Ellery found that the militia leader had a lot of respect for President Kiir, but was much more critical of the SPLA and other members of the government. Having once integrated into the SPLA, but later defected because of the way the Army had treated him, Yau Yau was very sceptical. Ellery estimated that some 30–40 per cent of the 500 militia were children as young as 12. But he was unable to get a firm response from the commander himself, perhaps because hardliners among his people, some with close contacts in Khartoum, held him back. Ellery went to see the 'rebel' leader five or six times in various places in Pibor County, but the militia's leadership group would not agree.

The SPLA launched its military operation on 5 March 2013. I made the difficult assessment that the SPLA, after these efforts, could not have been persuaded otherwise. I had thus engaged at the highest level, providing the government and SPLA with a position paper on the need to respect the Geneva Conventions and human rights. The Defence Minister and SPLA leadership made it clear both would be followed. I saw the order to the relevant commanders; suitable instructions had been given. In a separate press statement, I urged the government to make sure that this commitment was honoured on the ground.[88] Of course I was criticized by some foreign observers for not publicly opposing the military operation itself, but I felt that this would have been counter-productive.

At the same time, a last-ditch effort was now made to get agreement with David Yau Yau. On 13 March James Ellery flew to Pibor County and tried to get his consent to a 48-hour ceasefire. The UNMISS team handling this flew into unknown territory, often to untested landing sites and at great risk in light of the lack of credible communication channels within the militia. All this was not in accordance with our aviation procedures, but we had the green light from Kigali for the Rwandan helicopters to undertake such an operation. Despite these efforts, Ellery did not succeed. The answer was non-committal. There would be more fighting in Jonglei.

## Counter-insurgency on the loose

The SPLA's counter-insurgency efforts would take place in the most challenging terrain, and against a force that was part militia and part armed youths. Civilians had already fled the towns for the bush. Some vulnerable ones remained but, as so often, it was very difficult to distinguish combatants from civilians, making the counter-insurgency operation fraught with high risk.

UNMISS had small contingents at Pibor and Gumuruk. These forces patrolled the towns and surrounding areas, but did not seem to have established deterrence. They found it difficult to stop SPLA abuse of civilians. I ordered a more robust posture, and much more frequent patrols, including at night, but this did not seem to help much. At times, civilians were also caught in the middle of skirmishes, unrest and abuse in the vicinity of the towns, and they fled to the small UN bases for protection, whether Pibor or Gumuruk. At first there were 250 or 300, often for just a few days. Later the numbers increased to over 1,000.

The SPLA's operation against David Yau Yau's forces soon raised serious concerns. Although my attempt to ensure compliance with international humanitarian law and human-rights obligations had initially worked, at least on paper, and the President had publicly emphasized the importance of these commitments, the SPLA engaged in looting, abuse and harassment, and failed adequately to distinguish between combatants and civilians. Five civilians were killed and ten wounded at Pibor and Gumuruk on 1 April; four civilians were killed a week later at Manyabol; a woman and her two children were killed in the vicinity of Pibor; and several more civilians in Budi County in Eastern Equatoria. On 8 April I held a press conference in Juba to express concern over these developments and urged the government to abide by its legal obligations.

This, too, seemed not to have much impact. Soon new violations took place in south-eastern Jonglei. In Boma, an incident of extrajudicial killing was perpetrated in mid May. Among those killed were one of the President's confidents from years back.[89] These incidents prompted President Kiir to issue a press statement on the 17th expressing concern over violence against civilians.[90] But just a week later we were informed of another episode in which 14 civilians were killed and 100 women beaten in the SPLA barracks at Manyabol. Human rights investigation teams were deployed, and we reported the abuse to the Security Council. Within a few weeks in May and June a number of incidents of looting and destruction of civilian property took place in Pibor town. I issued another statement, expressing concern about human rights violations in the context of military operations.[91]

In public speeches on 29 June and Independence Day, 9 July, as well as in his speech to the forces at the General Parade a bit later, the President repeated his criticism of the SPLA. He also ordered action against perpetrators, leading to courts martial and the punishment of a number of soldiers and officers. UNMISS's advisers on military justice and the rule of law, working with the Judge Advocate General of the SPLA, registered a significant increase in the number of officers apprehended for abuses during the military campaign in Pibor.[92] The follow-through on the cases was slow, however, which led to questions about the real level of commitment to accountability.

Small towns in Pibor County were assumed to accommodate some 40,000 people; these civilians were now on the move into safer places in the bush, or suffering as IDPs in hostile environments. Others had gone to Juba or across the borders to Kenya, Ethiopia and Uganda. At about this time tens of thousands of Murle were registered in these three countries combined. A major operation was launched to assist the displaced. Distribution points were organized in government-controlled areas, but access to areas where David Yau Yau's forces were operating was restricted. This did not go down well with the humanitarian community, the UN or international donors. We intervened at the highest levels to bring about a change in policy.

Even from a military perspective the SPLA's operations went badly. They had lost the symbolically important town of Boma to David Yau Yau's forces in early May, an embarrassing defeat, and suffered reverses elsewhere. While the number of SPLA killed is unknown, there were clearly serious problems both with the command and the conduct of the campaign. Soon the government's forces would be confined to bases in the urban centres during the rainy season, while the militia controlled major parts of rural Pibor County, their home territory. For the SPLA, this was a mirror image of the civil war, when the SPLA was the mobile force that moved over vast territory and held rural areas, while the Sudanese Army was confined to garrison towns.

Counter-insurgency operations seldom offer opportunities for military victory. In this case, efforts to reach out to David Yau Yau resumed, and we were asked to help. Consultations started with the government and Murle community as to who would be best positioned to mediate, and consensus formed around the clergy. Meanwhile, concern mounted over the fate of the Murle civilian population.

In South Sudan ethnic slurs were part of the everyday parlance even of high officials and religious leaders, albeit in informal settings. But a common denominator among almost all other ethnic groups in South Sudan was negative rhetoric about this small semi-pastoralist group, the Murle.[93] The case against them often included their tradition of child abductions, allegedly related to infertility – a slander scientifically refuted years ago[94] – and various cultural characteristics.

Anti-Murle bias had been deepened by that people's position during the civil war. Pibor County had been under Khartoum's control for a very long time, and the Murle were seen as collaborators;[95] a Murle militia had indeed fought against the SPLA. Even now community leaders were split between those who had held positions on Khartoum's side and those who had supported the SPLM/A. That David Yau Yau likely received support from Khartoum – and there were multiple reports to this effect – only confirmed anti-Murle prejudices. The possibility that this bias contributed to abuse and harassment during the disarmament campaign and military operations of the SPLA could not be ruled out.

Murle leaders, however, simply did not believe that any other communities had been disarmed. When the SPLA operation got under way, they talked of genocide. Although there was no doubt that the SPLA committed atrocities, there was no evidence of the intent and systematic methods that would justify such a term. But definitions were small comfort, and tales of the 'disappeared Murle' persisted.

The obvious biases of government officials and army officers led many foreign observers to speculate whether, indeed, ethnic cleansing was taking place. No public charge was ever made, but this was the talk of the town among NGOs and some ambassadors. Fingers started pointing at UNMISS, which seemed to some too timid in our approach and too acquiescent in the government's restriction of access. Allegedly, the SPLA would want no witnesses to atrocities, so denial of access became the focus of observers' suspicion; that the leadership of UNMISS might be 'in the pocket' of the government only made matters worse.

There were major flaws in this line of reasoning. The vast area of swamps, rivers and muddy terrain during the rainy season was a problem for the SPLA. It also exacerbated our chronic mobility problems, but my attempts to explain this met with only limited success. The humanitarians' aircraft did not have the same safety constraints as we did. This was related to security incidents, and the strict rules applied after the shoot-down of the helicopter in December 2012. That they could take more risk, unfortunately reinforced the case against us.

We were fully aware that government delays in flight assurances could be used to keep the UN out of areas where counter-insurgency operations were taking place. The SPLA often claimed that locations were insecure and that our safety could not be assured. In some cases it was likely true, but the risk we said was ours to take, not the responsibility of the government.[96] Outright denial of access seldom happened.

At the same time, I had an obligation to avoid unnecessary casualties among our peacekeepers. Not only had a helicopter been shot down, and several shot at, but the ambush of a Mission convoy in Pibor had left five of our peacekeepers and a number of civilian contractors dead. This incident had a major impact on the Indian contingent and necessarily affected the way the Mission conducted its operations. We had to establish channels with both sides to make sure that advance notice was provided of our movements. We eventually came to an arrangement with the government whereby we would assess risk ourselves, and not blame the government if something happened to missions or patrols in 'insecure' areas. This facilitated movement of our patrols and humanitarian operations, particularly in militia-controlled areas.

## The 'disappeared' Murle

On 14 June 2013 Doctors Without Borders (usually abbreviated as MSF, from its French name) issued a press statement[97] about a humanitarian crisis affecting 120,000 desperate people. We were soon in the midst of a media frenzy. When I arrived in New York to brief the Security Council at the end of the month, I was told that MSF representatives had been making the rounds saying that more than 100,000 Murle had 'disappeared'. The story had currency in Juba, too, among diplomats and NGOs. Members of the Security Council were told that the UNMISS leadership could not be trusted – we were 'too close' to the government. This was ironic at a time when my deputy, Toby Lanzer, had been subjected to repeated bashing from government officials for his insistence on humanitarian access; I had certainly had my share of run-ins. Few of these episodes reached the media or, if they did, made headlines.

UNMISS had taken the fate of the Murle very seriously, and had continued careful monitoring, making use of all available satellite photography and working with community leaders to get more information. We had tried to access all relevant areas of Pibor County, despite our mobility constraints and the rains. As an anthropologist by profession, I had read the Murle literature, and had commissioned further research into each of the three communities in Jonglei State.[98] Our Civil Affairs team also did a lot of valuable analysis. However, Murle leaders declined to tell us where people might have fled for safety. I consulted others quietly about traditional survival mechanisms and migration routes. Where could they have gone during the rainy season? What did the Murle normally do when under threat? Could the SPLA pursue them into the bush?

The answers I got were clear. Although the Murle were usually in cattle camps during the dry season and returned to semi-permanent homesteads during the rains, when there was trouble they left the towns and avoided population centres, trekking farther into the bush. Potential areas were identified on the map. They would at such times use hideouts across the rivers and in the swamps that only they knew about, usually close to the Ethiopian border. This pattern had been followed during the civil war whenever the Murle felt threatened. My interlocutors assumed that these were where a major part of the population was now hiding. The SPLA had never been able to get there, they said, and never would.

The MSF press release had surprised me too by expressing concern about how the rainy season could adversely affect the Murle's health. For all communities in the region, and particularly pastoralists, most of the rainy season provides much better living conditions than the dry season. With adequate grazing opportunities and an abundance of water, they were better off, not worse. From July to November there would be good pasture for cattle and an abundance of milk.[99] Murle pastoralists supplemented their diet by fishing, and by hunting and gathering.[100] If they had fled without their cattle, the story would be different. This, however, was unlikely, since it appeared that they had not returned from the cattle camps once the military operation was under way. They were most likely in the hinterland, far away from soldiers, and from aid workers.

I was worried, however, about the townspeople, recent returnees from Sudan, and other more vulnerable, less mobile civilians.[101] They might have lost the planting season owing to insecurity, and might have less capacity to survive in the bush. This was why we pressed for humanitarian access to locations where people were likely to be able to come forward and pick up food assistance, then leave again.

While we hoped that our limited presence could deter some attacks or the worst violations, we had no capacity to engage militarily to protect civilians in the bush. We therefore had no choice but to provide physical protection by opening our bases, patrolling the vicinity, and providing protection for humanitarian operations. Civilians fled for their lives many times during the operations in the Pibor area, and women, children and vulnerable people often (at least 11 times) sought refuge in our bases.

The less numerous Murle on the Boma plateau were probably also vulnerable. They were subsistence farmers. Having fled Boma town, they were in the bush relying on traditional coping mechanisms for survival. The fighting had come close to them when the SPLA tried to re-take the town. UNMISS made a number of attempts to get to Boma, where we planned to establish a base. The rains made access almost impossible, however, as trucks broke down on the road, and helicopters could not provide sufficient supplies to sustain our presence: take-off and landing were too challenging. Only a few patrols and integrated assessment missions managed to get to the town to see what could be done to assist civilians. The humanitarians managed to fly in supplies after some time, but they also faced logistical difficulties.

We knew, in any case, that although the rainy season prevented us from moving, it likewise held back the SPLA from any operations that might deliberately target civilians. This was hostile and difficult terrain for any army, and the ill-equipped government, with no air force and no vehicles that could move in swamps and mud, did not stand a chance. As the rainy season wore on, the SPLA was confined to bases. Whatever the government's intentions, the Murle and David Yau Yau's forces, with their local knowledge and experience, were likely to outsmart the SPLA.

At a breakfast meeting organized by Norway in New York for the 'Friends of South Sudan' on 28 June, the situation in Jonglei was high on the agenda. A number of ambassadors and deputies had inquired about the humanitarian crisis in Pibor. I explained our effort to access remote areas and people in need, including through the use of satellite photography. Then I added a few points about the rainy season and the Murle's coping mechanisms, from a more anthropological perspective. This proved to be a mistake. Although this was a private event, an EU note-taker reported to Brussels a version that was misconstrued as insouciant, and this in turn was shared with the 26 member states, where the MSF allegations about UNMISS's lack of seriousness about the humanitarian situation in Jonglei had already been circulating. Naresh Perinpanayagam, who had lived in Jonglei as a UN field officer, remarked diplomatically afterwards that the level of understanding appeared very mixed.

## Stuck in the mud

When I returned to South Sudan in early July another crisis was brewing. The Lou Nuer were on their way to Murle territory again. Two enormous columns, each with as many as 8,000 armed youths, had been observed moving towards the Pibor area. The military operations against David Yau Yau had been at their most intense, and the rainy season had just started. Would we now see cooperation between the White Army and the SPLA? The attack on Walgak in February had not yet been avenged. But where were the Nuer heading?

I was briefing the Council by video link when we first learned the size of the Nuer columns and the likelihood of a large-scale attack. Again I explained our mobility crisis; we were almost stuck in the mud. As the counter-insurgency operations in Pibor were under way, UNMISS had developed worst-case scenarios (as we had done in 2012). In one of these, for the rainy season, even by maximizing the use of our air assets we could bring no more than 700 troops to one location in a high-risk area such as Pibor, in addition to the 150 already deployed. The greater problem, however, was that the deployment would take nine days and could be sustained for only a day or two. This made such a deployment a merely theoretical proposition. As a practical matter we could keep about 300 troops in Pibor for about two weeks.[102] During the dry season we could deploy as many as 900 peacekeepers, but in seven days. The possibility for a peacekeeping mission to protect civilians in urgent situations of rapid escalation was therefore limited, to put it mildly.

In the closed session I told the Security Council that UNMISS was in no position to protect civilians if 6,000–8,000 armed youths attacked. Even if we had been able to deploy our worst-case maximum of 700 peacekeepers at this time to a given place, we would be vastly outnumbered. Despite our requests, we had not been provided with other assets, such as riverine units and all-terrain vehicles – not to mention force multipliers – to compensate for our low troop strength. I told the Security Council point blank: UNMISS could not implement its mandate to protect civilians under these circumstances.

While there was genuine fear that the Lou Nuer columns would pursue the Murle far into the bush, they let it be known that their objective now was David Yau Yau's militia. There was much speculation that they might have been prompted to venture south – and been armed – by SPLA commanders.[103]

With our mobility restrictions and aviation safety regulations, we had no access to the area along the Nanaam River where reports indicated that fighting was going on. Although not verified, one of the columns of armed Nuer youth reportedly fought with the SPLA against David Yau Yau's forces. The column did not advance further. The other column appeared to be primarily pursuing cattle and did not attack the main Murle towns before turning homewards. Although people most likely had left the area, it is likely that vulnerable civilians were affected by the advancing columns in settlements on the way and in the Nanaam area. We could not get credible and corroborated information about this, however.

A returning column came to Manyabol on 18 July, and we were requested to help evacuate their wounded. With a few peacekeepers and a registered landing strip, this was possible. Our humanitarian colleagues hesitated, claiming that they were not in a position to fly in. UNMISS decided to help, but immediately reached out to David Yau Yau through other channels to offer the same assistance. We did not want to be seen as taking sides on a humanitarian issue. Rumours were that the forces on both sides, including the SPLA, had suffered a large number of casualties, but we could not get credible information.

On 19 July, after persuasion by community leaders, the entire column passed Manyabol on their way home. A video made by a young Indian UN soldier was later uploaded on YouTube, purportedly showing our 20 peacekeepers 'standing idly by.' Some people tried to use this to illustrate the Mission's apparent lack of response. But the UN's mandate was to protect civilians under threat, not to shoot attackers after the fact, nor to apprehend perpetrators. We had no mandate to take on police functions. And if we had been given such a mandate, a platoon of 20 peacekeepers could do nothing against a column of thousands armed to the teeth.

Concern about the lack of access for humanitarian operations and the crisis facing the Murle population continued. My friend Kristilina Georgieva, the EU Commissioner for Humanitarian Affairs was soon on the phone. She had received reports from New York and from the field, and wanted my assessment. We had worked together during my time as a minister, and when I was in charge of humanitarian operations for UNICEF. Kristilina's statement of confidence was gratifying. She knew me well and referred to my strong humanitarian background, saying she trusted my judgement and the way I handled the crisis. Both of us noted the positive meetings my deputy SRSG and the Humanitarian Coordinator, Toby Lanzer, had had with the SPLA's Chief of General Staff, James Hoth Mai, which had resulted in a letter providing humanitarian access to the whole territory, but at our own risk. This approval was now fully used to access the most remote areas of Pibor County.

NGOs and members of the diplomatic community remained concerned, however. The speculation about ethnic cleansing did not subside. Diplomats in Juba had monitored developments in Jonglei for months, and conveyed their concerns to South Sudanese authorities, the SPLA and UNMISS. The US had been particularly worried about grave human-rights violations by SPLA officers. This was reflected both in visiting delegations to South Sudan, the latest in June 2013, and statements at the Security Council. The US was also monitoring developments very closely through various sources. The alleged supply of arms to Nuer armed youths was a topic of serious concern. On 8 August the US Government informed President Kiir that punitive measures would be taken against a few individual SPLA officers on the basis of their conduct in Jonglei.[104] These included travel restrictions, and convening of the 'Atrocities Board', a new entity championed by Ambassador Samantha Power (when in the National Security Council). A Human Rights Watch report, 'They Are Killing Us: Abuses against Civilians in Pibor County',[105] also got the administration's attention.[106]

By this time, in August–September 2013, the first humanitarian missions had reached the areas of Pibor where David Yau Yau was operating and were providing assistance. When at the end of July they got to the remote locations of Labrab and Dorain, they found 25,000 people needing assistance. As they measured levels of malnutrition, the humanitarian workers were surprised to find the civilians in pretty good shape. They did need food, though, and distribution started. When other areas of Pibor County were accessed, tens of thousands of people turned up at distribution points. All were registered by name and location, according to procedures of the World Food Programme. We started doing the numbers. In a matter of two-to-three months, the number of civilians reached in this way was significant. When we added the Murle who had registered as refugees in neighbouring countries, and the likelihood that several thousand had fled to Juba and other areas in Eastern Equatoria, we reached a total not far from the 100,000 that allegedly had 'disappeared'.[107] The Murle appeared to have been true to tradition. As the anthropologist Jonathan E. Arensen found years back:

> The Murle people have an in-depth understanding of their territory. They know when and where to move at the appropriate time of the year. During the SPLA takeover of the Murle towns, most of the Murle simply vanished into the bush, away from the sources of conflict. After several years some NGO workers went out into the remote regions to evaluate food security. They expected to find people starving and in need of food aid. Instead they were surprised to find that nobody was starving, but that they were in good health. It was obvious that the Murle knew how to live off the land.[108]

Despite the good news, I remained concerned about our limitations. We had a strong mandate to protect civilians. We had to be able to do more, despite the rainy season. I had repeatedly instructed our troops to patrol daily, including at night, and had requested weekly reports from the Force Commander that this was indeed happening. With the rains, our troops could not go far, but they could venture farther than they had been going. But I continued to get negative feedback that the patrols of our contingents were limited in reach, not frequent enough, and did not happen during the night in Pibor town. This had been a regular complaint, and I had raised it many times internally.

The units were clearly cautious in their approach, especially after the terrible ambush in April. While investigations had not been conclusive, it was clear that that had been well organized and likely carried out by an armed group of more than 200. The incident prompted delivery of new and better equipment to the contingent, which was long overdue. But I insisted that we take a much more active and robust approach. Despite the mobility crisis, in August we launched a foot patrol campaign in Pibor County to build confidence. From mid August onwards, therefore, contingents deployed to Pibor, Likuongole, and Manyabol went on foot patrols in the surrounding areas.[109]

From satellite imagery, which we obtained through other sources, we were able to comb virtually the whole Pibor area. It was not possible to see signs of villages, huts or settlements systematically burnt down or other indications of deliberate targeting of civilians in a way that showed a pattern of attacks. On the basis of this satellite photography we selected areas of particular interest and sent peacekeepers on foot patrols to follow up. At this point we were still trying to locate Murle civilians, and to establish what had unfolded during the SPLA's operations. In the course of four weeks our patrols covered areas of some 10,000 people and engaged with more than 2,000 civilians. We included human-rights monitors and civil-affairs staff on many of the patrols to make sure we gathered as much information as possible.

The 'patrol campaign' continued for several months, systematically working to build confidence among the local population. By mid October nearly 100 patrols had gone out. People started to return from the bush to the towns, helped also by humanitarian assistance provided in the vicinity of Pibor town and Gumuruk. UNMISS got positive feedback that people felt safer. We had been hoping to take the campaign far into the remote areas of the county, where more people were likely to be found, but logistical challenges related to aviation safety and the absence of credible landing sites made this difficult.

## Making peace

I wanted to get to the bottom of what had happened in Pibor during the military operations. We therefore requested that our human-rights officers accompany humanitarian flights to get information. The humanitarian agencies denied such cooperation, lest the government stop their operations altogether. Our investigations on human rights violations in Jonglei would have benefited from this information. A year had passed since the famous Jonglei human-rights press release and the consequent fall-out. It was time to release a new Jonglei report.

Since the incidents in July, there had been no serious fighting between the SPLA and David Yau Yau. This seemed to indicate that both sides had become more interested in finding a political solution. Feedback indicated that he wanted a change of mediators, and this time Murle leaders approached three bishops, Paride Taban, Paul Yugusuf and Arkangelo Wani Lemi. Bishop Paride was senior, had a strong position among the Murle, and therefore had a decent chance of achieving results. The SPLA too respected him from the days of the civil war, as did President Kiir, who had sought his advice from time to time. The President gave their efforts his blessing, and UNMISS was requested to lend support. I had known Bishop Paride for almost two decades, from the time I was a member of the Board of Norwegian Church Aid, had met him regularly throughout the years, and as minister had supported his peace initiatives. I was pleased that he was now given this important task.

The first meetings took place in late August, in the bush, where David Yau Yau received the bishops with a rally of almost 1,000 people. The bishops had met his associates in Addis Ababa, who outlined their main demands. At the same time, others now seemed eager to assume a mediating role or at least gain profile out of supporting one, including international NGOs. The Governor of Central Equatoria, Clement Wani was particularly zealous. David Yau Yau and the bishops fielded telephone calls even from foreign capitals, offering sites for talks and support. UNMISS was under pressure to transport delegations to meet the rebel leader; we said no to all, unless advised otherwise by Bishop Paride and the parties.

I was concerned about all this activity. 'Forum shopping' was problematic. From experience, I knew that too much attention given to militia leaders and warlords could lead to inflating the price for peace and make it more difficult to reach agreement, particularly if foreign engagement was at high levels. Negotiations in world capitals could incentivize 'per diem' talks, with endless negotiations for merely personal financial benefit. In this environment it would be difficult for the bishops to stay united in their resolve to keep everything confidential. In one of his more frustrated moments Bishop Paride sighed, shook his head, and with an ironic smile said: 'It is tempting to call these people the vultures of peace.'

By this time the Murle population had started to return to the towns. Whether as a result of our repeated advocacy at the highest levels, the behaviour of commanders in the area was also beginning to change. Some had been replaced, some reprimanded, and others court martialled, apprehended or facing charges for misconduct.

On 4 October, after a month of relative calm, President Kiir gave orders to the SPLA to cease pursuit of David Yau Yau's group. The negotiation process would go on for a long time, and would require many more visits to Pibor County to meet the leader before talks eventually started in Addis Ababa. These concluded in an agreement only in May 2014,[110] long after the civil war had broken out in South Sudan, and provided for creation of a self-governing, semi-autonomous Murle administration.

## You don't care about our human rights

Meanwhile the cycle of violence continued, unabated. The Lou Nuer attacks on the Murle in July had not yet been avenged. But three months later, it was a different community's turn, the Dinka. On 20 October 2013, still during the rainy season, several hundred Murle attacked two places in Twic East, in western Jonglei State – the home area of John Garang. Again the Murle had moved stealthily, by night, and very few signs of trouble had been picked up. It was a brutal attack. The Murle killed some 80 civilians and wounded another 88. Women and children were abducted, houses burnt down, schools and the only operational clinic destroyed. The community fled. UNMISS urgently assisted with medical evacuation and I immediately deployed a fact-finding mission that included human-rights investigators.

We were faced with another situation in which the Mission was perceived to have failed. Now it was the Twic East Dinka's turn to confront the UN. A community meeting of Greater Bor, which was attended mainly by elected leaders from Juba, was tough. This was not the first time I had been told to pack my bags and leave the country: it had happened in such community meetings before. But this meeting did not end in a common understanding. The message was that UNMISS cared only about violations perpetrated against the Murle.

A draft human-rights report on Jonglei covering key incidents during disarmament and the military operations of the SPLA was almost ready for first review when the attack in Twic East happened. We had promised the Security Council that the report would be issued on 1 December. By then, UNMISS had issued more than 50 press statements on human rights issues in South Sudan, including on violations by the government and its security forces. Still, the line pursued by some NGOs and diplomats was that we were unwilling to criticize the government publicly. As a member of Amnesty International since I was 16 and as the first human rights minister in the world (1997–2000), it was astonishing to be under continuous onslaught by allies. The full backing of the High Commissioner for Human Rights, Navi Pillay, during this period was all the more important. I was keen to see the Jonglei report finished and published.

I knew that if the report came out without covering the Twic East attack, however, the Mission would lose credibility, and not only in the Dinka community of Greater Bor. Human-rights obligations include the duty of the state to protect its citizens against any violations of their rights, whether by its own security forces or from the violations by others. The latter included non-state actors, such as armed groups of citizens. We had issued public reports about the gravest of the attacks against the Lou Nuer and the Murle, and the lack of protection of these communities. We had to cover Twic East. Before we managed to complete the Jonglei report, the crisis of December 2013 had broken out, and we were overtaken by a much larger human-rights crisis. As expected, for this we were criticized by NGOs, including in the subsequent report of Human Rights Watch.[111]

Many South Sudanese however, held that UNMISS was far too negative. Ordinary citizens, women's groups and elders, church leaders, student leaders and civil society representatives, as well as party cadres asked me why I criticized the government and the SPLA so much on human rights. They seemed insulted. On a few occasions, civil society activists thanked me for the Mission's diligence on human rights, but the norm was criticism. I worried that South Sudanese ownership of the whole human-rights agenda could be lost; the surest way to dismiss human rights was to call it a Western invention, forced upon the people by former colonial powers. And government hardliners were getting close to succeeding in creating such a perception. After all, many citizens had spent years in Khartoum or elsewhere in the North, where such propaganda was fed to people every day. It was difficult for the Mission to meet the expectations of human-rights activists internationally without losing the South Sudanese along the way.

At the heart of the freedom fight of the South Sudanese for the last 50 years was the right not to be treated as second-class citizens; it was fundamentally about their rights. Whenever I highlighted this, people started nodding, and seemed to come around. Human rights was not a Western conspiracy against them after all. But this was a fragile understanding, one that needed to be nurtured and strengthened.

From July onwards, the political crisis in the country worsened. This affected UNMISS. Throughout the life of the Mission, we had experienced many security incidents and constraints on our freedom of movement. The Status of Forces Agreement was violated frequently, at all levels. The breakdown in command and control within the SPLA and the police service made our situation even more difficult. This was not only a matter of patrols stopped, flight assurances delayed, or staff denied access to detention centres. It also included harassment in customs and taxation, and mistreatment of staff; there were problems on all fronts.

Tension peaked when our Indian contingents were getting new equipment in mid November. We had for a long time struggled to get old and dysfunctional APCs and military equipment replaced, not least for our operations in Jonglei. When the contractor responsible for the transport managed to move a large number of APCs into Juba one night, without prior notification of the timing, people thought tanks were being brought in. There was panic in an already volatile situation.

And it would soon get much worse.

# 5

◆

# THE LEADERSHIP

The power struggle within the ruling party had now escalated. The two main protagonists were Salva Kiir Mayardit, chairman of the SPLM and President of South Sudan, and Riek Machar Teny Dhourgon, his deputy. They were the prime drivers behind the conflict. But there were other players in this game, and many different agendas. It is in these dynamics we find the origins of the political crisis in 2013.

## The two foes

Salva Kiir was catapulted into the chairmanship of the SPLM/A following Dr John Garang's death in 2005. At Garang's funeral the Archbishop of Juba, Joseph Marona, said that Moses had led them out of Egypt to the Promised Land. Now it was up to Joshua to lead the people through the difficulties that lay ahead.[1] The prelate called on all Southerners to support their Joshua, Salva Kiir, in his important mission. South Sudanese adopted this narrative. But who was Joshua?

### Salva Kiir

I had known Salva Kiir since 1998, when he led an SPLM delegation to Oslo. Norway had for many years been sympathetic to the Southern Sudanese. NGOs such as Norwegian People's Aid and Norwegian Church Aid had over decades of tireless work laid a solid foundation for this engagement. I was minister for international development and had taken on the role of chairing the group coordinating efforts to end the civil war, the IGAD Partners Forum. Salva, as we called him, was then deputy chairman of the SPLM/A and Chief of General Staff.

When Salva Kiir first walked into the room, a tall, lean man – he appeared more modest and less imposing than Dr John, quickly taking charge of discussions, speaking softly and with less eloquence than his chairman. But he still got his message across. Later I would meet Salva in the field on several occasions. While my engagement in the peace efforts necessarily brought me much closer to Dr John, Salva's visit to Oslo began a friendship that would last more than 15 years.

Salva and Dr John were the only survivors of the core group that founded the SPLM/A. Garang's death in 2005 was for Salva a significant personal loss. He certainly felt the weight that had suddenly been put on his shoulders.

Although he was long thought to prefer independence over unity, Salva pledged to follow in Garang's footsteps, pursuing the vision of a New Sudan, and working diligently to implement the CPA. However, if unity had ever been attractive, its allure was certainly fading by the day as soon as their visionary leader passed away.

Salva Kiir knew that unity of the Southerners was essential for the referendum to be achieved. This would characterize his presidency. He pursued vigorously his 'Big Tent' approach. As we have seen, this led to the Juba Declaration of 8 January 2006, laying the basis for unifying virtually all militia and splinter groups with the interim government.

Like many leaders of the SPLM/A, Salva did not have higher education, but was trained at the Military Academy of the SAF before defecting. He was less interested in politics, negotiating processes and international diplomacy, preferring to remain in the background dealing with military affairs. Despite misgivings, and his own frustrations, Salva stayed loyal to Dr John. Events in Rumbek in November 2004, widely depicted as a coup attempt or mutiny against Garang, were in the end about the conduct of leadership rather than grasping for it. Others around Salva pushed him. But this was still the most serious leadership crisis in more than ten years, and it had a lasting impact.

While Salva's election to succeed Dr John was undisputed, he had expected a contest. His suspicion of some cadres' loyalty continued throughout his chairmanship and presidency.

Salva's background and training as a military intelligence officer, and tendency to be sceptical, had made him circumspect; he avoided conflict and confrontation, preferring indirect communication. Trust came slowly, usually only after years. Early on, his closest associates were from a variety of backgrounds, but in later years he relied more on his own community and kin, assistants, bodyguards and a few friends who had been with him for decades.

In his private life Salva was quiet, almost an introvert, and strikingly deferential, with an aura of dignity and humility. He was commonly regarded as honest and modest. I remember meeting him in Juba in 2005, after Dr John's death. He had let Garang's widow remain in the 'Governor's House', while he stayed in a much simpler residence; it had just rained, and buckets were positioned in the dilapidated living room. Salva remained in that house for several years, with only minor changes to its interior.

Here he would gather those closest to him. A night owl, he would play cards, tell stories about the years of struggle, crack jokes, and drink whisky or wine. As a guest I sensed nostalgia. Several times he told me that the struggle had been easy compared to the challenges of running a country.

Within the movement Salva Kiir was respected rather than feared. One rarely saw him angry. He often spoke of having personally intervened to stop abuse and mistreatment of soldiers and civilians during the struggle. But it was difficult to reconcile that response with the inaction he at times showed as president against perpetrators and people who abused their authority.

As president he focused mostly on big, strategic issues, relations with Sudan, national security and defence. Salva seldom went into details. Giving speeches was a duty, not a pleasure, and his limited direct communication to the people or through the media made everyone wonder what was going on. Remoteness undermined his credibility and authority.

Salva was slow to make decisions and often reflected on possible long-term implications, a characteristic of intelligence officers. Rumination could last weeks, even months. It has been said that slow decision making is typical of the Dinka chief,[2] who is supposed to listen to people, hear their complaints, reflect, and hold his own counsel. The longer it takes for a decision to be revealed, the more independent the chief is thought to be, and the wiser his eventual ruling. Salva would listen and nod to all the delegations coming to see him, even at times saying 'yes, I agree'. But that never implied that a decision was made. The final decision, if one came, might be different. Actions spoke louder than words.

Some decisions, however, cannot be put off. Waiting too long can limit options and force emergency decisions in haste. This was certainly the case in South Sudan, especially because the capacity for implementation was so limited. Promises were made, but not acted upon. This was a problem not only with the President: it was typical of Southern Sudanese in office. Implementation was very slow. The President also had a tendency to walk back on positions he had taken. If a decision proved more costly politically than had been foreseen, and it was opportune to change a position, he would do so with a straight face. A close adviser calls this character trait 'tactical avoidance'.[3] But it meant that no decision seemed final, and one seldom knew what 'policy' really was.

Over time, Salva Kiir's modus operandi started to undermine an assessment of him as basically a good man who wanted to do the right thing. While many problems were attributed to the team around him and to 'bad advisers', confidence in his leadership eroded. Old tensions within the SPLM leadership resurfaced. Lack of access to the President, including for some ministers, did not help matters. He also seemed more available to community leaders of various ethnic groups than to his own SPLM colleagues. Salva trusted almost no one, but appeared to do little to reach out to these cadres and inspire trust in himself.

The mystery of who had access to the President and when was often blamed on gatekeepers. But he did use access as a tool in the power dynamics around him. This is not uncommon in Africa; it ensures that no one can claim permanent proximity to power and keeps people on their toes. As an observer said, 'they are like clouds, and they shift almost daily'. There were a few with constant presence in Salva's office, but whether they constituted an inner circle is a different story.

Any Special Representative needs to establish good working relations with the President. While commitments of close cooperation were made on both sides, and collaboration initially was good, it was not always easy. The complicated dynamics surrounding Salva affected all interlocutors, national and international, myself included. When the conflict broke out in December 2013, our relations were probably saved only due to personal ties from decades back.

## Riek Machar

Riek Machar Teny was a different character altogether, almost the opposite of Salva Kiir. A Nuer, he was charismatic and cavalier, a force of nature. He could rush into decisions too quickly, but came across as shrewder and more calculating; rough around the edges. A big man – in every way – he would dominate a room. Riek could be flashy, with expensive watches and the latest gadgets, although he toned things down during his last years as vice president. Indeed, the two leaders seemed to be opposite numbers.

Action-oriented, and eager to show his capacity to lead, Riek wanted to handle problems on the spot, big or small, and particularly when he had an audience. He could resemble a different kind of big chief, sitting in his office or compound with an entourage, listening to complaints and predicaments for hours on end, or showing visitors that he could fix things, picking up one of his many phones to give instructions. Although he was familiar with the principle of delegating authority, he often abused it, giving orders about rather trivial matters; he was often accused of micro-managing. Sources in the SPLM/A-In Opposition, Riek's most recent political vehicle, have also pointed to a tendency to get involved in things that had already been delegated, or that were far too detailed for his level.

But this flaw also had a positive side: people would resort to him when they were tired of waiting for a decision elsewhere, and they would often go away relieved that something finally had been done.

I first met Riek in 1998 when I was visiting Khartoum. After meetings with Sudan's senior officials, they insisted that I meet him too in his capacity as president of the Southern States Coordinating Council and senior advisor to President Bashir. Machar had taken up this position after his breakaway faction of the SPLM/A, under various rubrics, had failed militarily to overthrow John Garang.

My suspicion about the extravagance of Riek's titles was confirmed when I was taken to his office. Unlike other officials I had met he operated from a small colonial-era house in a back alley away from the Palace. There was not a single paper or file in sight. There were no books, no computer or any other equipment, a rarity for an academic like him, and no activity. He seemed to have nothing to do.

Machar was soon – or already – looking for ways to get out of this dead end. But all possible avenues seemed to require rapprochement with Garang, his arch-rival, with whom he had been at odds for a decade, with disastrous consequences for the SPLM/A. In his empty office he had little to bargain with, and in 2000 Riek decamped to re-establish his own militia group, the Sudan People's Defense Forces/Democratic Front (SPDF). Only after he had signed a reconciliation agreement with Garang in 2002 did I meet him again.

By then the Norwegian Government and others had been actively engaged in promoting reconciliation for quite a long time; conferences included as many as possible of the seven political groupings that had come to terms with Khartoum. A great deal of work went into the reconciliation process with Riek.[4] Many were involved, including church groups, friends of the SPLM/A abroad, and individuals on all sides. The Americans and General Sumbeiywo, the Kenyan Special Envoy and Chief Negotiator of IGAD, were kept informed. Agreement between Riek Machar and Garang would likely not have happened without such intervention and support.[5]

In return for unity Riek Machar demanded the second position in the SPLM/A, above Salva Kiir, then Garang's deputy. This was denied him; even his accession as number three was controversial. At the Leadership Council's meeting in Yei in November 2003, this reportedly provoked one of the most heated debates the SPLM leadership ever had.[6] Salva had initially opposed Riek's return in any leading position, let alone as number three. Deng Alor and Nhial Deng were among those arguing that Riek should be made number three as a way of promoting southern unity.[7] After hours of discussion, James Wani Igga, the current third-place holder, agreed to relinquish his position, and Garang ruled accordingly. It is against this background that the 2015 power-sharing negotiations chaired by IGAD should be seen.

It was only after the CPA was signed in 2005 and the interim Government of Southern Sudan was formed that I really got to know Riek Machar, the person behind the reputation. During this period

I visited Sudan and Southern Sudan regularly. Salva was commuting between Juba and Khartoum, and there were suspicions that Riek was trying to build up his personal powerbase. He was very active, ran day-to-day affairs of government, and acted for the President whenever Salva was away.

Riek Machar came across as intelligent and sharp. He had an academic PhD, yet he was also practical, and one of the few in the leadership who tried to use basic management tools, made sure that records were made of meetings, and kept substantial files. Whereas Salva did not always do well in selling himself to foreign audiences, and seemed anyway not to care, Riek made a real effort, and seemed effective and credible to Western eyes, at least superficially.

Although as Special Representative my primary contact would always be with the President himself, Riek became UNMISS's most important interlocutor. A Joint Implementation Committee, set up to ensure that problems were dealt with at the ministerial level, and co-chaired by the two of us, was critical for sorting out problems between the Mission and the government. I realized from the outset that I would have a challenging balancing act, and made sure to brief both the President and the Vice President about issues of concern, lest any perception of bias take hold.

Riek had long been widely regarded as ambitious, always eyeing the top job, and was reputed to be power hungry, even Machiavellian. No one had forgotten his attempted coup against Garang in 1991, which to many seemed an act of personal betrayal. Worst of all, in this view, was his having joined hands with the enemy, Khartoum. Given this history of perceived flip-flopping, most SPLM/A leaders distrusted him. His return to the movement had been strained and formal; feelings remained raw. A clear sign of tension was the Transitional Constitution's rules for succession. Article 102 (2) stated that in the event of a vacancy the Vice President would assume the presidency for a maximum of 60 days before the governing party made a permanent appointment.[8]

The Bor massacre of 1991 – in which Riek's Nuer forces killed many Dinka – followed him like a shadow. The Bor Dinka waited two decades for an apology, which he finally offered in April 2012[9] and repeated on several occasions later. But their leaders told me that this had not been done in the right way: Riek had never gone to Bor. Nor was a formal apology ever conveyed to the SPLM/A. In other words, Riek appeared not to have been forgiven, and the wound continued to bleed, after more than 20 years. Indeed, the 1991 massacre would play an important role in the crisis of 2013–15.

Although Riek appeared to understand better than most the way international diplomacy works and the 'do's and don'ts' of national leadership, he still made remarkable errors of judgement. One was to aver publicly in July 2013 that it was time for the President to leave office, and that he would contest a consequent election.[10] This could not be an off-hand remark, but a calculated step on his part. But he did not appear to understand its gravity. To many observers this indicated that the reputation for impatience and hunger for power was deserved, his interest after all being first and foremost Riek Machar, and much less the country.

## Digging deeper: Long-standing tensions within the movement

Those closest to John Garang in the early years of the SPLM/A were often called 'Young Turks'[11] or, later, and unflatteringly by various faction-alists, the 'Garang Boys', and were from many ethnic backgrounds. The Garang Boys were among the most ideologically focused members of the SPLM, engaging with liberation movements elsewhere and learning from them. They comprised most of the SPLM's team during the CPA negotiations in Kenya, and were well known to international audiences. Leading members were Pagan Amum, Deng Alor Kuol, Nhial Deng Nhial, Oyay Deng Ajak and Gier Choung Aloung. Among others, Kosti Manibe and Cirino Hiteng Ofuho, never SPLA commanders, were also in the group.[12] Majak D'Agoot, a Dinka from Twic East, although Salva Kiir's adjutant in 1982–5, was later more closely associated with the Garang Boys. Most of them became critical of Salva as president and were detained for several months during the crisis that broke out in mid December 2013.

Paul Malong Awan, Kuol Manyang Juuk, Daniel Awet Akot, Oboto Mamur Mete and Pieng Deng Pieng all belonged to the mainstream SPLM/A.[13] In conversations in Juba most did not consider themselves Garang Boys. During the 2013 crisis they and several Garang Boys in the Army remained with Salva Kiir, while those characterized more as 'politicians' broke ranks.

An important group of cadres and commanders hailed from the Nuba Mountains and Southern Kordofan, Southern Blue Nile, Eastern Sudan and Khartoum. They too were closely associated with Dr John, having joined the Movement as early as 1985–6, attracted by his commitment to fight for justice for all marginalized peoples of Sudan. They did not constitute a separate faction, and if anything resented that many comrades seemed to be Southern nationalists, primarily wanting independence for the South. Most important among this group were Yousif Kowa, Abd al-Aziz al-Hilu, Malik Agar, Yasir Arman and the former Foreign Minister Mansour Khalid.

Relations were tensest between those in Garang's inner circle and those furthest away, often from the Greater Upper Nile, and mostly Nuer. Riek Machar and Lam Akol, a prominent Shilluk, who openly split from Garang in August 1991, were followed by William Nyoun Bany and Gordon Koang Chol, and later by Kerubino Kuanyin Bol, a Dinka from Bahr el Ghazal. This 'Nasir faction' was named after the Nasir Declaration, which preceded the split, advocating for Southern independence, and criticizing Dr John's reform agenda, but competition for power was likely their primary motive.[14] Nasir in Upper Nile State soon became the headquarters for Riek Machar and his opposition forces. Most of the faction's followers were Nuer, but during the 1990s almost all broke ranks with Riek, including Lam Akol, and started their own militias or parties.[15] Animosity between the Dinka and Nuer fuelled a revolving door into and out of the SPLM/A, at times involving deals with Khartoum. As we have seen, although Riek returned to the SPLM/A in 2002 with only a few soldiers, he was still a political force to be reckoned with.

A third faction developed in consequence of the leadership dynamics. The Bahr el Ghazal community came to believe they were bearing the brunt of the conflict but without the influence they deserved.[16] People who saw themselves as core SPLM, but were disgruntled and disagreed with Garang's leadership style, also joined in.[17] By the mid 1990s Salva Kiir himself felt increasingly sidelined, and the so-called 'Yei faction', named for the town where he was stationed, emerged. Instrumental roles were played by Bona Malwal and Dominic Dim, both widely considered close to the ruling party in Khartoum.[18] From this group came encouragement for a coup against Garang in November 2004 after a rumour had circulated that Salva would be replaced by Nhial Deng Nhial as second in command. A common denominator was opposition to Garang's vision of a 'New Sudan'; they were mainly separatists. Some, such as Aleu Ayenyi Alieu and Telar Deng, would play important roles in the 2013 crisis.[19]

When telling the story of 2004, Salva Kiir has stressed that the crisis was triggered by his dissatisfaction with Garang's leadership, not to stage a coup. He blames lack of communication and rumour mongering by 'hardliners' trying to split the Movement. They had all crossed swords with Garang, and wanted Salva to contest the leadership.[20] Dominic Dim and Salva Mathok were in Yei at the time, the former reportedly claiming that Salva already had taken his decision to make his move against Chairman John Garang and that others now had to decide whom they would support.[21]

Disaster was averted by timely intervention. Several delegations visited Salva in Yei,[22] and although he still feared for his safety and thought he was about to be arrested, he agreed to meet Dr John.[23] At Garang's house in Rumbek, sources say, a true reconciliation took place. The subsequent commanders' meeting ended in a unified SPLM/A, ready to sign the peace agreement with Sudan.

The ruling party in Khartoum, the NCP, had a hand in the Yei crisis. Some Southerners were on Khartoum's payroll in 2004, and onwards; – information that is corroborated[24] from NCP and other sources.[25] In particular they wanted to sabotage the CPA and prevent Garang's accession to the First Vice Presidency of Sudan, which was an integral part of the deal.[26] Many in Sudan's military-security establishment saw Garang's 'New Sudan' and the structural reforms in the CPA as threats to their power base. They would be happy to base a final agreement on the Machakos Protocol and proceed directly to self-determination.[27]

## History repeats itself

When analysing the reasons for the 2013 crisis, the best starting point is therefore not 1991, but 2004.[28] Subsequent developments in the

Movement were almost cyclical, with the same characters involved in the struggle for power and control in the party and, later, in the country. The most surprising thing is how little changed, despite the achievement of independence. The lack of genuine reconciliation led to deepening mistrust rather than to a strengthened sense of common purpose. With the last crisis, the SPLM had come full circle again. Another constant was the involvement of Khartoum.

A leadership crisis was avoided when Salva Kiir became chairman of the SPLM/A in 2005.[29] But Garang's nomination of Pagan Amum for secretary-general and the return of Riek Machar as deputy chairman and number three had sown seeds of tension within the SPLM, another precursor for the 2013 conflict.

The Yei-crisis still haunted the SPLM. After Dr John's death Bona Malwal and his network continued to push their same agenda, and those who had negotiated the CPA found themselves isolated.[30] As Peter Adwok Nyaba says, the group that Garang had marginalized now surrounded his successor, Salva Kiir, and were in control.[31]

For Khartoum, these squabbles were very opportune. Those gaining control in the SPLM and the government wanted independence and cared little about the 'New Sudan'.[32] This suited NCP's agenda, leaving an impression of collusion with the Islamists in Khartoum. In relation to the Government of National Unity, observers would say that the SPLM was outmanoeuvred by the NCP.[33] SPLM cadres complained that the CPA was being disregarded and that not *bona fide* members of the SPLM had more influence in the party than them.[34] Several Garang Boys threw in the towel, left Sudan, and only returned much later.[35] Renewed efforts were made to regain control from the Yei group.[36] Rapprochement between the Garang Boys and Salva Kiir made investigations against Telar Deng Riing, Aleu Ayenyi Aleu[37] and Lam Akol – for different reasons – possible. The first two were expelled from the SPLM in 2007, while Lam Akol says he never received formal notice. He was replaced as minister of foreign affairs in October 2007.[38]

It was also during this period that the SPLM suspended participation in the Government of National Unity. When they returned, it was with stronger representation of the Garang Boys. But underlying problems had still not been addressed. At the SPLM Convention in 2008 the group around Salva Kiir (and other members of the Political Bureau) attempted to replace Pagan Amum with Taban Deng, Governor of Unity State, a Nuer seen as a Salva loyalist. A thinly veiled attempt to demote Riek Machar was a proposal to have one deputy chairman from the Northern sector, and one from the Southern, which would have made Taban the highest-ranking Nuer in the SPLM.[39] Salva Kiir's group and the Garang Boys would replace Riek with James Wani Igga, who had stepped down after his return in 2002.[40] It was at this point in 2008 that Riek signalled his interest in competing for the chairmanship.[41] Stories were whirling about that he had been making handouts to rally support even before the convention, but this was never confirmed.

In its political appointments the SPLM mirrored the military hierarchy of the liberation struggle. The top five positions were firmly established, and a change in ranking was problematic. When Riek formally declared his candidacy against Salva Kiir, a major crisis was averted only by the last-minute intervention of the elder statesmen Abel Alier and Joseph Lagu. The elders of Greater Bahr el Ghazal also talked to the chairman.[42] Both counselled against changes that could risk the unity of the South and jeopardize the referendum. This led to agreement not to vote on any of the proposals.

The more things changed, the more they remained the same. With the 2010 elections scheduled to take place in April, Salva's group and the Garang Boys were still promoting Taban Deng, now for re-election as Governor of Unity. The SPLM in Unity State put up Angelina Teny, Riek's wife, a seasoned politician and former official in the Ministry of Petroleum in Khartoum, for the governorship. Although Taban was senior, and hence seen as more entitled to run, another factor in his eventual nomination was others' wish to prevent the Machar-Teny family from controlling Unity State. Nicknamed 'Mr. 2 percent' on the widespread assumption that most of the state's 2 per cent of the oil revenue ended up in his pocket, Taban was unpopular. When the elections took place, and Taban was declared the winner against Angelina Teny (running as an independent), violence ensued and many people were killed. Rather than mobilization through rebellion, however, she chose the peaceful route. Her formal complaint achieved nothing, but Teny urged her supporters to eschew armed opposition and accept the result.[43] It is likely that the proximity of the 2011-referendum weighed in.

The 2010 elections were mired in controversy. Some 370 members of the SPLM stood for election independently, in protest at the way the National Elections Strategy Committee had handled the nomination procedure.[44] The SPLM was subsequently accused of rigging several gubernatorial races. International observers noted irregularities, but drew no firm conclusions.[45] In a couple of cases the SPLA intervened violently. Rightly or wrongly, many felt marginalized and disaffected by the electoral process and its results. A resurgence of armed militia activity ensued. An 'All Southern Sudan Political Parties Conference' in Juba in November 2010 helped to calm things down,[46] and efforts were made to bring the militias and all political parties into the fold. No faction wanted to risk blame for putting the referendum at risk. Southern Sudanese were united as they went to the polls in January 2011.

## Power struggle – under Garang's shadow

All SPLM cadres gave Salva Kiir credit for keeping South Sudanese together during the interim period. Without his leadership, independence would not have been achieved. But soon speculations were rife about the new cabinet. Many of the same old tensions in the leadership reappeared. Pagan Amum and Salva had never seen eye to eye. On Independence Day, Salva accepted Pagan's resignation from the cabinet and party. But after others intervened, Pagan agreed to stay on as secretary-general of the SPLM and chief negotiator with Sudan.

After observing the way things worked during the interim period, people would jokingly say that Juba had not one government, but several. There were most certainly several power centres. Would this change with independence? Although the new cabinet did not imply much change, as early as September 2011 senior ministers expressed concern that 'non-SPLM' people appeared to be gaining influence in circles around the President. By this they meant the Yei faction and individuals perceived to be close to Khartoum. Although the status quo prevailed in the cabinet, real decision making often lay elsewhere. The impression was that a 'kitchen cabinet' had emerged. 'T & T' was the acronym applied to the presidential advisers Telar Deng Riing, an Atout Dinka from Lakes State, whose personal animosity for the Garang Boys was reciprocated, and Tor Deng Mawien, a Dinka former Governor of

Warrap with a long history with the NCP in Khartoum and only recent membership of the SPLM. They were easy targets, however, and their enemies may have overstated their influence.

Although he had maintained the status quo in the cabinet, Salva Kiir was soon frustrated; he privately accused many of the ministers of not delivering,[47] and even questioned their loyalty. They repaid the compliment: on numerous occasions one heard ministers, particularly Garang Boys, badmouth and belittle the President behind his back. They criticized him for failing in his political leadership, performing poorly abroad and listening to the wrong people. As for the latter, an old SPLM official quoted Garang: 'If the mosquitos get into your net, you are the one to be blamed, not the mosquitos.'[48] While this likely referred to Khartoum sympathizers in the South, the interviewee was talking about the network around Salva.

### A dangerous slip of the tongue?

During this period it was widely assumed that Salva Kiir would run for another term in 2015. At a dinner he hosted in August 2011 for Thabo Mbeki and Pierre Buyoya, conversation turned to governance in Africa. Deng Alor, Kosti Manibe, Paul Mayom Akec and Cirino Hiteng were among those present. They asked for advice about how South Sudan as a new country could avoid mistakes.[49] Thabo Mbeki reportedly emphasized that the issues they raised were about leadership, and the conversation turned to African leaders' renewing their presidential terms unconstitutionally.

Salva Kiir said that by 2015 he would have been in power for ten years. That was enough; he would not run again.[50] Mbeki responded that many had said the same, and had changed their minds; he would not be surprised if the President had a different view in due course. Salva insisted he was serious. The ministers were surprised. Deng Alor shared this information confidentially with two other high-ranking comrades in the SPLM Political Bureau. He wanted to see what could be done to change Salva's mind or find a solution that would not destabilize the country.[51]

Whether Salva's avowal was off-hand, or designed to test the loyalty of the cadres, or gauge reactions, is difficult to tell. Others had heard him say such things privately in the past, when he talked of his desire to return to his village and the simple life. This had not been taken seriously. Saying it in a setting like this was different, in a formal dinner in the presence of two former presidents. Whatever the case, the subject of succession was no longer taboo. When it later became clear that Salva indeed intended to run again, Deng Alor was blamed for misleading others, and when he tried to explain his motives, he was rebuffed.[52]

The 'factions' from 2004 started emerging again, but tensions with Khartoum kept things in check. The ministerial corruption crisis in June 2012 changed this.[53] Salva characteristically avoided direct confrontation. Rather than legal proceedings, or calling in ministers one by one, confidentially sharing what he knew about their malfeasance, demanding reimbursement, and pursuing those who did not cooperate, he chose a different route. Repercussions from the debacle continued for months. But a crisis of confidence had made relations between the President and many ministers even worse, and may have been a first precursor of the 2013 crisis.

However, it was when the leadership debated the constitution of the SPLM as a political party that the most severe tensions surfaced. The Political Parties Act had been passed in March 2012,[54] and the SPLM had to be registered, meaning in turn that a SPLM Convention should be held. This was originally planned for April or May,[55] and would involve elections for the party leadership. Members of the SPLM Political Bureau and the secretariat of the Party expressed frustration over delays in drafting a party constitution and other relevant documents. Few meetings were called. Repeated appeals to Salva Kiir as chairman to speed up the process were not heeded.

Blame also fell on the secretary general, Pagan Amum, for weak management of party affairs and squandering resources. But with regard to the latest delays, Pagan had appealed several times to Salva to convene the party organs so that registration of the SPLM could take place.[56] On 21 June Salva Kiir finally ordered formation of four committees, including members of the SPLM Political Bureau, to prepare this process. Time passed. When the committees eventually got down to work, disagreement emerged. All the issues were in one way or another related to the leadership.

These included whether voting for the chairmanship should be by secret ballot or a show of hands; whether the chairman of the party should be permitted to nominate the list of members for appointment to the Political Bureau; whether the National Liberation Council would elect members of the politburo and the deputy chairman of the party, instead of having the chairman appoint them; and whether the chairman would have the mandate to appoint 5 per cent of the delegates to the National Convention, thus giving him greater control over its outcome. While 5 per cent may not seem much, these votes could be very important if selected carefully.

Salva Kiir wanted to retain the powers granted him in the existing party constitution. The other two main factions in the SPLM, Riek Machar and his allies and the Garang Boys wanted the mooted changes, and they tabled amendments accordingly, which they depicted as democratizing. The party secretariat had already got permission to consult the grassroots, a move championed by the deputy secretary general, Anne Itto.

Consultations were carried out all over the country in June-August 2012. Party cadres travelled to their constituencies and participated. Surveys showed widespread dissatisfaction with the SPLM and the government. The leadership expressed shock, but to many of us it was not surprising. In all 10 states and close to 20 counties, we had contacts with local authorities, civil society and citizens. There was a lot of disappointment and discontent. People did not see the dividends of peace and independence. Opinion polls also confirmed this.[57] Predictably, too, the results of the consultation became ammunition in the internal power struggle. Some were accused for orchestrating the outcome to put the President in a negative light; others used the result to point fingers at him.

As we have seen, fundamental reforms were not implemented, and performance of critical state functions was slow. This was owed in part to extremely weak government structures,[58] but it was also the result of a dysfunctional leadership team. Paralysis at the highest levels could not continue if South Sudan was to become a successful state. As SRSG, I had to get involved personally to try to move things forward.

I pressed for a retreat for the SPLM leadership, to address internal tensions and various issues of governance.[59] The first time I discussed this with the President was in July 2012. From my one-on-one-conversations with the top four of the SPLM-leadership there was full support, and repeated attempts were made for the retreat to happen. Three times tentative dates in early 2013 were agreed with the President,[60] but the retreat never took place.

## Comrades on a mission

Other attempts were made to bring the leadership together. In August 2012 James Hoth Mai, Taban Deng Gai, and Ambassador Ezekiel Gatkuoth Lul met informally and agreed that a dialogue between Riek and Salva was needed. While all three were Nuer, they warned Riek against contesting the chairmanship of the SPLM. The intention was to prevent the issue from becoming a problem. Taban discussed the need for such a process with the President, who agreed; Tor Deng was his contact point.[61] James Hoth Mai eventually brought the two leaders together for an inconclusive discussion that lasted three or four hours.[62]

In late 2012/early 2013, with Salva's and Riek's agreement, an informal group of three met regularly to discuss succession issues.[63] A possible compromise was discussed, by which the President would be re-elected in 2015, resign the chairmanship of the SPLM at the convention in 2018, and step aside at the election of 2020. But it was not clear what the President himself wanted to do. Riek, on the other hand, began talking to SPLM leaders individually, criticizing Salva. The President and his entourage knew that such conversations were taking place; National Security was monitoring.

When news broke that succession was on the agenda, candidates started to declare. Riek said he would run. Others included Pagan Amum, James Wani Igga (if Salva decided not to stand), and Rebecca Nyandeng, Garang's widow.

Relations between the President and Vice President were now increasingly affecting the government. I continued to push for a retreat. As late as 25 February 2013 I urged Salva to move ahead with this before the SPLM Political Bureau convened in March. In my view, an informal retreat could prepare the ground and prevent a major confrontation at the party meeting. The President and other members of the leadership reacted positively, but again nothing happened.

I was nonetheless encouraged when members of the leadership met to resolve the problems, with delegations going to see both Salva and Riek, who had agreed on the composition of a committee: Deng Alor (chair), Nhial Deng, Taban Deng Gai, John Luk Jok, Kosti Manibe, Paul Mayom and James Kok. Informally, Deng, Nhial and Taban were most active in trying to prevent an escalation.[64]

The committee met twice for consultations, then met with the Vice President alone, and finally the President. Riek Machar presented them with six criticisms of Salva Kiir, points he had listed privately with others.[65] This was seen as an attempt to rally support for his bid for the chairmanship. Committee members pointed out Machar's own responsibility for many of the problems he raised, and asked why he had decided to run against the chairman. They advised him to wait. Riek was reportedly 'furious' at this suggestion.[66]

Subsequently Salva Kiir asked Deng Alor to organize a meeting with Riek and the other declared candidates, Pagan Amum and James Wanni Igga. The meeting was held on 5 March with Deng Alor in the chair, and lasted seven hours. Harsh words were exchanged. Riek presented his encyclopedic 'points' against the President: inaction against corruption; tribalism – a tendency to give preference to his own community; lack of reform of the security sector; the economy; foreign relations – and the loss of support for South Sudan internationally; and lack of vision and direction for the SPLM. Riek was again told by Deng Alor and others in the meeting that he bore a major responsibility himself, having been vice president throughout the period. At the same time, Salva Kiir was also confronted by Pagan Amum and others present.

The meeting was inconclusive. Salva asked Deng to make a summary for review; the latter assumed that instructions would follow. Little is secret within the SPLM leadership, and the gist of the discussion was soon known to a number of people, including me. Vice President Wani Igga later gave a lengthy account of the meeting, its lack of protocol, and how failures in several areas were put on Salva Kiir, while in his view the blame was squarely on the disaffected participants and Riek Machar, all of whom had managed the government during the interim period.[67] The meeting had a very negative impact on the dynamics in the leadership, and was in many ways a turning point for Salva.[68]

For anyone who had followed South Sudan since 2005, the country's problems were pretty obvious. But this was hardly the President's responsibility alone. During the interim period Riek Machar had chaired most cabinet meetings and had significant delegated powers.[69] Senior figures in the committee agreed that they needed to convince Riek to pull back. Now he was open to a plan whereby Salva would continue until 2020, but anoint Riek as successor. Deng Alor waited in vain for an opportunity to come back to Salva Kiir and convey this.[70]

Be this as it may, it seemed that other leading members of the Political Bureau had encouraged Riek. Some of those hailing from Bahr el Ghazal had made negative comments about the President, including at the seven hour-meeting, and Riek might have thought he had a good chance of getting their support. If in this he misread the situation, it would not be the first time – or the last.

## Tensions escalate

On 6 March 2013 Salva Kiir finally convened the Political Bureau. On the agenda were reports from the four committees; the objective was to achieve consensus on proposals for the new party constitution and other key documents. The President now announced that he would run for re-election in 2015. Riek Machar likewise declared his candidacy, reiterated his 'points', and said it was time for change. Pagan and Rebecca Nyandeng followed suit, but neither was seen as a serious challenger. Owing to Salva Kiir's statement, James Wani Igga would not be a candidate. The meeting ended in failure, as members of the committee disagreed on key issues.

Salva could not be sure of the outcome from the Political Bureau after this, and he seemed to entertain alternative strategies to ensure support for his positions. He decided to convene the obsolete 'High Command of the SPLA' and endow it with decision making authority. With Dr John long gone, the members were Salva, James Wani Igga, Kuol Manyang Juuk, the Governor of Jonglei, Daniel Awet (deputy speaker of the legislature), and the aged Lual Diing, who was hospitalized in Nairobi. Salva turned to this group for regular strategy meetings during the months that followed.[71]

During March and April, there were no meetings of the leadership committee, although informal discussions continued.[72] I continued to encourage them to resolve their differences, but I started to ask whether it was time for an external mediator. We discussed the possibility of bringing in leaders from the region to help, and considered several. But the committee members still thought they could handle this. I continued to urge the President to convene the leadership to sort out the problems.

On 15 April the President issued a decree stripping Riek Machar of 'all duly delegated powers' under the 2011 Transitional Constitution.[73] From other sources I later learned of an initial plan to replace Riek with another Nuer, although this has never been confirmed.[74] There had apparently been consultation with people in the Nuer community, and Salva had been warned that this could lead to instability; curtailing the Vice President's powers seemed a more judicious route.

On the same day, Salva Kiir suspended the National Reconciliation Conference that Riek had been championing. There had been legitimate concerns in many quarters about the way he had been leading that effort, and about the danger that the national reconciliation process itself was being politicized by the power struggle between the two leaders.

Riek was left applying unsuccessfully for interviews with the President.

## Go-betweens in trouble

Riek's humiliation raised fears that the Nuer would react violently. This prompted church leaders to get involved. Gier Chuong Aloung, a government minister, called the Anglican Archbishop Daniel Deng, and asked him for help: 'We have tried, but we have come to a dead end', he said. On 26 April Deng, the Catholic Archbishop Paulino Lukudo, and the Moderator of the Presbyterian Church, Peter Gai Lual Marrow met Salva and Riek separately, then together, at the presidency. Abel Alier accompanied the clergymen.

They briefed me immediately afterwards. The religious leaders realized that they had but scratched the surface. Despite their attempts, both Salva and Riek had recited platitudes about working together; there was no true reconciliation. Nevertheless, they all appeared on televison that night, embracing each other, and things calmed down, for a while.

According to the 2008 SPLM Constitution, the third convention of the SPLM should be held no later than 20 May 2013. The mandate of the current leadership was therefore running out. The deadline passed, however, and the whole party apparatus continued to operate without a legal basis. No one seemed to pay any attention to this, and Salva Kiir, as chairman, gave no sign of doing anything. But with the atrophy of the SPLM and the apparent conflation of party and state there was no institutional mechanism which could intervene. As a leading veteran of the SPLM put it: 'When they needed the party to resolve their differences, they didn't find it. The SPLM was almost dead.'[75]

During the first week of June, the President told me there was little likelihood of a solution to the impasse; experience showed that Riek would not be curbed. Salva cast doubt too on Deng Alor, who had been chairing the leadership meetings. I was very worried. Four days later I sat down with Deng to discuss what could be done. Should we bring in regional leaders? The Government of South Sudan had reached a political standstill, and so it seemed, had the leadership of the SPLM.

That the President had concerns about Deng Alor became clear on 17 June when he suspended the minister and Kosti Manibe on account of corruption. In a Republican Order he lifted their immunity from prosecution, and by a separate Order launched an investigation into alleged irregular transfer of $8 million to Daffy [sic] Investment Group for procurement of safes for government offices.[76] The two were temporarily suspended from the cabinet, pending further investigations. The security organs had reportedly been on the case for months. The initial investigation cleared Kosti Manibe, but the case against Deng Alor was referred for criminal investigation.[77]

The donor community had for long requested action against corruption through investigations and prosecution. As we have seen, scandals involving hundreds of millions of dollars had come to light. If by the action against Deng Alor and Kosti Manibe the President was initiating a legal crackdown, observers would have raised fewer questions.[78] But when there was no movement on bigger cases, the perception was unavoidable that the two ministers had been targeted primarily for political reasons.

## Riek goes public against the President

Riek Machar certainly did not make things easier. On 4 July he gave an interview to the *Guardian*, explaining his decision to challenge Salva Kiir for the presidency:

> Even in your own country, Margaret Thatcher had to leave after leading the Conservative party for a very long time. Tony Blair also had to leave after winning three consecutive elections and give way to the next generation.[79]

Theirs was an example that Salva Kiir would do well to follow, he said, while rejecting any comparison between himself and Gordon Brown. He also said:

> To avoid authoritarianism and dictatorship, it is better to change. Our time is limited now. I have been serving under Salva Kiir. I did my best serving under him. I think it is time for a change now.[80]

This would mark Riek's third try for leadership of the Movement.

Two days later Salva Kiir dismissed Taban Deng.[81] On 7 July Joseph Nguen Monytuel, whose brother led the main militia operating in Unity, was appointed new Governor, raising hopes that the newly integrated South Sudan Liberation Movement would remain in the fold.[82] This followed a similar move against Chol Tong Mayai, Governor of Lakes State, accused of sympathizing with Riek.[83] Taban had recently returned from the US where, some sources allege, he had been less than loyal in his comments. It was anyway clear that Taban had lately become suspiciously closer to Riek,[84] who now publicly denounced Taban's removal as unconstitutional.[85]

## International firefighters

In his address to the nation on Independence Day, 9 July 2013, President Salva Kiir did not even acknowledge the presence of his Vice President. Later that day the BBC aired an interview with Riek Machar, who repeated the message of the *Guardian* interview.[86] Pagan Amum, who for the first time was absent from Independence Day celebrations, also publicly criticized the President. Thabo Mbeki and President Museveni of Uganda, in Juba for the anniversary, stayed on for an extra day, and speculation was rampant; was Museveni advising Salva Kiir to remove Machar? The truth about their conversations will probably never be known. Mbeki, for his part, met both leaders individually, advised a moratorium on public statements and an extraordinary meeting of the SPLM Political Bureau to resolve the problems. Both agreed, although no date was set.[87] General Sumbeiywo of Kenya had also called on Salva, with a message from former President Daniel Arap Moi.[88] Their discussion too remained confidential, but was directly linked to the leadership crisis. Sumbeiywo would return repeatedly over the next few months.

On 17 July Tedros Adhanom, the foreign minister of Ethiopia, arrived in Juba.[89] I briefed him late in the evening at his hotel, shared ideas of a compromise that had been discussed in Juba, and urged him to propose a face-saving solution. We agreed that ethnic violence was very likely otherwise. Tedros recommended that Salva Kiir be re-elected as chairman of the SPLM, that he run for a new five-year term as President of South Sudan in 2015, but that he agree to step down two years early, allowing the SPLM Convention in 2018 to choose a new chairman and for early elections to be called. The SPLM Convention would guarantee fulfilment of the plan.

The idea was reportedly shared with the two leaders before Tedros met them separately to discuss it. When he expressed a fear that even the Army could split along ethnic lines the President took exception, but he accepted the plan.[90] Riek likewise, in his meeting with the Foreign Minister, dismissed the possibility of ethnic violence and downplayed the gravity of the current situation. As for the succession plan, Riek would 'think about it'. And that was the end of that. A year later, after the crisis of 2013, Tedros asked why he never got back and took the deal. Machar referred to Salva Kiir and said simply, 'I didn't trust him.'[91]

Only a few days later, on 23 July, Salva Kiir made his next move: he dismissed the entire cabinet, including Machar.[92] There was now a full-blown national crisis under way. By another presidential decree, Pagan Amum, secretary general of the SPLM, was suspended, on account of mismanagement in office, with investigations to follow.[93] A high-handed separate order instructed Pagan meanwhile not to travel or address the media.

A restructuring of the government had been in train for a long time. The President had initially wanted a cabinet of only 18, which would require major reorganization. Donors had also been pressing for a leaner and more effective set-up. But there was still astonishment at the wholesale housecleaning. Yet by not singling out Riek Machar, the most prominent Nuer leader, Salva hoped to avoid ethnic violence. And if the new cabinet was appointed quickly and its composition adequately balanced, the clean sweep might not be as drastic as it appeared.

Riek's reaction made a good impression. He publicly stated that the President had acted within his authority, and that it had nothing to do with ethnicity. He worked hard to contain the Nuer community, urging them, and especially the youth, not to respond. He intended to take up his seat in the legislature. I told Riek of the favourable international response to his message of calm and his management of the crisis, and urged him to continue in the same way.

The President did not now resort to personal rule. He regularly convened the former High Command of the SPLA, and discussed next steps with James Wani Igga, Daniel Awet and Kuol Manyang Juuk. On the basis of nominations from the ten governors and the political party leaders they came up with a list of ministerial candidates.[94] Contrary to widespread fears, the President did not dawdle; the new government was appointed within a week. He delivered on his long-standing goal of a smaller, more streamlined cabinet, yet one relatively representative in ideological and ethnic terms.

Several ministers were reappointed, but there were two important political differences. One was the absence of anyone associated with the two other factions, Riek Machar's closest associates and the Garang Boys. What many of the latter had feared had now occurred; they were all out. Another change was that other parties got more prominent positions; among the newcomers were not only technocrats, but also former associates of the ruling party in Khartoum (now new members of the SPLM). Very few remained from the days of the struggle. The President told me and others that he intended to use former ministers as envoys or for special assignments.

The Garang Boys perceived the final outcome as even worse: the President had not used party organs to form the cabinet, and had not advanced the younger, second generation of SPLM cadres. This was regarded a marginalization of the 'real' liberators. They now turned to the National Legislative Assembly. If it rejected the new cabinet, there would be a constitutional crisis. But there the President's whips had the upper hand, and except for Telar Deng, who was personally unpopular and was blocked from becoming minister of justice, the entire list went through. The Garang Boys and Riek Machar had to swallow a bitter pill.

It is not clear whether relations with Khartoum influenced the choice of ministers. In April, President Bashir had made his first visit to Juba since independence, and as we have seen, a page had been turned in bilateral relations. In any case, the new cabinet was greeted with enthusiasm in Khartoum. Several of the Garang Boys had been regarded as hardliners and red flags in Khartoum.[95] Bashir returned twice to Juba after the change of cabinet, and several high-level meetings took place, cementing implementation of the 27 September oil agreement.[96]

With the benefit of hindsight, many donors regarded the dismissal of the whole cabinet as a trigger for the 2013 crisis. Yet many of them had called for a much smaller and more streamlined cabinet, and had complained about SPLM domination and the need for political inclusiveness. This would necessarily mean very significant changes. And the move had public support; people wanted change.

All now depended on how the President managed the predictable fall-out from his move, first and foremost in the SPLM. I therefore continued to engage with the President, and to stress the need for reconciliation, including convening the Political Bureau. While it was good that a government had been formed quickly and there seemed to be competent people on board, resolving the crisis within the SPLM was now critical. I urged the President to meet the leadership and former ministers.

On 23 August the President appointed James Wani Igga, then speaker of the Assembly, as vice president. He was confirmed three days later. Riek Machar refrained from running for the speakership, and in September Manasseh Magok Rundial, a Nuer and former NCP official in Khartoum, got the post. Salva Kiir later appointed Telar Deng his

Senior Advisor for Legal Affairs, another provocation to the Garang Boys and leading SPLM cadres.

In late August seven Political Bureau members and former ministers, not including Machar, had a meeting with the President.[97] Over dinner they reportedly had a very good discussion; it lasted until midnight.[98] They agreed to follow up with a retreat of Political Bureau members and of others the President wanted to include. This meeting in turn would agree on a process to resolve remaining issues, including those related to the SPLM constitution. There was also reportedly agreement that Riek should be encouraged to wait, and not run now.[99] Everyone felt they were now on the right track.

In early September the President told me that he wanted to bring former and current ministers together in a retreat to brainstorm on the future of the SPLM. I encouraged him to move forward with this as soon as possible. The President was supposed to follow up with a date. But we heard nothing after this. It appeared that the whole initiative had come to a halt, in the same way as similar plans we had discussed had a year and six months before. Some people around the President did not seem to want any reconciliation and Salva did not appear strong or committed enough to push it through.

On 18–27 September, the President went on a tour of the Greater Bahr el Ghazal region. During his visits to the state capitals, Wau, Aweil, Kwajok, and Rumbek, he made speeches explaining his decision to appoint a new cabinet. But in doing so he ridiculed and slandered former colleagues and those who had attended the reconciliation meeting. At home in his region, and speaking Dinka and Arabic, he probably thought that his crowd-pleasing message would not be widely retailed.[100]

In Rumbek the President had unaccountably been particularly provocative. 'The "Tiger" has now taken out its claws and is ready to crush their faces. Blood will flow,'[101] he told a crowd of Agar Dinka youth. 'Tiger' was Salva Kiir's *nom de guerre* from the beginning of the struggle. He reminded the largely Dinka audience of Nuer raids in the 1990s,[102] and called on them to be ready to defend themselves again. When I learned of all this I reminded him that such language could be interpreted as incitement.

Still, efforts at reconciliation continued. Several former ministers had individual meetings with the President in the next couple of months, including Nhial Deng, Paul Mayom, Gier Choung and David Deng Athorbei. Deng Alor would have two separate meetings later. Partly as a result of these efforts, some were offered positions. Nhial Deng, former defence minister and foreign minister, who had been seen for years as one of the Garang Boys, ended up as the government's chief negotiator. He would later occupy the key negotiating position in talks under the auspices of IGAD to resolve the crisis that erupted at the end of 2013. In October the President pardoned several people who had been accused of rebel activity, including Lam Akol, the former foreign minister and chairman of SPLM/Democratic Change.[103] While Salva thus seemed open for reconciliation, there seemed to have been an irremediable breakdown in relations with Riek.[104]

On 8–12 October South Africa's ruling party, the African National Congress, with its deputy chairman, Cyril Ramophosa at the helm, held a seminar with the Political Bureau of the SPLM on internal dynamics in party structures. This had been scheduled earlier, but was now utilized to address the current leadership crisis. Almost everyone in the SPLM Political Bureau attended, including Riek Machar and except only Salva himself, whom the ANC-leader met separately. However, Ramophosa did not succeed in finding a solution.

I still held the view that things could be sorted out. In New York in mid November for consultations, I suddenly got a message from Juba that Salva Kiir had announced the dissolution of the SPLM, including the highest organ of the party, the Political Bureau and the National Liberation Council. This appeared to be another spur-of-the-moment gambit; the party apparatus had lapsed because the National Convention had not met before the mandated five-year deadline. While legally and factually this was correct, the demarche was generally perceived as a far-fetched political maneuver, particularly since the office of chairman and the Secretariat were to remain operational.[105] But soon we heard from the Minister of Information that Salva's remarks had been misinterpreted: the organs of the SPLM would continue to function.[106] That it was not even a spokesperson for the SPLM who clarified what its chairman had meant to say showed that South Sudan still had a long way to go in making the necessary distinction between party and government.

In the Security Council on 18 November, I noted that while the transition to the new cabinet had been smooth, and Riek Machar had handled the situation well, a key determinant for developments in the country would now be management of schisms within the SPLM. I stressed that the country was at a crossroads, and that the way the preparatory process for the all-important National Convention was handled would indicate where things were heading.[107] In separate briefings with Permanent Representatives I highlighted that this could go either way. The SPLM leadership had usually been able to sort out such crises, however, often at the last minute. I was committed to continue to engage with the leadership to help find a resolution in the context of the upcoming meeting of the National Liberation Council.[108] Otherwise, things could deteriorate.

By the end of November, delegations from neighbouring countries and other 'friends' from around the world had not been able to make progress. Thabo Mbeki had not heard from the President. Two visits to Juba, the latest the last week of November, did not produce results.

I had met Machar only once in September, and he seemed then to have accepted the state of affairs and be motivated to work from his seat in the legislature. Now, however, in November I was told that he had become more confrontational, particularly when speaking to Nuer audiences in private.[109] I also heard about some meetings of ex-ministers, at times with Riek, at the houses of Deng Alor, Cirino Hiteng, and Oyay Deng. Such gatherings were very common, so I did not pay much attention to this. I was scheduled to meet Riek again in early December, as usual to urge patience.

## The two triggers: Press conference and party meeting

Two unexpected events would change the dynamics in Juba dramatically.

By December, the majority of former ministers had still not heard from the President, and the rumour was that the National Liberation Council might be called without a conclusive meeting of the Political Bureau having been held first. I met with Pagan Amum, who told me about the plans: a number of SPLM leaders were going to hold a press conference, likely the coming Friday (6 December), followed by rallies on 14 December. The intention was 'mass mobilization' against the way the SPLM was being led. They would not ask for the chairman's resignation, but would criticize his leadership. Those behind the initiative were several members of the SPLM Political Bureau, former ministers, Riek Machar, and the two governors who had been dismissed. They could achieve a majority in the Political Bureau, they claimed. Never before had cadres gone public like this about their disagreements.

Upon learning from Pagan of these plans, and concerned about the fall-out and potential violence, I went to see Deng Alor. He and Pagan were among the most senior members of the SPLM Political Bureau. To both of them I appealed for more time before they went public with the conflict. I was worried about violence, and in particular of ethnic violence, as well as their arrest. The plans for a rally, to 'mobilize the masses', were a major concern. I had no illusions that this could be contained, despite their promises; the security forces were also incompetent at crowd control.

Just as Salva Kiir had apparently given up on Riek, so Pagan and Deng Alor told me that leading cadres had now given up on Salva. After my discussions, and unsuccessful attempts to delay the press conference and avoid the rally, I got in touch with Akol Kuor, one of two Directors of National Security,[110] who was regarded as very close to Salva. It was critical that the government now did what could be done to contain the situation, and avoid escalation.

I had a meeting with the Minister of Interior on the 5th, the evening before the press conference, to make sure that the police or security forces would not disrupt the media event or arrest the participants. The location also mattered; a change was organized in contact with Riek Machar and his team the same evening. I later heard that others had made similar efforts.[111] The President was in Paris, at the France–Africa Heads of State summit; holding a press conference in his absence was deeply provocative in my view.[112] Salva Kiir called Juba, reportedly overruling several ministers who had advised taking a hard line.[113] The press conference was held at the SPLM headquarters.

On the 6th some 15 leading members of the SPLM cadres,[114] constituted a rather surprising and powerful public alignment of Riek Machar and the Garang boys. Their statement referred to 'anti-Garang elements inside and outside the SPLM [who had] encircled comrade Salva Kiir Mayardit's leadership of the SPLM and the Government of Southern Sudan'.[115] That Riek Machar had agreed to this text was interesting, given his animosity towards Dr John. A new political alignment had been formed. The President's power base was narrowing.

According to the statement, the SPLM's crisis had 'started immediately after the tragic death of the SPLM historical and eternal leader Dr. John Garang de Mabior',[116] with all subsequent troubles linked to this. It rehearsed the weakening of the SPLM to the benefit of regional and ethnic lobbies around the SPLM chairman; and promotion of 'recent converts' from the Khartoum regime to leading positions. The statement denounced Salva Kiir for unconstitutionally dissolving SPLM organs, allowing the party to become dysfunctional, and for impeding transformation of the Movement from a liberation movement into a mass-based political party:

> The deep-seated divisions within the SPLM leadership, exacerbated by dictatorial tendencies of the SPLM Chairman, and the dysfunctional SPLM structures from national to local levels are likely to create instability in the party and in the country. For these reasons, and out of our sincere concern about the future of our people, we the SPLM members of the Political Bureau and the Leadership of the party are obliged to inform the public about the true state of affairs in the SPLM and how General Salva Kiir is driving our beloved Republic of South Sudan into chaos and disorder.[117]

Strong public criticism of the President and SPLM chairman at a press conference of prominent members of the leadership was unprecedented, and represented a radical shift in the history of the SPLM. The reference to possible chaos and disorder can be interpreted as either a worry or a threat – or both.[118] Although the statement was clearly provocative, participants did not call for precipitate changes at the top, which likely would have triggered an emergency. Instead they demanded that Salva Kiir, as chairman, convene the Political Bureau prior to the meeting of the National Liberation Council.[119] The signatories seemed to assume that they could mobilize support in a way that would force Salva Kiir to cave in.[120] In this they misjudged the situation.[121] Their move was widely seen as evidence that they regarded themselves as indispensable, as entitled to lead the party. This did not go down well in all quarters.

In the absence of the President, the new Vice President James Wani

Igga returned the favour. Instead of calming things down and taking discussions behind closed doors, he held his own press conference the next day and made a provocative retort.[122] Whether he had the President's blessing to do so is not clear, but it certainly contributed to making matters even worse.

It was now Salva Kiir's reaction that people were waiting for. His management of the crisis would be decisive. He returned from Paris and wisely decided not to utter a word. I tried to see him before he left for South Africa for the funeral of Nelson Mandela, but time was too short. We knew that invitations for the meeting of the National Liberation Council on 14–15 December had been sent out, and that he had thus decided to leapfrog the Political Bureau meeting and convene the NLC directly.

Unable to see the President, I scheduled other meetings to try to prevent an escalation that could lead to violence. I met Riek Machar; the minister of national security, Obote Mete Mamur; and senior people around the President, including the director of national security, Akol Kuur; and Daniel Awet, another of the old 'High Command'. I asked them to make contact with the President prior to the NLC, and do everything possible to prevent violence in connection with the upcoming meetings and possible rally.

I also went to see Telar Deng, who was now back in the presidency as Legal Advisor. In the absence of the Minister of Presidential Affairs he was likely in charge of preparing Salva Kiir's speech for the opening of the NLC. We did not know whether the rally would go ahead on 14 December as planned, or whether a Political Bureau meeting might be called at the last minute. What we did know, however, was that the chairman's opening statement would be very important. He had not appeared in public since before the 6 December press conference.

I told Telar that this was a decisive moment. The President, despite the criticism, needed to be inclusive and conciliatory, not confrontational, I urged him to keep the interests of the country and the presidency itself at heart. If there was to be no Political Bureau meeting before the NLC, the President needed to convey willingness to debate, to listen, to have transparent processes, and to give people the feeling that he welcomed different views. Telar listened, and said he would take this into consideration and pass it on.

During the week, I actively engaged the main actors around the President, encouraging them to convene the Political Bureau. It could still be called at the very last minute, and the NLC could also be delayed for a few hours to allow discussion about the SPLM constitution. According to one source, there was in fact an attempt to hold a meeting of the cadres during the week, but misunderstandings around timing and invitations resulted in poor attendance and it was cancelled.[123] The day before the NLC was supposed to start, Riek Machar issued a statement that the planned rally would take place one week later, on 20 December.

Salva Kiir returned from South Africa on the 13th, the day before the National Liberation Council meeting. Given the importance of the presidential speech, I wanted to talk to him directly upon his return. I was in touch with his office several times, but was unsuccessful.

At dawn on the 14th Juba was full of security forces. It was Saturday and the National Liberation Council (NLC) was to be opened. The assembly hall at the Nyakoron cultural centre was filling up. In the usual South Sudanese way, people greeted each other warmly, hugged, patted each other's backs and laughed, whatever their ranks or animosities. Riek Machar, the deputy chairman, arrived to warm applause. But the atmosphere was tense. While things looked normal on the surface, the empty diplomatic seats were witness to the true mood: most ambassadors stayed away for security reasons.

Another sign was that many members of the SPLM Political Bureau were absent. Pagan Amum stayed at home.[124] Deng Alor and several others were at an award ceremony in Addis Ababa, and could only fly in later. All eyes were on the President when he arrived. The atmosphere was charged.

When the religious leaders arrived on stage in their robes, the gravity of the crisis and its possible implications were brought home. The highest representatives of the Church and Muslim community in South Sudan[125] offered prayers, and a strong appeal not only for peace, but – strikingly – for delay of the NLC itself. Going through with it could lead to unrest. It was better to wait, they said. Similarly, they called on those behind the press statement not to organize any rallies, and make sure that the streets of Juba remained quiet and peaceful. The room was dead silent.

The church in South Sudan carries a lot of weight. Throughout the civil war, the clergy played important roles in reconciling Southern factions and communities, and they ran 'people-to-people' peace processes that yielded impressive results. That the church leaders spoke out in this way was significant. After them I was asked to greet the audience. While I had not prepared anything to say, I repeated the strong appeal of the church leaders for peace. Referring to how the government had consolidated peace by reintegrating those who had rebelled, the disagreement was now in words and not with arms. I urged the leadership to find ways to reconcile with each other. I was later told that people around the President took this as confirmation that I was supporting Riek Machar; another example of the charged atmosphere at the time.

The chairman of the SPLM, Salva Kiir, was then invited to take the podium. It was time to break the silence. Did he know how decisive this speech was? I was not sure. I recalled a similar situation at the Commanders Conference in November 2004, when Salva Kiir had been the one challenging Dr John Garang, and where many of the same accusations had been thrown at the chairman. Dr John had ended up reconciling with his old comrade.[126]

It soon became clear that Salva had not seen any links between the two leadership challenges and their responses, or – for that matter – with the late President Mandela's management of foes and adversaries. Instead, the chairman launched a frontal attack on the SPLM cadres who had 'challenged his executive decisions', that is, those behind the press conference. He made a strong reference to 1991, and the massacre of the Bor Dinka:

> I must warn that this behavior is tantamount to indiscipline which will take us back to the days of the 1991 split. We all know where the split took us from that time. This could jeopardize the unity and the independence of our country and we must guard against such things, my dear comrades. I am not prepared to let this happen again.[127]

Warnings against repeating 1991 had been conveyed to Riek Machar several times before, but the context now was different. While there were also positive messages of democratic process and unity of the party in the speech, the damage had already been done. A woman in the audience started singing, and the President joined in. I got the meaning of this song only later. It was a liberation song, a call to action, urging that it was better to fight and die than to be humiliated. Some heard this as a signal; for those critical of the President, his speech had thrown down the gauntlet.

The rest of the NLC proceedings echoed these dissonant views. The internal conflict in the party was not discussed. The members mechanically went through proposals for the SPLM constitution. The President's lieutenants had lobbied to make sure that loyalists dominated the audience. All alternative proposals for the constitution failed. There was no attempt to reconcile the other factions, and none of them turned up for the second and last day of the Council meeting.

Was it the chairman's speech and the NLC that triggered the violence that erupted the following day? Or were the shooting incidents part of a pre-planned operation by Riek Machar and his allies in an attempt to seize power? The Government claims the latter, but it also seemed to have been prepared for such an eventuality.

Whatever the case may be, all factions of the SPLM had, intentionally or not, played with fire. Together, all these events triggered the violence that erupted on Sunday evening, the 15 December.

# 6

◆

# THE NIGHTMARE

On 15 December 2013 violence erupted in Juba. I had just finished a meeting at about 10.30 p.m. and heard gunshots in the distance. A while later a text message came in from the Chief of Security of UNMISS: 'Fighting broken out at SPLA HQ Military barracks in vicinity of Giyada'. There appeared to be fighting among the Presidential Guard.

Was this a barracks brawl, or something much bigger? Soldiers had gone on the rampage before. Although the atmosphere had been tense at the meeting of the National Liberation Council, and Riek Machar and several others had stayed away on the second day, there had been no sign at this time that any faction would turn to violence. A South Sudanese friend texted me from the town centre. He had passed the President's compound on his way home. Soldiers and check points were everywhere. Tanks were moving. Shooting and explosions were becoming louder and closer.

## Dark December night

Was there anything I could do? I had agreed with the President that in a crisis of national magnitude we would immediately be in touch. But I heard nothing from him, the government or his people. Should I call him? I started scrolling my phones. Not knowing the scale of this, I decided to get in touch with the security people before I disturbed the President. I should be able to get hold of them. Reports from UN Security indicated that the fighting was within the security forces. I checked my watch. It was close to midnight.

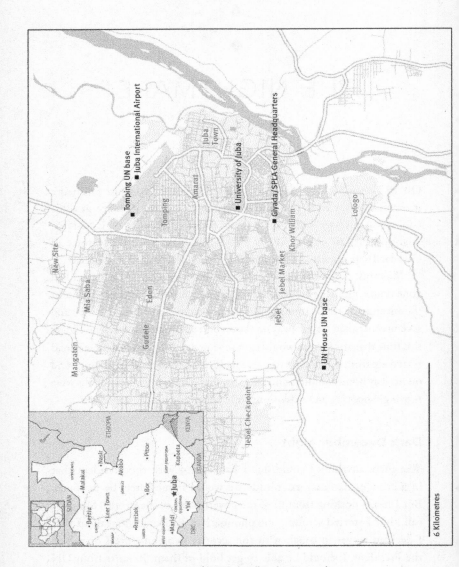

6 Kilometres

Juba Map © 2014 John Emerson Human Rights Watch. All Rights Reserved

At around 00.15 the shooting seemed to abate. Was the situation coming under control? Were those involved regrouping? One of my phones rang. It was Majak D'Agoot, the former deputy defence minister and a former SPLA general:

> If this is what it seems [...] it can trigger major ethnic killings. Hilde – you have no idea what can happen in this country, but this can set off ethnic violence between the Dinka and the Nuer which can drive us all down. This can become another Rwanda.

I had never heard Majak like this. He urged me to call both the President and Riek Machar and ask them to make a public statement calling for restraint and for an immediate cessation of violence. 'You are the only one that can reach both of them and convince them', Majak said. He thought if their respective forces heard such an instruction from their leaders, they would stand down.

Before I managed to reach them, Deng Alor, the ex-minister, called with the same message. The fighting was now surging, and seemed close. It was about 1.15. I told him that I was trying to reach both leaders, but that their mobile phones were either off or busy. Although I also used the satellite phone, the network was terrible, probably because of the emergency. Communication with senior staff to help with high-level phone calls was close to impossible.

An hour or so later I finally managed to talk to Defence Minister Kuol Manyang Juuk; Minister of National Security Obote Mamur Mete; and the Foreign Minister, Barnaba Benjamin Marial. They all said that the President was managing the crisis, and was not available to talk. They seemed to be together in some kind of operations centre. I urged that the President come out strongly calling for calm and asking all forces to stop the violence. I told them that I was calling for Riek Machar to do the same.

I tried to get to Riek on the five or six mobile numbers I had for him. The phones were either switched off or unanswered. I sent the same text message to all the phones, asking him to call me back. At 3 a.m. my phone rang. It was Riek, from a new and unknown number. I urged a public statement calling for calm and asking forces loyal to him to stop the violence. He asked whether the President was going to do the same.

I told him that I had spoken to the key security ministers and that I expected to speak to the President very soon. Riek said that he would consider a statement if the President would do the same. He said that his situation was now so serious that he had considered seeking refuge in a foreign embassy. He did not ask for UN protection or other assistance from UNMISS, and I made no offer. I still thought it possible to stop the violence, and said that he now was needed to take control of forces loyal to him and to prevent further bloodshed. At that point we had not yet received reports about any targeted ethnic killings.

At about 5 a.m. I was able to get through to the President, and told him of my conversation with Machar. Kiir listened carefully to my entreaties and said that a public statement would come soon, but that he needed to control the security situation first. I urged him to make the statement now, and not wait, but he was unmoved. I tried to call Machar back, but his phones were switched off.

At the crack of dawn on the 16th the sound of heavy fire resumed in full force. At 6.30 a.m. shooting broke out near the Nyakuron area. UN Security texted that fighting now appeared to be taking place not far from the western gate of the UNMISS Tonyping base, close to Bilpam, the SPLA headquarters. It was spreading. This was also near the UNMISS Residence, where I was. At 7.20 a.m. the house shook from artillery fire. I could feel the impact, but I continued working the phones. I was not afraid for my own safety. Although there was a risk of indirect fire, it was still a distance away. At this juncture I had no bodyguards and only local UN security at the gate, but I considered the risk of being directly targeted as minimal.

In the early morning UNMISS received reports that as many as 300 SPLA soldiers were engaged in the fighting, and that it involved Nuer and Dinka elements of the Presidential Guards. The violence appeared to go both ways. Shootings appeared to be concentrated around the Nacor area (south-west of the John Garang Memorial), at Giyada (SPLA headquarters) and in the Bilpam area on the western side of UNMISS Tomping. We were later told that the shooting during the night had been a major firefight at SPLA headquarters, where government forces, combining elements of the Presidential Guards, SPLA Commandos and some men of the SPLA's 2nd Division had fought renegade Nuer soldiers.

We soon got reports from security that civilians were fleeing for their lives and assembling outside the UN. During the night, hundreds had gathered around the gates both at UN House in the Jebel area and at Tonyping near the airport. They seemed in a desperate state, at Jebel even starting to cut the fences to enter. At 7.30 a.m. I instructed that we open the gates at both locations and provide refuge. It was clear that people were fearing for their lives. Not long after this, I also had my first conversations with UN headquarters in New York, briefing them about the situation.[1]

Close to 9.30 a.m. President Kiir sent out Philip Aguer, the SPLA spokesperson, with a first statement:

This situation is under control. People should not panic. The general command is acting and this situation will fully be brought under control any moment from now.[2]

He called on all soldiers to report to their barracks and announced that the President would speak to the nation later in the day. This was not the message I had been hoping for. I issued a statement calling for cessation of hostilities, which was immediately broadcast on radio.[3]

Around 10 a.m. I finally got through to Machar again. He appeared to have moved from his previous location. I told him I had talked to the President, referred to Aguer's statement, and said that an address by Kiir was likely to come soon. I urged him to come out strongly now with his own message of calm and restraint. I offered Radio Miraya, the UN station, to record such a statement immediately over the phone. He temporized; the overnight violence against the Nuer made such a statement difficult. He told me that he would call Radio Miraya if he decided on a statement or interview. Although we knew civilians were fleeing the fighting in large numbers, at this time, information about killings of Nuers had not yet reached us.

I learned later that fighting within the Presidential Guards had spread with lightning speed throughout the barracks. The noise I had heard near my residence had probably come from near the SPLA ammunition store in the New Site area, not far from the main Bilpam barracks. A firefight had occurred between loyal Presidential Guards and predominantly Nuer renegades. In the early morning hours the fighting had spread to nearby residential areas. Supported now by government soldiers with tanks, the security forces pushed the renegades southwards, out of New Site and surrounding neighbourhoods.

### 'Attempted coup'

At 11 a.m. President Kiir, who had always worn civilian attire since 2005, appeared on television in full military apparel. He wore the Tiger uniform (the Presidential Guard was called the Tiger Battalion). Kiir stated that an unidentified person had the night before fired into the air near the conference centre where the NLC was completing its two-day session, and that subsequently a group of soldiers allied with Riek Machar had attacked the SPLA's General HQ.[4] The President went on to affirm that the security situation was under complete control and that the SPLA was pursuing the attackers. He announced an immediate curfew from 6 p.m. to 6 a.m. until further notice. The security organs would conduct a full investigation into the attacks, and hold the perpetrators accountable.

In situations like these, it is important to note what is not said. At the time of his televised address, Kiir must have known how the military operations had been affecting civilians, and that civilians were fleeing to UN bases for protection. Yet he did not explicitly order his forces to protect civilians or express regret for those killed. This came only two days later. Instead, he again invoked the highly emotive 1991 split in the SPLM. After this we could expect no call for restraint from Riek. A national crisis was unfolding before our eyes.

The Chief Security Advisor of UNMISS wanted me to evacuate. As there was no immediate risk, I requested delay while I completed critical calls. I later went to the base, a short drive away, with military escort and force protection, together with the visiting deputy military advisor from New York, Adrian Foster. Little could I know that six months would pass before I spent another night in the Residence.

I knew that intervention at the highest levels was needed, and decided to contact Uganda. Now was the time to see whether President Museveni could influence events, given his close relations with President Kiir. I called Sam Kutesa, his foreign minister, both old acquaintances, and urged him to ask Museveni to advise the South Sudanese President that a political solution was needed, not a military one. Sam agreed to follow up. I was also in touch with the Kenyan ambassador to see whether his president could intervene.[5] But President Kenyatta had already called Kiir. Later in the day I was in touch with UN headquarters in New York to update them about what was unfolding, and to seek advice.

In the afternoon of the 16th Foreign Minister Barnaba Marial Benjamin and his deputy gave a briefing to the diplomatic community. Security was extremely tight; we barely managed to pass the numerous checkpoints from the UNMISS base to the presidency, where the briefing was held. A couple of times tense soldiers seemingly under the influence of alcohol or drugs made things difficult. Some of the security forces were uninformed about the meeting, and they repeatedly told us we should not be out in the streets, even with force protection.

The Foreign Minister reiterated the points made by Kiir that morning, and stated that the government had been subjected to an 'attempted coup' by Machar and forces loyal to him. The deputy foreign minister, Bashir Banda, briefed us on the proceedings of the National Liberation Council, including the decision to remove Pagan Amum, the SPLM secretary general.

The Government's version of subsequent events was that at 1830 on 15 December, during the closing of the Council meeting, unidentified persons had fired into the air near the Nyakuron Cultural Center, and escaped. This was a signal for an attack on the Giyada military barracks by soldiers of the Presidential Guard loyal to Machar. According to the government, these had first tried to get keys to the arms depot, failing which they attacked a group of Republican Guards loyal to the President to break into the armoury.[6] In the process an officer was shot and killed. Fighting then broke out. This was followed by an attack at Bilpam and, in the early morning hours, on other SPLA posts. The attackers broke into arms depots and stole arms and uniforms at both HQ locations. To the government this confirmed planning rather than a spontaneous outburst.[7]

Another version of events was that President Kiir had decided to disarm Nuer members of the Presidential Guard, and that they had resisted.[8] They broke into the armoury, where their weapons were stored, and fighting started. Machar's group and others loyal to him adopted this version. They linked an increased number of Dinkas in the

Presidential Guard to these events, all of which were part of an elaborate plan, they said, with coordinated attacks and killings in predominantly Nuer neighbourhoods. The very same new Dinka recruits, from Luri, were alleged to have had a leading role in the attacks against the Nuer. They claimed that the 'attempted coup' was just a cover for these actions.

Another possibility was that a random shooting incident simply got out of hand and led to the escalation. Concluding his briefing, Foreign Minister Marial said that anyone implicated in this (i.e. the attacks and 'attempted coup') would be arrested. He advised diplomats to deny entry to embassy premises to all South Sudanese nationals. The Government would respect the inviolability of embassies, but countries sheltering anyone suspected of a role in the attacks must inform the government of their presence. The hunt was on for Riek Machar, who remained at large. Later in the day, the US embassy, through its Twitter account, denied rumours that he had taken refuge in its compound.

When the minister further suggested that diplomats sheltering South Sudanese civilians should advise them to go home, I wondered whether this was a tacit reference to the UN. We had been sheltering people at our bases since early morning.

## Protected: The UN opens its gates

On the streets of Juba civilians were now in danger. But almost all UN forces had been deployed elsewhere in the country, and not least to Jonglei, where civilians had until now been under greater threat. Although our planning exercises had included worst-case scenarios for Juba in the event of a crisis, our forces there were few and lightly armed. They were mainly soldiers guarding UN assets and staff, as well as engineering, aviation, logistics and transport units. They had limited capacity and equipment.[9] Of infantry soldiers we had only about 120 who could engage in military operations outside the two bases.[10] Given the scale of violence raging in Juba, affecting thousands of people, not much could be done to protect them in the streets.[11]

UNMISS had a mandate to protect civilians under imminent threat. In my view, we had to give protection to those in need. Opening the gates was therefore a last resort. This had also happened before. During the Mission's table-top exercises on Protection of Civilians in November

2011, we had tested options for action in situations of large-scale threats to civilians. In Wau in December 2012, the thousands of civilians protected within our base returned home after a few days. In Pibor County, Jonglei State, as we have seen, hundreds of civilians had sought refuge a number of times, but not for long. This experience and the agreed procedures were critical, but never before had we been faced with the numbers that would now confront us.

It was my firm decision that leaving civilians to their fate outside the gates, where they were likely to be killed, was out of the question. In a matter of hours, thousands had flocked to us at Tonyping and UN House. When we had identified areas within our base that were suitable, the crowds were guided to the western gate, screened for weapons, and let in. During the morning of 16 December, approximately 8,000 sought refuge at Tonyping, and some 1,000 at UN House where, when firing resumed nearby later in the day, another 4,000 or 5,000 poured in. During the afternoon the total number passed 10,000.

On the 16th there was shooting on and off all day within the Bilpam barracks and in pockets elsewhere, as government forces attempted to clear areas and gain full control. They entered the residential areas of Khor William, Lologo and Jebel Market with tanks, and conducted house-to-house searches, reportedly looking for Nuer men. They also went on the attack throughout the north-eastern part of town, close to the military headquarters.[12] It was particularly from this period onwards that much of the violence against civilians took place. It turned ethnic.

At about 4.30 a.m. on the 17th sporadic shooting resumed in the Tonyping and Jebel areas. We were told that the SPLA was conducting widespread searches, sweeping neighbourhoods and targeting Nuer civilians. In Tonyping the firing became more sustained and included mortar shells. During the day the violence spread to other areas, with significant impact on civilians. I remember being in the office and hearing heavy fire on and off. It was clear that the fighting was not over, whatever the President had announced the previous morning. The numbers of displaced fleeing to our gates were increasing, as were the horror stories.

There were women with babies, elderly with walking sticks – barely managing to get to the camp; children clinging to their parents, crying; teenagers with fear in their eyes. Civilians with gunshot wounds were carried bleeding into the UN hospital. Women in despair had lost their husbands and children. Exhausted men in ragged uniforms were obliged to leave their firearms, fatigues and insignia behind as they entered the gate and became ex-combatants. By the following day the number of people in our two bases had reached approximately 16,000.

Mission staff worked around the clock to manage the crowds, check those entering the base for weapons and sharp items, organize water and sanitation facilities, make sure the wounded got treatment, pregnant women were assisted and the elderly did not collapse. It was a herculean effort. Humanitarian agencies had not yet moved in, so Mission staff had to handle everything. Maintaining the supply of water was extremely difficult. The bases and their infrastructure were not designed for such numbers.[13] At UN House, water soon ran out and more had to be trucked in several times daily, in the midst of insecurity, and with force protection from the other UN base. We had crisis meetings twice a day.

We redeployed forces to Juba as soon as possible to guard the multitudes under our protection. The initial expectation was that people would start returning home as soon as the violence abated, as had happened after the Wau trouble. But on 18 December, we realized that with this scale of violence people would not leave any time soon; we entered discussions with humanitarian colleagues to start food distribution. Until then we had been giving out only water. Soon an operations structure with the humanitarians was set up.

Civilian staff were restricted to the two UNMISS bases. There was still fighting in some neighbourhoods, random shooting and tanks operating. At check points soldiers were rough, unpredictable, sometimes drunk. Our soldiers who escorted the water trucks observed numerous bodies in the streets. In many places there was clear evidence of extrajudicial killings of whole groups of civilians. A number of them had clear Nuer markings in their face; it appeared that government security forces were responsible. Our human-rights officers gathered similar information from those fleeing the attacks. The following account of human rights violations and atrocities is based on corroborated information from UNMISS Human Rights Division.[14]

## The genie is out of the bottle

Several eyewitnesses reported that on the morning of 16 December Nuer men, all civilians, had been ordered out of their houses in Gudele and lined up. Any who resisted were shot. They were tied together and told to raise their hands and start walking.

At least 300 Nuer men, possibly as many as 450, were rounded up in this way. According to some reports, the group included men from New Site, Mangaten and Mia Saba. They were brought to a police station used for joint military-police operations and locked in a room. When some asked why they had been detained, the response came quickly. They were Nuer.

After dark, at about 8 p.m., unknown individuals started shooting through the windows. As one survivor states: 'they fired at everyone ... The room was very bright with bullets, sounds of PKM [a standard-issue Russian machine gun], and from an AK 47'.[15]

This procedure was followed several times during the night, for several minutes each time. Afterwards men in uniform went into the room with flashlights to see if anyone was still alive. Most were dead. Those alive were shot again or stabbed to death. A few, reportedly 12, were shielded under the dead and survived to tell what had happened. Of those a few escaped and the others were released when National Security officers discovered the gruesome site.[16] This massacre of civilians in Gudele is rightly known as one of the gravest incidents during the Juba violence.

In June 2014, after our human-rights report had been released, a source within the security forces told me that those in charge of rounding people up that day had gone to their superiors for instructions.[17] It was only when they returned several hours later that the massacre began. In other words, the mass murder was premeditated, deliberate and authorized, not perpetrated on the spur of the moment by soldiers who had suddenly gone crazy or were fired up by ethnic hatred.

Another very credible, high-level SPLA source later told me that on 16 December a retired general had been called in to lead the operation at the SPLA armoury in New Site that morning, using the reserve force of Presidential Guards from Luri and SPLA.[18] Not long after the Nuer soldiers had been subdued, government soldiers, in uniform and speaking Dinka, entered the neighbourhood nearby. They came in big numbers in tanks and on foot. My source says that the forces under the retired general's command were responsible for killing many innocent civilians there.

One witness reported that, after the soldiers entered the New Site neighbourhood, 18 men were ordered to stand in line and were tied together with rope. They were directed to walk for about 15 minutes until they reached a place with several tukuls (huts). As many as 200 Nuer men were detained in these tukuls and taken in groups to be interrogated in Dinka, or in Arabic if they could not speak Dinka. In a few cases, following the interrogation, men were returned to the tukuls; in the majority of cases they were not. Gunshots could be heard throughout the night. Those who remained the next morning were reportedly released into the custody of National Security personnel and thereafter detained and interrogated for some days. About eight men survived who spoke Dinka or other languages. None of the survivors had Nuer facial markings.

At about 2 p.m. on the 16th, government forces entered the Mia Saba neighbourhood. They were organized 'in big groups' and were 'collecting' Nuer civilians from the streets and houses, tying their hands behind their backs and taking them on foot to other places. Three lines of civilians were treated in this way, each of between 10 and 20 people. They were taken away, and no one knows what happened to them.

Several other people in Mia Saba reported having been taken from their houses by Dinka SPLA in a group of about 40 men, all Nuer, tied together with bed sheets, and forced to walk to the New Site cemetery. Smaller groups of between four and eight men were shot dead as they walked. When the main group came across a dead soldier, four or five men from the group were shot to death. This happened two or three times during the walk. Some 20 of those who reached the cemetery were then shot. Those not shot were detained for three days and then released.

During house-to-house searches in many neighbourhoods of Juba, soldiers asked the men in Dinka which language they spoke. If they responded in Nuer and not in Dinka or Arabic, they would be shot, or arrested, or beaten up. If they had Nuer facial marks, their fate would often be sealed.

Although we did not have such details on 17–18 December, stories of summary executions, abductions, arrests and killings began to circulate. The first sources were victims themselves, the wounded in our clinic, and those streaming through our gates, some of whom had even been chased right up to the base by would-be killers. Numerous other sources later came forward, both witnesses and survivors, as well as those telling what had happened to relatives and friends.

The Nuer, and particularly Nuer men, seem to have been by far the main victims throughout the capital, with the government's security forces, primarily Dinka, appearing to be the culprits. What clearly had been at first a fight between forces of the Presidential Guards loyal to the President and those siding with Riek Machar had degenerated into a deliberate massacre of Nuer, and particularly Nuer males. While the objective at first might have been to arrest Machar's partisans (in hiding or in civilian clothing), government security forces basically turned on the civilians.

## Calling for leadership: This has to stop

On Tuesday, 17 December, what we knew was anecdotal at best. Without any certainty of the scale of the targeting of civilians, I issued another press statement calling for an end to ethnic violence.[19] Urging restraint, I underscored all parties' responsibility to seek a peaceful conclusion to the crisis. Church leaders and the South Sudan Human Rights Commission made statements along the same lines.[20]

The violence continued. A woman in the UNMISS clinic who had given birth told me what had happened to her. 'Anna' was Nuer. The soldiers came to her house at night, in Mia Saba; they went through the whole neighbourhood. As they entered her house, they shouted at her husband in Dinka, then shot him dead. 'Anna' was afraid they would go after her and their children as well, so she ran as fast as she could out of the house, down the street towards the UN base, with her children. Two of the children got lost in the chaos. She had not been able to trace them since. A third was with her in the camp. Now her baby girl would grow up without her father.

Some women were raped during the violence, but the targets were usually men. Later sexual violence would be a regular feature and used as a weapon of war.[21]

191

At this time, on the 17th, it began to dawn on us what was unfolding. Majak's stark warning still rang in my mind ('this could become another Rwanda'). While the international community, the UN system and I personally had clearly failed to stop the fighting and contain the violence, we at least could give protection. Thousands of lives had been saved by the decision to open our gates. We even saw members of National Security, the SPLA, and government officials bring people to the UN bases. In many cases these were civilians they knew personally and wanted to protect. Or their protectors were simply good-hearted individuals who wanted to save people's lives. Later, government officials and SPLA would themselves turn to the UNMISS bases elsewhere for protection.

The director-general of external security, Major General Thomas Duoth Guet, a Nuer, now advised all Nuer in Juba to go to UNMISS for protection.[22] SPLA and National Police vehicles were dropping off relatives throughout the day. It was indeed a very bad sign that even the government's own security people feared for their families' lives. They were right to do so. Groups of SPLA soldiers took positions on the roadside leading to the UN base and attacked people who were fleeing there. In other cases, they snatched people and drove away with their prey, who were never seen again. It was deeply disturbing to hear of civilians who had been killed on their way to us, or been attacked when venturing from the bases for food, only to be harassed or raped. UN forces were too few to protect individuals who went out on their own. Although we tried to send patrols through town, to help deter such threats, our main concern now was to make sure that the 16,000 people inside the bases were safe.

I tried to get hold of the President and security ministers the whole day, but all were inaccessible. The centre of Juba now seemed relatively calm, with the violence localized in residential areas, where security forces appeared to have met stubborn resistance by forces loyal to Riek Machar or were conducting military operations among the civilians. The defected forces were expected either to regroup and return, or to retreat.

At the same time, reports that civilians were being targeted on an ethnic basis in these areas were deeply worrying. It was only in the evening that I was able to get in touch with government officials. I first spoke to Foreign Minister Barnaba Benjamin Marial and then to the legal advisor to the President, Telar Deng. I shared the information we had received so far and urged them to do what they could to stop the ethnically motivated violence, which seemed out of control. The same message was conveyed to security ministers.

The minister of defence, Kuol Manyang Juuk, was central in this regard. He expressed concern about the incidents of ethnic violence, attributed these to 'criminals', and promised that each officer would be held accountable. The minister of national security, Obote Mamur Mete, concurred, and said that many who had engaged in ethnically motivated violence, including SPLA soldiers, had been apprehended. He mentioned 200, but was vague, and I could not get this number verified by anyone else. Regarding casualties Kuol Manyang had said that the Red Cross had collected 260 bodies, while the SPLA had collected 70. It was impossible to verify any of these figures.

In any case, the scale of violence we had seen and heard about indicated that the numbers were likely much higher. I was later informed that security forces had been instructed to bury bodies as quickly as possible, and that they did so during the night in several mass graves. Separately, the Minister of Cabinet Affairs Martin Lomuro informed us that he had worked with the Red Cross to make sure that bodies were buried according to internationally recognized procedures, and he was ready to show us the records. While we never got access to these records, it is likely that those buried by the Red Cross in this way were only a fraction of the civilians killed.

At this time, information about what was happening was patchy and piecemeal. The Security Council held its first emergency meeting on South Sudan, late on the 17th, and a first statement of grave concern was issued.[23]

On 18 December our human-rights officers were able to venture out. Teams visited Juba University, Malakia, Tonypiny, the area around the presidential palace, the market behind the John Garang Memorial, and Gudele. Our military patrols had been out the day before and seen civilian bodies, some blindfolded, most with hands tied, and with gunshot wounds in the back of their heads. They had also quietly evacuated civilians hiding in several churches, as well as at Juba University, bringing them to UNMISS bases.

Now, in the morning of the 18th, with more reports of atrocities, I met President Salva Kiir. Foreign Minister Marial was there, too. I called on him personally to order all ethnically motivated violence to stop immediately.

The President assured me of his concern and said that instructions had already been given. He committed to redouble his efforts and make sure there was accountability for abuses; he had conveyed the same to the UN Secretary-General who had called him the evening before. Criminals had taken advantage of the situation, and they would be held responsible. He said that he had already that day met Nuer leaders to clarify 'misleading information' that the Nuer were being targeted as a community. I stressed the need for his willingness to participate in reconciliation efforts with Riek Machar.

While such promises were made, the President wanted to know whether the UN was hiding the former Vice President. Since I had been able to reach Machar during the night of the 15th–16th, it seemed that many thought we were protecting him. I said we were not, and that the UN, according to procedures, was indeed obliged to inform government authorities if a person of this importance sought our protection. I had nothing to tell the President in this regard; we had no idea of Machar's whereabouts. He nodded and seemed satisfied.

It was a positive step that the President in his press conference later that day called for calm, confronting tribalism, and the arrest and trial of anyone found attempting abuse, looting or killing.[24] The further announcement, in the evening, of his willingness to enter into dialogue with Riek Machar was another encouraging development.[25]

Not everyone was happy with the latter statement. Many people, including close advisers of the President, wanted to hunt down Riek Machar – literally – and not to reconcile with him. The President's question about the UN's protecting Machar was a first indication of a controversy that would envelop me personally. Much later I learned from credible sources that an email I had sent to UN headquarters on 16 December had been intercepted and brought to the President, allegedly proving my support for Machar. Most of the senior people in the security apparatus apparently wanted to declare me persona non grata. I have saved this email, and its innocent and impartial content tells a lot about the paranoia of the day.[26] The President stood firm, however, saying that such an action was simply out of the question. But this would not be the last time he was confronted with a demand to have me removed.

Hardliners around Salva Kiir now seemed to have a personal animus against anyone who opposed their agenda. The cadres around the President, and key members of the cabinet, wanted Machar out of the way. Cadres arguing for more nuanced positions had a tough time. But this did not prevent James Wani Igga from repeating the President's message of dialogue in a press statement the following day.

At this time, the sequence of events around the beginning of the crisis was still confused. In the Mission we remained unconvinced that an attempted coup had taken place. To make an authoritative 'ruling', however, would have required consultation with the UN's Office of Legal Affairs, and put the Mission at odds with the government. This could have had dramatic consequences at a time when our presence and protection were most needed. It might also have caused difficulty in relation to some neighbouring countries.

Extrajudicial killings and ethnic targeting were our main preoccupation. It was time to sound the alarm. This was better done at higher levels. The High Commissioner for Human Rights, Navi Pillay, issued a strong statement on 19 December, as did the Secretary-General of the UN.[27] With information provided by UNMISS the Security Council followed suit. On 20 December the Council condemned the targeted violence against civilians and specific ethnic communities.[28] Four days later the Security Council went further, condemning the ethnic violence perpetrated by both armed groups and national security forces.[29] I raised similar concerns in the Christmas message broadcast on most radio stations in the country the following day.

## 'Wanted' – the comrades

Evidence we had collected of the deliberate targeting of Nuer civilians was reinforced by the full details we later learned. The security forces were hunting down not only Machar and his family, but also everyone on his team, advisers, security guards, even secretaries – any person known to be associated with him. His houses in Juba were targeted, even after he was known to have got away. One indication of the level of personal

195

revenge was the attack on the former Vice President's residence, which he had still occupied after his dismissal from office.

On 16 December forces from the Tiger Battalion had deployed around the perimeter of the residence, and ordered the security guards to disarm. They complied. No one was subsequently permitted to leave the compound. Machar was nowhere to be seen. The following morning, after the troops surrounding the compound were reinforced, a mixed force of heavily armed SPLA troops, National Police, and even Wildlife Service wardens attacked. At least two tanks broke through the walls of the compound, and pick-up trucks mounted with machine guns and other heavy weapons followed. Three named senior government officials were observed on site, monitoring the assault, according to an eyewitness.[30]

The security forces shot directly into the residence, where as many as 60 civilians were staying, and a number of those, including women and children, were later reported to have been killed. Five unarmed soldiers were also killed, and at least five more wounded. The shooting went on for hours and only after it stopped were the injured taken to hospital, and some people arrested. Later the interior minister, Aleu Ayeny Aleu, explained that the raid had been part of a security operation to 'clean the area' of those suspected of being loyal to Machar.[31] I had also been told that there had been shooting from the roof of the house earlier, in the direction of the President's compound.[32] The former Vice President's other houses were also attacked, and people there killed.

Security forces continued to search elsewhere for anyone affiliated with Machar. But not to arrest them, it appeared; most of those found were killed. One was Lam Chol Tishore, Machar's private secretary, a competent and reliable young professional whom I knew well. He had fled during the turmoil and gone into hiding. Security forces tracked him down in a Juba hotel, and he was killed in cold blood together with his brother.

High-profile Nuer politicians, soldiers and security personnel, none of whom had joined the renegades, were also targeted.[33] They were pursued all over Juba during the following week. Some were arrested, others killed. A number fled to the UNMISS base for protection. For months, we had members of the Legislative Assembly, former ministers and officials under our protection.

We were concerned that other members of the SPLM leadership could be next. It seemed that anyone associated with the notorious press conference of 6 December was at risk. They seemed to be 'wanted, dead or alive'. As early as the evening of the 16th Majak D'Agoot had spoken live on the BBC; security forces had visited his house and told him to remain there until he was 'picked up by Government agents.'[34] He told the BBC he was about to be arrested.

Local media soon referred to arrests of unidentified 'disgruntled soldiers and politicians'.[35] On the 17th Information Minister Michael Makuei confirmed in a statement that ten people had been arrested for 'interrogation' following the purported coup attempt, and he provided a list:[36] all had participated in the press conference on the 6th, including Deng Alor Kuol, Kosti Manibe, John Luk Jok and Oyay Deng Ajak. The whereabouts of former SPLM Secretary-General Pagan Amum, former Unity State Governor Taban Deng Gai, former Minister Alfred Ladu Gore and former Minister Peter Adwok Nyaba, remained unknown. Pagan managed to telephone me at one point, and seemed calm. Later he and Peter Adwok were arrested.

## Friends on all sides

Among those now in detention were thus many prominent figures. While some were 'Garang Boys'; others had been very close to Kiir. A couple had fallen out with him or become sympathetic to Machar. Rebecca Nyandeng seemed to be under house arrest.

Many were held at the house of Pieng Deng Kuol, the inspector general of the National Police. He was a neighbour of Machar's, and the detainees worried that the attack on the vice-presidential residence might be directed towards them as well, or that they could be hit by indirect fire. Rebecca called me on their behalf, and I took up the matter with the President at our meeting on the 18th.

I was in a very delicate position. I had colleagues of long standing on all sides, in government, among the detainees, and those who had fled, presumably to join Machar. Some I had known for 15 years. They would all expect me to take their side, or at least support their cause one way or another. But my duty was to implement the mandate of the Security Council, and emphatically not take sides.

This would be the most challenging balancing act I had ever faced as a SRSG.

In my meeting with President Kiir on 18 December I raised the issue of the detainees. I asked for international access and protection of their rights. The President assured me that his old 'comrades' were fine and would be well treated; he also promised me that the Red Cross would have access to them (which never happened). He insisted that the detainees would be subject to due process – immediate release was out of the question. At a second meeting a few days later, I had the President's permission to visit them.[37]

Meanwhile the Minister of Information took pains publicly to explain that the fighting in Juba did not have ethnic overtones. As evidence he pointed to the ethnic diversity of both those in government and those accused. Any apparent ethnic targeting had been the result of misjudgement by individual soldiers. Announcing that the airport would be re-opened on the 18th, he called upon the population to resume normal activities.

On 18 December Riek Machar gave his first interviews to various national and international media, from an undisclosed location. He denied that he had tried to stage a coup, and accused President Kiir of inciting tribal and ethnic violence to cover his own failings.[38] He blamed the fighting on a conflict between members of the Presidential Guard and made it clear that he would not leave the country. The following day he declared that, if required, he would lead the resistance against Kiir, and was quoted as calling on the SPLM 'to remove Salva Kiir from the leadership of the country'.[39] Following events in Juba, the targeted attacks on Nuer, and this statement from Machar, reconciliation seemed much more difficult. If we now had a declared armed resistance, the ballgame had shifted.

I also needed to do my utmost to make sure nothing happened to those in detention, and see what more could be done to help. I had lost contact with Machar, who was clearly trying to avoid being traced by the security apparatus. But through South Sudanese contacts abroad I was able to establish a channel of communication with him on 20 December. My meetings with the President were initially frequent, at least once a week, and I would usually call Riek the same day. I kept a record to make sure there was impartiality even in this.[40]

## Domino effect

If there had been any expectation that things would get under control, it was instantly contradicted by events. Bor, the capital of Jonglei, had already fallen to opposition forces on 18 December; in Bentiu, capital of Machar's home state of Unity, they took control on the 21st. The Government lost Malakal, capital of Upper Nile State, on the 24th, although fighting continued for days thereafter. Within ten days, therefore, forces loyal to Machar controlled three state capitals; within two weeks considerable territory beyond also seemed under their sway, despite some back and forth at Bor. Concern was voiced that Riek's forces might move southwards and even attack Juba. At the same time, he issued a statement to the effect that Salva Kiir was no longer the legitimate leader of South Sudan.[41]

There were three underlying reasons for these startling developments. First, the SPLA was fracturing along ethnic lines, with defections by Nuer soldiers and officers on all fronts and remaining forces performing poorly in the field. Secondly, the killings in Juba had united the Nuer in a way that generated significant support for Machar, including among armed youth and the 'White Army'. They needed but one motive for involvement now: revenge! This was enough for massive mobilization, and it added tens of thousands to Machar's numbers. Their objective was to make the Dinka suffer, just as the Nuer had in Juba. Thirdly, whether in pre-arranged concert or reaction to events, the large majority of security forces in Jonglei, Unity and Upper Nile States defected to Machar. The Greater Upper Nile region was the epicenter of the fighting after Juba, and forces loyal to Kiir in these critical states were few.

## Bor falls

The security situation in Bor had begun to unravel as soon as the fighting started in Juba. A seemingly isolated incident within the South Sudan National Police Service Auxiliary Forces sparked shooting at Pakwau. On the night of 16 December some 500 civilians arrived at the UNMISS compound in Bor. The next morning Peter Gadet, still commanding the SPLA's 8th Division, paraded through the town and urged calm. But on the 17th fighting among the security forces continued and we received reports that they were splitting along ethnic lines. Gadet had switched sides during the night, taking a number of soldiers, their armoured vehicles and heavy weapons with him. A former militia leader from Unity State, he had been reintegrated into the SPLA only in 2012, held grudges against the leadership of the SPLA, and had needed preferential treatment to remain in the fold. Now he had taken the first opportunity to re-defect and join Machar. Gadet soon became a major figure in mobilizing forces against the government.

By the morning of the 18th Gadet and his men had seized control of the SPLA's Panpandiar barracks in Bor, and made their way towards Bor town. By this time, Nuer members of the auxiliary police had already entered the town and started shooting randomly.[42] Apparently by coincidence, the various defectors now joined forces. At the same time, there was an exodus of civilians, with some 12,500 seeking refuge at the UNMISS compound.

On the same day, the 18th, the Jonglei State Governor, John Kuong Nyoun, a Nuer, returned to Bor from Juba to handle the crisis. Upon arrival, he was escorted from the airfield to his compound by UNMISS force protection. The Governor convened a meeting, during which his compound was attacked.[43] UNMISS had to escort him to the base in Bor. By then almost the whole state cabinet had sought UNMISS protection. This was the first time – there would be many more – that government officials sought the protection of the UN in the areas where fighting was going on. They would often in future also deposit relatives and others they thought at risk. At times the clearest sign that a town was about to fall would be government officials coming to UNMISS with wives, children and other relatives. It was thus all the more ironic later to be accused of sheltering only 'rebels'.

Fighting continued in Bor. On the morning of 19 December, sustained heavy gunfire, including RPGs, lasted for two hours. The situation was chaotic; eyewitnesses say that at times it was difficult to know who was fighting whom. Defected Nuer, both police and SPLA, moved in in big numbers. The speed with which Bor fell was shocking. It also had symbolic importance. Bor was where the liberation movement had started in 1983, and close to the home of John Garang. The town would become the site of some of the worst violence against civilians during the first month of the conflict. Within two weeks forces loyal to Machar would exert control over the majority of the counties in Jonglei and two counties in Upper Nile.

We soon had 14,000 people in our base at Bor. But before we could address their needs, beyond mere physical protection, and anticipate the next move by opposition forces, we had another crisis at our hands.

## Akobo crisis

On 17–18 December we received reports of intra-SPLA and communal violence at Akobo and Waat (Nyriol County) in northern Jonglei. Our small support base at Akobo was under threat, and I ordered evacuation.[44] This took longer than expected,[45] and I was surprised to hear that it had not yet been carried out when the base came under attack by some 2,000 armed youths. Approximately 30 Dinka civilians had been sheltering there, protected by a small number of lightly armed peacekeepers.

A survivor explains:

> There was no way to escape, the compound was very small. I was inside. Many people were killed in my presence. I got confused and hid with the UN peacekeepers in a small place. They [the attackers] called us out, there was no way to run [but] someone saved my life by saying this man is not Dinka, he is an Equatorian; the rest of the youth they were dancing, shouting that they have killed all the Dinka.[46]

UN investigations later concluded that the attack had been orchestrated by defected Nuer of the SPLA, police and prison services, together with Lou Nuer youths. Two of our peacekeepers had been killed; one international UN staff, and among the Dinka civilians 11 were found killed. It is not clear how many survived. The UN would soon be under attack elsewhere too.

Press statements condemning the Akobo attack were issued by UNMISS, the Secretary-General and the Security Council. Two days later, Machar acknowledged command of the 'White Army' elements, and regretted the incident. I told him that these attacks were a grave violation of international law. He promised to control the armed youths, but I had my doubts that he could.

Within a couple of days Gadet had strengthened his grip in the Bor area and reportedly withstood an air strike on 21 December. The SPLA did not have helicopter gunships; this was the first hint of foreign support for the government. President Museveni had visited on the 19th and pledged support to Kiir.[47] After the first observation of Ugandan forces on South Sudanese soil – the next day, in Juba – ostensibly to protect strategic locations and assist the evacuation of Ugandans,[48] MiG-29s were seen bombing rebel positions near Bor.[49]

The United States decided to remove its nationals from Bor,[50] and all other embassies subsequently implemented evacuation plans, most of them pleading for our assistance. While we were dealing with the Akobo crisis and evacuations, we received reports that Gadet's forces were attacking villages south of Bor.[51] They burnt everything, looted extensively, and took the cattle. Civilians fled, and by the 23rd the number classified as Internally Displaced People (IDPs) in Awerial County, across the Nile, had reached over 28,000. By now, Gadet's forces had control over vast areas of Jonglei State.

The Government could not accept the loss of Bor. Forces were sent north from Juba. On 24 December there was heavy fighting, and by the next morning it appeared that the government had re-occupied the town. At the same time, the majority of Dinka who had sought refuge in the UNMISS base, reaching 15,000, left the compound, and those remaining were mainly Nuer.

But Bor remained a battleground. Credible reports of killing, rape, abduction and threats to life, including of foreigners, suggested a pattern of targeting by both government and opposition forces. Civilians leaving the UN base as the town changed hands were also killed. By the time opposition forces recaptured the town at the end of the month it was almost empty; Dinka were at risk if found. These forces included many more armed Nuer youths than during the previous assault, and the destruction they caused was even more indiscriminate.

The most widespread targeting of Dinka civilians took place during the first two weeks of January. Places of past safety became targets. Civilians seeking refuge at St Andrew's Church and Bor Hospital were killed, between 10 and 20 in each location. A witness described the killers as men 20 years old or younger.[52] At St Andrew's, the majority of those killed were women, and included clergy; the female church attendants were sexually abused first. This caused widespread outrage among the Dinka.

The total number of people killed at Bor has been contested; UNMISS later found that 2,000 people in Bor County seemed a reasonable estimate. The numbers of displaced south of Bor multiplied, as they fled the town. They ventured across the Nile for safety, reaching close to 90,000 in the area of Awerial alone within a few weeks.

On 24 December, the President issued a statement calling for an end to all ethnic violence, characterizing recent developments as 'unacceptable'. While referring to 'terrible acts committed by unruly and undisciplined soldiers and the killing of innocent people', and promising accountability. The statement fell short of condemning such acts.[53] Four days later, the National Police established a committee[54] to investigate the Juba violence; the SPLA would follow suit.[55] It soon became clear that the commander-in-chief's appeals went unheeded.

## Ethnic killings in Bentiu and Malakal

By 16 December hostilities had already spread to Unity State. On that day fighting broke out among staff at a base camp of the Greater Pioneer Operating Company in the Unity oil field. Fighting spread to the 4th Division,[56] and soon there were violent incidents at a number of SPLA barracks. Many soldiers and officers were killed.

Witnesses reported incidents of killing and looting in Bentiu on the night of the 19th. Security forces entered houses, sometimes stole valuables, and killed or wounded civilians and unarmed soldiers. The perpetrators were Nuer, the victims Dinka. At Rubkona on 20 December there were shootings by what witnesses referred to as 'Nuer SPLA', and two days later some 30 dead bodies were seen in the market area. We had reinforced perimeter security at our Bentiu base, including around the area where civilians had sought shelter and hundreds of civilians had arrived in the afternoon of the 19th. The number quickly multiplied on the following day; Dinka civilians had been killed near the oil fields, and others taken to our base for protection.

There had been skirmishes at the Rubkona airstrip, in the vicinity of Bentiu town, and near our base. But when on the 21st the commanding officer of the highly regarded SPLA 4th Division, Major General James Koang Chuol, declared his support for Machar, and announced that he was now the interim Governor, Bentiu fell to the opposition. Most of his personnel went over with him. Although previously regarded as a loyalist, he was thought to have had no choice but to change sides or be killed.

The loss of Bentiu and major parts of Unity State was a big setback for President Kiir, who was reported to be responding with military deployments from the neighbouring states and Northern Bahr el Ghazal. At a meeting of the National Liberation Council on 23 December, he admitted that Riek Machar and the opposition were now in control of two states.[57] It was still not clear which side the mainly Nuer members of the newly integrated South Sudan Liberation Army would take. The militia had reached agreement with the government just six months before, and many expected them to join the opposition, but for now they stayed loyal to Kiir, a decision that would prove very important.

Bentiu changed hands several times, and the ethnicity of civilians seeking refuge in our base varied accordingly; early in the crisis the number reached 5,000, but it would increase to 40,000 within a few months.[58] On each occasion the killing, abuse and impact on civilians grew worse. Rebels from Darfur, elements of the Justice and Equality Movement, opportunistically joining the SPLA, were seemingly prone to attack women and children and engage in sexual violence, being responsible for grave atrocities.

At the same time as Bentiu fell to opposition forces, Machar took control of Nasir in Upper Nile State. By 22 December, Bor and Bentiu were now under opposition control, as well as a number of counties in all three states in the Upper Nile region. Fighting also intensified at Malakal, and there were indications that a split might occur within the SPLA there at any time.

Upper Nile State was of fundamental importance to the government: 85 per cent of South Sudan's oil was there. Should Machar succeed in gaining firm control of the state, including its oil fields, the government would suffer a major setback. The stakes were very high.

Heavy fighting took place in and around Malakal on 24 December. The SPLA's 7th Division at Fashoda split, and opposition forces took the town, although the government still seemed to hold the airport and the Paloich area. The UNMISS base had been in the crossfire, and shells hit our Level II Hospital, leading to casualties. Fighting nearby involved tanks, anti-aircraft guns, mortars and heavy machine guns. Thousands of displaced people were allowed into the inner compound for better protection, while many civilians were killed in the crossfire outside. Opposition forces conducted house-to-house searches in the town, looking for alleged collaborators. Gross human rights abuses, including killings and sexual violence, occurred, and houses were looted and destroyed.

Such house-to-house searches affected all ethnic groups, Dinka, Shilluk, Nuer and others. Twelve thousand civilians sought refuge in our Malakal base at this time. After two days of heavy fighting, government forces recaptured the capital on the 28th, and lethal revenge attacks and other abuses ensued. The number of people taking refuge in our base increased exponentially.

From late December onwards, the two sides' forces swept back and forth through Baliet County, fighting for control of Malakal and other areas in Upper Nile. As they moved through the county, Nuer armed youths from Nasir and defected SPLA left a path of destruction. Hundreds of civilians were reportedly killed, many seemingly at random, entire villages were destroyed, and livestock and food looted. Survivors were left isolated and without food, water or shelter, and thousands tried to find protection in three makeshift camps.

Despite some government successes, the amount of territory that opposition forces had captured within about ten days was astounding. As I will show later, this seemed to be less a result of Machar's personal leadership than of decisions by individual commanders to take matters into their own hands. Observers found it hard to believe that the national Army, the SPLA, had so quickly lost control in so many places.

## Threat against Juba?

As fighting raged in the states we received information about a massive mobilization of Nuer armed youths. It had usually taken weeks for large columns to form. But now several were already marching from locations in Jonglei State and assembling at Gadiang, north-west of Bor. Some had allegedly been mobilized for revenge attacks against the Murle, but with the killings in Juba, their target appeared to be Bor, and possibly Juba itself, for revenge. They were led by Bor Doang and the Nuer prophet, Dak Kueth, who was reported marching in the general direction of Bor and possibly to assembly points farther south. It was clear that Riek Machar had established links with them. On 28 December he told me on the telephone how they had reached agreement, both on objectives and on a code of conduct, and he claimed that they were fully under his command. This was my third conversation with him since 16 December, and I immediately reported this affirmation of control over the White Army to the UN Security Council.

Would Machar succeed in pushing southwards? The Nuer were united in their desire to avenge the killings of their people. If major columns moved beyond Bor, towards Mongalla and the southern counties, the national capital could be at risk. Speculation ran high. Multiple sources reported a column of armed youths, as many as 25,000, heading towards Bor.[59]

It appeared that the loyalist SPLA was too weak to repel an attack of such magnitude. The Ugandan People's Defence Force (UPDF) had in the meantime moved in with ground troops. Whether the Ugandans could prevent an attack on Juba no one knew. The President confirmed as much on 28 December during my fourth meeting with him since the crisis started. Although the government had regained control of Malakal, I knew that they were about to lose Bor again. But he was most concerned about the possibility of a massive attack by the Nuer column on Juba, and what that would imply, which in his view was a 'tribal turn' in the conflict, with devastating consequences.

After that meeting, Riek Machar confirmed to me on the telephone that a major column was indeed on the way to Bor, and might push farther south. I implored him to halt the offensive, reminding him of the many unsuccessful attempts in the past to control such columns, and the risk that thousands of civilian lives could be lost. Riek repeated that he was in 'full control' and that every effort would be made to avoid civilian casualties.

## The UN under attack

'From today on, we shall have no excuses or scapegoats to blame.' So said Salva Kiir to his people and the world on the day South Sudan's independence was declared in 2011. But his words would not hold.

When the violence exploded in Juba in mid December, speculation about Riek Machar's whereabouts had immediately begun. He had clearly fled his residence during the early morning hours of 16 December. Soon the rumours had it that the UN (and the US?) had helped him to safety. It was not true, of course. It was only several days later that I was made aware that this story was circulating, and that most people in Juba believed it. When the President confronted me, I had no idea what he was talking about. Kiir's security people knew that Machar had escaped through Jebel Ladu on the outskirts of Juba, across the Nile, and on foot from there. Information later from the cell phone networks confirmed his coordinates.[60]

But within the President's circle, many still averred that I had helped Machar and others to escape. Stories began to circulate that I was even sending weapons to him. That I was seen as close to the detainees added to suspicion. All my movements and phones were monitored. Instead of engaging in public advocacy for the detainees' release, which would only have made it easier for hardliners to compromise my position, I worked behind the scenes. The same applied to our preliminary assessment of whether there had been an attempted coup. I kept quiet. Being declared *persona non grata* at this point would not have served any useful purpose.

## Wild stories

Reinforcing hardline perceptions was the opening of the gates to our bases. We were, it was said, protecting rebels, not innocent civilians; they had hidden their weapons within the bases, and were ready to attack the capital. The proximity of the most important UNMISS base to the airport now assumed sinister implications.

Ironically, as we have seen, at the same time, government politicians and even soldiers had sought refuge along with civilians in our bases at Bor and Bentiu, and would later do so at Malakal. As in

Juba, members of the security forces needed to leave their uniforms and weapons behind before being allowed in, and they thus entered as ex-combatants. Everyone was searched going into and out of a base. But our protection of Dinka civilians and government officials seemed to go unnoticed, and the story of our 'rebel support' continued unabated.

We knew we had the facts on our side. The protection of civilians within our bases followed strict international procedures. Our demographic information derived from registration for food distribution, conducted by the International Organization for Migration and the World Food Programme by name, age and gender. Although there was always a risk of error, the lists gave a very good picture of whom we were protecting. The vast majority at all our bases were women and children: at Tomping in Juba 77 percent, and at UN House in the Jebel area more than 80 percent.[61] The figures were even higher at bases elsewhere. This meant that only a relatively small number could possibly be men of 'fighting age'. We also counted uniforms and weapons handed over at entry, and reported the statistics to the authorities. But our information was either ignored or dismissed as false.

With time, the fictitious stories were fuelled by statements and badly disguised allegations by government officials in the media. We were repeatedly accused of harbouring rebels, and of acquiescing when UN vehicles were taken or UN premises looted by opposition forces. Even more bald-faced was criticism of the UN for not condemning the attack on our base at Akobo, when of course the Secretary-General, Security Council, and UNMISS had all issued statements immediately.[62] The Government's communications team seemed to be orchestrating all of this, clearly with the intention of building their case that the UN was on the opposition's side. For this reason, I had tried several times – unsuccessfully – to schedule a meeting with Information Minister Michael Makuei to refute these allegations with the facts.

With the SPLA on its back feet during the first weeks of the crisis, and suffering some astounding defeats, government officials were on the defensive. Scapegoats were needed. When Riek Machar and other opposition leaders, including Hussein Maar, the former deputy governor of Jonglei State, managed to evade arrest at Bor, UNMISS was said to have airlifted them out. It was a joke. That accusations such as this came from cabinet ministers showed the level of propaganda that had been reached.

After the government had retaken Bor in mid January, Minister Michael Makuei, himself a Bor Dinka, jumped on the first flight in. The minister had been advised that he would be welcome at the UN base, where community leaders of the displaced people were ready to receive him. At this time Nuer predominated because most of the Dinka had decamped into town now that the SPLA had regained control. At division headquarters the minister asked that a number of soldiers accompany him to the camp. Even some SPLA commanders wondered why such a large detail was needed for a meeting with civilian refugees under UN protection, but they conceded.[63]

Soon, therefore, five or six 'technicals' – pick-up trucks carrying about 60 soldiers – drove up to the gate of the Protection of Civilians site within the UNMISS base. According to eyewitness accounts, they behaved in a threatening manner. And when Makuei was told that TV cameras would not be allowed to accompany him, owing to the qualms of refugees, a verbal confrontation ensued. Makuei insisted that, as a government minister of a sovereign nation, he had the right to enter with media.

One of the soldiers cocked his weapon and pointed it at Ken Puyoma, our State Coordinator. A few others attempted to go past him into the base, but were stopped by UNMISS personnel. The minister was furious. He claimed that UNMISS was hiding rebels, in uniform, and with weapons, which of course was not true. The situation was very tense, and could quickly have got out of control. Ken was firm, kept his cool, and Minister Makuei departed, fuming that the UN had not heard the last from him about this.

After Ken, on the line from Bor, had told me what had happened I knew there would be political fall-out. The minister had clearly abused the inviolability of UN premises, as stipulated in the agreement between the UN and the government and according to international conventions. I knew the reaction in New York would be very strong. I also knew Michael Makuei well enough to be sure he would pursue the matter. I tried to telephone him, but he was inaccessible, as was the President. I called Kiir's private secretary, as well as the Minister of Cabinet Affairs and the Minister of Foreign Affairs, and requested that they inform the President as soon as possible that this incident would lead to strong reactions at UN headquarters. The sooner the government could find a way to regret the incident, the better.

Watching the televised local news, my staff who had witnessed the whole debacle were quite upset. The version presented did not chime with what they had experienced. Instead, Minister Makuei was now the victim, and the UN was accused of disrespecting him and denying him entry to South Sudanese sovereign territory. That same evening, the UN Secretary-General issued a firm statement condemning the incident. I met Minister Makuei in his office early the next morning, and used the opportunity both to refute previous allegations against UNMISS – providing evidence through facts and a series of statements – and to discuss what had unfolded the day before. I urged him to prevent a public dispute about the matter. But he demanded an apology from the UN. This was difficult. The statement by the Secretary-General made him even more furious.

President Kiir had scheduled a press conference later in the day, and I was worried that things might get worse. We contacted his spokesperson, explained our side of the story, and encouraged him to help calm matters down instead of escalating the situation. We did not succeed. A question had been planted with a journalist: he asked about the Bor incident, and the President immediately pulled out a piece of paper. What he read included the following:

> I think the UN want to be the Government of the South [Sudan] and they fell short of naming the chief of the UNMISS as the co-president of the Republic of South Sudan [...] And if that is the position of Ban Ki-moon, they should make it clear that the UN wants to take over South Sudan.[64]

This was not an off-the-cuff remark. This was deliberate, and not for the first time. I was shocked that the President could use such language again, in such a volatile situation, and especially since he knew better than anyone how far-fetched it was. It was a surreal accusation.

## Unleashing the beast

The following day, demonstrations started. There was every sign that the government had organized them; I knew that the security people often paid youngsters to take to the streets, at times with the help of members of the SPLM youth league.[65] The attacks were also very personal. In Rumbek, in Lakes State, flyers indicated that I was the girlfriend of Riek Machar. In other state capitals, posters demanded that the UN in general, and I in particular, leave the country. Many marched to UNMISS bases, handing over letters of protest. The media were full of allegations. And as before, South Sudan TV provided headline coverage. The President, for his part, used the opportunity to appear on Al Jazeera, saying that the UN was giving support to the rebels.[66]

UNMISS operations were severely affected. There was no point in protesting the accusations, for this would just escalate the tension. Security incidents were now involving both national and international staff. We had to move two senior staff from the mission area after they received direct personal threats and were deemed in New York to be at very high risk. Patrols were interfered with, movement was denied, and in Bor there were no fewer than four attempts by SPLA soldiers to gain forced entry into the base. Church leaders were encouraging us, however, and one said, 'It is better to be persecuted for saving lives than being praised for having allowed the killings to happen.'

I knew that the President was the only person who could stop the anti-UN campaign. I managed to schedule a meeting with him after five days through the help of senior officials concerned about the situation. At the same time, Gayle Smith, Senior Advisor to President Obama, a friend very familiar with the South Sudanese leadership, flew in. She told Kiir that this had to end; relations with the UN had to be restored. There was also concern for my personal safety. I told the President he was lucky that no UN staff member had been killed so far, and that he had to make a public statement, requesting respect for the UN, UNMISS and its personnel.

Up to this point I had been one of the few Special Representatives in a UN Mission without a personal security detail. The UN's risk assessment in 2011 had concluded that I did not need bodyguards, owing to my relations with the government and the population at large. Now, however, the situation had turned around. The risk was assessed to be very high, peaking around the time of the demonstrations. I was becoming a target. A full personal security outfit was requested with immediate effect.

The President issued a statement on 24 January calling on the security forces to ensure that the UN and foreign nationals were protected.[67] Things began to improve, though slowly, but the Mission was still largely confined to base due to security concerns.

Within a short period of time the number of civilians under our protection had reached 70,000 in the outlying bases, and continued to increase in Juba as well, although the security situation there had improved. We worried that weapons might be smuggled into the bases, increasing the risk of violence. After we got armed police from the UN's Stabilization Mission in the Democratic Republic of the Congo in late December, our military and police conducted frequent, unannounced cordon-and-search operations. We also used our de-mining team, with metal detectors, to search the bases and surrounding areas. In these operations very few weapons were found.

We shared the figures with President Kiir, relevant officials and later also in writing with the cabinet;[68] they were welcome to verify these through visiting the weapon storage facilities. But facts appeared to be of limited interest. The assumption was that our figures were wrong, and the allegations continued. One issue that infuriated them and the President was the fate of confiscated weapons. They expressed alarm that 'rebels' within the bases could attack our stores, take the weapons, and join forces to attack Juba. They insisted that all confiscated weapons were the property of the government, and should be handed over – not an unreasonable demand.[69]

For the UN this was problematic, however. Handing weapons back to parties at war was a difficult. Things would have been different if a ceasefire were holding, or a peace agreement had been signed. We were caught in the middle. Every time opposition forces took control of Bentiu and Malakal armed youths and defected soldiers demanded the return of weapons we had confiscated when they had sought our protection. On several occasions opposition forces surrounded our bases, and threatened to attack if they did not get their weapons back. But we held our ground. Angry field commanders of opposition forces thereupon denounced UNMISS for siding with the government.

The worst was yet to come. On 23 December the Security Council had approved reinforcing UNMISS with 5,500 troops. The Mission was dangerously overstretched, with close to 100,000 civilians under our direct protection. But despite support from New York headquarters and colleagues in other UN missions that had been requested to provide support, deployment was very slow. We should have had five more battalions within a few weeks, but six months into the crisis we had received only one-fifth of the promised number. We needed more police units as well. Much of the equipment we had been promised was also delayed. This was the UN at its worst.[70]

In early March the first units of a Ghanaian battalion were finally on the way. They were meant for Bentiu, where we were short. The troops would be flown in, but their equipment had to be transported overland. Owing to insecurity, however, we had already established a practice of shipping all arms and ammunition by air. On 5 March an UNMISS convoy on its way to Bentiu was stopped south of Rumbek for a government security check. Although this was a violation of the agreement on freedom of movement, UNMISS had nothing to hide; our people decided to open the containers.

All necessary permissions to bring in the military equipment had been given by the government, and the paper work was correct. Unfortunately, the transport papers for the consignment did not match the cargo. And weapons were found in a container labelled incorrectly. The Ghanaians had mixed things up. The following day more weapons were found. This was terribly embarrassing. I immediately called relevant ministers, including the Minister of Information, to explain the mix-up, and asked them to pass the message to the President. I also immediately sent a letter, explaining what had happened, to them.

A press statement was issued, to the effect that UN headquarters would at once launch a high-level investigation. We had hoped for a joint investigation, but the government in the end decided to launch its own. Ministers all seemed to understand that the incoming battalion had made an error. I was later informed that our early intervention had helped, and that there had been agreement among senior ministers not to make too much of the issue.

But the temptation to exploit our embarrassment was too strong for government hardliners to resist. On 8 March Minister of Information

Makuei, against the advice of some colleagues, went to Rumbek with a number of local and foreign journalists.[71] There he claimed that land mines and air defence systems had been discovered in the trucks, none of which was true. A new round in the propaganda campaign against the UN had begun. The story line across the country was that weapons were being smuggled into the country for the rebels, and that I was involved.

Rallies and demonstrations followed.[72] Government officials gave inflammatory speeches to a crowd in Juba, saying that South Sudan had been 'colonized' by the UN, that we were supporting the rebels, and that the international community wanted to replace President Kiir, who also was present at the rally. Vice President James Wani Igga similarly railed against the UN and the international community, saying the intention was to take over the country. Only a couple of weeks earlier I had been in his office with factual evidence refuting the allegations that had been circulated, and Wani Igga had offered to help clarify the issues and get our relations back on track. Now, instead, he did the opposite. The political winds were blowing in a different direction.

That the demonstrations were well organized was clear. The many large photo-shopped posters of me pointing a gun at people could not have been produced by private individuals or civil society organizations; they looked like ads for an action movie. This was pretty advanced, and had to have been orchestrated by elements in government. Slogans such as 'Why Hilda Kills People of South Sudan', 'Why Hilda supports rebels', and 'Why [is] UNMISS importing land mines' were further evidence.[73] This marked the start of a campaign that would run on South Sudan TV for the next week or so, with even more fabrications. The lurid comments by the President at the press conference of 20 January – which he later retracted – were also run again and again. The atmosphere was poisonous, and the security situation was worse than ever, for Mission staff, patrols and me personally.[74]

I knew that this was not about me, but about them, about South Sudanese fighting each other, and looking for someone to blame. It reminded me of an Equatorian saying a SPLA general once told me: 'Don't throw your spear against your own shadow.'

In January, when things heated up, I had created what I called my 'crazy file'. In this plastic folder I put printouts of the most far-fetched and ludicrous press statements and allegations. I included several speeches of government officials. Now I had new treasures for my file: the latest reports and pictures from the demonstrations. As I joked to my staff, if they wanted to put me on a poster with a gun, and send me worldwide on the news wires, it was good that they at least had used a decent photo.

What worried me much more were reports I received from the field and from friends with their ears to the ground. This time, I was told, many people really believed that the UN had been involved in danger- ously underhanded activity. In doing so, they said, we had made a very stupid mistake, so now we deserved the opprobrium we were getting. It was clear that the government's propaganda was beginning to have an impact.

Before leaving for New York and the Security Council on 16 March, I went to see the President again, and appealed to him to calm things down. He promised to issue a statement the following day, and I informed headquarters and the Security Council accordingly. They were waiting for it, and so was I. No statement emerged. This questioned the President's control and credibility.[75] The security threats against the Mission prevailed.

By the end of the month the results of the UN investigations were published. The UN's high-level independent committee had concluded that procedural mistakes had been made on several fronts, and was rightly critical of the Mission in this regard. But it concluded that there was no basis for the many other allegations that had been made.[76] Having returned to Juba I held a press conference on 3 April, sharing the findings and refuting 12 of the gravest allegations against UNMISS.[77] A fact sheet was handed out to the media, providing factual corrections one by one. Although the conference was packed, and a lot of media covered the story, the government-run SSTV was nowhere to be seen. This was the first time in my almost three years as SRSG that I had noticed its absence from a major press event.

A few weeks later, the UN findings were confirmed by the govern- ment's own investigations. Although critical of our handling of transport, it produced no evidence for UN support of rebels, for the charge about land mines, and the rest. The Government made no attempt to publicize these findings. Only later, when the Secretary-General arrived, was there coverage of this important conclusion.

## Despair: South Sudan in civil war

In mid January Uganda finally admitted its role in fighting alongside the SPLA. On the same day, its parliament passed a motion in support of the deployment. A few weeks later South Sudan's minister of defence, Kuol Manyang, confirmed publicly that South Sudan was paying the Ugandans,[78] whose role by then was significant. Their intervention was probably the main factor in deterring the opposition from advancing towards Juba, and in the absence of anything more to loot, the White Army temporarily withdrew.

While the situation seemed therefore to have stabilized in Juba and the Equatorial states, fighting continued in all three states of Upper Nile region. The taking and retaking of the state capitals, numerous times between January and April, involved untold human suffering, with abuses and atrocities on both sides. Women and children were severely affected and grave incidents of sexual violence became a regular feature. Villages were looted and burnt, and thousands fled their homes. Everywhere, civilians bore the brunt of the conflict.

The Government had also recruited Darfurian militia to help them in the fight against opposition forces.[79] When they entered Leer, Riek Machar's hometown, at the end of January, they burned most of it, including the hospital, in what many saw as solely an act of revenge. Forty thousand civilians seeking refuge there were again forced to flee. Later, places such as Mathiang and Duk north of Bor in Jonglei were subject to similar retaliatory destruction by opposition forces.

Among the worst incidents were attacks by both government and opposition forces on civilians seeking sanctuary in places of worship and hospitals in all three state capitals, with numerous witnesses reporting that armed men would enter, in some cases nearly every day, harassing and looting, targeting individuals on the basis of ethnicity, killing, abducting, and in some cases sexually violating women and girls. Gang rape also occurred.

The courage and dedication of individual peacekeepers and humanitarians was noteworthy. In Bentiu, UNMISS peacekeepers rescued hundreds of civilians hiding in churches, mosques and hospitals on several occasions during this period. They also did so under fire, while fighting was going on. Through the use of trucks they were able to transport people to safety. Humanitarian corridors were created to make sure that thousands were able to get to the protection sites within our base.

In Malakal several thousand people had sought refuge in St Joseph's Cathedral, Christ the King, two Catholic churches, and the Presbyterian church. We learned of desperate cries for help from Christ the King Church, through families calling us, worried that their women and young girls would be raped and killed. Several thousand people had sheltered there while elements of the White Army were roaming the town. I instructed our forces to assist. Beyond the hundreds extracted from the church, safe passage was provided to many more, and all came to the UNMISS base for protection.

## Broken promises – large-scale attacks

In mid April opposition forces moved in and again took control of Bentiu. Their behaviour this time proved even worse than before. On the 15th they attacked and killed several hundred civilians at the mosque. The killings seem to have occurred in several stages. Around mid morning, a score of soldiers accompanied by armed civilians entered the mosque compound and began shooting at civilians in the yard. People inside the mosque then locked the doors.

A second group of fighters then arrived. After extorting money and other belongings from civilians, they began shooting into the mosque. Multiple shooters were identified by witnesses, including one with a machine gun and one with an AK-47. Ethiopians and Eritreans were escorted out of the mosque, while the attackers especially targeted Darfurians. (It was well known that Darfurians had been active in fighting on the government side.) This was their revenge.

That evening, over 200 bodies from the mosque were reportedly loaded onto military trucks and taken to a place about a two-hour drive from Bentiu, in the direction of Kaljak.[80] UNMISS staff who arrived at the mosque later observed dead civilians outside, in the market place and along the road. The number of people killed might have been as many as 400, although this figure could not be verified. But a death toll of at least 287 civilians sheltering in the mosque was later confirmed. It was an abomination. Astoundingly, Riek Machar did not take responsibility.[81]

On the same afternoon as this horrific incident, an individual claiming to be SPLM 'Secretary-General of Unity State' came on the air of Radio Bentiu and stated, in a mix of Nuer and Arabic, that Dinka SPLA and allied Darfurian fighters had raped Nuer women, who were now pregnant. He called upon young men to meet at the SPLA's 4th Division headquarters the next day in order to do what the Dinkas had done to their wives and girls. Another individual, claiming to be acting Commissioner for Rubkona, later reiterated the same message and advised all Dinkas to leave Bentiu.

When I heard about this I recalled my visit, as Norwegian minister of international development, to the International Criminal Tribunal for Rwanda in Arusha ten years before. This was the first time media professionals had been tried for inciting ethnic violence, resulting in genocide. In a groundbreaking verdict, the so-called 'Media Case' in 2003 ended in the conviction of all three defendants. Broadcasting hate messages, inciting violence, was now a very serious crime under international law.

In Bor the situation had been largely stable for weeks when another shocking attack on the UN took place. On 17 April a group of at least 200 individuals, including Dinka youths, approached the UNMISS compound under the guise of a peaceful demonstration. They claimed that they intended to present a petition demanding evacuation of 'Nuer White Army youth' from the camp within 72 hours.

By this time, virtually all other groups had left the UNMISS base, leaving only Nuer behind. Several thousand civilians were under our protection. They were afraid to leave. Tensions were still high in the town, and both the local authorities and SPLA were uneasy with – and at times hostile towards – UNMISS and the refugees. Opposition forces had just retaken Bentiu, and many of the displaced were celebrating. This provoked the local population and Dinka youths.

As the group advanced on the UNMISS compound, they did not proceed to the main gate as expected, but instead moved directly towards where the displaced were located. Uniformed SPLA and National Police nearby did nothing. It was later clear from witness statements that those personnel knew what was going to happen. Local authorities had tried to talk to the youths before, but did not succeed. As the mob approached, they began to throw rocks and other objects over the walls, followed almost immediately by small-arms fire.

When the mob breached the perimeter of the protection site UNMISS military returned fire, from both fixed and mobile positions. Several attackers were killed, causing the mob to retreat and thus saving many lives. But due to unfortunate delays in response at least 51 people, almost all of them Nuer civilians, were killed in the attack, most of them within the UNMISS compound.[82]

The slaughter of civilians under UN protection was totally unacceptable. The President told me how angry he, personally, was. In a public statement on 20 April he condemned the attack,[83] and he later vowed to investigate the matter and hold perpetrators to account. But despite the fact that the identities of many individuals involved in the attack were known, no arrests have ever been made.

The events in Bentiu and Bor sparked international condemnation and fear that the fighting and ethnic killings would lead to a new cycle of revenge attacks that could get totally out of control. We arranged visits by the High Commissioner for Human Rights, Navi Pillay, and Special Adviser to the Secretary General for the Prevention of Genocide, Adama Dieng.[84] Following this came John Kerry, the US secretary of state,[85] and the Secretary General himself, Ban Ki-moon, on 6 May. The pressure on both sides increased. In many ways the events in Bentiu and Bor were a game changer for international engagement.

In a press conference with the Secretary General, President Kiir said that they had clarified 'misunderstandings' between the UN and the government. The investigations of the Rumbek incident had both concluded that the UN had made a mistake, but that there had been no intention of supporting the rebels. He said that he appreciated the efforts of SRSG Johnson, although I noted that he used the past tense. But the atmosphere changed after the Secretary General's visit, easing the tensions.

At the same time, our human-rights investigations had the highest priority. One of the main problems was to get a grip on the numbers and scale of killings in the various places where the worst atrocities had been committed. Our human-rights team had done their utmost to get such data and identify the mass graves that would have made possible more credible estimates. Difficulties of access arose, however, in particular when these were near military installations from which our staff were barred. Numerous localities suggested by witnesses were visited, but proved to be incorrect. In many cases witnesses pulled back at the last minute, afraid to help. Security conditions were in other cases not conducive to deeper investigation, given the risk of reactions by security forces.[86]

All this made it difficult to provide a credible estimate of the number of people killed, both in Juba and elsewhere. Also the AU Commission of Inquiry, later able to access more sites of mass graves with forensic expertise, had problems estimating the number of civilians killed in Juba and overall in South Sudan.[87] Without such verification, numbers would be only approximate. Several thousand people had been killed, but providing a substantiated figure beyond this was impossible. On 8 May we released as scheduled our UNMISS Human Rights Investigation Report covering the period 15 December 2013 to 1 May 2014. This concluded that there were reasonable grounds to believe that war crimes and crimes against humanity had been committed during the conflict, by both government and opposition forces. Further criminal investigations would be necessary to establish the scope of the violations and responsibility of perpetrators.[88]

That South Sudan, in only its third year of existence as an independent country, could be subject to international justice for mass atrocities perpetrated by its own leadership against its own people was something that none of the liberators, or international observers, could ever have expected.

## 'Crisis is opportunity' – to steal

But there were other things that also astonished some of us. While the country was in economic difficulties and more than a third of the population was in dire straits, the corruption problem increased. A Crisis Management Committee (CMC), established five days into the crisis and chaired by Vice President James Wani Igga, was eventually tasked with assessing the political, social, economic, security and diplomatic aspects of the conflict. It was also to assess the impact – and mitigate the effect – of the purported coup attempt, and was given wide administrative responsibilities. According to very credible sources, functions normally delegated to the Ministry of Finance and the Ministry of Labour and Public Administration, including even salary payments, ended up under the auspices of the CMC.[89] To some, it appeared to be a parallel government.[90]

There were thus ample opportunities for mismanagement and misappropriation of financial resources. Sure enough, after the worst fighting was over and the government had contained the situation in Juba and most state capitals, stories started to circulate about what the CMC had been up to. As a saying goes: crisis is opportunity. And in this case the crisis seemed to have been used to the maximum degree possible. The amount of money allegedly syphoned away was shocking, even for South Sudan. A government insider with knowledge of the committee's operations warned the President of 'a new Dura scandal'.[91] The figures reported from confidential sources went beyond most of the corruption scandals of the interim period. This information has been corroborated. Transfers were made directly to the foreign accounts of at least two senior government officials on the committee.

The sums involved were in the hundreds of millions of South Sudanese pounds.[92] People started to call the CMC the Corruption Management Committee. Indeed, it presided over a slush fund used for all sorts of things, from mobilization of new recruits to the customary servicing of patronage networks. While the latter was probable during a period of conflict, to ensure the loyalty of officers and men, the figures appeared to go far beyond that. Ironically members of the CMC appeared to be grabbing so much for themselves that a likely result of its work could be a deepening of the security impact of the crisis it was supposed to 'manage'. If, for example, the delays in salary payments to the SPLA could be attributed to this malfeasance, with the inevitable increase in disaffection, the CMC made an already tenuous security situation worse.

Whatever the case may be, the leadership hardly seemed to care. By this time South Sudan had received a total of US$19 billion in oil revenue between 2006 and 2014.[93] Now, they were using crisis money to cater for themselves. In April the deputy chairman of the committee, Daniel Awet Akot, said that some members were being investigated for misappropriation of funds, and that some had been suspended for misconduct. On 1 May President Salva Kiir, after proposals to abolish the CMC had languished for some time, finally dissolved it.[94]

But crisis was opportunity also in other ways. Most of the staff of the foreign banks had been evacuated by their embassies, some without time to put their affairs in order. One day an ambassador from a neighbouring country came to my office in shock and said: 'Our bank has been stolen!' I responded, 'A bank robbery? Here in Juba?' With the current security situation and crime levels it would not have been so surprising. But the ambassador continued, 'No, not in that way; the people in the Central Bank have taken it.' I raised my eyebrows, and he told me the most astonishing story.

A commercial bank from his country had been established in South Sudan with an investment of $7 million. It had registered with the Central Bank, got permission to operate, and filed the necessary paperwork. During the crisis, however, when the management and staff had been evacuated, documents were altered. The same thing happened to a foreign exchange bureau owned by the same people. The ownership of both the bank and the forex bureau was transferred to South Sudanese individuals. The ambassador was very discreet, and wanted to deal with the issue confidentially, so the story never reached the public domain. Whether he succeeded through quiet diplomacy in getting the bank and exchange bureau returned to their rightful owners I do not know.

The President did nothing to stop the misappropriation of funds or to hold culprits accountable. Although the CMC was dissolved, those alleged to be involved are still in office – apparently with their bank accounts intact. It is likely that the increasingly narrow political base of the President, who had alienated the leadership of the other SPLM factions, meant that his room for manoeuvre was very limited, and still is. He could not afford to confront or marginalize his remaining political allies, and now more than ever he would need to retain his networks of loyalty. Credible information indicates that large sums were paid to some individuals just to keep them in the fold.[95]

## The grip of fear: No return home

At the same time as resources were literally syphoned away from the government coffers, almost 100,000 people were still seeking protection in UN bases. With the rainy season upon us, things deteriorated further. In a very short time, the bases became swampy and flooded,[96] and people were literally forced to live amid mud and pools of infected water. One of our greatest fears was cholera. A major cholera epidemic would likely lead to thousands of deaths. Impressive collaboration had already developed with humanitarian partners, whereby they took responsibility for management of the protection sites within our bases and provided basic services. Cooperation in this regard was unique. The Humanitarian Coordinator, my deputy SRSG, Toby Lanzer, had experience in both peacekeeping and the humanitarian and development side, and so had I. This helped us navigate the very difficult political and operational landscape to ensure an adequate humanitarian response within our bases.

Humanitarian partners worked around the clock with UNMISS logistics colleagues to keep the UN bases cholera-free for a very long time. Following the first cholera cases, however, two government ministers blamed UNMISS and cited the experience of Haiti, where peacekeepers had been blamed for being the origin of the epidemic. This comparison was factually incorrect; the South Sudan outbreak began elsewhere, and our bases remained cholera free for much longer than other areas. It was also deeply unfair to all the UN staff and humanitarian partners who had worked so hard, day and night. As a response to this and a host of other challenges within our bases, new Protection of Civilian sites were established, allowing improvement in living conditions. As the fighting showed no signs of abating, most civilians were too afraid to return home and remained under UN protection. They were in a grip of fear.

The US had decided to pursue targeted sanctions against individuals alleged to have been involved in atrocities and human rights abuses.[97] The EU followed suit.[98] The conflict had at this time, according to established definitions, reached the threshold of civil war.[99]

How could this happen? And how could the conflict escalate so quickly, and seemingly take on a life of its own? To understand this, we need to take a closer look at the security sector.

It is the heart of the matter.

# 7

◆

# THE HEART OF THE MATTER: SECURITY

Weak security institutions always carry risk of internal fragmentation and instability. South Sudan, with its history of divisions within the liberation movement, and of militia and proxy forces supported by Khartoum, was especially vulnerable. While it was not unexpected that a political crisis could lead to violence, its speed, scale and scope can best be explained from within the security forces, dating back to 2005.

After the CPA, the leadership of the SPLM/A decided not to change the names of the Movement and Army. Retaining the SPLM – just as other liberation movements had done elsewhere in Africa, would also help to keep public support for the party. The SPLM was a strong 'brand'. Opinion polls confirmed this. Whatever their dissatisfaction on issues, the South Sudanese population's support was rock solid. For the same reason, 'SPLA' retained credibility for the majority of people. During the interim period, few trusted that the war was over, least of all the SPLA-commanders, and it made sense to nurture the perception that the liberating force was still in full operation.

Come independence, however, I raised the issue of a name change with the leadership. A 'South Sudan Armed Forces', for example, would signal a professional, conventional force. I was told that this would come only after the transformation process had been completed. While this can be seen as a 'chicken-and-egg' issue, hesitation might simply have been fear of weakening the SPLA and its capacity to mobilize the cadres and people. The legacy of the liberation movement was anchored in the bones of every SPLA soldier and officer. They would not easily let go of their identity as freedom fighters. And when the border clashes with Sudan took place, they seemed to be back in their comfort zone; they would readily leave the irritating paperwork of the office and set out for the bush.

Disturbingly, this appeared to be the case also when the civil war broke out in December 2013. As we have seen, it started within the SPLA, at its two headquarters in Juba. The former Sudanese Armed Forces barracks south of the city, at Giyada, close to Nyakoron, is the main operations centre. The other, expansive headquarters, with most of the administrative departments and the Ministry of Defence is at Bilpam. A huge statue of John Garang looms above them, in his SPLA uniform, reminding every visitor that the SPLA remains a liberation army at the core. It was in the shadow of this image that leaders of the SPLA ended up fighting each other in a cycle of violence that literally spun out of control.

To understand what happened in the security forces, we need to look at the CPA-period, the failed integration efforts, lack of reforms, corruption and the crisis itself.

## Ready to fight – again

After the CPA was signed, security was of highest priority. This was reflected in budgets, salaries as well as policies in relation to Khartoum. As late as in 2009, during a visit I paid to Juba, relations with the North were strained, and the issue of Abyei was particularly difficult. At a dinner Salva Kiir and three or four senior ministers made it clear that if the situation did not improve they would go back to the bush and fight. I was shocked. They did not need nice houses, cool cars and luxuries, they said; they had managed on nothing and could do so again. My attempts to remind them of the costs of war for their people and future generations failed miserably. In later discussions with members of the international community who believed the referendum or independence could be delayed, I recounted these and similar conversations. I knew that the alternative to enforcing the timetable in the CPA was not a better-prepared independence, but another war.

Budgets during the interim period reflected this. The overwhelming importance of external security justified the salaries of various forces. In 2006 a private was paid $125 per month. This was more than three times what his counterpart would have earned in the neighbouring Democratic Republic of the Congo. Officers of medium and high rank made between $2,000 and $4,000 a month. These munificent salaries – and politically important veterans' pensions – explain why, from 2006 onwards, the SPLA alone accounted for over 40 per cent of the national budget. The overall security sector took up more than this, of course, but no one knows the true figures. After the austerity budget of 2009, official figures showed defence expenditure at 37 per cent of the total. Capital projects, including major procurements, were a major expense too, while relatively little went to operations and training. By April 2011, when privates' pay had risen to about $220 a month,[1] over 80 per cent of the defence budget was allocated to salaries.[2] Ironically, soldiers' pay was often in arrears, which contributed to instability in the ranks.

During the interim period it seemed to be assumed that military strength was measured by the number of soldiers, rather than by capacity and quality. A trained, well-equipped and mobile fighting force would likely have been much more effective in defending South Sudan where, however, as indeed elsewhere, reductions in personnel could be politically risky.

The CPA called for each side's forces to withdraw from the other's territory, and for establishment of Joint Integrated Units (JIUs). The latter had been championed by Garang and First Vice President Taha, but with Dr John dead and Taha sidelined in Khartoum, fully integrated units were never formed. Instead, the JIUs were to a large degree used for placement of forces of least priority for both armies; many of them former militia.

Indeed, as we have seen, ten days after Dr John's death Salva Kiir took steps towards implementing his Big Tent strategy: offering militia leader Paulino Matip return to the SPLA under generous conditions.[3] With the Juba Declaration of 2006, thousands of militia from multiple groups reintegrated with the SPLA. While Dr John also integrated some militia and probably would have seen the strategic wisdom in such a process, sources agree that he would not have done so on such a scale and in the same way:[4] they claim that he would have been more concerned about the security risks and weakening the SPLA.[5]

Most militia leaders were from the Greater Upper Nile region, from Jonglei, Unity or Upper Nile State.[6] One very credible source later reported that the number of actual fighters integrated in 2006 was wildly inflated. According to information obtained in Khartoum, the true number of militia was 15,000, not the reported 50,000. 'We integrated shop-keepers, not soldiers', he said.[7] And while most militia leaders re-joined the SPLA, a few remained defiant;[8] reintegration efforts continued through 2014.[9] In numbers, Nuer predominated, and this affected the overall ethnic composition of the Army. These multiple reintegration processes depended on promotions in rank and economic incentives, nothing more. There was no reconciliation through dialogue, no settling of grievances.

Khartoum had always used cash and supplies of arms to buy loyalty and support from disgruntled local leaders and ethnic communities resentful of Dinka leadership of the SPLM/A. Now, it appeared, the South Sudanese had entered the market. Sudan's former National Security Chief Salah Abdallah even complained in 2010 that southern militia had become so overpriced that Khartoum could not afford to compete![10] Left unsaid, but widely understood, was that leaders who had changed sides several times in the past were liable to do so again. The loyalty of these cadres to the SPLA – and to the President – was weak and opportunistic.

Reintegration of the militia had another worrying aspect. The intake of thousands of militia seemed to render the Army a social welfare system, taking care of old cadres and veterans. Edward Lino, a long-time SPLA commander, clearly frustrated by the 2013–14 crisis said that the SPLA had 'never been a robust united force' since it 'started to incorporate militia' in such 'appalling numbers'; 'each soldier was almost free ... to choose' his commanding officer: 'there was nothing called "SPLA" It was divided and shredded into tribal formations adhering to individual commanders ...'.[11]

While he may have exaggerated, the essence of Lino's statement rings true for those who have closely monitored the poorly managed integration process of the SPLA.

## Lost window for SPLA reform

After the Juba Declaration in 2006 a strong reform programme was formally adopted. The goal was a more professional national army, and a multi-ethnic Presidential Guard, trained together, streamlined and cohesive. The SPLA Commandos were formed as multi-ethnic units and trained to conduct special operations.[12]

Initial plans of creating a multi-ethnic Presidential Guard soon faltered. The President himself distrusted such an arrangement from a security perspective.[13] In the end he, Riek Machar and Paulino Matip all had their own personal security details.[14] Matip's Nuer forces were never properly integrated.[15] Even cabinet ministers did not want to relinquish their numerous handpicked bodyguards, and in effect a system of personal militias was accepted at the top.

For the SPLA as a whole, it was hoped that the example of the Commandos could be replicated. Plans were drawn up for amalgamating former militia into various units of the Army. But the process of absorption and reintegration across all units, training tens of thousands of soldiers, was so challenging that it soon met major capacity constraints. Senior officers were very concerned. In 2008 the SPLA leadership made serious efforts to stop additional reintegration; further dilution of the SPLA without progress in amalgamation and training would only serve Khartoum's interests.[16] 'We were buying peace, it was a disaster to us,' one officer said.[17] But soon Salva Kiir and Riek Machar pushed for further integration of militia, lest Khartoum use those remaining outside the fold.[18]

From 2005 to 2011, adhering to impartiality between the two parties, the UN peacekeeping operation did not assist in this area. Programmes for demobilization, disarmament and reintegration (DDR) which were part of the UNMIS mandate, were not linked to such reform efforts, for example as an alternative to integration to the Army. Analysts have since pointed out how resource constraints prevented SPLA training plans from being implemented, and not least inhibited the successful integration of the other armed groups.[19]

At this time, support from key international players was also inadequate. Regional neighbours had the manpower, but not the resources, while it was the opposite with the donors. Only very late in 2007 and in 2008 did key donors start focusing on some types of SPLA reform programmes. But the window for defence reform and transformation is usually open for only a short time in post-conflict countries. And so it was in South Sudan. The motivation had been there at the outset, but the momentum was soon lost.

There were three important factors in the delay of reforms. One was relations with Khartoum. The need for a cohesive and effective fighting force in the event of another war had been a major incentive for early reform at the outset. By 2008, however, people in the leadership had started feeling that the CPA might be more sustainable than they had expected. One of the greatest incentives for SPLA reform therefore appeared to have been weakened. The second factor was the scale of the challenge. Multi-ethnic training and reorganization of units, as well as establishment of a professional command structure required more capacity than South Sudan could muster.[20] The third factor was directly related to economic benefits. Budget allocations within the SPLA were not transparent, and allowed misappropriation of funds with impunity. Reforms would necessarily imply cleaning up the system; there were no offsetting financial incentives to do so.

## 'Retail' politics – corruption within the ranks

Corruption within the SPLA was not new. During the civil war there were no salaries, so cadres found other solutions, both for the Movement and for themselves. In such situations, food was like money, and could be traded for most other things, including arms. The World Food Programme needed, for example, one of the most extensive and advanced security operations in the humanitarian world to protect their convoys. Some comrades could acquire much wealth, and the top leadership of the Movement was at times characterized as a 'military aristocracy'.[21] Indeed, leading cadres themselves could in moments of lucidity admit that their generation was a 'lost case' when it came to management of financial resources; only a new generation of SPLM/A leaders would be able to set things straight.

## Ghost soldiers

After the signing of the CPA, opportunities for malfeasance were particularly lucrative as the military absorbed large numbers of armed elements, in the absence of proper registration processes. In 2006–7 the SPLA was estimated to employ 140,000 people, but the 'core' – soldiers – numbered only about 68,000.[22] As independence approached, personnel numbers increased, with a spike during the last months to as many as 207,000.[23]

Credible sources have indicated that in December 2013 the SPLA's payroll comprised approximately 230,000 soldiers. However, experts who did audits could not identify more than 170,000.[24] At the same time, the government's estimate for DDR also seemed unrealistically high.[25] To date, the SPLA has not undergone a proper registration of all forces under its command. The SPLA's own internal audit suggested a minimum of 40,000 'ghost soldiers' whose salaries were either used to pay operational costs or pocketed by commanders.[26]

I discussed this in January 2012 with late Prime Minister Meles Zenawi of Ethiopia, with whom I had many conversations since the days of the CPA negotiations. Meles cautioned against going too far too fast: 'The SPLA is not an army', he said. 'It has been there to keep people "salaried".' He worried that major clean-up efforts would backfire. It was a difficult dilemma. As Alex de Waal puts it:

> Military commanders were both rewarding and defrauding their followers, by putting them on the payroll and cheating them of their full pay. For both patronage purposes and to lessen the dangers of the mobilization of the aggrieved, commanders assembled military units on tribal lines with the aim of maximizing personal loyalty. This is one reason why three attempts to institute a centralized roster of SPLA soldiers were thwarted.[27]

The opportunities for graft were also very significant. In the absence of proper procurement procedures, shady deals were easy to do. The international arms market is itself famously corrupt, and thrives on opaqueness.[28] Both the seller and the buyer have an interest in secrecy.

It is rumoured (but not verified) that the first opportunity for big kickbacks came in 2006, and related to acquisition of Ukrainian T-72 tanks, a deal worth hundreds of millions of dollars.[29] More Ukrainian tanks were purchased in 2007–8, and in 2010 several transport helicopters.[30] Most of those interviewed aver that kickbacks were involved in all these deals, although a central source denies.[31] A deal was also made in 2009–10 to procure 120 trucks at approximately $120,000 each. There are two versions of how many were delivered, 39 and 60. At least half of those paid for were therefore never delivered, the difference in cash having been syphoned away.[32]

In 2008 the Southern Sudan Government purchased air defence systems from Ukraine, a deal worth between $116 million and $199 million (the figures vary with informants).[33] The price should have been much lower. According to credible accounts, about $71 million was deposited in Kampala and shared by three prominent members of the South Sudanese leadership. The air defence systems were never made operational, however, as some parts were not delivered, reportedly requiring an additional investment of another $40 million.[34] When the border clashes with Sudan took place in 2012, other members of the leadership were furious that the SPLA had not acquired such deterrent capacity, despite the major investment that had supposedly been made several years before.

But the incentives to continue with the status quo were overwhelming. While reports and papers were produced, such as the White Paper on the SPLA in 2008 and the SPLA Act 2009, and decisions were made on critical issues such as enlistment age, service limits, retirement age, and pensions, there was little implementation. Regarding DDR almost nothing was achieved during the interim period.[35]

At the same time, defence spending continued to increase. In the 2013 audit of 2008 financials, only seven of 40 SPLA divisions reported payroll figures as required, even when repeatedly instructed to do so.[36] Only in 2013 was the Auditor General given formal permission to review the overall accounts of the SPLA, but in early 2016, when this book went to print, nothing had happened.

## Nuer sway within the SPLA

From 2008–9 onwards, the Big Tent approach became increasingly controversial. There were tensions between senior commanders and former militia leaders who were inflating the officer corps and being promoted above them. Some of these latecomers had been in the service of Khartoum during the struggle, and it seemed unfair that they should do as well as or even better than comrades of long standing. Observers had started to refer to 'rent-seeking rebellions',[37] by which commanders flip-flopped between Khartoum and the SPLA, trading their loyalty for a higher price in rank or funds. Their grievances might have been genuine, but so were suspicions about their manoeuvres, which called into question the whole Big Tent approach.

SPLA commanders blamed Khartoum for wanting 'the SPLA to be diluted.'[38] But the President consistently held the line on integration, convinced that this would consolidate peace and prevent Sudan from using militias to fight proxy wars against the SPLA and the South. Although there had been efforts at creating multi-ethnic units,[39] some former militia commanders appeared to retain old networks that could be mobilized at short notice, or even kept former soldiers in close proximity. Primary loyalty continued to run through patronage or ethnic identity or clan and sub-clan affiliation. This led to an army fragmented and porous in structure and command, which could easily fracture along ethnic lines. Inflation of ranks was another factor; the SPLA reportedly had more than 700 generals.

Furthermore, the Big Tent approach left the whole integration process to the military. The political avenue was not used to address grievances, including ethnic concerns. As Edward Thomas says: 'The SPLA was given the unmilitary task of providing a framework for national identity and national reconciliation.'[40]

Some SPLA soldiers granted leave to visit families ended up joining local units for convenience and local affiliation rather than returning to base. Some units lost many soldiers in this way, and therefore started in turn to recruit locally. This happened, for example, to the 4th Division, which was originally based in Eastern Equatoria, and composed mainly of Dinka and Equatorian soldiers and some militia. After it was transferred to Unity State, many soldiers drifted home, prompting local recruitment.[41] The ambition to develop a competent multi-ethnic force in Unity, the critical oil-producing state, slowly gave way to a mostly Nuer force of uncertain quality.

While no one would share information about the ethnic composition of the SPLA, it is reasonable to assume that the perceived Dinka domination had declined and the proportion of Nuer risen significantly. Early in 2014 senior government officials claimed privately that former militia had constituted a majority of the Army by December 2013, and that that was at least one reason for the SPLA's problems on the battlefield.[42] Upon further analysis, that argument seems overblown. Crude but independent estimates indicated that approximately 40 per cent were likely to be Nuer, with the rest consisting of Dinka (probably about 35 per cent), Equatorians and others.[43] Many of the Dinka and Equatorians were regarded as core SPLA, having been at the centre of the struggle throughout the civil war.

Whatever the case may be, the SPLA was less effective as a national army than it had been as a guerilla or liberation force. According to security experts, deterioration occurred primarily in 2006–7, when thousands of militia forces came in and efforts to integrate and train them properly faltered.[44]

## International efforts – too little, too late

International support for reform came late, and focused on infrastructure and technical issues rather than on developing a multi-ethnic and cohesive force through systematic training at scale, revision of command structures, etc.[45] A comprehensive strategic review early on would have helped, if supported by important donors and regional governments.[46] While the UK and the US supported efforts to reform the SPLA, they did so late in the day. Pressure for a SPLA Transformation and Research Directorate established in 2010 was one such intervention. But it did not work effectively. External experts appeared not to understand the SPLA's internal dynamics well, many cadres preferring a different approach.[47] As we have seen, the inability of the European Union, including the UK, to provide direct support to military training because of sanctions against Sudan was one of the reasons.

After independence more efforts were made, and UNMISS tried to get an overview of the support provided to the SPLA now that it was a national army.[48] The Mission was not mandated to play a role in this regard, and the US and the UK continued as main contributors. We were, however, mandated to support security-sector reform and had the main responsibility for assistance in DDR. Coherence among all stakeholders and coordination with other security-sector interventions were all the more important after independence for security sector reform to succeed.[49] But in practice the exchange of information was limited, which was symptomatic of hesitation to coordinate. Regarding support from other sources, and in particular from the region, no government wanted to share details. There was no systematic transparency or complementarity of effort.

An ambitious programme was drawn up under the leadership of the DDR Commission and with support from us and others, but without real interest within the SPLA leadership. The programme was anyway too costly and rather unrealistic, and not adequately adapted to South Sudanese conditions.[50] No consideration had been given to alternative approaches such as a pension fund and resettlement. Full registration of the SPLA was still on hold; transformation plans were adopted, but not implemented.[51] By the time of the crisis, in late 2013, I had started discussions with security ministers on how these plans, including a total revamping of the DDR programme, could be moved forward. We were also discussing how security-sector coordination could be improved.

There was no high-level commitment. The leaders of both Government and Army seemed to prefer a more comfortable (and lucrative?) route, and hesitated over politically risky decisions. A country's security situation is also often an impediment to reform, whether external or internal.[52] Only in the absence of violent conflict can reforms, such as increasing civilian control of the military and implementing DDR, be pursued successfully.[53]

That the war with Sudan might re-erupt at any time could have reinforced the urgency for transformation of the SPLA to a professional national army. But the security threats and tensions were immediate and now had the opposite effect. They were a disincentive to reform and DDR. Experience immediately following independence, with military overflights, bombings and ground incursions provided a shaky basis for reform efforts, let alone for full transformation. Violence in Jonglei and militia activity in the border areas also complicated such efforts.

## Other security forces – rule by gun, and not by law

After the signing of the CPA, the Southern Sudan Police Service (operating under different names after independence), the Prison Service, the Wildlife Service and Fire Brigade were also established. In their development many similarities with the SPLA were evident.

John Garang wanted all the cadres of the SPLM/A to have some kind of job after the peace agreement had been signed. In 2004, as Norway's minister of international development, I brought in my friend Ashraf Ghani, who had then completed his tenure as finance minister of Afghanistan, to advise Garang and the leadership on critical transition issues. Ghani was adamant that peace could best be consolidated by ensuring that those who had participated in the struggle got some kind of pay or pension, at least for a transition period.[54] This advice backed Garang's strategy. The decision was soon made to provide all the old cadres, including veterans, with a salary by establishing various uniformed forces. It was a way of buying peace.

There was a clear hierarchy among the new services. To put it crudely, the perception was that first-class soldiers remained in the SPLA, second-class went to the police, and the rest ended up in the Prison Service, the Wildlife Service and the fire brigades. Transfer was not a matter of choice, and many soldiers found themselves demoted and unhappy. A number of militia were also integrated into the police after the Juba Declaration of 2006; several thousand police were transferred from the North and similarly integrated. Disabled veterans were formally assigned to the various services.

A clear illustration of this tiered system was the difference in salaries. By 2012, the disparity in salaries at all levels was significant, with SPLA colonels paid three or four times more than the National Police of comparable rank.[55] Other terms of service were different, too.[56] The Army carried much more prestige, both within the Movement and among the population at large. This led to disaffection in other security services.

## Other security forces – same challenges, same 'diseases'

Development of a competent police service was fundamental for Southern Sudan, a cornerstone for the rule of law in the semi-autonomous region during the interim period. In the territories under its control during the liberation struggle the SPLA had been police, investigator, judge and prison warden, with no independent oversight or checks and balances; the local commander was everything. Establishing a judiciary and police independent from the military was a major step.

But the nascent police service was incapable of dealing with internal security challenges, and the SPLA was forced to assume responsibility on many occasions. Internal security and protection of civilians and their property was not the military's forte, with rather bad and heavy-handed management of security challenges and of inter-communal violence. But police primacy could be affirmed only when the capacity of the police service had been adequately developed.

Having very limited education, if any, and no training, new recruits to the police were also poorly motivated. Senior police officers told me that many recruits still saw themselves as soldiers, 'on loan' and awaiting return to the SPLA. This feeling was even stronger among former militia.[57] That most security services still operated with military ranks, titles and hierarchy did not improve matters. Their uniforms, while different from the SPLA, were still military in design. This added to the feeling that they really belonged in the Army, and that their current situation was temporary.

With this background it is unsurprising that bad habits of the SPLA showed up, and even multiplied, in the other services. Not only was there less command and control and less discipline, but police personnel were also frequently accused of serious misconduct, drunkenness, unnecessary force, assault, bribery and extortion, all, of course, in an environment lacking transparency and accountability.

A case in point was a shooting incident in the troubled Tri-State area of Unity, Lakes and Warrap on 1 February 2012. After communal fighting had resulted in 78 deaths, a meeting of local authorities, state police leaders and relevant security services of Unity State took place at the Mayendit County authority's compound, to prevent revenge attacks and a cycle of violence. UNMISS's State Coordinator for Unity, several United Nations Police (UNPOL) and other staff were also present.

After the meeting started, four pick-ups arrived with armed men who started shooting indiscriminately. Uniformed personnel joined in. There were later rumours that soldiers from the SPLA's 6th Division had joined the fighting, which continued for two hours. An estimated 50 people were killed, including many civilians. While some saw this as a revenge attack, others discerned ethnically motivated violence within the forces. UNMISS staff were caught in the crossfire, and one UNPOL officer was wounded. Only after several hours was one of our helicopters able to land to rescue them. Government officials told me that the whole thing was a misunderstanding: one side thought the other was attacking them, when no one was. Be that as it may, the incident certainly illustrated problems of command and control in the uniformed services.

While reform plans were written up for the security services, in particular the police and prisons, resistance from within was significant. Transformation of the Southern Sudan Police Service (SSPS) would ultimately involve at a minimum compiling accurate numbers and adjusting the size of the force.[58] The same was true of the Prison and Wildlife services. While these services offered less scope for manipulating procurement contracts, there were ample opportunities for corruption in relation to payroll.

Critical measures were therefore delayed for years. Former UNMIS focused more on monitoring and less on capacity building. There was not much donor engagement, although the UK and US provided support. The SSPS was still embryonic, and could have been steered in the right direction. Observers regard this as a missed opportunity.[59]

It was only ahead of the elections in 2010 that a major reform effort was made. While UNPOL estimated the total number of police at 33,000 – but at most 60,000 as 'useful and deployable'[60] – efforts were made to train new recruits at Rajaf. As many as 6,000 recruits – men and women – were sent for training. Unfortunately, living and training conditions were bad, and accusations of human-rights violations soon ensued, forcing the UN Mission and donors to withdraw support.[61]

Recruitment continued to the SSPS and increased throughout 2011. Transformation of the SSPS to the South Sudan National Police Service (SSNPS) was imperative.

## Transformation of the South Sudan Police

In late 2011, after independence, the South Sudan National Police Service was assumed to have approximately 50,000 personnel, although we knew of many 'ghost' names on the lists. Some personnel even kept two uniforms, and claimed salaries from both the police and the Army.[62] Many officers in charge in rural areas were former militia who had been integrated into the SPLA after the Juba Declaration of 2006.

It was also only now, under the new minister of the interior, Alison Magaya, supported by UNMISS Police Commissioner Fred Yiga, that the registration process began. They made interesting discoveries. One police officer turned out to be a bull. A grandmother in her 70s had been listed as a captain – and a man; she claimed entitlement to the salary of her long deceased son. Colonels who were 12 years old were discovered, too – people had just added their children to the lists.[63] The registration process was completed under the new Inspector General of Police Pieng Deng, who was appointed in January 2013 and was very supportive in this final phase. In an excellent example of what was possible, UNMISS had assisted with correcting the payroll, in cooperation with UNDP. The SSNPS had in fact 35,633 personnel. More than 16,000 'ghosts' were identified, a number that reportedly translated into tens of millions of dollars, money that was now reallocated for equipment and infrastructure.

Getting the payroll right was only one important step. Now, a major transformation process was needed. The new inspector-general of police requested the support of UNMISS and UNPOL to assess the state of the police and provide data to help accelerate the transformation process. The UK's Safety and Access to Justice Programme, in collaboration with UNPOL and other partners, had already led important strategic reforms, and these combined efforts ultimately helped to change mindsets.

On the basis of the newly registered personnel, the joint assessment included an analysis of literacy and language capacities and competence levels, disaggregated by rank, and identified five areas critical to the transformation of the SSNPS, including training gaps, capacity inadequacies, and institutional deficiencies.[64] (When police cannot read the Penal Code, or check procedures for arrest, major problems ensue.) The assessment, made public in early 2013, revealed that only one-third of the police were literate in English, and one-sixth in Arabic. The rest were illiterate in all languages. In Unity and Jonglei as many as nine of ten officers were illiterate. And there had been a huge inflation in rank: the ratio of non-commissioned officers to constables was almost 1:1.

The assessment identified major challenges and recommended reforming the whole SSNPS, its legislative framework and operational systems (command and control, accountability standards, a standardized training system, etc.). The Service adopted all the recommendations, as did the new interior minister, Aleu Ateny Aleu, in August 2013. Soon thereafter, a Training of Trainers course began for 300 university-educated police personnel. The process of streamlining command-and-control structures commenced. In early October, all ten governors and the cabinet were briefed and approved a roadmap for transforming the SSNPS.

The director of the Prison Service approached UNMISS for similar support. During 2012–13, in line with the Mission's mandate regarding the rule of law, we drew up strategic plans for the Service that for the first time included significant reforms. Early on, the minister of wildlife conservation and tourism, Gabriel Chansong Chang, had also requested UNMISS help in registration and cleaning up the payroll, but we had to complete the Police process first because of limited resources. The minister went ahead anyway, and was under serious threat of violence several times from his own staff and officers, illustrating the challenges such transformation processes could entail.

Reform of the entire National Security Policy in 2013 showed considerable promise. Contrary to prior efforts, donor countries, their experts, UNMISS, and advisers from the African region worked together in advising the government, under the leadership of the minister of national security, Oyay Deng Ajak. Through extensive consultations in all ten states and with civil society and international stakeholders, a truly inclusive process was completed, across party lines, and facilitated by the Mission. The draft National Security Policy that resulted was locally owned and, in its last draft, seen as one of the most advanced in Africa.[65] It would ensure coherence across the various sectors, under the overall supervision of a National Security Council.

Before the crisis broke out, the policy was about to go to the President and cabinet, but it was stalled thereafter, presumably by the new minister of national security, Obote Mamur Mete, and the national security directors, who appeared to prefer a different approach. National Security legislation was instead presented for parliamentary approval but was, as we shall see, almost totally different from the pre-crisis draft.

With the violence in Juba in December 2013, the window of opportunity for reforming the SSNPS from top to bottom was closed, and challenges in the security sector increased exponentially. All security services subsequently divided along ethnic lines. The institutions were too weak; command-and-control lines too porous; and ethnic identity too strong for any of the security services to resist the tidal wave that now rolled over them.

## Playing with fire – other developments prior to the crisis

In the absence of a robust army and transformation of the other security forces, the situation was very fragile. With a significant part of the Army comprising poorly integrated Nuer, the loyalty of the SPLA to its commander-in-chief, the President, a Dinka, would be in doubt in an escalating crisis. For the President, this was a risky situation. For others, this might have been seen as an opportunity.

In 2012–13 other factors came into play. After the events in Heglig in 2012, when clashes on the border prompted South Sudan to occupy this oil-producing area, the government called for a national mobilization of able men. Each state recruited 5,000 soldiers. Governor Paul Malong of Northern Bahr El Ghazal recruited more than his share. After the mobilization was cancelled, he wanted to retain the recruits in a training camp at Pantiit in Aweil North. Numbering as many as 14,000, they were all young Dinka and came primarily from the Governor's state and neighbouring Warrap, the President's home state.[66] They were called 'Mathiang Anyor', a Dinka name for predator cat.[67] The force was not funded by the SPLA, since it was not part of the Army, but was supplied by the Governor and the Bahr el Gahzal community with their own resources.[68]

On 14 February 2013 Salva Kiir issued a decree placing 117 senior officers on the paid reserve list. These included two lieutenant generals, two major generals, and over 100 brigadiers.[69] Some had been serving in the civil administration; in fact 8 of 10 elected governors were ex-military.[70] This, on top of the removal the previous month of some 35 senior officers, constituted the biggest shake-up in the Army leadership since independence. Those in civilian positions remained in office. Although seemingly a dramatic move, it had been long in the making. According to the SPLA's highest officials, the relegations were the work of a committee, not 'political' in any way, but part of the reform effort.[71]

When it was proposed that a number of new recruits from Pantiit should reinforce the Presidential Guards in Juba, some senior officers in the SPLA and Ministry of Defence preferred reinforcement through internal redeployment. They suspected a hidden agenda.[72] Paulino Matip's forces, which had been officially under the auspices of the Presidential Guards, but had largely remained separate under his control, were divided after his death in 2012. Some were reportedly integrated into the SPLA proper, while others remained in the Presidential Guards. According to most informants, this meant that Nuer were now a majority in the Guards.[73]

Paul Malong and President Kiir appear to have agreed that a number of 'Mathiang Anyor' would be transferred to Luri, the SPLA training centre outside Juba, and become Presidential Guards. This was not the first time the Governor had stepped in to enhance the security of the President. In 2005–6, when Kiir had been concerned about plans for multi-ethnic presidential security, which included taking on a number of Garang's bodyguards, Paul Malong and General Salva Mathok, Kiir's relative and deputy chief of staff in the SPLA, had stepped in and recruited closer to home.[74] Now, as danger threatened, Malong appeared to have taken action again. Tensions with Riek Machar were increasing, Malong worried that Nuer would dominate the Presidential Guards, and he wanted to restore balance with a large number of new recruits. When these were transferred to Luri, outside normal SPLA deployment plans,[75] one senior security official said, 'We smelled a rat.'[76]

## 'Dot Bany' – rescue the leader

While the first batch of recruits sent from Pantiit in Northern Bahr el Gahzal to Luri was a battalion of 800, senior officials at the time said that the total was three battalions.[77] A smaller number appeared to be trained to become Presidential Guards,[78] with others to be assigned to different duties in the Army. Major General Marial Ciennoung, the commander of the Presidental Guards, told another senior official that those graduated to join the Tigers later in 2013 were 700, almost a battalion.[79] A number of interviewees claimed that the number was higher; others lower. Whatever the case may be, the special recruitment and training arrangement for Luri, as well as ethnically based loyalties, probably combined to strengthen the protective forces around the President, whatever duties they were assigned.[80]

The recruitment for the Presidential Guards at Luri led to tensions with the Army leadership and senior officials in the Ministry of Defence, strains that increased further when funding from the SPLA also was requested.[81] It is not clear how the training of the recruits at Luri was funded. Some say the President had a separate security fund for miscellaneous purposes,[82] or through fungible off-budget funds of National Security; others claim that fundraising efforts among the Bahr el Ghazal community helped; and others again that funds were diverted from the SPLA 5th and 8th Divisions, leading to delayed salary-payments.[83] It might be that money came from all these sources.

Recruiting and training extra forces for the President's protection was probably seen as an additional security measure at a time when tensions within the SPLM were rising. Prior to the rescinding of the Vice President's delegated powers, Paul Malong was quoted as saying that he had sufficient forces to prevent Riek from ever leading the country. If Riek did not relent, Malong said, 'Mark my words: I will push Riek and the Nuer to the other side of the river.'[84] Whether this was just 'tough talking', is not easy to say. There were no other witnesses, which has made corroboration difficult. However, on two later occasions Malong made similar comments to others, increasing the likelihood that the information might be credible.

After Riek's statement on 4 July in the *Guardian*, that 'he was ready for a fight', things only got worse. Some thought he was preparing militarily. A very senior figure immediately confronted him.[85] Riek responded that by 'fight' he had meant only a political showdown, not a resort to arms. Despite encouragement to publish a clarification, however, he let it go. A number of people around the President seemed to take Riek at his (literal) word.[86] The many Nuer in the Presidential Guards now only added to concern.

The forces trained at Luri to become Presidential Guards got special Dinka names, used interchangeably: 'Dot Bany', meaning 'rescue the leader' and 'Gel Bany' ('protect the leader').[87] Sources say that a close confidant of Salva Kiir, former Chief Justice Ambrose Ring Thik, gave the Luri forces these names, either when they were brought to Luri,[88] or on 16 December, as the crisis erupted.[89] In 2012–13, and together with a few community leaders, he had reconvened the so-called Dinka Council of Elders, which in the 1990s in London had served as a focal point for resistance to John Garang. Now consisting mainly of well-connected people from Warrap, Kiir's home state, they resented the political threat posed by Riek Machar.[90] They often met in the President's house.[91] Sources are clear that the group planned a strictly political confrontation with Riek.[92] The question remains whether they had links to others from the Bahr el Ghazal network in the security apparatus discussing what to do if things got out of hand – and whether such discussions included mobilization of the 'Luri boys'.

Having picked up rumours from various sources, I raised questions with the President and ministers. We were told that although the first recruits were from the Bahr el Ghazal, the expanded Presidential Guard would be multi-ethnic. While there was arguably no need for expansion, most African presidents tend to have extensive personal security, so the repeated explanation was plausible. It proved not to be true. I followed up with security ministers, and got the same response. We should have pressed further. Towards the end of 2013 Paul Malong was spending more and more time in Juba, away from his home state.

The Presidential Guards were easily identifiable from their tiger-striped uniforms. The Imatong Tigers were the unit Salva Kiir first commanded in 1983. As we have seen, his code name during the struggle was 'Tiger', hence the name of the Presidential Guard and the choice of uniform for the press conference on 16 December. The Luri boys, or 'Dot Bany' were provided with different uniforms, also easily recognizable, but were still under the Tiger Battalion's command.

The Luri boys' arms and ammunition appeared to have come from contractors other than those supplying the SPLA, and most likely arranged through National Security. Their newest weapons may have come from China or Israel.[93] The arrival of weapons from China led to speculation that something had been planned. However, these imports had been ordered long before the 2013 crisis.[94]

Most 'Gel Bany' spoke only Dinka. They were active during the fighting in Juba on 16–20 December, and easy to discern from their distinct uniforms and insignia.[95] Both Tiger and Luri forces have been identified as perpetrators during a number of 'sweeping operations', house-to-house searches, targeted killings and atrocities against civilians.[96] While some other units of the security apparatus tried to contain the situation then, others went on the rampage. Numerous eyewitnesses noted that many soldiers involved in the atrocities knew only the Dinka language. A well-placed source in the SPLA claims that Chief of General Staff James Hoth Mai was sidelined at this time, and that Paul Malong commanded units directly, both during the crisis in Juba and later. This involvement included circumventing normal command lines, directly commanding lower ranks and officers in the field.[97] This has not been fully corroborated.

A number of credible sources with intimate knowledge of the events before and during the crisis avow that the SPLA leadership was not involved in any way. It appeared, however, that a network of old and retired commanders outside the formal SPLA command structure, all Dinkas originating from Northern Bahr el Ghazal and Warrap, immediately turned up and started giving orders.[98] Four names were highlighted to me by very credible sources early on; later firmly corroborated through a number of interviews.[99] These generals are believed to be in the inner circles of power. All of them had been put on the reserve list or relieved of their rank earlier in 2013. The AU Commission of Inquiry quotes Defence Minister Kuol Manyang referring to 'a shadowy "group [that had] organized itself as *Rescue the President*. It killed most people here [in Juba] – from 15th to 18th. It was even more powerful than organized forces."'[100]

It seems clear that the SPLA senior command was not involved. James Hoth Mai, SPLA Chief of General Staff and a Nuer, was immediately engaged in trying to contain the violence and regain control in the capital and other affected areas.[101] He worked closely with Paul Malong, who had already relocated to Juba and SPLA headquarters, where he remained throughout the crisis. Some of those alleged to be involved in directing the most violent operations during 16–18 December in Juba had reputations for brutality.[102] They were also regarded as close to the President. The above-mentioned four had already (on 20 December), three days into the crisis, been reinstated in their former military ranks along with some Nuer commanders, presumably so the latter would not defect.[103] That this happened can be seen as public acknowledgement of their performance during the crisis.

While there have been many accusations that the killings in Juba resulted from elaborate advance planning of almost genocidal intent, supported by the fact that Juba had been divided into sectors,[104] this has been impossible to substantiate. The capital had earlier been divided into sectors by the security agencies and forces in response to rising crime rates. The question is rather whether killings and atrocities were planned with the use of Dinka forces, whether from Luri, the Tiger Battalion, or the SPLA, all combined, or whether such forces got totally out of control.

On 12 December, three days before the crisis erupted, Oyay Deng, Pieng Deng and Taban Deng were invited to dinner at Governor Paul Malong's house in Juba. Conversation centred on the political crisis. Paul Malong did not want Riek Machar to contest the chairmanship at the SPLM Convention (which was still expected in April or May 2014). He wanted Salva Kiir to stand in the 2015 election, and reportedly said that Riek could take over in 2020. If Riek refused, there would be fighting, he stated. The discussion was animated.[105] On the 15th Malong went to urgently see Oyay Deng before noon, saying that he should abandon the others and join the President and that the division in the Movement would last a long time.[106] Oyay rejected the offer. Paul Malong appeared to be aware that something was going to happen.

At around 7 that evening I met one of the security ministers at his house. I was very concerned about the developments at the National Liberation Council, and wanted him to talk to the President about trying to reconcile with the dissidents. He seemed amenable. In my presence, the minister got a call from security headquarters; he was needed urgently. He later told me that the security organs of the government knew that something was going to happen that evening.

The findings of the subsequent UNMISS human rights investigations suggested 'coordination and planning' had taken place in relation to some violent incidents.[107] According to the African Union Commission of Inquiry:

> The evidence thus suggests that these crimes were committed
> pursuant to or in furtherance of State policy [...] [proving]

[...] the 'widespread or systematic nature' of the attacks. The evidence also shows that it was an organized military operation that could not have been successful without concerted efforts from various actors in the military and government circles.[108]

Did civilian leaders and military commanders instruct forces to carry out attacks on Nuer civilians? This can only be clarified through independent criminal investigations.[109]

## Political rallying turns violent

What was the situation on Riek Machar's side? Was there planning, as some have alleged, for a military coup? There had long been fear that Riek would raise a rebellion, and there was unease whenever he ventured to areas in the Upper Nile region. UNMISS was confronted several times with rumours that we were going to transport him to certain places in one of our helicopters. But we followed UN rules, which stipulated that only travel that could be justified by the mandate of the Mission could be facilitated; Riek did make requests for transportation after leaving office, but since these were usually not justifiable they were rejected. That this matter went all the way to the President, and that he personally confronted UNMISS leadership, showed how tense the situation was.

After Riek Machar and his colleagues were dismissed, stories had begun circulating in Juba about the possible acquisition of arms and equipment by his followers. The allegation was that Taban Deng Gai had started operating when he returned from Dubai, about a month after he was ousted as Governor of Unity State, that is, in June 2013,[110] before Riek Machar was dismissed. Such activities supposedly increased from September 2013.

There was nothing new in rumours like this. Machar had already been accused at least eight times of planning a coup, Majak D'Agoot six times, Oyay Deng four, etc.[111] In July 2012, when Riek Machar, Oyay Deng, James Hoth Mai and Majak D'Agoot were all at the airport to bid the President farewell on one of his trips, a security officer became suspicious when they huddled in a car. Their desire for air-conditioning was soon inflated into coup plotting. Security forces were put on high alert, and checkpoints were established all over the capital. It took almost two weeks to calm things down.

South Sudanese have an incredible ability to spin rumours, and not least, conspiracy theories. As with their Sudanese brothers in the north, the security and intelligence apparatus are among the worst at this. Competition between services results in a race to be first to the top with the latest – often unverified – information, thus feeding a sense of paranoia. I experienced many examples of this unfortunate tendency, leading at times to faulty decisions.

To what extent this played out in the case of Riek Machar is difficult to tell. His movements and conversations were monitored. A lot of his activities seemed suspicious to security officers and government officials, including his speeches to the Nuer community, and two senior officials cautioned him in October and November 2013.[112] SPLA commanders of Nuer origin were often observed coming to see him. Machar himself claims that all such meetings were purely political, and had nothing to do with plots or suspicious activity.

As early as June, in Dubai, after having been dismissed as Governor, Taban Deng Gai had told a comrade in reference to the President that they 'must do something'.[113] Several people heard him talking this way.[114] One credible source puts Taban Deng in Riek's house very often during this period, and 'pushing very hard'; Riek in turn was overheard several times saying that he did not want a repeat of 1991,[115] and that Taban Deng was a 'loose cannon'.[116]

Several sources in Khartoum, including within the security apparatus, and others within the SPLM leadership refer to contacts with Taban before the crisis. Apparently, he was asking for military support through a business colleague with close links to military intelligence in Khartoum.[117] I was unable to interview Taban about this. Interestingly, Khartoum rejected these requests, at least at the time. Most inter-viewees confirm that Taban was mobilizing. The extent to which he was trying to start a rebellion through acquiring weapons is disputed, however.[118] Such attempts could also be part of an effort to rally support in the event that things deteriorated further and a confrontation was unavoidable. In other words, these are not necessarily evidence of a plan to oust a President from power, but may have been preparations in case of conflict.

It is interesting that friends and foes alike – excepting members of the current government – agree that Riek would not try to orchestrate a military coup, not least because of his limited following in the military and even among the Nuer. But a number of them are less certain about Taban. One has said, 'Taban is the best mobilizer, and can be dangerous.' Two people close to the President had warned him before his dismissal as Governor, recommending that Kiir reconcile with him for this reason.[119]

Taban Deng and Riek Machar are related by marriage, and were on the same side during the 1991 SPLA split and for years later, though at times they ended up in different factions. In 2013, having both been ousted from government positions, they reconciled and were natural partners.[120] But we cannot know the extent to which Riek was aware of, and agreed with, everything his comrade was up to.

One source claims that Taban mobilized some Nuer commanders, and particularly officers who were angry about having been taken off the reserve list and were with the President.[121] I have not been able to verify this. Sources also claim that Taban and Riek 'did the numbers' with regard to the overall percentage of Nuer among SPLA commanders and potential backing in the event of a full confrontation.[122] As one senior leader in the Movement from the mid eighties onwards explained to me:

> There is no political powerbase in the SPLM without military power. Whoever takes the SPLM, takes the SPLA. The distinction is not there. This implies that you cannot rally political support only. In the SPLM you will automatically also rally military support. The commanders discuss politics. Any political division within the SPLM will eventually lead to a military division. There is no culture to resolve conflicts politically. Hence, they will in the end be resolved militarily.[123]

This statement is closer to the truth than some may like to believe. It was certainly how Taban and Riek's activities were interpreted on the government's side. Meetings with other members of the SPLM Political Bureau were seen in the same light. One prominent minister used the military term 'regrouping' to describe the frequent meetings at which planning for press conference and rallies took place, which was seen by him and those close to the President as discussing 'how they could remove Salva'.[124] Several key players on the security side told me that they had evidence of coup plans, but when I asked to see it none was forthcoming. Nor was any such documentation produced during the ensuing court case, which probably means that such plans were never discovered.

Rapid mobilization of Nuer commanders on 16–18 December has been taken as evidence of pre-arranged plans. Peter Gadet has been accused of advance mobilization of the 'White Army'.[125] While prior contacts cannot be ruled out, they appear unlikely, as we shall see. Nuer commanders may, however, have interpreted political rallying as a prelude to military action. A message to several commanders from Taban along the lines that Salva Kiir was trying to humiliate Riek Machar, and that the Nuer should not accept this, could have mobilized some of them. According to some sources, such messages were in fact conveyed.[126]

Furthermore, at about the time of the 6 December press conference, Taban Deng contacted Nuer members of the Presidential Guards and told them that he, Riek, and others might be arrested, and that they should do what they could to prevent this.[127] Sources say that during the week of 10–15 December, Taban spun a rumour that the force at Luri was being deployed to disarm Nuer Presidential Guards.[128] Apparently, he was also talking to former bodyguards of Paulino Matip. Several sources from different camps, including two very senior SPLA officers, independently state that rumours of Riek's arrest from 6 December and the 'impending disarmament of the Nuer' escalated the situation. They see this as a major trigger for what happened.

On 15 December at around 3 p.m. a junior officer in the Presidential Guards telephoned Taban Deng with the news that some 120 armed Dinka soldiers (one company) had just arrived at their barracks and made inquiries about the armoury.[129] The Guards on duty thought they were about to be disarmed and arrested. According to two eyewitnesses Taban Deng, on the telephone, urged calm and asked a third, a senior general, to do likewise.[130] Taban was in Oyay's house at the time, with Majak and a few others. They requested a top official of one of the security agencies who also came by to alert the President of a serious problem at the barracks and ask for the President's intervention. He promised to do so. None of the three interviewees are sure whether this was done.

Following the arrival of the armed Dinka soldiers (presumably from Luri), it seems clear that no one at the top level did in fact act to reassure the Presidential Guards that they were not under threat. The exact sequence of events during these early evening hours is uncertain. Later, however, there were a number of phone calls between Taban and Nuer Guards. The security apparatus has referred to transcripts of these conversations as evidence of plans, and they used some in the later court case. These include Taban calling about preparedness, access to arms, and late Sunday evening also directing action. However, from my copies these are selected quotes, in summary form, and hence less accurate.[131] As the AU Commission of Inquiry also says, 'the evidence does not point to a coup'.[132]

The same SPLA sources allege that the reckless warnings by Taban of their likely arrest triggered the whole situation among the Presidential Guards.[133] One account states that a Nuer soldier tried to grab a gun from a sentry, and the sentry himself was killed by another. This action might have been precipitated by an attempt to access the Armoury or by a desire to defend it. A second officer was also shot.[134]

Whatever the case may be, the atmosphere was like a powder keg, and things got out of control. Dinka and Nuer soldiers started shooting at each other.[135] Late evening, following reports from Nuer Presidential Guards, Riek Machar gave the order to break into the armoury.[136] Both Dinka and Nuer soldiers took guns from the stores.[137] Fierce fighting ensued between soldiers loyal to Salva Kiir and those loyal to Machar. Military intelligence officers were sent in to try to stop the fighting. The source says, 'it was just chaos; no one knew what the other was doing'.[138] The fighting then spread to Bilpam. The Nuer forces took more weapons and uniforms than their own, as they had done elsewhere, reconfirming – in the minds of the President's people – that a grand scheme was under way.

While the most likely explanation for the outbreak of violence on 15 December was a series of incidents that spiralled out of control, two individuals, one on each side, Paul Malong and Taban Deng, appear to have played important roles in prompting them. They also appeared not to have been entirely unprepared.

## SPLA collapses like a house of cards

While the first shots resulted from an escalation seemingly caused by risky decisions and reckless behaviour of a few people, the fighting then exploded. Why was it not controlled?

No message of calm was sent out from either of the two leaders, and the President's press conference at 11 a.m. did not help. With their subsequent actions, government forces fuelled the fire. As they ventured into the neighbourhoods on 16 and 17 December, where the targeting and mass killings of Nuer were perpetrated, and as forces 'cleared' areas presumed to contain Nuer males and civilians, the message was clear to everyone. And as we have seen, during the first few days that followed, key Nuer commanders defected, together with tens of thousands of Nuer soldiers, many of them former militia. The SPLA divided along ethnic lines.

With Juba in turmoil, Bor falling to the opposition, and Bentiu and Malakal following suit, the feeling was of an army imploding, collapsing like a house of cards. The fear that even the capital might be attacked was real. During these critical hours ethnicity trumped everything. Whatever loyalty Nuer soldiers may have had to the SPLA as an institution, or to its commander-in-chief, quickly dissipated. And the forces expected to be loyal to him were fewer in the Greater Upper Nile region than anywhere else.

The most important mobilizing factor was the scale of the killings in Juba. I discussed this later with several of Riek Machar's commanders; some had been at SPLA headquarters at the time, others in the field.[139] They all said the same: they had had no contact with Riek or Taban Deng prior to the crisis. If there had been such contact from Machar's side, they said, they would not have considered joining him. It was the killings of their own that had mobilized them. 'When the Nuers were killed like fish, children, women, elderly, and officials and the military were targeted and killed; that is when we realized – this is a tribal war.' One commander said that it was desperate phone calls from relatives and others in Juba that made him and his force defect and march towards Malakal to fight. He had no contact with Machar for weeks.[140] 'We mobilized ourselves,' several said.

Sources with intimate knowledge of the SPLA agreed: Riek's authority over Nuer commanders was limited.[141] 'What Salva Kiir has done, not even the Arabs would do against us; we had to fight back,' one said. A Nuer politician put it differently, however: 'This is the war of Paul Malong; Salva Kiir was just dragged into it.'[142]

Ethnic loyalties were a strong motivator, but personal feelings of marginalization and betrayal probably played a part, fuelled by the desire for revenge. It is also likely that many ex-militia simply followed their old commanders. Former militia leaders defected during the height of the crisis in order to fight the Dinka, the President and the SPLA. This contributed to the surprisingly speedy escalation of the fighting and the SPLA's losses in the first ten days of the conflict. Reality far surpassed any scenario anyone might have entertained.

The SPLA units most vulnerable to defections were in Upper Nile region and dominated or commanded either by former militia or by Nuer. UNMISS estimated the number of soldiers who defected at 40,000. Since the majority were in the Upper Nile region, the effect on the SPLA was dramatic. The 1st Division in Upper Nile State, the 4th Division in Unity, the 7th Division in Upper Nile (and in particular the units on the west bank of the Nile) and the 8th Division in Jonglei were the most vulnerable, losing much or even all of their strength and a great deal of equipment. Some commanders might have been killed if they had not changed sides: General James Kuong, the commander of the 4th Division in Unity State, is an example; other anecdotal evidence was difficult to verify.[143]

Forces loyal to the President now had to be moved in from other parts of the country. Recruiting from the regions least affected by conflict resulted in a more Dinka dominated SPLA than in earlier years. The Big Tent had collapsed. It had failed also as a strategy to consolidate peace. The way it had been implemented led to the opposite. Absorption onto the SPLA payroll did not mean integration. With virtually no attempt at addressing grievances politically or personally, loyalties remained with old commanders. This contributed to the domino effect that led to the implosion of the Army.

This development was not of Riek Machar's making. A very senior SPLA official at the time says, 'It is Salva who has mobilized for Riek.'[144] Once events were in motion, however, Machar willingly and enthusiastically took command of an opposition movement defined more by its grievances than by its membership. He soon took the decision to capitalize on an upsurge of anger and revenge, using the opportunity of massive mobilization. For angry Nuer commanders, their own retaliation and Machar's decision to topple the President were motivation enough to spur further action. The AU Commission of Inquiry nevertheless concludes that there was an element of coordination 'that hardly seems possible without forethought' also on the opposition side.[145]

The director of SPLA military intelligence, General Mac Paul Kuol Awar helped clarify this important issue. When he gave evidence in the trial of four SPLM detainees, he denied that a coup plot had existed and that this had been the reason for the outbreak of fighting in December 2013.[146] Mac Paul was the only major witness not from Kiir's Bahr el Ghazal inner circle, and his testimony undermined what was widely perceived as an already weak case. Interior Minister Aleu Ateny Aleu, expected to be another key witness for the prosecution, chose not to testify.[147]

## The security dilemma

The Government and the newly minted SPLM/A-In Opposition (SPLM/A-IO), thus blame each other, whether for a coup or for ethnic cleansing or worse, claiming that their reactions only were defensive responses to aggression of the other. In my thorough research on these hypotheses, I have not found enough evidence to indict either side for sole blame.

Many commentators have rejected both sides' stories and focused instead on two other explanations for the eruption and escalation of civil war. On the one hand, there has been a tendency to resort to simplistic ethnic explanations, reminiscent of former colonial powers' description of events in tribal terms: this is a war between the Dinka and the Nuer. On the other hand, the focus has been on the two intransigent leaders, whose selfish ambitions and greed for power have driven the country to total disaster. Neither explanation holds water.

First, the crisis was primarily a political one, and not driven by ethnic agendas. Ethnicity became a factor exacerbating the crisis, first through events in Juba, and later through revenge in other places in the Upper Nile region. Ethnicity and its representative structures ('tribes') emerge as the consequence rather than the cause of conflict.[148] And while greed in terms of power and resources most likely played a part in escalating the political crisis, it does not explain the explosion of violence.[149] While these factors probably contributed to the obstinacy of both leaders and prolonged the crisis, they do not answer the question of why the mutual escalation was not stopped.

In an environment without a culture of resolving conflicts politically, no mechanisms within the party to do so, and a polarized environment and virtually no credible and impartial mediators, the stakes were high. Instead of choosing the route of reconciliation and compromise, each side counted on the other to succumb to political pressure through a showdown. Preventive action was taken, particularly by Paul Malong and Taban Deng, in the expectation that the other side would resort to violence. What originally could be characterized as a political crisis very quickly became a security crisis.[150]

Another explanation for these developments may be found in what has been called 'The Security Dilemma' in an article by Barry R. Posen:[151]

> what one does to enhance one's own security causes reactions that, in the end can make one less secure [...] All fear betrayal [...] they are unaware that their own actions can seem threatening [...] [nevertheless] [...] The nature of their situation compels them to take the steps they do.

These actions can trigger a preemptive response. Posen applies this idea to situations where central authority collapses in new states that are governed by a multi-ethnic leadership. Indeed, those who emerge as leaders of any group and confront the task of self-defence for the first time will doubt that the group identity of others is benign. The result is that groups see each other only as threats, and will 'arm' – militarily and ideologically – against each other. These dynamics can produce incentives for preventive war, and can even lead to a drive for security so great that it produces near-genocidal behaviour.[152]

Salva Kiir and his closest allies were convinced that Riek Machar and his network were preparing to act militarily. There are no traditions in South Sudan for violent military coups; more likely would there have been a mutiny, with those loyal to the President losing control. This probably explains the increase in Presidential Guards through the Luri forces, loyal to the President largely on ethnic grounds, and the military recruitment. With the press conference on 6 December, the security forces in Juba were on maximum alert, and Presidential Guards and other units were, according to some sources, armed at critical points all over town. There had been unconfirmed reports about a potential showdown. They remained at this level in the run-up to the meeting of the National Liberation Council.

While we international observers noted increased military presence, the ethnic identity of the soldiers was difficult for us to detect. Sources have indicated that the armed soldiers deployed in town were primarily Dinka.[153] At this particular time, tensions between the President and Riek Machar were at their peak. As one could expect, Dinka domination among the forces in the streets created concern among Nuer commanders and soldiers in the barracks.

The President and his allies were so suspicious of Riek Machar and his capacity to mobilize the Nuer that they took precautionary measures. As a credible Sudanese source with intimate knowledge of the dynamics at the highest levels in Khartoum said to me a few months into the crisis: 'The people around Salva Kiir have a security mentality; Juba has become just like Khartoum.'[154] The behaviour of Taban Deng probably gave them reason to believe that something was afoot. Antagonism between the two factions, and historical grievances between the two communities were so great, that every move was interpreted in the worst possible way. 'They must assume the worst, because the worst is possible.'[155]

As a credible source has said, in the SPLM you cannot rally political support only; you will be assumed also to rally military support. Any political rift within the SPLM will imply a military rift.[156] Engaging in risky behaviour, as all the factions of the SPLM did at this point, was very dangerous at a time when Juba was like a tinder box. Already, Juba was rife with rumours that the Dinka and Nuer were going to fight.

It is likely that both sides made their own calculations of support in the Army, should things deteriorate. This might explain the additional Dinka forces deployed to Juba, and particularly to the Presidential Guards. On Machar's side, calculating the numbers of commanders presumed to be on 'his side' could for example be used as political pressure against the President and chairman of the SPLM at the right time, and especially when well planned. What is clear, however, is that such calculations in themselves can contribute to escalation. One can lose control over what follows. In a tinder-box environment, any incident can light the fire. And in Juba on 15 December an incident in the Presidential Guards did.

Exactly what happened during the night of 15–16 December can only be clarified through independent investigations. The same is true of what lay behind the targeted ethnic killings, massacres and atrocities by Dinka security forces, in particular 16–18 December.

## Game changers in battle

More thorough analysis will also be needed to achieve full under-standing of how and why the violence spread beyond Juba. One simple but important factor must be mentioned: the seasons. If these develop-ments had happened at another time of the year, it is unlikely that we would have seen the scale, speed, and duration the conflict reached. That the crisis erupted when the dry season had just started made it possible for fighting to spread quickly.

Evoking unavenged killings is one way of mobilizing a clan or ethnic group in Nilotic cultures. After the massacres in Bor by Riek Machar in 1991, which killed at least 2,000 people, no one had been held accountable. Nor had there been revenge. '1991' was a terrible nightmare recurring in the minds of many SPLA cadres. It was perceived as a mobilizing factor for the violence in Juba during these December days, and a reference point for a lot of public rhetoric, from the President's speech to the National Liberation Council on 14 December, in the press conference on 16 December, and in other commentary from leading government figures during the crisis. It was repeatedly said that Riek was at it again. This accusation may itself have incited ethnic violence. Whether this was intended or not is difficult to tell. That '1991' seemed to have become code for targeted killings of Nuer among some Dinka forces seems nevertheless to be the case.

I discussed ethnically motivated killings with President Kiir many times, expressing grave concern. He agreed, underlining that he had not used ethnicity as a mobilization tool against the opposition. Kiir stated that if he had done that, the whole of the Dinka of the Bahr el Ghazal would be on the move, and there would be total havoc in the country.

This was a conflict fought by government forces against a rebellion, and nothing else, he claimed. But the Dinka recruits from Luri who were devoted to his protection, and the rhetorical use of '1991' were still important mobilization factors on ethnic grounds. Revenge was an important reason for the massive response on the Nuer side, as we have seen.

Together, the personal grievances and the gravity of atrocities seem to have constituted a groundswell of movement from below. Riek Machar certainly took opportunistic advantage of this. But he was not himself the game changer. To quote one prominent Nuer:

> What happened in Juba, the killings, changed everything with all the Nuer. Riek was not a popular figure, and would normally not command support from all the factions of the Nuer. But with the killings in Juba, and the fact that Riek himself almost got killed by the Government forces, the sympathies went in his direction, and the Nuer factions joined in and rallied behind him.[157]

The scale, speed and duration of resistance cannot be explained by Machar's actions. There is no way he would have the personal gravity and unifying force among the Nuer to make this happen at his own merit, or the capacity to orchestrate such enormous opposition, leading to massive defections in Bor, Unity and Malakal in just a few days.[158] As he was fleeing for his life from the SPLA, whose units were literally hunting him down, he was not in a position to direct multiple actions in far-flung locations – even if he had wanted to.[159] According to several credible sources, Machar only narrowly escaped government forces outside Juba and was almost ambushed by the SPLA elsewhere within the first 48 hours.[160]

The Bul Nuer commander of the 8th Division in Jonglei State, Peter Gadet, was assumed to play a more important role.[161] When Bor fell so quickly to opposition forces it was presumed that he had orchestrated it in advance, in cooperation with Machar. Gadet's absence from the commanders' conference in November had even then been seen as suspicious, and he had to be persuaded to come to Juba.[162] Government sources also refer to reports from the commander in Waat indicating that

Gadet engaged in suspicious activities there; it was later assumed that he had started mobilization of the White Army at this time.[163]

Others familiar with Gadet's thinking say that his reluctance to come to Juba resulted from his escape from an ambush the previous April. He feared another attempt on his life.[164] But there was no love lost between Gadet and Riek Machar,[165] and Gadet and Taban Deng were also mutually hostile.[166] It must be noted, however, that on 20 November 2013 Taban and Gadet are alleged to have had a private meeting in the margins of the commanders' conference. I have not been able to confirm what they discussed, but afterwards Taban started to talk again about arrests, and of the likelihood that Gadet would be arrested.[167]

Nuer members of the Auxiliary Police were the first opposition forces to enter Bor town, and their actions were reportedly decisive in determining what happened later. Their move appeared to be spontaneous, as UNMISS reports also indicated. According to eyewitness accounts, Gadet went to Bor to try to calm things down.[168] It was only later, after the events in Juba on 16 December, that he decided to switch sides, team up with the police, and take over the town.[169] Whether this was part of a plan or a spontaneous move, as several of Gadet's colleagues – as well as foreigners in touch with him at the time – claim, is now not possible to verify.[170] According to the account of people in Riek Machar's convoy, and Machar himself, driving to Bor – after a very hazardous journey, much of it by foot, – developments in the state capital were as surprising to the former Vice President as to the government.[171] Whatever the case may be, upon arrival on 24 December Machar met Peter Gadet, Hussein Maar (the Nuer former deputy governor of Jonglei, who had sought refuge in the UNMISS base), and a number of other government officials. Hussein and the former County Commissioner Goi Yol joined Riek Machar's convoy heading north from Bor. In Mathiang, the home village of Kuol Manyang,[172] they were caught in an ambush on 25 December, and only narrowly escaped before proceeding to Gadiang.[173]

While Gadet's actions were important, it appears that the government's forces' own actions precipitated reactions that united the Nuer behind Riek Machar, and made it possible for him to assume command. But as one of Machar's old compatriots from the Nasir faction (who did not join him now) says: 'The mistake Riek made was to take over a rebellion he didn't plan. And when they committed atrocities, he was responsible.'[174]

There were two branches of the White Army, one of the Lou Nuer in the north-western counties of Jonglei State, and the other in the south-eastern parts of Upper Nile. Although the White Army originally were Nuer armed youths mobilized by Riek Machar in the early 1990s, it was not owing to his efforts that they gathered now. According to credible sources, the attacks by Murle armed youths in the county of Twic East, as well as in Lou Nuer areas in past months, had led to a major mobilization of Lou Nuer youths and the White Army at the beginning of December.[175] One source, a young Lou leader, says that many armed youths were already gathered at Gadiang when Riek Machar arrived. They were several thousand, and more were on the way.[176]

From Riek Machar as well as from other sources, it has been made clear that extensive discussions took place with the White Army leadership over several days.[177] On command and control, discussions were difficult, but Gadet got them to agree to his military tactics despite their reluctance.[178] The White Army leaders in Jonglei also agreed to refrain from attacking women and children and innocent civilians. That these arrangements helped initially seems clear,[179] and more so than with the armed youths in Upper Nile State.[180]

I doubted that Machar would be able to control the White Army and warned him about the prospect of their attacking civilians, and women and children in particular.[181] The opposition leader seemed unrealistic about his capacity to keep them in check, and claimed that they would behave as they moved southwards towards Bor, which at this point was part of the plan. The mobilization of thousands of angry armed youths and the White Army was a factor to be reckoned with, and soon the stories began that their next target would be Juba. For them, loot was a major motivator beyond the desire for revenge, and it did not take long before codes of conduct were violated.

## Unexpected allies

Foreigners made contingency plans for worst-case scenarios for Juba, including evacuation of all – or all non-essential – staff. Some had already completed evacuations in late December, others followed suit.

For UNMISS it was critical to remain, albeit with adjusted numbers, but the Mission revised its own plans and prepared for the worst.

The speed and scale of the violence and the mobilization of the opposition led the government to request support from the outside.[182] The prompt deployment of the UPDF on 19 December, to Juba and beyond, seemed to be based on the SPLA's fear of imminent defeat. While Ugandan protection of strategic installations in Juba received IGAD's blessing, the engagement of the Ugandans in Bor and surrounding areas was more controversial.

Without the UPDF deployment, including its air capabilities, it is not clear what would have happened. It was a game changer. The most decisive factor from a military perspective was the Ugandans' use of heavy artillery, which effectively dissuaded Peter Gadet and the White Army from advancing on Juba.[183] Ugandan support therefore gave the government time to stabilize the situation and regain the initiative. Following the attacks on Bor and operations in some other places, but with no supplies and nothing more to loot, the White Army returned to their respective communities. White Army elements operating in Upper Nile State similarly withdrew, at least for now.

Two other factors, not as decisive, were still important. Two militia leaders who had recently been reintegrated into the SPLA remained loyal to President Kiir. This was quite surprising, given the history of their relations. Both the SSLA militia leader Bapiny Monytuiel and the commander of the Shilluk militia Johnson Olonyi signed an agreement with the government only six or eight months prior to the crisis. The former SSLA's control over important areas in Unity was essential for the government's ability to hold the state. The new Governor, Joseph Nguen Monytuiel, had broken ranks with Riek Machar, with whom he had previously been close, and joined the government in April 2013. It is likely that he did his utmost to ensure that his brother, the newly integrated SSLA militia leader Bapiny, also remained on side. Defection by the former SSLA could have had a huge impact in Unity State.

Complicating the alphabet soup, the South Sudan Democratic Movement and Army (SSDM/A), Upper Nile faction, often called Johnson Olonyi's forces or the Shilluk militia, accepted the President's amnesty after significant pressure, not least from the Shilluk *reth* (king), in June 2013. But while Olonyi returned to Juba, his troops stayed in the field as negotiations of the terms dragged on.[184] The group remained loyal to the government for more than 16 months into the conflict, until an incident perpetrated by the SPLA caused them to jump ship. What then ensued, the loss of Malakal to the opposition, showed what might have happened if Olonyi's forces had joined the opposition earlier.

If the White Army had moved on Juba, and the militia groups had gone over to the opposition, the SPLA could not have held. This would have been a dramatic turn of events. That this did not happen, and the UPDF remained on South Sudanese territory, no doubt prevented havoc in Juba. But it also permitted the conflict to continue unabated. It was prolonged not only with the availability of arms on both sides, but mobilization through the ethnic card, with stereotyping, scapegoating, dehumanizing rhetoric and creating a sense of victimhood through 'reproduction' of grievances.[185]

In the battlefield, the two sides continued to pursue a tit-for-tat approach, often avoiding direct confrontation, focusing on control of strategic locations in the Upper Nile region. Civilians bore the brunt. As so many times in South Sudanese history, the security forces, whatever their allegiance, did not act as protectors of their people, but as predators.

That innocent South Sudanese should go through these nightmares once again, after they had finally won their independence, was bad enough. But never before, even under Khartoum's leadership, had anyone seen such atrocities committed by South Sudanese against South Sudanese. Never before had the towns of Bor, Malakal and Bentiu seen such destruction. Thousands and thousands had been killed. Never before had the sanctity of churches, mosques and hospitals been violated in this way, not even under attacks by Khartoum-recruited militia.

On Independence Day two years before, the President had said:

> We the people of South Sudan have experiences what it is to be a refugee. We hope that this has been our last war and that our people will never again have to cross our borders in search of security.[186]

By July 2014, 1.5 million were displaced. Hundreds of thousands were refugees in Kakuma and across the Ethiopian border and, even more shockingly, in Sudan.

The country was also at risk of breaking another record, of seeing the worst famine in its history unfold. Predictions were clear: in 2014 close to 4 million people were estimated to be in urgent need of food aid[187] because of this manmade disaster.

The question was: would any of the antagonists be ready to come to an understanding? What were the incentives for agreement? Would they – in the end – be willing to put their people and the future of their country, and peace, above their own personal interests?

# 8

◆

# WAGING PEACE IN
# SOUTH SUDAN

Kofi Annan proved right when he said that waging peace is always much harder than waging war.[1] IGAD mediators and leaders of neighbouring countries knew this long before December 2013. In this chapter we will examine how the circumstances of the conflict that erupted then have complicated matters since. For making peace does not take place primarily at the negotiating table. The lack of a clear strategy for building the new nation fostered the very forces that pulled it apart. It is this lesson that now must be learnt before new efforts to wage peace have a chance to succeed.

On 19 December 2013, as the horrors of war recurred, the region's foreign ministers arrived. The first IGAD delegation led by Ethiopia's Tedros Adhanom landed in the middle of chaos. Counterparts from all the member countries, including the foreign minister of Sudan, Ali Karti, accompanied him. They hoped to intervene before things escalated, to 'nip it in the bud', so to speak. I briefed them on the situation, and warned of the animosity between the leaders and the gravity of the problem.

General Sumbeiywo, President Kenyatta's envoy, with whom I had worked on the CPA, had arrived the day before. During the liberation struggle, when Sumbeiywo was chief of general staff of the Kenyan Army, he had assisted Salva Kiir personally on several occasions and knew him well. Sumbeiywo and I discussed how to calm the situation and get the detainees released; Riek Machar had already indicated unwillingness to talk to the government unless they were all set free.

This major stumbling block had to be overcome. Sumbeiywo and I quietly worked on face-saving options. He, rather than I, sat with key players on the government side; because of their expressed suspicion of UNMISS support for Riek Machar. I could talk to the President and a few others, but not government hardliners. Sumbeiywo, on the other hand, had no access to Riek Machar, with whom I was in touch by phone. Sumbeiywo kept the Ethiopians, chairing IGAD, informed about our efforts. When the IGAD foreign ministers arrived in Juba, they went directly to talks with President Kiir.

## The IGAD peace talks: A bumpy road

Although the foreign ministers had been promised access to the detainees, this was denied, and they left the same day without having made much progress. By 20 December, as we have seen, I was able to reach Riek Machar, but he was available by phone only to the Americans and me. With his permission I gave his number to Tedros Adhanom who managed to get hold of him from Addis Ababa.

Riek informed the media on 23 December that he had spoken to Tedros Adhanom and called for the political detainees' safe passage to Addis Ababa. Machar had agreed to send a list of delegates to the talks the Ethiopians wanted to hold in Addis, premised on the release of the detainees, most of whom would represent him in negotiations that could commence immediately.

On the same day, our acting state coordinator and senior military adviser in Bor, Mike Chadwick, received a message from Peter Gadet that Riek wanted to see him. They met at the airstrip, where Machar handed over his list of delegates for the talks. He wanted us to send it by email to the Ethiopians, which we did immediately. Interestingly, the designated head of the delegation was Pagan Amum; most of the people on the list were in detention: all had been at the press conference on 6 December. I knew that Riek could not have been in touch with them. That he took their support for his rebellion for granted was surprising, and an error in judgement that would haunt him later.

The Government was unwilling to release the detainees. Sumbeiywo was still working on options we had discussed, and an IGAD summit was in the works. The Kenyans wanted to host the IGAD talks, while the Ethiopians expected Addis to be the site. It was critical to avoid a turf fight and make sure that the process, not the location, had priority. This may be seen as the start of the difficulties IGAD would face in creating a united front for the South Sudan peace process.

At the same time, other foreign officials began to arrive in Juba. On 23 December, President Obama's special envoy Donald Booth, came to meet President Kiir on condition that he be allowed to see the detainees. The Americans had been in regular contact with Machar from the beginning, and were thus working the phones with both sides, as I had done. Three days later the Ethiopian prime minister, Hailemariam Desalegn, and President Kenyatta came to Juba to meet Kiir. They also visited the detainees who were being held in good conditions at a ministerial residence.

## Worried neighbours

On 27 December the IGAD summit took place in Nairobi. The leaders of Kenya, Uganda, Djibouti and Somalia attended alongside the First Vice President of Sudan; South Sudan's foreign minister, Barnaba Marial Benjamin; and the deputy chairperson of the African Union Commission. Neither Salva Kiir nor Riek Machar was present.

A final communiqué condemned all unconstitutional actions, in particular any efforts to change the Government of South Sudan through the use of force. It commended the expressed commitment of both sides to engage in dialogue, requested face-to-face talks with all stakeholders in the conflict by 31 December, and welcomed South Sudan's commitment to an immediate cessation of hostilities, while calling on all other parties to do the same, in the absence of which within four days the summiteers would consider 'further measures'.[2] The communiqué also called for a review of the status of the detainees. Ambassador Seyoum Mesfin of Ethiopia, General Sumbeiywo and the Sudanese general, Mohammed Ahmed Mustapha al-Dabi were appointed as IGAD's Special Envoys for South Sudan.

The Ugandan military engagement was now supported by IGAD, specifically to secure and protect critical infrastructure and installations.

Some foreign observers commented that to them it seemed that Uganda was acting beyond that mandate. These tensions would later disturb relations between several IGAD countries.

On 27 December President Kiir met the ambassadors from the Troika countries (the US, UK and Norway) and told them that most political detainees would be released. Later that evening it was announced that two, Peter Adwok and Deng Deng Akon,[3] were already out of custody. However, it soon appeared that hardliners, including Legal Advisor Telar Deng and Interior Minister Aleu Ayieny Aleu were digging in their heels over further releases. Both bore personal grievances against some detainees. At the same time, almost all civil society organizations were united in favour of release, as the detention without charge was seen as unconstitutional. The rationale of the international community, however, was the – possibly misguided – assumption that release would contribute to an early peace.

On the 29th Sumbeiywo and the Ethiopian Foreign Minister returned to meet the President and other officials. Now that IGAD had formally taken on the mediation, my role of engaging directly with the parties in relation to the political process was over. I would support IGAD's efforts, help if I could, but not facilitate talks.

The urgency of the IGAD engagement to end the fighting could be illustrated by recent events in Bor alone. At least 13 separate incidents had been reported in which minorities and their own citizens were targeted, including Ethiopians, Eritreans, Kenyans and Ugandans. There were also allegations of extrajudicial killings, rape, abduction and other abuses. What had unfolded during the last two weeks had clearly alarmed the region. Neighbouring countries knew that civil war would hit them hard, with refugee flows and a serious impact on their economy and security.

A few hours before the stipulated deadline both sides declared readiness to talk. Delegations moved to Addis Ababa to start the negotiations on 2 January 2014. A main challenge for the IGAD mediation was that member states had differing national interests; coordination was a problem. Nor were the parties really ready to talk after all. Military victory might be impossible, but each side wanted to position itself better before serious negotiations started. Nevertheless, with international pressure mounting, the parties realized that they at least had to attend.

When the delegations arrived, despite the unresolved detainee issue, there was endless discussion about the talks, the agenda, the format, participation, and so forth, and little about substantive issues. The delaying tactics showed lack of commitment.

Apart from a declaration on principles and processes, including humanitarian access, the main outcome of the meetings was the first Cessation of Hostilities Agreement on 23 January.[4] Only two days later incidents occurred, followed by an increase in fighting; the agreement was repeatedly violated by both sides. There was no mechanism for monitoring it in any case, so no way to hold the parties to account.

## Release of the detainees

Although Riek Machar had set release of detainees as a precondition for negotiations, after international pressure his SPLM/A-In Opposition had attended anyway, and President Kenyatta and Prime Minister Desalegn visited the detainees (I followed suit). Ahead of an AU summit in late January, however, the government knew it would be under serious pressure, and before its delegation left for Addis Ababa on 27 January, 7 of the 11 detainees were released,[5] This was widely seen as a break-through, after which they were quickly whisked off to Nairobi. Now, four remained.

Surprising both parties, but not many others, the released detainees expressed no desire to join either camp, insisting that they be a 'third' party in the talks. They were most concerned, they said, about stopping the war. For Riek Machar this was a blow: he had counted on their support, and their independence made his SPLM/A-IO seem that much more Nuer-dominated and, for that reason, weaker than he had foreseen.

Following another IGAD summit in the margins of the AU,[6] a second round of negotiations started on 10 February. The SPLM/A-IO delegation had threatened to stay away until the Cessation of Hostilities and Status of Detainees Agreements had been implemented in full, including participation of all detainees in the peace process and the withdrawal of Ugandan forces. But eventually they came around.

Following consultations with the parties, IGAD tabled three documents on 21 February. These included a framework and agenda for political dialogue. Beyond implementation of what had already been agreed in January, the most interesting development was the reform agenda. This comprised restructuring the security sector; justice and accountability; review of the Transitional Constitution; national reconciliation; transparency; and reforming and restructuring the civil service. In addition, a declaration of principles was proposed to guide the entire peace process. A parallel track was devoted to the SPLM reunification process by members of the Political Bureau.

During this round, the question of inclusiveness and the format for the talks were debated. It was agreed to establish a Monitoring and Verification Mechanism to ensure compliance with the cessation of the hostilities agreement. While UNMISS could have taken this on rather quickly, the parties opted for regional responsibility. If the goal was to avoid establishment of an effective monitoring mechanism, and to preclude reporting of violations to the Security Council, this clearly was more convenient.[7] That the IGAD-mediators did the same was more surprising.

The round ended on 3 March with the signing of implementation modalities for the cessation of hostilities agreement and some progress on finalizing a declaration of principles. As expected, the monitoring mechanism was slow to be established, and had very limited capacity, which permitted the parties to continue to violate the agreement with impunity. Worse, the mechanism would be operational only from 1 April in Bor, and with a minimal presence in two other places later the same month. It was entirely dependent on logistical support from UNMISS, and was initially weak in confronting serious violations. At the same time, fighting continued, as we have seen, with some of the worst violence happening in March and April.

Another IGAD summit on 13 March ended with a communiqué reaffirming the need for an inclusive political dialogue which would involve the former detainees, political parties, civil society and other stakeholders. The former detainees were recognized as positive contributors to the peace process.[8] President Kiir participated. Upon his return to Juba, however, the government claimed that it had protested this part of the text, which should not have been included. This position was subsequently disputed by the IGAD secretariat and chairman of IGAD, Prime Minister Hailemariam Desalegn, who reportedly made it crystal clear in a letter to Kiir, copied to all heads of state in the region.[9] This was not the first time a delegation would walk back on commitments it had made. Riek Machar, on his part, was upset with the proposal to deploy an IGAD protection force. Neither party was keen to attend the next round of talks.

The participation of other stakeholders in the negotiations was a contentious issue. From the onset of conflict, South Sudanese civil society organizations had demanded a part in the peace process. IGAD mediators consulted a number of them, and other South Sudanese political forces, to establish a means for participation. The former detainees, now calling themselves the Group of 11,[10] claimed a place at the table. Including them and others was controversial, despite the backing of all IGAD heads of state, and would later become a source of intense debate between the mediation and the two parties.

During this period, the trial of the four remaining detainees, Pagan Amum, Oyay Deng, Majak D'Agoot and Ezekiel Lol Gatkuoth took place. They had been charged under the Penal Code Act of 2008, chapter five, with 'treason, incitement of the masses, causing disaffection among police forces or defence forces, defaming the Government of South Sudan and undermining authority of or insulting the President.'[11] Some of these charges carried a maximum penalty of death. For the first time in South Sudanese history, a national court procedure allowed access to the public and the press, which to many observers seemed a breakthrough in judicial practice.

The detainees remained in custody until almost the end of the trial. It became clear that the case against them was very weak. Key witnesses chose not to turn up, and others, such as the SPLA's chief of military intelligence, General Mac Paul, undermined it by flatly stating there had been no attempted coup.[12] The case collapsed. On 24 April the government withdrew the charges – in 'the interest of peace and reconciliation' – and the detainees were freed.

## Preventing another cycle of violence

Meanwhile the political process focusing on the SPLM, which was led by the African National Congress and the Ethiopian People's Revolutionary Democratic Front, was delayed. The intention had been to contribute to the solution of issues within the party through dialogue among members of the SPLM Political Bureau, since tensions there had sparked the crisis in the first place. The party process convened for the first time on 5 April 2014, soon faced some of the same difficulties as the IGAD negotiations. There was an apparent lack of commitment: despite everyone's agreement, participation was poor from at least two of the factions, and the status of members such as Riek Machar and Taban Deng was moot.

In mid April two of the gravest spikes of violence since the crisis started took place: the massacre in the mosque and surrounding areas of Bentiu, killing hundreds, and the attack on the UNMISS base at Bor, killing more than 50 people. There was grave concern that the vicious cycle could get totally out of hand. The international outrage was loud enough to bring both Salva Kiir and Riek Machar to Addis Ababa. For the first time since the crisis broke, there was a glimmer of hope.

The third round of talks under IGAD auspices had opened on 28 April, and both the government and the SPLM/A-IO now had to show that they were serious. Discussions culminated on 9 May with Kiir and Machar publicly committed to resolving the crisis and implementing the cessation of hostilities agreement with immediate effect.[13]

The two-page agreement was described as a possible 'breakthrough', but the presence of the two leaders was more important than the substance of their commitments. Sure enough, as soon as they returned to their home bases, they complained of undue pressure from their Ethiopian hosts, who had been chairing IGAD.[14] This was not well received.

There was nevertheless hope that agreement between the two would lead to a 'month of tranquility', so that planting for cultivation could take place, preventing a famine later in the year. A Humanitarian Conference in Oslo in May mobilized donor support. But South Sudan's representatives, particularly Foreign Minister Barnaba Marial Benjamin, angered donors with an apparent unwillingness to take responsibility for the humanitarian crisis in the country. Although $600 million was pledged at the Oslo conference, the agencies had hoped for more.

Another cycle of revenge through mass killings was avoided after the terrible incidents of mid April, but violence rose sharply at the end of May. Following another round of intense negotiations, at the IGAD summit on 10 June Salva Kiir and Riek Machar agreed to set a 60-day deadline for arranging a permanent ceasefire and establishing a transitional government of national unity.[15] While they had refused even to greet each other on 9 May, this time they at least shook hands. The deadline for agreement on the transitional government was now set for 10 August.

IGAD mediators had continued to push the parties to allow participation by other opposition groups and civil society representatives. A Multi-Stakeholder Symposium was hosted in Addis Ababa prior to the IGAD summit.[16] There was a lot of noise over selection of civil society participants, however, and to what extent they were truly representative or were compromised by association with any of the main factions.[17]

The SPLM/A-IO refused to participate in the next round of talks from 20 June on the grounds that the inclusive framework undermined the mediation process. They wanted to negotiate only with the government, and to consult other stakeholders separately. The meeting had to adjourn.[18]

The talks had been fraught with challenges from the start. The mediators had weighed the options of a narrow peace agreement between the belligerent parties and a comprehensive agreement that addressed the 'root causes' of the conflict. The so-called Single Negotiating Text did indeed list a number of fundamental challenges facing South Sudan,[19] but with the problems facing the inclusive approach little progress was made. Instead the discussions centred on the agendas of the two warring parties, composition of a transitional interim government of national unity, and the SPLM/A-IO's demand for federalism.

The parallel negotiation process for reunification of the SPLM never got off the ground. Following the request of the ANC and the South Sudanese parties, the Tanzanian ruling party, Chama Cha Mapinduzi (CCM) later took charge of the process, yielding much better results. The lack of coordination between the IGAD mediation and the reunification process of the SPLM in Arusha would later pose a problem, however.

I left South Sudan in July 2014 after completing my contractual period as SRSG. I had stayed on longer than most in these assignments. It also followed the new and very different mandate for UNMISS, where state-building and peace-building was replaced by a focus on crisis management and protection of civilians.[20] As I departed, I hoped that both sides would take the new 60-day deadline seriously. But it passed without any substantial developments. A new deadline of 15 August was set for agreement on the transitional government.[21] A preparatory meeting of the leaders of Uganda, Kenya and South Sudan – but without the chairman of IGAD, the Ethiopian Prime Minister – ratified a prior agreement among the three for transitional arrangements, during which Salva Kiir would remain president.[22] The Ethiopians had little choice but to join the consensus, in what was only the latest of many examples of disharmony within IGAD.

From the outset of the process the IGAD leaders had been united in calling for respect for the cessation of hostilities agreement and for humanitarian access. They had joined in expressing dismay at the multiple violations by both sides, demanding release of the detainees, and stressing the need for inclusivity in the talks. Later they agreed on the establishment of a regional protection force, establishment of a transitional government, and the need for fundamental reforms in South Sudan. But on other issues the mediators needed mediation.

## Neighbours and others: Peacemakers or troublemakers?

Each country in the region had its own strategic interests. The venue and leadership of the talks were initially a matter of tension between Ethiopia and Kenya. More serious was disagreement over the approach to the negotiations. Seyoum Mesfin emerged as chief mediator, although such a term never existed, and he made most decisions on strategy.[23] This led to tensions not only within the mediation team, but to some extent also between IGAD governments. The first sign of these challenges was tension between Uganda and Sudan. Uganda had the full backing of IGAD for its limited military engagement,[24] and in December and January its intervention probably prevented an attack on Juba by opposition forces. While the degree of Ugandan military support for the SPLA was contentious, some observers quietly noted that this prevented an even worse scenario from unfolding. An opposition attack on the capital could have involved heavy loss of civilian lives, with possible irreversible national implications.

There was a difference between strategic support at a critical juncture, however, and continuous military engagement. While members of IGAD did not publicly criticize, the main concern was that this engagement could prompt Sudan to enter the conflict on Machar's side. Sudan and Uganda had been in dispute for a long time. The danger of internationalization of the conflict led to demands for withdrawal of Ugandan troops.[25]

It did not help that South Sudan had also quickly solicited support from the Justice and Equality Movement (JEM) in Darfur, particularly in Unity State where the SPLA was especially weak. This provoked Khartoum; Mohammed Atta, the head of the national intelligence and security services, was fuming about this when I met him in June 2014.

Sudan soon appeared tacitly to adjust its policy. Having supported Salva Kiir and his new, and in their view more Khartoum-friendly cabinet, Bashir's government reportedly rebuffed early overtures from Riek Machar's side,[26] just as he had rejected similar approaches through business contacts and military intelligence prior to the crisis. The Sudanese President therefore continued to reassure Kiir of his support, including through sales of military hardware. (Twenty-four armoured personnel carriers were purchased in Khartoum for the SPLA as late as March 2014.)[27] With excellent contacts in the South Sudan Government, Khartoum could still exert effective influence.

When they defected to the opposition, many SPLA units had taken their hardware with them. The SPLM/A-IO also captured significant assets during the ebb and flow of battle. Still, external support was critical for the continuous supply of ammunition and to confront better equipped government forces. Chinese weapons ordered by the SPLA before the crisis, in 2013, worsened the opposition's long-term predicament.[28]

In due course, indications of support for Riek Machar and the SPLM/A-IO from across the border were discernible. Sudan had an obvious interest in the security of oil supply lines, but Uganda's intervention and the involvement of the Darfurian rebels seemed more important in determining Khartoum's next moves.

Rumours multiplied of arms deliveries to the opposition via Eritrea, as well as direct Eritrean involvement. Later there were more substantial indications that Sudan and Iran were providing direct support, and that Qatar was contributing financially.[29] (Sudan's collaboration with Iran would later switch to alignment with Saudi Arabia.) SPLM/A-IO attacks in areas adjacent to the Sudan– South Sudan border, where supplies would be easily accessible, showed at least passive support from Khartoum. Sudan was probably playing both sides up to mid/end of 2014, but there was clearly an increasing tilt towards Machar's camp.[30]

Khartoum's support for the opposition has been confirmed by two important sources. Firstly, London-based Conflict Armament Research has documented direct airdrops of weapons and ammunition from Sudan to the SPLM/A-IO.[31] It appears that Iranian weapons may have been trans-shipped through Sudan.[32] Secondly, very reliable sources have provided information from security meetings in Khartoum[33] in which their support to Riek Machar Teny and the SPLM/A-IO was mentioned.[34]

Hardliners in Khartoum have always seen developments in South Sudan as a zero-sum game. This is a legacy of decades of civil war, and the mentality remains; the weaker the Southerners, the better for Khartoum. As we have seen, long-time support of proxy militia was publicly acknowledged by Sudan in September 2012 in the context of the AUHIP negotiations. The signing of the CPA was the only exception to this approach, of divide and rule. After John Garang died and his counterpart, Vice President Ali Osman Taha was sidelined, elements in the military-security apparatus deliberately and systematically under-mined its implementation, and reverted to old strategies.

Riek Machar and a number of his commanders had at times been allied with or supported by Khartoum. The military-security apparatus there now revitalized contacts, and established a network of direct links with Riek's commanders, some of whom went to Khartoum for meetings. This strategy would enable Khartoum to keep proxy militia operating in the Upper Nile region even if Riek Machar returned to the fold.

During the IGAD talks, it was reported that Sudan's leadership several times advocated giving the parties more time,[35] the only member state that seemed in no rush to reach an agreement. While representa-tives of the Sudanese Government continued publicly to express deep concern about developments in South Sudan, there was no urgency at all, and other elements of the military-security apparatus seemed to be making full use of this opportunity for their own ends.

On the military side, there appeared to be several tacitly accepted red lines between the neighbouring countries. Credible sources warned that if Ugandan forces were to engage farther north, beyond Gadiang, a reaction from both Sudan and Ethiopia might be triggered. Similarly, if Sudan moved in ground forces – for example to assist the SPLM/A-IO to occupy oil fields in Upper Nile State, strong reactions might be expected from the neighbours. In this way, the IGAD countries watched each other and had a deterrent impact, preventing any of them from overstepping the line.

## Other strategic interests: Carrots and sticks

As the conflict continued and the IGAD peace process faced increasing difficulties, it appeared that tensions in the region itself were impeding progress. There was hegemonic competition in relation to South Sudan (Ethiopia versus Uganda), and competition over the lead role in the peace process (Ethiopia versus Kenya). There was direct support to opposing belligerents (Uganda versus Sudan) and at times directly opposing national interests of several neighbouring countries in South Sudan (Uganda, Sudan, Ethiopia and Kenya). The refugee crisis in South Sudan was also creating problems in the neighbouring countries, affecting Kenya, Uganda, Ethiopia, and Sudan, with a total of around 450,000 at this time, a figure which would increase exponentially.[36]

Ethiopia's economic interests in South Sudan were predominantly in the property markets and hotel and restaurant business, rivalled only by Kenyan interests in the financial sector. Ethiopia has a large Nuer population, and given the history of conflict in the region the Ethiopian Government had to tread carefully.[37] Riek Machar was based in Addis Ababa.

Ethiopia pushed for a joint protection and deterrent force, the mandate of which would be to ensure full implementation of the cessation of hostilities agreement, support the Monitoring and Verification Mission, protect civilians, and help to prevent any attempt to occupy or attack the South Sudanese oil fields. Indirectly, this was also intended to provide the basis for a Ugandan withdrawal from South Sudan, which the Ethiopians saw as a prerequisite for a meaningful peace agreement.[38] The Ethiopians would provide forces and be joined by units from Kenya and Rwanda; Uganda and Sudan were seen as too involved to participate in such a force.

Uganda had significant security interests in relation to South Sudan, revealed through its military engagement. As early as 18 February

Uganda stated a preference for invoking 'the African Capacity for the Immediate Response to Crisis', a security mechanism under development within the African Union, enabling a progressive withdrawal of Ugandan forces. This was not a realistic proposition at this time, however. A 'lighter' deployment, such as regional forces within an UNMISS framework, was another alternative which could provide for increased protection.

Riek Machar and the SPLM/A-IO had called for Ugandan withdrawal from the very outset, but also opposed a separate regional protection force. Machar claimed that extra forces to be deployed under the authority of the UN through UNMISS would be more than enough; his resistance was likely linked to proposed deployment near the oil fields.

The IGAD countries could not fund the joint protection and deterrent force and requested assistance from the UN. But the Security Council would only agree to fund additional forces if these were under UN command and control, integrated within UNMISS and under the same mandate. Since additional forces for UNMISS were delayed, however, units from the IGAD countries ended up constituting the reinforcement of UNMISS and not a separate protection force. It had never been clear whether Uganda really would withdraw if the regional force materialized, and they now remained on South Sudanese territory. But Ethiopia's influence was ensured as the country pressed for, and got, the Force Commander position in UNMISS, and provided the majority of the additional troops.

At the same time, Ethiopia had a strong interest in maintaining good relations with Khartoum. Sudan supported the Grand *Ethiopian* Renaissance Dam (GERD) *on the Blue Nile,* a mega-project opposed by Egypt. It was critical for the Ethiopians that this support continue. While Ethiopia remained largely impartial in relation to the South Sudanese conflict, it therefore also had to be careful in confronting Sudan.

Kenya and Uganda had significant economic interests in South Sudan. South Sudan was Uganda's most important export market and second only to the UK as a source of remittances.[39] Kenya dominated the banking and insurance sector. Both countries enjoyed a significant surplus in trade relations with South Sudan, and both had citizens deeply engaged in business in Juba and beyond. For both countries South Sudan was a major market for manufactured goods and food. Quite a number of business partnerships had been formed between members of the SPLM leadership and influential individuals in both countries. To what extent this influenced the positions of their governments is difficult to tell.

As time passed without a settlement, the IGAD mediation increasingly faced challenges with resolving the impasse. An observer from the region, in close contact with the South Sudanese, put the blame on the Ethiopians, who were 'not behaving as mediators, but as prescribers'. At one point, the South Sudan Government urged not only a change of venue, from Ethiopia to Kenya, but also replacement of the (Ethiopian) chairman, Seyoum Mesfin, who had publicly criticized other IGAD states, with the experienced (Kenyan) Sumbeiywo.[40] The Kenyans did not take the bait. No change was forthcoming.

But it was not only neighbouring states that had political interests in South Sudan, and in how the conflict evolved. The stakes were also high for the Troika – the US, UK and Norway, with their critical role behind the CPA. They knew that a South Sudan in prolonged conflict was at risk of imploding and fragmenting, with a potentially destabilizing impact on the whole region. Their Special Envoys followed the talks closely and supported the IGAD mediation every step of the way. They also helped to fund the mediation effort and the Monitoring and Verification Mechanism of IGAD.

The US administration watched with growing anger and impatience as the conflict unfolded, and was the first to impose sanctions against individuals identified as responsible for the worst violence in South Sudan.[41] The European Union followed suit. The Security Council also discussed sanctions against individuals, but only later would the legal basis for such sanctions be formally approved.[42] South Sudan did its best to charm Russia, despite the unfortunate handling of the investigations following the downing of the Russian helicopter in December 2012, but did not succeed – at least at this stage.

China had the potential to play an important role in South Sudan. Chinese companies were the most significant oil producers in the country. The Chinese Special Envoy engaged actively with the parties to the conflict, and at times in consultation also with his counterparts in the Troika. But the Chinese operate discreetly and only they know which messages were conveyed to the South Sudanese parties. It was clear, however, that major Chinese commercial interests were at stake if the conflict continued; it would be in China's interest to help end it.

## True colours

That the two parties would criticize the IGAD talks was to be expected. Mediators can seldom avoid reproach. But the team trying to broker agreement between the South Sudanese warring factions faced intransigent leaders on both sides, who at times played the IGAD countries against each other, both through public statements and through their approach to the talks.

Conflict usually brings out the true colours of leaders. It turned out that the two principals in this conflict, Salva Kiir and Riek Machar, seemed willing to go to extreme lengths to gain or retain power. Salva Kiir's resolve was likely rooted in several factors. He had long been subject to pressure and spitefulness from his comrades, which probably reinforced his determination not to bend. Pressure from leading figures in his own community in the Greater Bahr el Gahzal, who wanted to maintain the status quo, was also likely involved. Besides, government hardliners hated Machar, and were unlikely to favour any compromise.

Riek Machar, with his long-standing ambition to be president, had been deeply provoked by the atrocities committed in Juba. The clear message from his side, and that of opposition forces in general and his own community, was that Kiir had forfeited legitimacy and had to go. This view was engrained in the minds of his key commanders, who had no loyalty to Kiir and no interest in extending his presidency.

The all-or-nothing position from each side made a power-sharing agreement extremely hard to achieve. Although neither leader was really tribalistic in his approach, each increasingly leaned on his own community for support, both as his political base and as a basis for personal security. Riek Machar's SPLM/A-IO was predominantly Nuer. Although the make-up of Salva Kiir's last cabinet was multi-ethnic, his presidency was perceived as progressively Dinka dominated, with Bahr el Ghazal elders taking centre stage. While this tendency was already obvious before my departure from Juba in July 2014, it was later much reinforced.[43]

At the same time, it is important to note that Salva Kiir during these critical months managed to contain the Greater Bahr el Ghazal community from large-scale ethnic mobilization against the Nuer. If the Dinka hardliners who hailed from his community had got a free hand, it is likely that the atrocities in Juba would have been repeated nationwide, in a scenario one could honestly compare with Rwanda. Although the atrocities that did occur were bad enough, this did not happen. Nevertheless, the way both leaders rallied their followers and sustained their backing is a central issue. Both, in the end, used ethnicity as a basis for continued support.

That both leaders signed on to commitments that they would not keep came as no surprise. Both had often been opportunistic. If commitments had a higher price than expected they could be broken. And as mentioned above, 'tactical avoidance' was a trait of President Kiir, one that, with the crisis, became much worse, as IGAD leaders and the UN would discover. But changing positions was more familiar to Sudanese traditional political culture than South Sudanese liberators would like to acknowledge. In this tradition, as the Southerners themselves complained many times, agreements were interim arrangements subject to renegotiation, depending on what seemed convenient at the time.[44]

After signing agreements on the cessation of hostilities, for example, government forces and the SPLM/A-IO continued fighting. When they promised humanitarian access, they did not follow through, at least according to their agreements. Among the leadership on both sides there appeared an inability or unwillingness to prevent atrocities. Key perpetrators were known to both leaders; none were held accountable. Officers were not even suspended pending investigation. This failure to act could hardly be interpreted as anything other than condoning such actions. Impunity prevailed.

The intransigence of the two parties was among the reasons for the mediators' insistence on broadening the peace process. Other stakeholders might have a greater interest in peace, and would push for fundamental reforms. But this strategy gave both sides a new excuse to delay, and it ultimately complicated the talks. A dilemma in all peace negotiations is the parties' interest in retaining control and avoiding anything that can hinder their chance of getting a deal on their own terms.[45] Yet inclusiveness could be critical for sustaining peace in the long run.

It was in this landscape the IGAD-mediators were navigating. To achieve peace, signatures on paper would not suffice; the South Sudanese leaders were in for a much longer journey.

## Sustainable peace: A longer journey

Waging peace in South Sudan was a multi-layered and complex process. Tensions undermining peace and national unity often had deeper roots, but the lack of willingness to deal with them in the past had made them worse. Furthermore, South Sudanese leaders had themselves contributed to widening the divisions in the country by playing the ethnic card in their own competition for power.

A basic aim in nation-building, one would assume, should be to avoid tearing a country further apart through ethnic politics. Divisive politics has consequences. When people have a lot of grievances and no political influence, they are more likely to resort to violence. Even statistical evidence collected by the SPLM Secretariat itself showed palpable dissatisfaction. Jok Madut Jok published a stark warning about this only a fortnight before the outbreak of violence in December 2013 and asked what happens:

> when people become so poor, desperate, unable to speak, insecure – and above all loose [sic] trust in their leadership? Such is the stuff with which civil unrest, protests, and even outright revolutions are made. The political leadership in South Sudan should not play with fire.[46]

But they all did. At the same time, processes that could have helped unify the nation and give people a say were not prioritized.[47] To successfully wage peace going forward, therefore, it will be essential to avoid repeating these mistakes. In the South Sudanese environment today, marred by newly exacerbated ethnic divisions, it is even more important to prevent such policies from gaining new momentum. In the IGAD talks, two of the most important reform processes were the new constitution and national reconciliation, both essential for building and sustaining peace in a divided South Sudan.

## A country is not a nation

With the goal of providing the young nation with a democratic permanent constitution, the Transitional Constitution outlines four stages through which that process should happen.[48] These include a National Constitutional Review Commission, National Constitutional Conference, the National Legislature, and the assent of the President. The drafting and adoption of the Transitional Constitution had been rushed and divisive, granting the President sweeping powers, and without consultation of all stakeholders; the process for the permanent document was meant to be different.

Owing to initial delays, appointments to the National Constitution Review Commission on 9 January 2012 were made haphazardly at the last minute. Although the chairman, the late Professor Akolda Maan Tier and his deputy were seen as impartial, there were complaints about lack of representation of civil society, non-partisan stakeholders and technical experts.[49] Under terms of the Transitional Constitution they had only one year to submit a report to the President, much less than constitutional processes had enjoyed elsewhere in Africa. Although this was clearly linked to the schedule for the next elections, from a nation-building perspective these timelines were a missed opportunity for South Sudan.[50]

The legitimacy of a constitution is of the greatest importance, and can be assured only by the greatest possible degree of public participation.[51] We advocated broad consultation across the country. But although his committee would consult the people as stipulated, the chairman considered that consultation at the county level, involving the grass roots, would be difficult, referring to the high levels of illiteracy. This was contrary to experience elsewhere on the continent, where grass root-consultations had worked well, and indeed in polls and focus group research in South Sudan.[52]

Despite extension of its timelines, the National Constitutional Review was caught up in the overall political paralysis of the country in 2013. The peace agreement will provide a golden opportunity to change the constitutional review process entirely, so that the constitution emerges as a document around which people can rally as citizens of a nation, above and beyond their ethnic identity. For that to happen they need to have a say and to contribute to it. The process should not be another missed opportunity for nation-building.

One topic that will be at the centre of discussion is federalism, which emerged as a very contentious issue in the IGAD negotiations.[53] As Douglas Johnson has pointed out, federalism has meant different things to different people at different times.[54] John Garang, for example, used the term 'confederation'. It was only when South Sudan got its independence, however, that the demand for federalism was revived, this time by Equatorian politicians feeling marginalized by larger Nilotic ethnic groups.

For this discussion to have any meaning, however, federalism needs to be defined. There are many models, with varying degrees of devolution of powers. For example, according to Johnson 'The SPLM/A-In-Opposition's proposal of making 21 states along the 1956 boundaries of the South's districts ... [would create] ... weak states unable to challenge or restrain whoever holds power in central government.'[55]

Increasingly, federalism has been associated with ethnicity. As a woman from Malakal said in a meeting after the explosion of violence: 'how can we live side-by-side with these people again?', 'Let them stay in their own area,' was her solution.[56] This sort of federalism would mean segregation rather than national unity.

It is impossible to build a nation out of a broken society that has not dealt with its past. When people primarily identify themselves with their ethnic group, and not the nation, ethnicity rather than the larger common good will drive their actions. While there were positive signs of an emerging national identity earlier,[57] the reverse happened during the recent crisis. And priority of ethnic identity will prevail, whatever the content of a peace agreement, unless very deliberate policies are put in place to counteract it.

## National reconciliation

Amnesty and accommodation, through political positions, military rank or other forms of benefit, is not true reconciliation. As Jacob J. Akol, editor of *Gurtong* writes:

Re-instating the situation before mid December 2013 and do little or nothing would be to bury our heads in the sand and continue the vicious cycle of rebellion, destruction, revenge and counter revenge even at a much larger scale.[58]

As Douglas Johnson says, a peace agreement that merely tinkers with the structures of government and the distribution of offices will not address the trauma that threatens to divide South Sudanese from one another. For peace to be sustained, major changes are needed in the way the leadership deals with the drivers of conflict, and in processes of reconciliation between communities and adversaries.

In the past, reconciliation did not have high priority in the SPLM-leadership. These provisions in the CPA were virtually ignored,[59] and tactical avoidance prevailed. Long-standing grievances between the SPLA and certain communities, and between opposing communities, remained largely unaddressed. If peace is to be achieved going forward, reconciliation not only at the political level between the parties in conflict and its leaders, but also in relation to these tensions, will be critical. However, reconciliation will have to occur in tandem with the healing and accountability processes.

They include not only the 1991 Bor massacres and the multiple rebellions of different cadres during the 1990s and post-election periods, but also the 1982–3 Kokora-violence in Juba,[60] participation in 'clearing' areas for Khartoum's oil-production in multiple locations, the mutual grievances of various ethnic minorities and the SPLA, and post CPA-conflicts between cattle herders and Nilotic communities and the Equatorians. These 'ghosts of the past' are conflict drivers, fuelling fresh conflict. If they are not confronted, violence – given its cyclical nature – will reappear.

Many have been of the opinion that the government itself cannot lead such a reconciliation process; it has to be home grown and independent.[61] In some cases it was the state – or the SPLA – that would stand to be accused. This would likely be the case for example for minority communities such as the Fertit, the Shilluk, the Murle. Mutual mistrust had led to grave violence in the past. Among the Equatorians, land grabbing and abusive behaviour against their communities by SPLA commanders were the concern. It would be difficult for a national reconciliation committee led by the government to be able to handle such issues with credibility.

When the President appointed instead the Committee for National Healing, Peace and Reconciliation, headed by Archbishop Daniel Deng Bul, there were no direct links to the government. The committee was dominated by church representatives and civil society, probably modeled on the earlier people-to-people processes in South Sudan. The committee soon faced difficulties, however, with lack of resources, inadequate capacity and question marks about its composition. Before the crisis erupted in December 2013, the committee had barely started its work.

Soon after the initial violence, the new Vice President James Wani Igga also saw the opportunity to play politics with reconciliation, and launched what many regarded as a competing initiative. While he had been asked by the President to coordinate the government's efforts, his initiative looked more and more like a strategy for political rallying. The plan was to combine a major reconciliation conference with a general amnesty. If anything, this looked much like a repetition of the past, and his National Platform for Peace and Reconciliation did not move forward.

The most recent fighting has not only torn the social fabric of society, but also further aggravated multiple grievances and tensions between communities and escalated local conflicts. It is this cumulative impact of the past and the present that now complicates the efforts of achieving peace. As Professor Jok Madut Jok says:

> The war experience, dating back over several decades, may appear unrelated to the immediate triggers of new violence, but is actually what draws groups of people into a new conflict, making any new conflict spread quickly, and more vicious in its brutality.[62]

As the conflict wore on, relations deteriorated to almost unprecedented levels, with the cycle of revenge killings spreading to communities uninvolved in the initial conflict. As Jok also underscores, peace will not return if people are not collectively given a chance to face the history of violence head on, to engage in dialogue about the communal conflicts that have wrecked ethnic relations and address the relationship between the state and the citizens. Lessons learned from elsewhere show that there is never a shortcut to reconciliation and restoration of social cohesion.[63]

In the IGAD talks, the parties agreed to establish a National Commission for Truth, Reconciliation and Healing, mandated to create a historical record of human rights violations, including the identification of victims and perpetrators, recording the experiences of victims, investigating the causes of conflict (and making recommendations on how to prevent the repetition of conflict) and facilitating local and national reconciliation and healing. In addition, there were discussions about compensation and reparation for victims.[64]

As South Sudanese scholars themselves have pointed out, it is not possible to reconcile people by merely telling them to forget the past and start a new page. Difficult histories need to be unearthed, facts of who did what to whom have to be considered, even if that does not result in punitive justice, as some communities may be willing to come to terms with their loss, if someone admitted culpability and expressed remorse.[65]

Traditional customary practices can contribute to reconciliation and healing, but also compensation mechanisms that can ensure justice for aggrieved communities, individually and collectively. Nevertheless, as the African Union Peace and Security Council stated as early as 30 December 2013, the gravity of the crimes and atrocities committed in South Sudan during the civil war would require a credible judicial mechanism.[66]

The African Union Commission of Inquiry, chaired by former President Obasanjo, was tasked with setting the course for this process. The Commission of Inquiry started its work on 12 March 2014, and was mandated to:

> investigate the human rights violations and other abuses committed during the armed conflict in South Sudan, and make recommendations on the best way and means to ensure accountability, reconciliation and healing among all South Sudanese communities.[67]

After the UNMISS Human Rights Investigation Report was released,[68] including our recommendation for an international process of accountability for the grave violations, atrocities and crimes committed against civilians, Secretary-General Ban Ki-moon recommended to the Security Council on 12 May that a Special/Hybrid Court for South Sudan be considered,[69] pending also the outcome of the AU Commission of Inquiry.[70]

At the time of my departure from UNMISS, the Commission had not yet submitted its report to the chair of the African Union. Nevertheless, it was clear to me that the gravity of atrocities committed meant that reconciliation would not be possible unless accountability was served. To many, peace would be a reality only when justice was in process, whether through inter-communal processes or international accountability measures. It was also clear to me that any attempt at skirting this responsibility, and relying on impunity for the perpetrators who had committed atrocities during the civil war would likely imply a return of new violence later, revenging what had happened to the victims, or in other ways making sure that the crimes were not forgotten. The cyclical pattern would continue.

As I left the region, I wondered whether South Sudanese leaders would be willing to do what was needed to save their country, not only from fighting, but also from failing. This meant not only achieving peace on paper, but also to achieve sustained peace; refrain from playing divisive politics, implement genuine and inclusive processes of reconciliation and healing, as well as constitution-making, and end impunity. Only then would South Sudan stand a chance of becoming a nation. I was not sure.

# EPILOGUE

Only we can determine how our vision will be read in history books generations from now. Will we let our challenges define us, or will we rise as a nation and define our own future? I believe that we will write a story worthy of the sacrifices of our ancestors and martyrs. If we work together, the story of South Sudan will inspire the world.

Salva Kiir Mayardit, Independence Speech, 9 July 2011

Up to this point, the story of South Sudan had not been much of an inspiration. The leadership had chosen division over unity. On 26 August 2015 Salva Kiir finally signed the Agreement on the Resolution of the Conflict in the Republic of South Sudan. Riek Machar and Pagan Amum, representing the Former Detainees and Other Stakeholders[1] had signed on the 17th. Salva Kiir, although present, had surprised the signing ceremony that day by suddenly requesting two more weeks to review the text. He subsequently raised a number of reservations that reinforced the perception of a leader under serious pressure. The reservations were later dropped, but illustrated the challenges of the IGAD mediation, with both parties voicing misgivings.

Machar had seen strong resistance to the agreement too, but he reluctantly signed. He had been seriously weakened militarily, with six of his commanders breaking ranks, including Peter Gadet.[2] Salva Kiir, for his part, signed, but tried to circumvent provisions in the power-sharing arrangements through his surprise decision to establish 28 states in South Sudan.[3] Also the closure of several media outlets by National Security,[4] the decisions to dissolve the SPLM General Secretariat and fast-track important party processes, [5] the detention of one governor and the sacking of several others, were clear indications of more authoritarian rule.[6]

However, in the end both leaders had no other choice but to succumb to the pressure and abide with the provisions of the peace agreement.

## South Sudan – beyond redemption?

While responsibility for the crisis rests with South Sudan's liberators across factions, the two belligerent parties have to share the blame for the grave acts of violence against their own people and the civil war. Regional dynamics also played a part in its continuation.

I knew the South Sudanese very well, from way back, and was aware of their tendency to dig their heels in. Yet I was surprised by the depth of intransigence. After numerous deadlines and 'last rounds', the two leaders had still been unwilling to come to an understanding,[7] preferring yet another round of fighting.

I recalled a warning prior to Independence by a Sudanese official.[8] I didn't believe it at the time, but it now rang true. The official in Khartoum noted what he regarded as a certain naivety on behalf of the South Sudanese leadership in the international community, and said to a UN colleague:

> We know our Southern brothers much better than you. We might appear very different. But you will soon be disappointed. We are like trees coming from the same roots.

In a statement at the airport prior to my departure from Juba on 8 July 2014,[9] I referred to this:

> If there are further delays, and the blame games go on, whether from those wanting to remain in office or those wanting to get back in, we can draw only one conclusion; that this is only about a scramble for power.
>
> There will be claims that there are different reasons (and) [...] other explanations, but – please – don't believe them. If they do not come to an agreement, it is because this – in the end – is only about them, and not about you, the people of South Sudan, or the country.[10]

Among those most angry and upset internationally were old 'friends' of the South Sudanese, those who had shared the struggle for peace and justice for all. Some were among those pushing hardest for international sanctions against those they saw as responsible and, as a last resort, also with an arms embargo.[11] Russia, however, was against the use of sanctions.

By April–May 2015, in the fourth year of independence, the Troika, and the US in particular, were close to giving up on the South Sudanese.

## As if people mattered

The blame game continued, however. We heard many reasons why the two factions could not come to an agreement, from leaders on both sides.

In the meantime, South Sudan was falling apart.

The Government tried to portray normality; the civil war was just a conflict in one part of the country, in the always difficult Upper Nile Region. The rest of the country was 'normal', they said. Towards the end of the dry season in 2015, fighting escalated significantly, particularly in Upper Nile. During this period, opposition forces captured both Malakal and Bentiu again, and threatened the oil fields through a new alliance with Johnson Olonyi's forces, effectively leading to fragmentation of the state into three areas.[12] About 750,000 people were affected by the violence in Unity state alone, and many of them were forced to flee their homes.[13] The military offensive in Unity resulted in the systematic displacement of a significant amount of the population.[14] SPLA checkpoints prevented thousands from getting to safety in UN bases.[15] The situation was certainly not normal. And later in the year it would get worse, with fighting escalating also in Western Bahr el Gahzal and Western Equatoria.

Another abnormal feature was the gravity of the violence. The UN Panel of Experts on South Sudan,[16] assessing the basis for sanctions, found that armed forces were 'intent on rendering communal life unviable and prohibiting any return to normalcy following the violence,' including 'by clearing the population from much of Unity state'. It concluded that, since April 2015, the intensity and brutality of the violence aimed at civilians had been greater than hitherto seen.[17] The

Human Rights report published by UNMISS in late June also gave a chilling picture of violence at a new level of brutality. The scope and level of cruelty suggests a depth of antipathy that in the UN's view 'exceeds political differences' and points to 'the further ethnicization of the conflict'.[18]

Burning of towns and villages, mass killings and other terrible atrocities were documented. This included an escalation of abduction and sexual abuse of women and girls, some of whom were reportedly burned alive in their dwellings after being gang-raped. There were abductions of boys as young as 10, some of whom were mutilated. UNICEF reported horrific crimes against children, including castration, rape and murder.[19] The stories outraged the world. Only further investigation can clarify whether the latter acts of grave violence were motivated as a generational attack on another ethnic group. Similar crimes and widespread use of sexual violence was reported in Unity state from both sides even after the peace agreement had been signed.[20] Recruitment of children also escalated.

The African Union Commission of Inquiry reported sexual violence as a weapon of war and extreme cruelty exercised through mutilation of bodies, burning of bodies, draining blood from people who had just been killed and forcing others from one community to drink it or eat burnt human flesh.[21] It was also reported that 50 people had suffocated to death in a container in Leer on 22 October 2015, with the SPLA being deemed responsible.[22] UNMISS Human Rights Report of 21 January 2016 documented further atrocities, committed by both sides.[23]

Outrages on this scale, committed by South Sudanese against South Sudanese, had not been seen before. Something had changed. To paraphrase the anthropologist Sharon Hutchinson, an expert on these communities: 'God it seems, was no longer watching.'[24] In an effort to understand such brutality, Christine Cheng refers to the 'emotional desensitization' that can happen during war, stimulating further aggressive behaviour.[25] An obscure pattern has also been observed elsewhere, where a society's stock of 'conflict capital' accumulates with its use, generating further violent behaviour.[26] In other words, violence breeds further – and often worse – violence.

Given the history of violence and war in South Sudan, additional 'conflict capital' had been accumulated, generating more fighting. Leaders will now have the difficult task of stemming this seemingly perpetual violence, reversing the trend, and re-sensitizing communities to the concerns of the other. This will be very difficult unless there also is accountability for the atrocities committed.

This will be an even greater challenge because the fighting has spread and engulfed the nation, ignited and reignited conflicts in many locations, as communal disputes increased, and old tensions between ethnic groups, clans and sub-clans resurfaced. Disagreements over borders and boundaries reemerged, whether across payams, counties or countries, and conflicts between cattle-herders and subsistence farmers and resident populations escalated. With the implementation of the presidential decree to establish 28 states, inter-communal violence is likely to increase further, adding fuel to the fire.

The UN Panel of Experts documented how the conflict spread to Northern Bahr el Ghazal and Western Bahr el Ghazal states,[27] the latter with increasing intensity. Traditional communal violence re-erupted, affecting Lakes and Warrap states in particular. The situation in the whole Equatorian region worsened, with an escalation of conflicts between cattle herders and farmers. This violent conflict in Western Equatoria was particularly serious, affecting tens of thousands of civilians,[28] a state which had been among the most peaceful in South Sudan in later years. Conflicts were soon spreading further; the authorities could no longer put out the fires. In early 2016 there were upsurges in violence also in Pibor, Wau, Malakal, as well as Western Equatoria. The already fragile fabric of society was torn apart.

## 'There is no more country'

This reminded me of a statement by the Catholic Bishops of Sudan and South Sudan early in the crisis. They quoted the Bible:

> And everyone who hears these words of mine and does not act on them will be like a foolish man who built his house on sand. The rain fell, and the floods came, and the winds blew and beat against the house, and it fell – and great was its fall![29]

Many had the feeling they were in a house built on sand, or even worse, that the house was already collapsing. One of them, John Kamis, put it this way: '*There is no more country*'.[30] The world, as he knew it, was falling apart.

South Sudan was already classified as one of the world's biggest humanitarian crises, and at this time the only one on this scale in Africa.[31] Counting all those whose livelihoods had been destroyed, and those facing food insecurity, almost half the population of the country was affected. Close to four million were severely food insecure,[32] having increased 80 per cent from September 2014 to September 2015, with famine likely in parts of Unity State.[33] By the end of January 2016, more than 2.3 million people had fled for their lives, around 650,000 of them across international borders.[34] Around 200,000 had sought refuge in UN bases in the country.[35] Historic levels of food insecurity and hunger were expected by mid year.

The economy was collapsing. Market prices had skyrocketed, preventing ordinary people from buying the most basic staples. The oil price plummeted, owing to global trends, and even more for South Sudanese crude than for others.[36] At the same time, the agreement with Sudan under the Transitional Financial Arrangements implied an automatic transfer of $26 per barrel, whatever the oil price in the market. It was an incredible deal, which implied that South Sudan was getting as little as $9-10 dollars per barrel in late 2015.[37] Paradoxically, it was Sudan that now benefited most from South Sudan's oil income; there was not even a clause for renegotiation should the oil price change dramatically. In addition, there was a reduction in oil production following the fighting. The oil fields in Unity were not producing, and parts of the Upper Nile fields were down too. The estimated deficit of South Sudan was said to be around $3 billion by the end of the financial year in 2015 (1 July).[38] The country was almost without income. The economic crisis was total, as reflected in the title of an article at the time: 'Dead Economy Walking in South Sudan'.[39]

It is worth highlighting that at independence, four years earlier, South Sudan had no public debt at all. This had dramatically changed. From 2014 South Sudan needed funds for basic government functions and money to finance the war, purchase arms and ammunition, and pay the Army. The only solution was to borrow; South Sudan engaged further in forward selling of oil. A loan was also obtained from Qatar in 2013, allegedly on commercial terms, of $250m per quarter, or a total of $1b a year.[40] In 2015 the funding needed to cover the government's payroll alone was three times its income.[41] In June, the ministry of finance and economic planning acknowledged that the debt had reached $4.2b.[42] According to my sources, the figure was likely higher. But the government still proceeded with expensive military contracts, acquiring Mi-24 and attack helicopters for close to $140 million, and plans of arms deals of another $50 million.[43] Indeed, even after the signing of the peace agreement both sides continued to acquire new weapons.[44]

While the Central Bank already had problems servicing the debt, it had provided credit lines to the government based on foreign exchange it did not have. The Bank resorted to printing money.[45] A huge gap between the black market rate and the official rate ensued,[46] and the pound lost half its value between January and July 2015.[47] The elite continued to pocket the difference. South Sudanese economists and scholars were now debating what to do with a currency worth almost nothing in the international market. Comparisons with Zimbabwe in 2008, and its decision to dollarize the currency, were frequent.[48]

South Sudan would never have an easy ride on the economic side, despite its oil income. According to Paul Collier, the country falls into all four traps that keep countries poor. It is struggling to emerge from conflict, gets most of its income from natural resources, is landlocked, and suffers from bad governance.[49] But the way the government had managed the economy during the crisis had further entrapped the country in an economically vicious cycle, almost leading to hyperinflation.

And it was getting worse. On 15 December 2015, two years after the civil war started, South Sudan finally unpegged the South Sudanese pound from the dollar, with all transactions following the market determined rate.[50] As one could expect, the value of the currency dropped like a stone.[51] Soon, the oil price fell even further. As this book went to print in early 2016, the net revenue per oil barrel was believed to be less than $5,[52] prompting new negotiations between senior officials of Sudan and South Sudan in early 2016.[53] There was no money. South Sudan had hit rock bottom.

## Saving South Sudan

The peace agreement called for a Transitional Government of National Unity, to include both parties, former detainees and other political parties within a period of 90 days.[54] President Salva Kiir would remain in office, Riek Machar, representing 'South Sudan Armed Opposition', would be first vice president, and James Wani Igga would remain as vice president, a model similar to that in Khartoum after the CPA. At the same time the majority of ministerial seats were divided between the conflicting parties. The former detainees and other parties would get a smaller share. For a 30-month interim period the transitional government would be responsible for implementing the agreement until elections.[55] With such a powersharing arrangement there would be very little difference between this government and prior ones. Those who had been responsible for the demise, would also be part of the transition. The question was whether change would now follow.[56]

Most critical for peace were the security provisions. Unification of forces and a Strategic Defence and Security Review were key commitments. With a stroke of a pen, the mediators had renamed the national Army, the SPLA, 'The National Defence Forces of South Sudan'. This was included in the government's list of reservations.[57] A similar renaming was attempted with the SPLM/A-IO, called 'South Sudan Armed Opposition', corrected in handwriting by Machar, but still minimizing any references to the SPLA in the agreement.[58] Despite the signing and agreement to end the fighting, the civil war continued. Only when details were agreed at a workshop on 26 October, and on the numbers of forces in Juba on 3 November 2015, was progress possible.[59] UPDF for its part started withdrawing its troops from South Sudan two weeks before.[60]

It would be in the reunification and transformation of the Army and the demobilization of many soldiers from both sides that the South Sudanese leadership would face their greatest test. A Joint Integrated Police was also supposed to be established, although the agreement did not include details about reforms either within the Army or the police.

The issue of reconciliation and accountability for atrocities was imperative for peace to prevail. On 27 October 2015, the report of the African Union Commission of Inquiry was finally published.[61] The AU had held back the report until a peace agreement had been signed; it was handed over a year before. A leaked draft had created consternation in early 2015. Despite clear provisions for the protection of witnesses and victims, that document included names of interviewees, in some cases with inaccurate statements attributed to them.[62] The final elaborate report was different, however. It found that a combination of an overall governance crisis, a militarized environment and a political crisis in the ruling party contributed to the outbreak of conflict. The Commission established that there were reasonable grounds to believe that war crimes and crimes against humanity were committed by both parties, and that these were committed in a 'widespread and systematic' manner.[63]

The report recommended that 'those who bear the greatest responsibility at the highest level [be brought] to account'. While the report did not list the perpetrators, the Commission has a highly confidential list which will be submitted in due course.[64]

In the peace agreement the parties had agreed to establish a Hybrid Court, and a Commission for Truth, Reconciliation and Healing.[65] About half the members of the Commission would come from other African countries. The AU Commission of Inquiry recommended something similar, an Africa-led, Africa-owned, Africa-resourced legal mechanism under the aegis of the African Union supported by the international community and the UN, to bring those with the greatest responsibility the highest levels to account. Such a mechanism should include South Sudanese judges and lawyers.[66] The lack of accountability by both sides strengthened the case for such a process. By the end of 2015, none of the two parties had taken decisive action against perpetrators and almost no one had been brought to justice for the atrocities committed.[67] The report also proposed the establishment of a Truth and Reconciliation Commission, and saw peace and justice as complementary, recommending a sequential approach.[68]

On 22 January 2016, the UN Panel of Experts issued its final report, with a very clear verdict:

> The Panel has [...] determined, on the basis of multiple, independent sources with first-hand knowledge, that there is clear and convincing evidence that most of the acts of violence committed during the war, including the targeting of civilians

and violations of international humanitarian law and international human rights law, have been directed by or undertaken with the knowledge of senior individuals at the highest levels of the Government and within the opposition.[69]

At the time of completion of this book, it was too early to say how the recommendations and findings of these two reports would affect the South Sudanese political equation.

## Saving South Sudan from failing

As I highlighted before my departure from the Mission in 2014, South Sudan has been afflicted by three 'diseases' since 2005: the cancer of corruption – with oil becoming a curse rather than a blessing; rule by the gun and not by the law, with impunity among security forces and services; and government by a self-serving elite for the elite rather than for the people.[70] As we have seen, these diseases were to a large degree self-inflicted. During the crisis they worsened, and curing the country would now be much more difficult.

It is therefore clear to most observers that a quick fix between political elites will not help South Sudan. Band-aids do not cure diseases.

South Sudan still has to get through its three challenging transitions, from war to peace, from liberation struggle to government, and from secessionist region to independent country. Amazingly, even on the last point, a number of issues remain. And with recent developments, the two other transitions had become more complicated; the civil war in South Sudan had further militarized and ethicized the South Sudanese society. As the UN Panel of Experts also points out, 'tribal fissures' have widened and ethnic based lobbying groups such as the Jieng (Dinka) Council of Elders have gained significant influence at the centre of power.[71] Most importantly, therefore, it is incumbent upon all South Sudanese leaders to nurture and develop a mindset of a nation, regardless of ethnic affiliation.

We have earlier shown the scale of the challenges South Sudan was already facing in relation to nation-building and state-building. With the civil war, these processes had gone in reverse and become even more complex. This was why the IGAD mediation emphasized an ambitious reform agenda, critical for peace. It included transitional governance arrangements; resource, economic and financial management arrangements; transitional security arrangements, implementation of a permanent ceasefire and security sector reform; transitional justice, accountability, national reconciliation and healing; and a permanent constitution process. This was very ambitious, and rightly so. As Jok Madut Jok says:

> Whatever the nature of the agreement will be [...] no peace agreement will bring peace to South Sudan. While the conflict is rooted in the lackluster state-building and nation-building programs, corruption, insecurity and injustice prevailing in the country since 2005, there is no denying that the events of December 15, 2013 were the tipping point, and patching them up in a quick fix style of peace agreements will not cut it this time, even if the principal parties sign a peace agreement. Any peace agreement that does not commit the warring parties to programs of (far-reaching) reforms, would be as good as an agreement to continue the war.[72]

As we have seen, it would take much more than signatures on paper for peace to be achieved – and not least – sustained, in South Sudan. Implementation of the peace agreement has so far been excruciatingly slow. Nevertheless, the country has likely been saved from fighting. Now it also needs to be saved from failing. This would imply fundamental reforms and a complete overhaul of some of the key state institutions. Most South Sudanese leaders did acknowledge this. South Sudan topped the lists of failed and fragile states in the world in 2014 and 2015.[73] IGAD had still struggled with getting a full commitment from the parties to several of the proposed reforms.

While some reforms are embedded in the agreement, both in relation to the security sector as well as in management of the petroleum sector and financial resources, an overall problem with the agreement is its complexity. The number of commissions, committees, authorities, mechanisms and roadmaps, as well as special funds – and their multiple governance arrangements and unrealistic deadlines is overwhelming. These would be difficult for any government to implement. For the

South Sudanese, with their limited capacity, they will likely be much more than can be handled. Conversely, a Constitutional Review which is expected to be completed within eighteen months is too limited to ensure inclusiveness and a broad-based nation-building process. This warrants further reflection.

The establishment of the transitional government was long overdue. By late 2015 all the former detainees had returned to Juba, except Pagan Amum. After more than two years of fighting, Riek Machar had yet to come back to join the transitional government. While his advance team and several hundred of his people returned to Juba in late December 2015, disagreement over the 28 states held him and the SPLM/A-IO back. The African Union Peace and Security Council and the IGAD ministers issued strong Communiques, calling on the parties to establish the transitional government with immediate effect.[74] On 3 February 2016, Riek Machar stated that he wanted to return and form the government of national unity as soon as possible, interpreting the IGAD Communique as supporting this formation while delaying the issue of the 28 states.[75]

In a surprise announcement on 11 February 2016, and without agreement on this issue, President Salva Kiir appointed Riek Machar as first vice president of South Sudan.[76] This was welcomed by the SPLM-IO. As this book went to print, Machar conveyed that he would return to Juba to take up his new position, along with his security.[77] Even with further delays, it seemed clear that the Transitional Government of National Unity would soon be established. South Sudan had come full circle, with Riek returning to another vice president position, after all the suffering, fighting and bloodshed. The two will now be in charge of a country at serious risk of fragmentation along ethnic lines, and implosion, with an economy in peril, indebted and without many prospects for improvement.

A fundamental question is whether a transitional government, consisting of many of the same characters, will have the political will and capacity to deliver. Will such a government build institutions and at the same time build the bridges necessary to unify a divided nation? Will such a government implement fundamental reforms? Will such a government be able to tackle the 28 states-issue and prevent tribalism? Or will we witness a largely dysfunctional government, only able and willing to implement what is politically most convenient, choosing tactical avoidance as their primary strategy? The latter is certainly most likely.

The negotiations revealed that while all the factions of the SPLM were at loggerheads on most issues, they were united on one. The international community had advocated more transparency and accountability over the management of financial resources, and not least the revenue from oil production. Proposals for stricter controls with international participation were discussed. Various ideas were considered, including stronger external oversight. When this news broke, all factions of the SPLM protested. This was not surprising, given the endemic corruption involving a large number of the cadres on all sides. However, it was disturbing, and it gave many people the feeling that in this area the status quo – and not reforms for financial transparency and accountability – was the priority, even after so many months of civil war. A weakened Economic and Financial Management Authority was the end result.[78]

Nevertheless, the establishment of the Joint Monitoring and Evaluation Commission (JMEC) under the leadership of former President Festus Mogae of Botswana is tasked with overseeing that Authority's work and making sure that the peace agreement is implemented to the letter, reporting regularly to the IGAD Chair and Heads of State, the African Union Peace and Security Council and to the Secretary General and the Security Council of the UN.[79] With the inauguration of JMEC on 27 November 2015, the IGAD mediation had completed its job, and with the highly respected former head of state at the helm the commission certainly had teeth.

International donors have often talked about the 'post-war moment' emphasizing the need to make use of the important window of opportunity after a peace accord has been signed.[80] This moment was largely lost in Southern Sudan after 2005 and after independence, as we have seen. The leadership of the SPLM squandered moments of opportunity. Much more could have been achieved. Following the return of Riek Machar and the establishment of the transitional government, South Sudan has got a second 'post-war moment'. This time, however, less support will be forthcoming, and much more will be expected of the South Sudanese themselves.

In this regard, it is important to be realistic about what can be achieved in the short term. As the AU Commission of Inquiry pointed out, it is critical to avoid an over-ambitious reform agenda.[81] With the limited capacity to manage and implement reforms, a sequential approach would be needed.[82] Setting clear priorities and getting the sequencing right would be critical, focusing on a few reforms at a time. International donors and stakeholders should also realize this, and apply lessons learnt from the past of supply-driven, uncoordinated aid, a tendency to favour technocratic blue-print approaches, and ignoring critical political dynamics.

Attention to the political economy of state-building[83] can give guidance for South Sudan's post-war efforts. Informal structures of power and personal interests crystallize during periods of protracted violence, with the 'recycling' of old networks whose interests may be served even by retaining a weak or 'failed' state.[84] New state institutions can often become instruments for continuation.[85] Informal networks also equal ethnic ties in many societies, as well as political and economic linkages that are resilient, adaptable and difficult to transform by outsiders.

No country can succeed in implementing major reforms in one go, and least of all South Sudan; they have to be moved forward in a prioritized manner. And no country can succeed in doing so on its own, operating in a vacuum.

For such engagement to happen, however, the process of fragmentation and implosion in the country will have to be halted by a leadership pursuing a unifying agenda, not a divisive one. Furthermore, South Sudan will have to make a major effort in restoring its own lost credibility. International partners will also have a significant responsibility. The peace agreement was a result primarily of international and regional engagement and pressure. Neither IGAD, the AU, nor the Troika can now walk away from South Sudan. Evidence from numerous peace processes shows that there is a high risk that agreements signed under external pressure will fail. The architects and midwives of the South Sudan agreement, the guarantors and observers, now need to make sure that this accord does not face the same fate. The international stakeholders have all signed the agreement in various capacities. They must now own up to their commitments. In this regard, JMEC, in close cooperation with the UN and its mission in the country will have decisive roles to play, as the new UNMISS' mandate also reflects.[86]

Furthermore, for South Sudan it is imperative that regional relations are repaired to avoid negative dynamics from undermining peace in the country. This includes refraining from any interference in the affairs of the world's youngest nation through proxies.

### Redemption – by whom?

The conflict in South Sudan bears the hallmark of a society held hostage by its bloody past.[87] After a civil war involving such unfathomable atrocities and a very repressive climate,[88] the divisions and wounds in South Sudan are deeper than ever. The gulf between the leaders and the communities is severe, and the animosity worse than we have ever seen at any point in South Sudanese history. A simultaneous process of healing and reconciliation, justice and accountability will be critical.[89] As a first step, reconciliation within the leadership is urgently needed, making it possible for a more unified leadership to take on the numerous daunting tasks of the peace agreement. This is also necessary to be able to lead a process of healing and reconciliation in a divided country.

One of the greatest risks in this regard is the temptation of leaders to continue with ethnic politics, building their powerbase from divisive strategies aimed at rallying their support base and antagonizing others.[90] This will undermine state-building, nation-building and peace-building processes. In South Sudan, the only alternative organizing principle to ethnicity has been the multi-ethnic SPLM. This was the case during the civil war, and this is the case now. When the party is weak, sectarianism takes hold, and becomes decisive. Short-sighted politicians playing to their own power base and ethnicity make this worse. That was why reunification of the SPLM was so important. Reconciliation within the leadership is key for implementation of the reform agenda and for the state- and nation-building processes in the country to succeed.

The cadres of the SPLM did agree on reunification of the party through negotiations in Arusha from late 2014, leading up to a ground-breaking agreement on 21 January 2015.[91] Unfortunately, the misgivings of some members of the IGAD mediation team against the Arusha process and lack of coordination led to lost opportunities in the talks. Both sides probably have to take responsibility for this. International observers have mistakenly seen the SPLM as the problem and the origin of the crisis in South Sudan. In fact, despite the recent political crisis and the fault lines among the liberators, the Movement is the only glue that can hold South Sudan and its leadership together across ethnic lines. Technocrats and competent leaders, including from other parties will be important, but a transformed and reinvented SPLM – or a similar multi-ethnic platform – may be the only mechanism that can prevent sectarianism and tribalism from fragmenting the country. For this reason, such a reunification process is still imperative, whoever provides the platform going forward.

This includes addressing the historical tensions within the leadership, and not least the critical reform and succession issues. They cannot now leap-frog over these essential processes. They must confront their past – for the sake of the future of their country. Most importantly, and for the first time, they will all have to address the origins of the cyclical tensions in the SPLM leadership from the 1990s onwards, and not least from 2004. Accommodation, 'buying' peace through positions or other means, and not reconciliation, will never solve the problems. Only confronting the past, followed by reconciliation and healing will. This will be vital to avoid a return to conflict in the long run. Even if there were to be changes in party affiliations, such a process is critical.

A unified leadership will have the best chance of unifying the country, and strong checks and balances are ensured, not least through the active engagement of the South Sudanese people – who after all, are the ones that now must have the greatest say over the direction of their country.

Leadership remains most critical, however. Recycling of old leaders will over time be counter-productive, even in reinvented versions. Indeed, not without reason, the reunification of the SPLM put the succession issues high on the agenda. The current leadership – across all factions – is now facing its greatest test. Even with the peace agreement, it is at risk of failing, failing their people, failing the struggle and ultimately failing their country – its primary achievement. There is not much time left to prevent the country from fragmentation and implosion.

On Independence Day in 2011 President Kiir asked: 'Will we let our challenges define us, or will we rise as a nation and define our own future?'

In the last four years the leaders of South Sudan let the challenges define them. And they let the challenges get the better of them. The liberators betrayed themselves and their people. South Sudan is now at risk not only of failing, but also of falling apart.

Archbishop Desmond Tutu says: 'Hope is being able to see that there is light, despite all of the darkness'. From a generational perspective, the story of South Sudan is yet to be told. The next generation of South Sudanese leaders is ready. They should soon be given the chance. It is likely that we will have to count on them to get that story right, a story worthy of the sacrifices of the ancestors and martyrs. If the current crisis can be overcome, and with strong partnership from regional and international partners, we hope they will be given a chance to win a different kind of war, a war against poverty, disease and ignorance, a war where lives are saved rather than taken, where prosperity is achieved rather than destroyed, where hope is brought, rather than despair.[92]

With such support, and with the people holding them to account, they may still be able to save South Sudan, both from fighting and from failing, and finally build the country their people dreamt of.

Only then can South Sudan rise as a nation.

# APPENDIX 1

## SPLM leaders 2011–14

### Members of the SPLM Political Bureau

Lt General Salva Kiir Mayaardit, SPLM chairman and commander-in-chief of SPLA

Dr Riek Machar Teny, first SPLM deputy, unity

Mr James Wani Igga, second SPLM deputy, Central Equatoria

Mr Pagan Amum Okiech, SPLM secretary general/secretary to Political Bureau, Upper Nile State

Mr Daniel Awet Akot, Lakes

Mr Kuol Manyang Juuk, Jonglei

Mr Lual Diing Wol, Northern Bahr el Ghazal

Mr Nhial Deng Nhial, Warrap

Mr Deng Alor Kuol, Abyei

Mr John Luk Jok, Jonglei

Mrs Rebecca Nyandeng de Mabior, Jonglei

Mr Paul Mayom Akec, Lakes

Mr Mark Nyipuoch Ubong, Western Bahr el Ghazal State

Mrs Jemma Nunu Kumba, Western Equatoria State

Mrs Awut Deng Acuil, Warrap

Mr Kosti Manibe, Eastern Equatoria

Mr Taban Deng Gai, Unity State

Mr Akol Paul Kordit, chairman of Youth

Dr Anne Itto, SPLM deputy secretary general

### SPLM ministers and senior advisors during 2011–14

(The list includes longer-term members of the SPLM of both Cabinets, 2011–13, and 2013 onwards; deputy ministers normally not included.)

Deng Alor Kuol

John Kong Nyuon (Deputy Minister Majak d'Agoot Atem acting periodically)
Nhial Deng Nhial
Oyay Deng Ajak
John Luk Jok
Michael Makuei Lueth
Kosti Manibe Ngai
Awut Deng Acuil
Michael Milly Hussein
Barnaba Marial Benjamin
Betty Achan Ogwaro
Gier Chuang Aluong
Agnes Lasuba
Peter Adwok Nyaba
Garang Diing Akuang
Alfred Lado Gore
Jemma Nunu Kumba
Madut Biar Yel
Stephen Dhieu Dau
David Deng Athorbei
Joseph Lual Achui
Paul Mayom Akec
Cirino Hiteng Ofuho
Emmanuel Lowilla
Telar Deng Riing
Rebecca Nyandeng De Mabior
Kuol Manyang Juuk
Obote Mamur Mete
Aleu Ateny Aleu
John Gai Yoah
Aggrey Tissa Sabuni
Paulino Wanawilla Onango
Beda Machar
Ngor Kolong Ngor
Kuong Danhier Gatluak
Nadia Arop Dudi
Awan Riek Guol
Rebecca Joshua Okwachi

# NOTES

## Preface

1   Hilde F. Johnson: *Waging Peace in Sudan: the Inside Story of the Negotiations that Ended Africa's Longest Civil War*, Eastbourne 2011.

2   Agreement on the Resolution of the Conflict in the Republic of South Sudan (ARCSS), signed 17 August 2015.

3   Transitional Government of National Unity (TGoNU), formed on 28 April 2016.

4   All figures from the United Nations Office for the Coordination of Humanitarian Affairs (UNOCHA), South Sudan, *Humanitarian Needs Overview 2018*, UNOCHA November 2017.

5   The mediator is the regional body for the Horn of Africa, IGAD (Intergovernmental Authority on Development), supported by the African Union (AU), the United Nations (UN) and the Troika countries (the US, the UK and Norway).

6   According to the Agreement: The Transitional Period shall commence 90 days after signing of this Agreement and the term of office shall be thirty (30) months preceded by ninety (90) days of a Pretransitional Period.

## Chapter 1: A Dream Comes True

1   Independence Day speech, 9 July 2011.

2   'SPLA Woyee!' has no translation; it signifies praise for the SPLA, battle or victory, and became a slogan for the SPLM as a party.

3   For a more detailed account see Hilde F. Johnson, *Waging Peace in Sudan: The Inside Story of the Negotiations that Ended Africa's Longest Civil War* (Eastbourne, 2011).

4   Alex de Waal, 'When kleptocracy becomes insolvent', *African Affairs*, cxiii/452 (2014), p. 350.

5   Douglas Johnson, 'Federalism in the History of South Sudanese Political Thought', Rift Valley Institute Research Paper 1 (London, 2014), p. 5.

6   United Nations, 'Report of the Secretary General on the Sudan', S/2005/57, 31 January 2005, p. 1, para. 3. See also http://www.un.org/en/peacekeeping/missions/past/unmis/background.shtml.

7   For this process and other 'people-to-people' processes see John Ashworth, *The Voice of the Voiceless: The Role of the Church in the Sudanese Civil War, 1983–2005* (Nairobi, 2014), pp. 151–67.

8   The phrase is Abel Alier's, *Southern Sudan: Too Many Agreements Dishonoured*, 2nd edn (Exeter, 2003).

9      African Union, 'Commission of Inquiry on South Sudan: Final Report of the African Union Mission of Inquiry on South Sudan' (Addis Ababa, 15 October 2014), pp. 20–1.

10    Breaking the tradition of taking time to mourn, Kuol Manyang and 'uncle' Elijah Malok, both Dinka Bor, immediately proposed Kiir. Interview 34, 21 April 2015, Interview 8, 29 January 2015; Interview 48, 24 June 2015.

11    Johnson, *Waging Peace in Sudan*, p. 215.

12    De Waal, 'When kleptocracy becomes insolvent', p. 354.

13    Interview with then SPLM Representative to the US, Ezekiel Gatkuoth, February 2015.

14    Statements by President Obama; President Obama in Ministerial Meeting on Sudan, 'The Fate of Millions', 24 September 2010. Available online: https://www.whitehouse.gov/blog/2010/09/24/president-obama-ministerial-meeting-sudan-fate-millions.

15    Reported in the *Guardian* on 4 January 2011. Available online: http://www.theguardian.com/world/2011/jan/04/bashir-south-sudan-independence-vote.

## Chapter 2: A Country without a State

1      A more common comparison is with France, which is roughly the same size but has thrice the population.

2      A census was conducted in 2008 in Sudan as a whole. It was controversial and not seen as legitimate in Southern Sudan, claiming a population in the semi-autonomous region of 8.26 million people.

3      Jok Madut Jok, quoted in Francis Deng (ed.), *New Sudan in the Making?* (Trenton, 2009), p. 458.

4      For example Ramciel, located where the three greater regions, Equatoria, Upper Nile and Bahr el Ghazal meet.

5      Edward Thomas, *South Sudan: A Slow Liberation* (London, 2015), pp. 60–1.

6      'Report from a Special Mission on the Economic Development of Southern Sudan', IBRD Report No. 119a-SU (1 June 1973), p. 5 (para 1.15) cited 'forcible spread of Arabization and Islam, the neglect of secondary education, curbs placed on Christian missionary activities, and, finally the expulsion of all missionaries in the South in 1964'.

7      Christopher Clapham, 'From Liberation Movement to Government: Past Legacies and the Challenge of Transition in Africa', The Brenthurst Foundation, Discussion Paper 8/12 (Johannesburg, 2012).

8      Ibid., pp. 5–6.

9      Ibid., p. 6

10    Ibid., p. 8.

11    'The "curse" of Liberation', *Sudan Tribune*, 16 February 2013, 15.02. Available online: http://www.sudantribune.com/spip.php?article45547.

12    Cherri Leonardi, '"Liberation" or capture: Youth in between "Hakuma" and "Home" during civil war and its aftermath in Southern Sudan', *African Affairs* cvi/424 (2007), pp. 391–412. Siri Torjesen emphasizes 'state capture' in post-conflict societies in 'Transition from War to Peace' in Mats Berdal and

Dominik Zaum (eds), *Political Economy of Statebuilding: Power after Peace* (London, 2013), pp. 48–62.

13   Øystein Rolandsen, *Guerilla Government: Political Changes in Southern Sudan during the 1990s* (Oslo, 2005).

14   SPLM, 'Peace through Development: Perspectives and Prospects in the Sudan', February 2000.

15   'SPLM Strategic Framework: For War-to-Peace Transition', SPLM Economic Commission, August 2004.

16   Ibid., p. 66.

17   This definition builds on John R. Common's *Institutional Economics: Its Place in Political Economy* (New Brunswick, 1990).

18   'SPLM Strategic Framework: For War-to-Peace Transition', p. 62.

19   Consequently, the country would be also denied the service of able citizens from numerically smaller ethnicities, see Thomas, *South Sudan*, pp. 278–9.

20   Clapham, 'From Liberation Movement to Government', p. 12.

21   Dan Smith (PRIO), 'Towards a Strategic Framework for Peacebuilding: Getting Their Act Together', Overview Report of the Joint *Utstein* Study of Peacebuilding, Evaluation Report 1/2004, Ministry of Foreign Affairs, Oslo, together with the Evaluation departments of UK DFID, the Netherlands and Germany, April 2004, p. 10; Dina Esposito and Batsheba Crocker, 'To Guarantee the Peace: An Action Strategy for a Post-Conflict Sudan', Centre for Strategic and International Studies (CSIS) (Washington, DC, January 2004), p. 8.

22   Barney Jopson, 'Fury at unspent funds for Sudan', *Financial Times*, 16 February 2010.

23   Lise Grande, 'Rescuing the Peace in Southern Sudan'. Presentation at an international donor forum in Brussels, 10 January 2010, p. 24.

24   *It's Our Turn to Eat* is the title of Michaela Wrong's book (London, 2009) about John Githongo, the Kenyan anti-corruption tsar.

25   Kenya Commercial Bank (KCB) was established in Southern Sudan in 2006.

26   Sources inform me that at least $30 million was pocketed by a number of SPLM leaders. After the suspension of Secretary General Pagan Amum Okiech in July 2013, this specific case was not investigated in detail. Amum sued journalists who accused him of corruption for defamation of character, and he won the case.

27   'Sudan Public Expenditure Review', Synthesis Report No. 41840-SD, Poverty Reduction and Economic Management Unit, the World Bank, December 2007, Executive Summary, para. 13.

28   One could, for example, have opted for an externally administered trust fund, with a governance framework which was nationally owned, as an interim solution until capacity was built.

29   SPLM leaders privately admitted this in, e.g. Interview 39, 24 April 2015.

30   Ibid.

31   Peter Adwok Nyaba, *The Politics of Liberation in South Sudan: An Insider's View* (Nairobi, 1996).

32   'Liberating Areas, Exploiting People: The "Old" SPLA', in *Food and Power in Sudan: A Critique of Humanitarianism*, African Rights, London, 15 July 1997, pp. 89–97; Alex de Waal, principal investigator.

33   Ibid., pp. 73–5.

34 John Prendergast, *Frontline Diplomacy: Humanitarian Aid and Conflict in Africa* (Boulder, 1996), p. 23.

35 *Sudan Tribune*, 'Text: Minutes of Historical SPLM Meeting in Rumbek 2004', Section: Confidential Report on the Rumbek Meeting 2004, 12 March 2014. Available online: http://sudantribune.com/spip.php?article26320. The Rapporteur, Telar Deng Riing has verified the minutes.

36 Ibid.

37 Ibid.

38 Ibid.

39 James Copnall, *A Poisonous Thorn in our Hearts: Sudan and South Sudan's Bitter and Incomplete Divorce* (London, 2014), p. 61.

40 Thomas, *South Sudan*, p. 139.

41 Audit Chamber, 'Presentation of the Report of the Auditor General on the Financial Statements of the Government of the Southern Sudan' (Juba, 2008), p. 7. The figure is 1.293 billion Sudanese pounds (SDG). I have used an exchange rate of 3 to the dollar.

42 OECD, Aid Statistics, Development Cooperation Directorate (DCD-DAC), International Development Statistics (IDS), CRS dataset, Paris, 2014. Available online: www.oecd.org/development/stats/idsonline.htm.

43 Information provided by Manuel da Silva, a former trade minister in Mozambique and subsequently a UN official, including in Sudan for many years, was particularly helpful: several thousand civil servants from Portuguese and Spanish-speaking countries were seconded to Mozambique to work under FRELIMO cadres and provide on-the-job training.

44 Seconded experts are imbedded in a national institution for a longer period, reporting to local authorities, and where the 'sending' institution takes responsibility for all costs related to the secondment.

45 Author's notes from conversations with Cabinet ministers.

46 For further details see numerous World Bank reports, including http://www-ds.worldbank.org/external/default/WDSContentServer/WDSP/IB/2008/01/16/000020953_20080116104133/Rendered/PDF/418400SD.pdf.

47 Interview 39, April 2015.

48 Report 41840-SD 'Sudan Public Expenditure Review', Synthesis Report December 2007, Poverty Reduction and Economic Management Unit Africa Region.

49 GoSS paper for High Level Meeting in Brussels on Core Functions, September 2010.

50 Copnall, *A Poisonous Thorn*, p. 132, uses the term 'federal government'. The Transitional Constitution does not provide a 'federal' system, so I use the term national government.

51 2012 statistics from the GRSS Ministry of Agriculture and Forestry, including Presentation for the Washington Conference, 31 October 2012. Even at independence about 83 per cent of the population lived in rural areas, according to the National Bureau of Statistics, http://ssnbs.org/.

52 World Bank, Poverty Reduction and Economic Management Unit, 'Sudan Public Expenditure Review', Synthesis Report No. 41840-SD, December 2007, Executive Summary, pp. iv, vi.

53    Copnall, *A Poisonous Thorn*, p. 113.

54    World Bank, Poverty Reduction and Economic Management Unit, 'Sudan Public Expenditure Review', Synthesis Report No. 41840-SD, Executive Summary, para. 13 (from an annual revenue of about $120,000 in 2005 to $1.7 billion in 2006).

55    Available online: http://farmlandgrab.org/uploads/attachment/20130304-Transnational-land-acquisitions-10.pdf.

56    World Bank, Poverty Reduction and Economic Management Unit, 'Sudan Public Expenditure Review', p. 67.

57    Ibid., p. 71.

58    Interview 39, April 2015, and eyewitness reports of cash handouts by Southern Sudanese security officials.

59    Interview 17, February 2015, verified by others, referring to kickbacks by senior officials, including a $50 million deal in May–June 2011, just prior to independence.

60    Interview 17, February 2015; Interview 40, March 2015; Interview 43, April 2015; Copnall, *A Poisonous Thorn*, p. 135. Some say the selling price was $300 million, others $185 million (of which $135 million in cash), and some claim that some of the money was transferred to the government.

61    Interview 17, February 2015; Interview 43, April 2015.

62    Telecom companies such as Zain and MTN had to pay tax; controversially, there was no income to the government from the sale of – or revenues from – Gemtel or Vivacell.

63    Interview 17, February 2015; Interview 43 April 2015.

64    In late July 2013 investigations were launched into this and other issues (management of the party and party finances), focusing on Secretary General (SG) Pagan Amum who was suspended from his position. The outcome was presented at the National Liberation Council-meeting of the SPLM on 14–15 December 2013, leading to the release of the Secretary General from his position.

65    Interview 17, February 2015; Interview 40, March 2015; Interview 43, April 2015.

66    Audits for 2005–6, 2007 and 2008, published from November 2011 onwards, show a clear pattern.

67    Interview 38, October 2014.

68    Interview 39, April 2115, states on the authority of several sources that a very senior official in Sudan handed out $11.5 million in cash every month.

69    Interviews 16 and 17, February 2015.

70    Interview 38, October 2014.

71    The Government of South Sudan's oil revenue is estimated at $8.66 billion in 2008–2011 (siteresources.worldbank.org/INTSUDAN/Resources/GoSS_Financing_Requirement.ppt+&cd=6&hl=en&ct=clnk&gl=us). Even with less annual oil revenue than average during this period, the total figure from 2005–2011 would likely be beyond $12 billion.

72    Available online: http://www.reuters.com/article/2012/06/04/us-southsudan-corruption-idUSBRE8530QI20120604, Copnall, *A Poisonous Thorn*, p. 137.

73    Audit Chamber, 'The Report of the Auditor General on the Financial

Statements of the Government of Southern Sudan for Financial Year Ended 31 December 2005'; equivalent – 'Ended 31 December 2006', equivalent – 'Ended 31 December 2007', equivalent – 'Ended 31 December 2008'.

74   Ibid., 2005, 2006.

75   This figure ($288 million) has been corroborated in Interview 15, February 2015; Interview 18, February 2015; and Interview 11, February 2015 without being reflected in the budget.

76   'Presentation of the Auditor General to the South Sudan National Assembly of the Audit Reports on the Accounts of the Government of Southern Sudan For the Years 2005 and 2006', 1 November 2011, p. 20. Hereinafter PAGSSNA.

77   Ibid., pp. 11–12, 21–2.

78   PAGSSNA, For the Year Ended 31 December 2007, March 2012, p. 16.

79   Ibid., p. 15; a 'weekend allowance' meant to simply give civil servants extra pay, on top of the normal salary, before the weekend.

80   PAGSSNA, For the Years 2005 and 2006, 1 November 2011, p. 10.

81   PAGSSNA, For the Year Ended 31 December 2007, March 2012, p. 15.

82   Ibid., p. 8.

83   PAGSSNA, For the Year Ended 31 December 2008, p. 8.

84   Payroll documentation provided by a senior official in Juba, 2012.

85   PAGSSNA, For the Year Ended 31 December 2008, pp. 5–6. The reports show overspending in most ministries: see 2007, pp. 8–9; 2008, pp. 5–6.

86   PAGSSNA, For the Year Ended 31 December 2008, p. 13.

87   Ibid., p. 13 states that the contracts awarded amounted to SDG 7 billion, against a budget of SDG 2.6 billion. The Finance Ministry later reported that the government signed 1,738 contracts for delivery of 50 million bags of dura and maize valued at SDG 6.2 billion. Later investigations also revealed various amounts of undelivered grain; and insufficient storage facilities for delivered grain, some of which was of poor quality.

88   After investigations conducted by the STAR-programme of the World Bank/ UNODC, the actual amount reported as fraudulent (on the so-called black list) was approximately $250 million. A summary of the outcome of these investigations is with the author.

89   Laws of the Republic of South Sudan, 'The Transitional Constitution', 2011, Article 144, (1) b: 'Without the prejudice to the powers of the Ministry of Justice in public prosecution, the Commission shall [...] investigate and prosecute only cases of corruption.'

90   Interview 39, 24 April 2015.

91   Donors would not provide budget support or direct assistance to the GoSS. Aid-funded programmes implemented by others, contractors or multilateral agencies, or channelled through trust funds administered by UNDP and the World Bank. The Compact did not change this.

92   Government of Southern Sudan (GoSS), 'Juba Compact between the Development Partners and the Government of Southern Sudan', Juba, 30 June 2009.

93   Ben French and Nicholas Travis, 'South Sudan: The Juba Compact', ODI Budget Strengthening Initiative. Country Learning Notes, July 2012, p. 4.

94    Interview 12, February 2015; Interview 28, March 2015; Interview 40, February 2015; Interview 39, 24 April 2015.

95    Interview 12, February 2015; Interview 28, March 2015. The author has had access to, or seen copies of, documents proving the accuracy of information in this paragraph.

96    Copnall, *A Poisonous Thorn*, p. 136.

97    *Sudan Tribune*, 18 November 2014.

98    Manibe failed to stop remittance of $8 million requisitioned by a prominent minister, Deng Alor, reportedly payable to the account of a relative in Nairobi for procurement of storage safes.

99    Recently the government started instructing ministers to move out of hotels, *Sudan Tribune*, 18 November 2014.

100   'Edward Lino: There was no Coup in Juba, Part I', *PaanLuel Wel* blog, 9 February 2014. Available online: http://paanluelwel.com/2014/02/09/edward-lino-there-was-no-coup-in-juba/ 2014.

101   Author's notes 2012–2013; Interview 40, February 2015.

102   Interview 40, February 2015. For the Chinese loan see https://www.imf.org/external/pubs/ft/dsa/pdf/2014/dsacr14345.pdf 38 country.eiu.com/article.aspx%3Farticleid%3D922349476%26Country%.

103   Interview 40, February 2015.

104   Available online: https://radiotamazuj.org/en/article/special-investigation-no-open-bidding-juba-roadworks;https://radiotamazuj.org/en/article/roads-built-abmc-never-handed-over-central-equatoria-govt.

105   Interview 4, 7 January 2015.

106   Transparency International, Anti-corruption Resource Centre, 'Overview of Corruption and Anti-corruption in South Sudan', U4 Expert Answer 371, 4 March 2013.

107   Interview 17, February 2015.

108   Interview 17, February 2015.

109   Interview 42, April 2015; Interview 17, February 2015.

110   De Waal, 'When kleptocracy become insolvent', p. 347.

111   'Public Expenditures in South Sudan: Are they delivering?', South Sudan Economic Brief, Issue no. 2, February, pp. 1–2. All figures from this report.

112   World Bank, 'Sudan – Strengthening Good Governance for Development Outcomes in Southern Sudan: Issues and Options', WB Report no. 48997_SD, April 2010, p. 102.

113   The rationale was to provide food-for-work programmes and deliver food aid by road rather than (more expensively) by air. Also see Copnall, *A Poisonous Thorn*, p. 128.

114   While disaggregated (pre-independence) Southern Sudanese data are difficult to obtain, some are available. See e.g. World Bank Report, 'Public Expenditures in South Sudan: Are They Delivering?', South Sudan Economic Brief, Issue No. 2, February 2013, pp. 10–11.

115   Ibid., p. 10.

116   GoSS, MOFEP, 'South Sudan Development Plan 2011–2013'. The figure

for Kenya: xv; figures also from UNICEF – www.unicef.org/southsudan/education.html.

117  World Bank, 'Public Expenditures in South Sudan: Are They Delivering?', p. 14.

118  Ibid., pp. 13–15.

119  'South Sudan Development Plan 2011–13', p. xv.

120  UNICEF statistics. Available online: http://www.unicef.org/southsudan/reallives_13025.html.

121  Southern Sudan Centre for Census, Statistics and Evaluation, 'Key Indicators for Southern Sudan'. Available online: http://ssnbs.org/storage/key-indicators-for-southern-sudan/Key%20Indicators_A5_final.pdf.

122  Thomas, *South Sudan*, p. 88.

123  Ibid., pp. 127–33.

124  Ibid., p. 143.

125  Ibid., p. 129.

126  SPLM Economic Commission, 'SPLM Strategic Framework: For War-to-Peace Transition', August 2004.

127  'GOSS Priority Core Governance Functions: An Action Plan for Rapidly Building Capacity', Presentation to Brussels High Level Meeting, 17 September 2010.

128  'South Sudan Development Plan 2011–2013: Realizing Freedom, Equality, Justice, Peace and Prosperity for All', Juba, August 2011.

129  International Republican Institute (IRI), 'Survey of South Sudan. Public Opinion 6–11 September 2011'.

130  The *Guardian*, 4 January 2011. Available online: http://www.theguardian.com/world/2011/jan/04/bashir-south-sudan-independence-vote.

131  Interview 41, 27 June 2015.

132  Transparency International, Anti-Corruption Resource Centre, 'Overview of Corruption and Anti-corruption in South Sudan', U4 Expert Answer 371, 4 March 2013.

133  As of late 2015 many companies hired to work on the celebration had not been paid.

134  Information from GOSS delegation at World Bank/IMF Spring meetings, 15–17 April 2011; the conversation took place on 14 April.

135  Author's notes.

136  See also Andrew Ssemwanga, 'South Sudanese Pound, Managed under Floating Exchange Rate Regime', in Samson S. Wassara and Al-Tayib Zain Al-Abdin (eds), *Post-Referendum Sudan, National and Regional Questions* (Senegal, 2014), pp. 189–91, 201–4.

137  Between 18 July and 1 September 2011, the Bank of South Sudan converted approximately 1,771 billion of the estimated 2.1 billion Sudanese pounds in circulation in South Sudan at a one-to-one exchange rate.

138  Available online: http://www.oanda.com/currency/iso-currency-codes/SDG.

139  The UN Country Team had helped identify projects that realistically could be completed within this time frame. The new Minister of Presidential

Affairs never helped to sell this achievement, and the government was criticized in the Assembly, *incorrectly*, for failing to deliver.

140 In possession of the author.

141 The Treasury Account is the current account used by ministries of finance or treasury departments around the world, and is normally held in the respective central bank.

142 UNMISS' Senior Advisor on Statebuilding and Peacebuilding.

143 This followed a brief period of auctioning, letting demand for foreign exchange allow the currency to 'find its level'.

144 IMF Country Report 14/345: 'Republic of South Sudan 2014 Staff Report for the Article IV Consultation', 7 December 2014. Available online: https://www.imf.org/external/pubs/ft/scr/2014/cr14345.pdf.

145 Ibid.

146 Confidential memorandum from some donors to the Government of South Sudan, in possession of the author.

147 Available online: http://www.bbc.com/news/world-africa-15000900; Statement from President's Office dated 19 September 2011 (copy in author's possession).

148 There followed Presidential Order 30/11, 'Declaration of Assets and the Prohibition of Private Business', 9 December 2011; and Presidential Order 32/11, 'Operationalization and Implementation of Five Points Measures for Accountability and Transparency', 12 December 2011.

149 Letters were sent to Heads of State and Government, as appropriate, in countries where banks were presumed to hold stolen assets, followed by contacts with the countries' authorities. Little progress was made.

150 Quoted in Victor Lugala, *Vomiting Stolen Food* (Nairobi, 2010), p. 2.

151 This forced the UN Security Council to cancel its planned visit to Abyei.

152 Ted Dagne, *Sudan: The Crisis in Darfur and the North-South Relationship*, Congressional Research Service, 15 June 2011, p. 2.

153 A Security Council Resolution was passed at the end of June, mandating establishment of a United Nations Interim Security Force for Abyei (UNISFA), SCR 1990, 27 June 2011.

154 Related to a multilayered complex of conflicts over land, and tensions from the Kokora period in Juba (1982–3), when a redivision into sub-regions resulted in exclusion of Dinka, ethnic clashes and killings (Rens Willems and David Deng, 'The legacy of Kokora in South Sudan', Briefing Paper, Intersections of Truth, Justice and Reconciliation in South Sudan, November 2015, pp. 13–16).

155 The coordinator of these efforts was our Senior Advisor on Statebuilding and Peacebuilding seconded to the presidency.

156 Security Council Resolution 1996 S/RES/1996 (2011), 8 July 2011, OP 18.

157 The first cabinet discussion of the Peacebuilding Support Plan (PBSO) was in mid November 2011.

158 The Peacebuilding Support Plan was largely based on the SSDP, and support programmes by UNMISS, the UN Country team and relevant bilateral and

multilateral donors; submitted in early March 2012 and considered by the Security Council in their meeting that same month.

159　See numerous references in Johnson, *Waging Peace in Sudan*, 2011.

160　Copnall, *A Poisonous Thorn*, p. 226

161　AUHIP report to the AU Peace and Security Council, November 30 2011, p. 8, para. 24.

162　'Survey of South Sudan Public Opinion', International Republican Institute, 6-27 September 2011, p. 9

163　'Building a Nation: South Sudanese Share Their Thoughts on the Creation of a Successful State', November 23, 2011; 'Governing South Sudan, Opinions of South Sudanese on a Government that Can Meet Citizen Expectations: Findings from Focus Groups with Men and Women in South Sudan', 22 March 2012, p. 5.

## Chapter 3: An Incomplete Divorce

1　Available online: http://www.rssnegotiationteam.org/past-agreements.html.

2　'Report of the Secretary General to the Security Council on the Situation in Abyei', 26 July 2011, S/2011/451, p. 2.

3　'Report on the Human Rights Situation during the Violence in Southern Kordofan, Sudan', UNMIS, June 2011.

4　Interview 17, 4 February 2015.

5　Copnall, *A Poisonous Thorn*, p. 150; Interview 17, 4 February 2015.

6　Interview 16, 5 February 2015.

7　Kiir to Obama, letter dated 12 October 2011, copy seen by author.

8　On 15 October 2011 the GRSS proposed to forgive debt by Sudan of $2.84 billion and provide transitional financial assistance of $2.04 billion for three years, totalling together $4.89 billion (or 94 per cent of Sudan's projected budget deficit).

9　Author's notes of conversations with GRSS delegation and mediators.

10　The meeting in Khartoum, 29 February 2012, was cleared by UNHQ in New York, as critical border issues related to the UN's operations could only be resolved at the presidential level.

11　Evidence submitted by UNMISS to the Security Council, November 2011, in possession of the author.

12　The GRSS preferred to call the package 'financial assistance', Khartoum preferred 'financial arrangements', a terminological dispute that became a major sticking point.

13　South Sudan stated a commitment to resolve all outstanding issues. Its conditions were that implementation of the transitional financial arrangements would be consistent with Guiding Principle 9 for the negotiations (8 February 2011) and: (i) Immediate, unconditional withdrawal of SAF troops from Abyei and agreement on a clear, time-bound process for resolving determination of the final status of Abyei; and (ii) Final agreement on a time-bound process for demarcation of the agreed borders and agreement on an arbitration process for the disputed areas. The final monthly payment schedule would be organized so that higher payments were made after demarcation of border areas was completed.

14  At this time, these demands were related to Khartoum's unilaterally stipulated user fee of $ 35 per barrel. Reportedly, Sudan intended to use the oil as payment 'in kind' in lieu of receiving $25 per barrel transfers from South Sudan.

15  See Chapter 6.

16  Interview 38, 24 October 2014.

17  Ibid.

18  Also see Statement by the President to the National Legislative Assembly, 23 January 2012.

19  Briefing by Kalonzo Musyoka in Nairobi, 5–6 March 2012.

20  Ibid.

21  Tweet by Reuters journalist Hez Holland, 31 January 2012.

22  AUHIP to Kiir ('Proposed Roadmap for Final Agreement on Oil'), 20 January 2012, in possession of the author; Kiir to AUHIP, 21 January 2012.

23  The meeting between the parties under the auspices of the Ethiopian Prime Minister took place prior to the main plenary meeting of the IGAD Heads of State on 27 January 2012.

24  De Waal, 'When kleptocracy becomes insolvent', pp. 363–4.

25  Meeting with Meles Zenawi, 30 January 2012.

26  De Waal, 'When kleptocracy becomes insolvent', pp. 363–4

27  De Waal claims that Pagan Amum 'overruled and humiliated his President' (ibid., pp. 363–4).

28  Interview 46, April 2015.

29  Author's notes of meeting of AUHIP leaders and UN officials, 30 January 2012.

30  Some ships were literally at sea for months with a cargo that no one wanted to buy for fear of litigation.

31  Available online: https://www.skadden.com/professionals/david-herlihy.

32  De Waal, 'When kleptocracy becomes insolvent', p. 364; Author's notes from meetings with World Bank officials.

33  The impact of these combined economic shocks could imply a projected increase in the poverty rate to 83 per cent in 2013 (from 50 per cent in 2009).

34  Budget support or loans could not be provided, given the GRSS' weak macro-economic performance and problems with transparent financial management.

35  If various instruments in the World Bank, African Development Bank and IMF were used to the maximum, they could provide no more than $100 million. Macro-economic performance is decisive for loans to be provided.

36  The loan, which was obtained towards the end of 2012 was in the order of $250 million per quarter, a total of $1 billion per annum (Interview 35, 23 April 2015).

37  In a letter from the chief negotiator of South Sudan, Pagan Amum to the Security Council, ambassadors and representatives in Addis Ababa on 12 March 2012, he substantiated in detail the basis for the statement that 'the

GoS [had] established that their oil fee demands were not based on cost or necessarily state practice or international law, but simply a government decision to secure no less than $9–10 billion from the RSS – whatever the source and configuration'. Copy in author's possession.

38    Available online: http://www.rssnegotiationteam.org/uploads/1/2/8/8/12889608/10_agreement_on_the_demarcation_of_the_boundary_13_march_2012.pdf and http://www.rssnegotiationteam.org/uploads/1/2/8/8/12889608/11._nationality_agreement_13_march_2012.pdf.

39    Author's notes of conversations; Copnall, *A Poisonous Thorn*, p. 238.

40    Interview 9, December 2014; Copnall, *A Poisonous Thorn*, p. 239.

41    It turned out that the SPLA had not 'taken Heglig'. They had approached, but not as far as capturing the oilfields or town proper.

42    Statement at public rally 4 March 2012. Available online: http://panafricannews.blogspot.no/2012/03/sudan-president-bashir-orders.html.

43    'Sudan suspends Summit with the South after border clashes', Agence France-Presse (AFP), 27 March 2012.

44    UNMISS's Matrix over reported and verified bombing incidents, reporting eight bombs in total in November 2011 and 1 in February 2012: 'Report of the Secretary General on South Sudan' S/212/140, p. 8.

45    According to UNMISS figures, by 18 April 2012, 13 civilians had been killed and 23 injured from bomb attacks on South Sudanese territory.

46    The Dinka name had always been 'Panthou', while 'Heglig' had been used by the Khartoum government since 1978. See Douglas Johnson, 'Note on Panthou/Heglig', 2 May 2012, published on 'Gurtong Net', 5 May 2012. Available online: http://www.gurtong.net/ECM/Editorial/tabid/124/ctl/ArticleView/mid/519/articleId/6915/Dr-Douglas-H-Johnson-Note-on-PanthouHeglig.aspx, and in summary form in the *Sudan Tribune*, 5 May 2012. Available online: http://www.sudantribune.com/spip.php?article42499.

47    Author's notes. See also Copnall, *A Poisonous Thorn*, p. 230.

48    Johnson, 'Note on Panthou/Heglig', 2–4, unpublished note, shared with the AUHIP negotiation team.

49    Ibid., p. 4.

50    Even in this revised map, the status of Heglig is not clear: Johnson, 'Note on Panthou/Heglig', p. 4.

51    Available online: http://www.pca-cpa.org/showpage.asp?pag_id=1306.

52    Reuters Industries, 'UPDATE 2-Sudan says Heglig oilfield repaired, pumping oil', 2 May 2012.

53    The National Legislature in the Republic of South Sudan consists of two chambers, the National Legislative Assembly and the Council of States.

54    Available online: http://www.newsudanvision.com/sudan/2574-south-sudan-president-addresses-national-legislature-on-sudan-attacks.

55    The term 'co-president' had been invented in September 2011 by government hardliners unhappy with the mandate of UNMISS and determined to undermine it.

56    Government statement, 12 April 2012.

57    Numerous statements, 11–14 April, in the archive of the author.

58   Available online: http://www.un.org/en/ga/search/view_doc.asp?symbol =S/PRST/2012/12.

59   In possession of the author.

60   Government of South Sudan to Security Council, 14 April 2012.

61   Border disputes between Sudan and South Sudan were not in the mandate of UNMISS. But discreet good offices on behalf of the Secretary General were part of any Special Representative's job.

62   UNMISS statement about the bombing in Unity and Warrap States, 16 April 2012.

63   According to UNMISS statistics 16 were killed and 34 wounded during the period 11–21 April.

64   Press Statement by UN Secretary General and UNMISS, 17 April 2012.

65   Available online: http://www.bbc.com/news/world-africa-17727624.

66   Speech recorded by Al Jazeera, published on 19 April 2012, and referenced in http://www.sudantribune.com/spip.php?mot422.

67   Copnall, *A Poisonous Thorn*, pp. 230–1.

68   Ibid., p. 232.

69   UNMISS statement on the bombing in Bentiu, Unity State, 23 April 2012; UN Secretary General: 'Secretary General Condemns Aerial Bombardment on South Sudan by Sudanese Armed Forces', SG/SM/14248-AFR/2380, 23 April 2012.

70   De Waal, 'When kleptocracy becomes insolvent', p. 364.

71   AUPSC statement, 24 April 2012. Available online: http://www.peaceau.org/uploads/psc-319-com-soudan-south-sudan-24-04-2012.pdf.

72   The agreement to establish the Safe Demilitarized Border Zone would demilitarize an area of 10 km on both sides of the so-called median line between the two countries. A border monitoring mission was supposed to oversee implementation.

73   SCR 2046 used the term 'additional measures under Article 41 of the Charter', which is code for sanctions.

74   To avoid accusations that the UN was predetermining the border, it abided by the map used by the former UNMIS, constituting our Area of Operations. The South Sudanese saw this as approximating Khartoum's position, and it was a constant irritant in our relations.

75   Riek Machar to Security Council, 3 May 2012.

76   Statement on Radio Miraya, 23 May 2012.

77   Available online: http://www.sudantribune.com/spip.php?article44006.

78   Available online: http://www.rssnegotiationteam.org/historic-september-27-peace-agreements.html.

79   Copnall, *A Poisonous Thorn*, p. 227.

80   Author's notes from conversations with senior officials, Juba, September 2012.

81   I was at Deng Alor's house when I got news about the final decision. The Security Council was meeting in just an hour, so we made sure that phone calls were placed for the latest government positions to be conveyed.

82   Available online: http://peacemaker.un.org/sites/peacemaker.un.org/files/SD-SS_130312_ImplementationMatrix.pdf, Section 5.4, pp. 11–12.

83   This was related to pipeline-differences.

84    Available online: http://peacemaker.un.org/sites/peacemaker.un.org/files/
      SD-SS_130312_ImplementationMatrix.pdf.
85    Available    online:    http://www.rssnegotiationteam.org/modalities-for-
      security-arrangements.html.
86    Oil exports from South Sudan through Sudan restarted on 5 May 2013.
87    It has not been possible to corroborate this quotation from an eyewitness.
88    Interview 33, 21 March 2015.
89    Available online: http://www.reuters.com/article/2013/05/27/us-sudan-
      south-oil-idUSBRE94Q0IL20130527.
90    Ibid.
91    Ibid.
92    Copnall, *A Poisonous Thorn*, p. 219.
93    *Sudan Tribune*, 5 May 2013, www.sudantribune.com/spip.php?mot2815.
94    The visit took place on 30 June–2 July 2013.
95    *The Guardian*, 4 July 2013.
96    'Human Security Baseline Assessment for *Sudan* and *South Sudan* (*HSBA*)',
      South Sudan Crisis Timeline 27 June 2014, p. 3, www.smallarmssurveysudan.
      org/fileadmin/docs/documents/HSBA-South-Sudan-Crisis-Timeline.pdf.
97    Available online: http://www.gurtong.net/ECM/Editorial/tabid/124/ctl/
      ArticleView/mid/519/articleId/12789/South-Sudans-Kiir-In-Khartoum-
      To-Avert-Oil-Shutdown.aspx.
98    HSBA, 'Small Arms Survey', 2014, 4; Interview 17, 4 February 2015.
99    Available online: http://www.securitycouncilreport.org/atf/cf/%7B65BF
      CF9B-6D27–4E9C-8CD3-CF6E4FF96FF9%7D/s_2013_627.pdf.
      Author's notes from conversations with Sudanese officials.
100   HBSA Small Arms Survey, 2014, p. 4.
101   'The referendum in Abyei is an ongoing challenge for the African Union',
      2 December 2013. Available online: http://www.issafrica.org/iss-today/
      the-referendum-in-abyei-is-an-ongoing-challenge-for-the-african-union.
102   *Sudan Tribune*, 28 October 2013. Available online: http://www.sudant-
      ribune.com/spip.php?article48606.
103   De Waal, 'When kleptocracy becomes insolvent', pp. 347–69.
104   Ibid., p. 349.
105   'Statement of H. E Salva Kiir Mayardit, President of the Republic of South
      Sudan to the South Sudanese People on Transparency and Accountability',
      21 September 2011, Juba, in possession of the author. 'South Sudan's
      President Salva Kiir to Fight Corruption', *BBC News*, 21 September 2011.
      Available    online:    http://www.bbc.com/news/world-africa-15000900;
      Press release 'Republic of South Sudan, The Office of the President.
      Anti-Corruption Measures', 1 June 2011, Juba, available in PDF-format
      on https://paanluelwel2011.files.wordpress.com/2012/06/anti-corruption.
      pdf; UN Security Council Report of the Secretary General on South Sudan
      S/2011/678, 2 November 2011, p. 3, para. 11.
106   Presidential Order 32/2011, 22 December 2011.
107   Presidential Order 31/2011, 9 December 2011, on the Declaration of
      Assets and the Prohibition of Private Business. While this had been part
      of the Anti-Corruption Commission Act of 2009, it had never been enforced.

108　Letter from The Republic of South Sudan, The Office of the President, signed by President Salva Kiir Mayardit, 3 May 2012, available in PDF-format on http://paanluelwel.com/2012/06/01/letter-from-president-kiir-on-corruption-4-billion-dollars-stolen.

109　Interview 47, 25 June 2015.

110　The President sent letters to eight Heads of State and Government, as appropriate, requesting repatriation of funds.

111　Informed sources confirm that there was a basis for dismissal in several cases, and information provided that would merit further investigation. According to Interview 28, 24 June 2015, the President was presented with the findings, and the proposed course of action, but did nothing. Press release 'Republic of South Sudan, The Office of the President. Anti-Corruption Measures', 1 June 2011, Juba.

112　'Letter from The Republic of South Sudan, The Office of the President, signed by President Salva Kiir Mayardit', 3 May 2012, available in PDF-format on http://paanluelwel.com/2012/06/01/letter-from-president-kiir-on-corruption-4-billion-dollars-stolen.

113　The letter was dated 4 May 2012, but hand-delivered to ministers and a few others at the beginning of June. The story hit the headlines on 5 June. Available online: http://www.theguardian.com/world/2012/jun/05/south-sudan-president-accuses-officials-stealing.

114　'The Report of the Auditor General on the Financial Statements of the Government of Southern Sudan for Financial Year Ended 31 December 2005; equivalent – Ended 31 December 2006'.

115　'Letter from The Republic of South Sudan, The Office of the President, signed by President Salva Kiir Mayardit', 3 May 2012, available in PDF-format on http://paanluelwel.com/2012/06/01/letter-from-president-kiir-on-corruption-4-billion-dollars-stolen.

116　Available online: http://www.aljazeera.com/news/africa/2012/06/2012652 33043136384.html.

117　*Sudan Tribune* (available online: http://www.sudantribune.com/spip.php?article46984) reported on 17 June 2013 that the President's Office had been robbed twice in March. The President formed a committee under the chief of the anti-corruption commission, Justice John Gatwech Lul, to investigate. Several officials were suspended. The committee recommended only administrative measures against them, not prosecution. In June 2015 one of these same officials was arrested and the other two suspended for using the Presidential seal, letterhead and forged signature to authorize transfers of money from the government to their private accounts.

118　'South Sudan Presidency seeks to resolve corruption case out of court'. *Radio Tamazuj*, 22 November 2015, reporting that National Security Director Akol Kuor approached the Chief Justice on the matter. Available online: https://radiotamazuj.org/en/article/south-sudan-presidency-seeks-resolve-corruption-case-out-court.

119　*Sudan Tribune*, 'South Sudanese court prosecutes senior presidential officials over money', 23 February 2016, http://sudantribune.com/spip.php?article58090.

120  Republican Order No. 30/2011 of December 2011 prohibited government officials, civil servants and constitutional office holders, from conducting any commercial activity or receiving remuneration from any activity other than government salary.

121  IMF Country Report 14/345: 'Republic of South Sudan 2014 Staff Report for the Article IV Consultation', December 2014, p. 9. Available online: https://www.imf.org/external/pubs/ft/scr/2014/cr14345.pdf.

122  IMF Country Report 14/345: 'Republic of South Sudan 2014 Article iv Consultation', December 2014, p. 7. Available online: https://www.imf.org/external/pubs/ft/scr/2014/cr14345.pdf. The report refers to 79 forex houses in South Sudan, almost as many as in Kenya, whose economy is five times larger.

123  The US State Department reported that of $1.3 million to be disbursed weekly from the Central Bank to commercial banks, only about $450,000 was delivered: the rest went to the parallel market. See 'Tracking Progress, Anti-Money Laundering and Countering the Financing of Terrorism in East Africa and the Greater Horn of Africa', Global Center of Corporate Security, March 2015, p. 47. Available online: http://www.globalcenter.org/wp-content/uploads/2015/03/Tracking-Progress-low-res.pdf.

124  IMF Country Report 14/345: 'Republic of South Sudan 2014 Article iv Consultation', December 2014, p. 7. Available online: https://www.imf.org/external/pubs/ft/scr/2014/cr14345.pdf, The Sentry, 'The Nexus of Corruption and Conflict in South Sudan', Washington, July 2015, pp. 9–10, www.TheSentry.org. Only imports of food, medicine, fuel and construction materials benefit from the official exchange rate.

125  Christopher Adam and Lee Crawfurd, Exchange Rate Options for South Sudan (Oxford, 2012), pp. 19, 25. The Ministry of Justice declined access to information on the owners of forex bureaus, citing confidentiality. According to one (uncorroborated) source (Interview 41, 25 June 2015), the Central Bank allocated funds to forex bureaus at the fixed rate, which sold them at the parallel rate.

126  Adam and Crawfurd, Exchange Rate Options for South Sudan, p. 3.

127  Radio Tamazuj, 18 June 2015, see https://radiotamazuj.org/en/article/list-south-sudanese-companies-accessing-dollars-preferential-rate-1.

128  Information from a source with personal knowledge. All details, including the criminal's name and the amount of money have been provided.

129  Available online: http://www.isn.ethz.ch/Digital-Library/Articles/Detail/?lng=en&id=177799. Two refineries were constructed during this period: at Bentiu, Unity State, in part by Safinat; and Thiangrial refinery in Upper Nile State, contracted to a Hong-Kong registered company, Frontier Resources Group. Neither was fully operationalized.

130  International Republican Institute, 'Survey of South Sudan. Public Opinion 24 April–22 May 2013', presented in November 2013.

131  Rumours of $4.5 billion in loans at commercial rates, reported in the Sudan Tribune on 4 May 2013, seemed to have less credibility.

132  The Government cut spending in half, although military expenditure remained at approximately the same level: Kosti Manibe, 'South Sudan,

challenges, reforms and a new partnership', presentation to the World Bank, Washington DC, 16 April 2013, p. 5.

133  For the New Deal Compact see http://www.g7plus.org/new-deal-document.

134  The president sent it back to the Assembly twice, objecting to the audit clause in what can only be seen as an attempt to continue mismanagement of the oil income. He finally signed a revised text in November 2014 (not 2013, as the Act as published states).

135  The rate on the black market at the time was 4.5 pounds to the US dollar.

136  Interview 35, 23 April 2015; Interview 40, 20 February 2015.

137  De Waal, 'When kleptocracy becomes insolvent', p. 366.

138  Austerity Budget, Ministry of Finance and Economic Planning, March 2012; Budget for the Fiscal Year 2012/13, June 2012; and Budget Speech by the Minister of Finance and Economic Planning, June 2012.

139  De Waal, 'When kleptocracy becomes insolvent', pp. 363–4.

140  Ibid., p. 353.

141  Ibid., p. 129.

142  Author's notes from several meetings in 2012. See also Thomas, *South Sudan*, p. 139.

143  President Kiir claimed not to have been fully consulted.

144  Cf. Thomas, *South Sudan*, p. 160.

145  According to the Local Government Act of 2009, Section 48, (2), the county commissioner should be elected by universal suffrage in the county.

146  GRSS Transitional Constitution 2011, Article 101 (r) and (s).

147  UNMISS Press Statement, 7 December 2012. Numerous condemnations and protests and massive funeral gatherings followed.

148  UNMISS Press Statement, 11 February 2013.

149  See 'Report of the UN Secretary General on South Sudan S/2013/140', 8 March 2013, paras 52–5; Amnesty International, 'South Sudan: Civil Unrest and State Repression, Human Rights Violations in Wau, Western Bahr el Ghazal State', February 2013.

150  UNMISS Press Statement, 13 December 2012. Available online: http://unmiss.unmissions.org/LinkClick.aspx?fileticket=eB_3VM0zatQ%3d&tabid=4041&mid=6878&language=en-US.

151  Information Minister Michael Makuei, press conference, 6 November 2013. Available online: https://radiotamazuj.org/en/article/transcript-south-sudan-information-minister-warns-press.

152  'Report of the UN Secretary General on South Sudan S/2013/366', 20 June 2013, paras 52–3

153  'Report of the UN Secretary General on South Sudan S/2013/140', 8 March 2013, para. 55; 'Report of the UN Secretary General on South Sudan S/2012/140', 7. March 2012, para. 63, 'Report of the UN Secretary General on South Sudan S/2012/820', para. 56, 8 November 2012.

154  'Report of the UN Secretary General on South Sudan S/2013/366', 20 June 2013, para. 57.

155  Available online: http://civicus.org/index.php/en/media-centre-129/

press-releases/1939-south-sudan-s-ngo-bill-is-needlessly repressive-civicus. While the NGO-bill was held up in parliament for a long time, it was finally approved and signed into law by the president in early February 2016, *Sudan Tribune*, 11 February 2016, http://www.sudantribune.com/spip.php?article57988.

156 Human Rights Watch, 'South Sudan: Abusive Security Bill', 15 October 2014; *Radio Tamazuj*, 10 October 2014. Available online: https://radiotamazuj.org/en/article/document-south-sudan%E2%80%99s-revised-national-security-bill.

157 A revised version was passed in October 2014 amid a walk-out of protesting MPs: 'S. Sudan parliament passes security bill amid protests', *Sudan Tribune*, 8 October 2014. Available online: http://www.sudantribune.com/spip.php?article52674.

## Chapter 4: Jonglei: The UN – Between a Rock and a Hard Place

1 'Speech of the Rt. Hon. Speaker/Lt Gen Wani Igga before the National Legislature of the Republic of South Sudan', p. 4.

2 In hindsight, it is a rather entertaining read: 'Millions of mabrukat [congratulations] to H. E Madam Hilde Johnson, the Norwegian Iron Lady who stood firm as a loyal servant of sisterly Norway behind the Naivasha-negotiations [...] She is in this hall as Special Representative of the Secretary General [...] I just wish the world has [*sic*] just ten solid ladies like Hilde' (ibid.).

3 Security Council Resolution 1996 (2011) Op para. 3 (a) (v).

4 The mandated level was 7,000 military personnel, of which more than 2,000 were enablers (engineers, administrative staff and others). The number of infantry was initially no more than 3,600, increasing to 4,600 in 2013.

5 The Anglo-Egyptian condominium that ruled Sudan (1899–1955) was headed by a British governor-general.

6 Thomas, *South Sudan*, p. 2.

7 See UNMISS, 'Human Rights Report Jonglei', June 2011, pp. 11–12.

8 International Crisis Group, 'Jonglei's Tribal Conflicts: Countering Insecurity in South Sudan', 23 December 2009, p. 1.

9 Ibid., p. 3.

10 UNMISS, 'Human Rights Report on Jonglei', June 2012, p. 6.

11 Ibid., p. 11.

12 South Sudan Bureau for Community Safety and Small Arms Control, 'Reports', p. 2012.

13 Jonathan E. Arensen, 'Murle Political Age Sets and Systems', Houghton College research paper, 2012, p. 5; Thomas, *South Sudan*, p. 292.

14 Thomas, *South Sudan*, pp. 223, 225.

15 Arensen, 'Murle Political Age Sets and Systems', 4; Thomas, *South Sudan*, p. 217.

16 'The History of the Murle Migrations', Houghton College research paper, 2012, p. 11.

17 Øystein Rolandsen and Ingrid Marie Breidlid, 'What is Youth Violence in Jonglei', PRIO Paper 2013, pp. 6, 9; Eddie Thomas, *South Sudan*, pp. 224–5.

18 Ibid.

19 Arensen, 'Murle Political Age Sets and Systems'.

20 Sharon Hutchinson, 'Nuer Ethnicity Militarized', *Anthropology Today* xvi/3 (2000), p. 8.

21 Ibid., pp. 10–11.

22 Thomas, *South Sudan*, p. 223. The scale of attacks originated from a modern version of the traditional mobilization of whole age sets (when the whole community was threatened, in conflict with other communities).

23 UNMISS, 'Human Rights report on Jonglei', June 2011; Thomas, *South Sudan*, p. 3.

24 These comprised a total of 288 long-duration, short-duration and integrated ground patrols during the period, as well as 243 special flights to specific destinations or dynamic air patrols.

25 These were regarded to be Pibor and Likuangole (both Murle) and Akobo and Walgak (both Lou Nuer).

26 Prophets have an important role to play in the Nuer culture. When a prophet emerges, owing to qualities of divination, he or she can lead the community on issues of security and protection. Prophets do not take on administrative functions, however, roles normally of chiefs.

27 This account is based on the UNMISS Human Rights Investigation Report on Jonglei issued in June 2012.

28 UNMISS Statement: Available online: http://www.gurtong.net/ECM/ Editorial/tabid/124/ctl/ArticleView/mid/519/articleId/6161/Hilde-F-Johnson-Condemns-Jalle-Incident.aspx.

29 See 'SPLA repulses Lou Nuer-attack on Pibor-barracks', *Sudan Tribune*, 2 January 2012.

30 UNMISS Press Statements, 16 December and 26 December 2011; 'UN urges South Sudan to Help Avert Possible Attack', *Bloomberg News*, 27 December 2011. Available online: http://www.bloomberg.com/news/articles/2011-12-27/united-nations-urges-south-sudan-to-help-avert-possible-attack.

31 A battalion usually has 850 soldiers.

32 The UNMISS Human Rights Investigation Report on Jonglei, p. 15, reports that 31 vulnerable civilians were evacuated by air by UNMISS helicopters.

33 Ibid. The last message was referring to Likuongole as the headquarters of the *payam*, which is the administrative level below *county*. The threat implied that the Murle were requested to depopulate the area, and hence, the headquarters of the local *payam* would no longer be there.

34 Ibid., p. 16.

35 The number of infantry had by March 2013 still reached only 4,931.

36 'Accounts Emerge in South Sudan of 3000 deaths', *New York Times*, 5 January 2012. Available online: http://www.nytimes.com/2012/01/06/world/africa/in-south-sudan-massacre-of-3000-is-reported.html.

37 According to the UNMISS 'Human Rights Investigation Report on Jonglei', 12, approximately 370 civilians were unaccounted for.

38 'Born in Unity, South Sudan is Torn Again', *New York Times*, 12 January 2012,

by Jeffrey Gettleman. Available online: http://www.nytimes.com/2012/01/13/world/africa/south-sudan-massacres-follow-independence.html.

39   The visit took place on 7 January 2011, a week after the attacks. They went to both Pibor town and Fertait, one of the villages rumoured to have experienced a massacre.

40   Hilde F. Johnson, in the *International Herald Tribune*, 'South Sudan: Old Enmities Test New Nationhood', February 2012, responing to the *New York Times* story of 12 January.

41   UNMISS Press Statement on civilian disarmament, 12 March 2012.

42   Some were unhappy about exclusion from the process, and the way the archbishop ran it. UNMISS was in continuous dialogue with all community leaders and politicians, but as a Mission we had to support the peace process organized by the government.

43   For the Peace Agreement of 5 May 2012, see http://paanluelwel.com/2012/05/06/jonglei-peace-conference-resolutions-held-in-bor-1st-5th-may-2012.

44   President Kiir had criticized the role of politicians in Juba as prime drivers of the violence. Author's notes from president's speech on 5 May 2012 and several meetings.

45   Available online: http://www.sudantribune.com/spip.php?article42491, 4 May 2012.

46   General Kuol Diem Kuol led the disarmament campaign in Jonglei. Appointment of General Peter Gadet to lead Division 8 in Bor led to erroneous assumptions that he was in charge.

47   'The Report of the Secretary General on South Sudan, the Security Council, S/2012/486', pp. 8–9 referred to 63 cases of reported human rights violations between March and June, 43 were in Pibor. These included six killings and 13 rapes, although the latter was presumably underreported.

48   6 April.

49   Akobo and Pibor counties were never disarmed: 'Report of the Secretary General on South Sudan, the Security Council, S/2012/820', p. 7.

50   'Report of the Secretary General on South Sudan, the Security Council, S/2012/486', p. 9.

51   Ibid., reports eight arrests, with detentions and one court martial.

52   Ibid., pp. 8–9.

53   UNMISS, 'Statement on Situation in Jonglei', 26 June 2013. Available online: http://unmiss.unmissions.org/Default.aspx?tabid=4041&currentpage=2&language=en-US.

54   'Report of the Secretary General on South Sudan, the Security Council, S/2012/820', pp. 11–12, reporting human rights violations between 15 July and 20 August, 27 involving torture or ill-treatment, 12 rapes, six attempted rapes, and eight unlawful arrests.

55   During 10–13 August ten abuses were reportedly committed in another place, including rape, torture, beatings and looting. In mid August, another killing was reported.

56   UNMISS Press Statement, 24 August 2012, 'Report of the Secretary General on South Sudan, the Security Council, S/2012/820', pp. 7–8.

57 'Report of the Secretary General on South Sudan, the Security Council, S/2012/820', p. 5.

58 Human Rights Watch, 'Open letter to President Salva Kiir', 23 August 2012, often referred to as 'the Human Rights Watch report'.

59 21 September 2012. Available online: http://sudaneseonline.org/cs/blogs/english/archive/2012/09/20/south-sudan-police-graduates-first-cadets.aspx.

60 13 September 2012.

61 The UN Human Rights Due Diligence Policy applies to all mission settings.

62 Ministry of Foreign Affairs and International Cooperation, Office of the Deputy Minister for International Cooperation, 19 October 2012, signed by the acting minister, Elias Nyamlell Wakoson.

63 The minister was clear that a full reversal of the decision for both officers was not going to happen.

64 In another letter from the Ministry of Foreign Affairs, dated 24 October 2012, and signed by the Undersecretary, Charles Manyang D'Awol, the decision on Richard Bennett was suspended.

65 UNMISS Statement, 4 November 2012.

66 Thomas, *South Sudan*, p. 230; Jonathan E. Arensen, 'Human Ecology of the Murle', Houghton College research paper, 2012, p. 7.

67 See 'Thousands of children to be gradually released from armed group in South Sudan', UNICEF, 27 January 2015. Available online: http://www.unicef.org/media/media_78936.html.

68 The small UNMISS contingent was attacked by David Yau Yau's forces; there were no casualties. The SPLA helped defend the base. The civilians departed Likuongole, and it became clear that it would take time before the environment was perceived secure enough for them to return. Several threats against the UNMISS-base made it difficult to redeploy the contingent to other locations; otherwise setting a precedent that UN forces could be 'chased out' of Pibor and Jonglei, thus undermining the protection of civilians mandate of the Mission.

69 A Murle Red Chief, 24–25 September 2012.

70 As many as 17 were reportedly killed in the vicinity of Manyabol and Gumuruk in November/December 2012. For other incidents, see Report of the Secretary General on South Sudan to the Security Council (8 March 2013, S/2013/140, 12) and Report of the Secretary General on South Sudan (8 November, S/2013/651, 10).

71 Øystein H. Rolandsen and Ingrid Marie Breidlid, 'What is Youth Violence in Jonglei?', PRIO Paper, Oslo 2013, p. 8.

72 The investigation report on the incident of 25 December 2012 recommended replacing the Commander of the SPLA in Pibor and accountability for the soldiers involved.

73 UNMISS called for accountability and the removal of the commanding officers from the area. Our investigators were blocked from doing their work, and an Investigation Committee appointed by parliament was impeded and unable to complete its report.

74 During the civil war the Tomm El Nur militia recruiting from these communities had been used by Khartoum as a proxy.

75    The UNMISS territory to soldier ratio was 98 square kms:1 soldier in late 2012 (including *all* forces); in 2011–2012, the figure had been even lower. For the UN African Union Mission in Darfur (UNAMID) the ratio was 29:1, and for the UN Operation in Cote d'Ivoire (UNOCI) it was 35:1. For the UN Mission in the Democratic Republic of Congo (MONUSCO), using its primary area of operations as comparator, Eastern DRC, the ratio was 17:1. If UNMISS were to move most of its forces to Jonglei, the ratio would be 19:1. All statistics from the United Nations Department of Peacekeeping Operations, DPKO, 2012, reflected in several UNMISS presentations, 2012–13.

76    Military helicopters usually have more flexibility in their operations than civilian aircraft. The civilian aviation companies offered voluntarily to enter into a special agreement with UNMISS, enabling them to take on most of the operations that the military helicopters had been conducting. An agreement was signed after this initiative.

77    'South Sudan admits it downed UN helicopter, killing four', Reuters, 22 December 2012. Available online: http://www.reuters.com/article/2012/12/22/us-southsudan-un-idUSBRE8BK0V720121222.

78    Without additional landing sites, the contingent could be 'trapped'. Its continued presence in Likuongole was based on military assessments and consultations with UN HQ. For further background on this, see footnote 72.

79    A source with close connections to Khartoum's military intelligence told me in January 2013 how the supplies were provided and dropped; the same source has been interviewed on other issues (Interview 17, 4 February 2015).

80    UN DPKO Aviation Safety Manual, Section V, Chapter 10.

81    The flight hours we had at our disposal also made continuous testing very difficult, so that many otherwise suitable sites could not be used.

82    'Uniting Our Strengths for Peace, Politics, Partnerships and People', Report of the High Level Independent Panel on UN Peace Operations, 16 June 2015, p. 59, para. 213.

83    'Uniting Our Strengths for Peace – Politics, Partnerships and People', Report of the High Level Panel on Peace Operations, which was made public on 16 June 2015; The Panel proposed changing the rules to remove constraints on military aircraft: available online: http://www.un.org/sg/pdf/HIPPO_Report_1_June_2015.pdf.

84    On 25–7 August 2012 UNMISS helped prevent thousands of Nuer youth from crossing the Warrap-Unity State border in the vicinity of Mayandit to attack Dinka communities.

85    UNMISS Human Rights Investigation Report, 'Attack on Lou Nuer pastoralists in Akobo, West Sub-County', April 2013, p. 7. Goi Yol had requested a UNMISS flight to Walgak to warn the community, but delays in flight procedures prevented this.

86    UNMISS Human Rights Investigation Report, 'Attack on Lou Nuer pastoralists in Akobo, West Sub-County', p. 10.

87    UNMISS Standard Operating Procedure (SOP), 'Movement of Casualties

and Medical Patients (CASEVAC and MEDEVAC)', 2013.01., 26 April 2013; following UN standards globally.

88 UNMISS Press Statement on the Situation in Jonglei, 5 March 2013. In possession of the author.

89 'Report of the Secretary General on South Sudan to the Security Council', 8 November 2013, S/2013/651, p. 10.

90 Office of the President, 'End Violence against Civilians', 17 May 2013.

91 UNMISS, 'Statement on the Situation in Jonglei', 26 June 2013.

92 Statistics from the UNMISS Military Justice Unit, working with the SPLA Legal Counsel show by mid November 2013 accountability cases against 115. Of these, 39 related to murder and rape (at least 32 to murder), while 53 were disciplinary cases (disobedience, mishandling of weapons, intoxication). Overall, there had been 92 convictions and 23 acquittals.

93 See Thomas, *South Sudan*, pp. 263–77; and Jonathan Arensen, 'Contemporary Issues Facing the Murle', Houghton College research paper, 2012, pp. 1–2.

94 Thomas, *South Sudan*, pp. 263–77, refers to several studies on health and demographics.

95 Arensen, 'Contemporary Issues Facing the Murle', pp. 2–3; Thomas, *South Sudan*, Chapters 6 and 8.

96 The Mission had legal freedom of movement anywhere in South Sudan according to the Status of Forces Agreement (SOFA). Flight assurances were not requests for approval but giving notice of movement. Some of our military still sought approval, despite clear instruction not to do so. Asking for permission undermined the SOFA.

97 In possession of the author; for a shorter version see http://www.msf.org/article243/south-sudan-120000-people-pibor-county-cut-aid, 13 June 2013.

98 Eddie Thomas (the author of *South Sudan: A Slow Liberation*, 2015), produced a series of research papers for UNMISS on Jonglei and on dynamics among the three communities.

99 Arensen, 'Human Ecology of the Murle', p. 2.

100 Thomas, *South Sudan*, pp. 35–7.

101 Ibid., pp. 255–7 notes how Jonglei's food economy has changed, particularly among communities that became more dependent on relief supplies and trade in goods. Such trends might have increased also in later years, affecting survival and coping mechanisms.

102 The lengthy time was due to dependence on helicopters (and the need for flight assurances), as well as logistical hurdles: all supplies had to be flown in. UNMISS contingents had almost no mobile equipment. Their massive tents and kitchen equipment had to be transported by truck, which was not possible in the rainy season. There were no mobile command office systems or sanitation facilities.

103 Stories were rife – but never corroborated – about the SPLA dropping arms in the bush from helicopters.

104 Copy in possession of the author.

105 September 2013.

106 'South Sudan Army Faces Accusations of Civilian Abuse', *New York Times*, 28 September 2013. Available online: http://www.nytimes.com/2013/09/29/

world/africa/south-sudans-army-faces-accusations-of-civilian-abuse. html?_r=0.

107 The Humanitarian Coordinator, Toby Lanzer and the OCHA team (Office for the Coordination of Humanitarian Affairs) added registered recipients of food in Pibor (75,000 by November 2013) and registered Murle refugees abroad (20,000). Murle who had fled to Juba and other towns had not yet been counted.

108 Arensen, 'Human Ecology of the Murle', p. 7.

109 My deputy SRSG for political affairs, Ray Zenenga, had the main responsibility to make sure that these instructions were followed through.

110 'Agreement on the Resolution of the Conflict in Jonglei State Between the Government of the Republic of South Sudan and The South Sudan Democratic Movement/South Sudan Defence Army (SSDM/SSDA-Cobra Faction)', Addis Ababa, 9 May 2014.

111 Human Rights Watch, 'South Sudan's New War, Abuses by Government and Opposition Forces', New York, 7 August 2014, p. 76.

## Chapter 5: The Leadership

1 The notion of John Garang as Moses was common. A former child soldier in Rumbek said in 2004: 'We consider John Garang to be like Moses, who took his people away from Egypt' (NDI/SCSE-report December 2004: 'On the Threshold of Peace', p. 18).

2 Interview 50, 23 March 2015.

3 Interview 47, 25 June 2005. In *South Sudan, The State We Aspire To*, np, 2011, 170, Peter Adwok Nyaba describes this habit: 'It was generally known that Gen Salva Kiir would make or be instigated to make a decision from which he would immediately distance himself.'

4 Information from Kjell Hødnebø, Royal Ministry of Foreign Affairs of Norway (1998–2005), 26 January 2015.

5 Machar and the SPDF had also been weakened militarily; an SPLA unit encountered Riek in the bush in 2002 with around 70 soldiers; they had run out of ammunition (Interview 34, 21 April 2015).

6 Interview 26, 7 February 2015; Interview 48, 14 February 2015; Interview 31, 18 March 2015; Interview 30, 18 March 2015.

7 James Wani Igga, a junior officer in the Political Bureau, had been promoted as an Equatorian alternative to Alfred Lado Gore. He, Kuol Manyang, Daniel Awet and Samuel Abu John sided with Salva on this issue; John Kuong (a Nuer), with Deng Alor and Nhial Deng favoured accommodating Riek. Wani Igga's concession spoiled the strategy, reportedly agreed in advance, of preventing Riek's ascendancy by reserving the position for an Equatorian.

8 Laws of the Republic of South Sudan, The Transitional Constitution, 2011, Article 102 (2), p. 56.

9 *Sudan Tribune*, 4 April 2012.

10 The *Guardian*, 4 July 2013; BBC, 'Focus on Africa', 9 July 2013.

11 Interview 48, 14 February 2015.

12    This group is now comfortable with the term being used, including for this book.

13    Paul Mayom Akec

14    Interview 48, 14 February 2015.

15    Lam parted ways with Riek in 1994 and started his own parties, SPLM-United and, later, SPLM/Democratic Change.

16    With Riek's departure in 1991, 'Elders of the Bahr el Ghazal region' formed (in London), with Bona Malwal at the centre, to build an alternative power base to Garang's. Similar groups, of youth, were formed elsewhere. The motive seemed to be to strengthen the position of the Greater Bahr el Ghazal within the movement.

17    These included Dominic Dim, Alieu Ayenyi Alieu, Telar Deng, Harun Ruun and later Dr Justin Yak.

18    Bona Malwal had never been 'core' SPLM, partly due to his failure to get along with Garang. In 2005 he was even a Senior Advisor to President Bashir, seen as operating very closely with the ruling party in Khartoum. The role of Dominic Dim was confirmed by Khartoum sources. After his death, $4.7 million was found in a bank account under his name in London. Bank officials provided the documents in Juba and inquired whether there were any rightful owners to the money. Two interviewees (Interview 12, 3 February 2015; Interview 9, 30 January 2015) claim the account held twice as much, $8–10 million.

19    Alieu as minister of interior and Telar Deng as senior advisor for Legal Affairs to the President.

20    Private conversations in Juba; author's notes. See also Johnson, *Waging Peace in Sudan*, pp. 163–5. Almost all members of the leadership interviewed confirmed Salva Kiir's intention not to stage a coup.

21    According to several witnesses, Dominic Dim told arriving colleagues that Salva would confront the chairman, in a bid for the leadership. They now had to choose. These are probably those Kiir referred to as 'hardliners'.

22    In addition to Paul Malong and Pieng Deng, the decisive role in convincing Kiir to go to Rumbek was played by three delegations to Yei, including (i) Kuol Manyang and Deng Alor, (ii) Oyay Deng Ajak, and (iii) Riek Machar and Malik Agar. Corroborated by Interview 31, 18 March 2015; Interview 9, 30 January 2015; Interview 18, 6 February 2015; Interview 34, 21 April 2015.

23    Oyay Deng Ayak connected Salva Kiir and John Garang by satellite phone after gatekeepers on both sides had prevented conversation. While the other delegations went ahead, Paul Malong, Pieng Deng and Oyay Deng accompanied Salva to Rumbek. Deng Alor, at Salva's request, escorted him, without weapons and bodyguards, to the chairman's house.

24    A high-level NCP contact within the presidency in Khartoum confirmed this: 'Dominic Dim was working with us under [*sic*] the Yei crisis in 2004'. Another key South Sudanese operative says that money changed hands. The individual, seen as instrumental in causing the crisis, also recently confirmed that 'Khartoum was involved,' and that money was paid. In Khartoum in 2007 General Bakry Hassan Saleh, minister of presidential affairs, referred

twice to working with Dominic Dim. Interview 47, 25 June 2015; Interview 13, 2 February 2015.

25    After his dismissal as head of National Security in Khartoum in 2010, Salah Gosh reportedly expressed disappointment that Khartoum's strategy with the SPLM from 2004 onwards had failed. Those cadres I have been able to reach deny such links. Interview 13, 2 February 2015; interview 47, 25 June 2015.

26    Some claim that money changed hands in this context, and indications of collaboration with the NCP are strong.

27    In April 2004 Bona Malwal returned to Khartoum, publicly affirmed the importance of the Machakos Protocol, and committed to work for the unity of Sudan. See http://www.sudantribune.com/spip.php?article2546. See Johnson, *Waging Peace in Sudan*, pp. 43–57.

28    Interview 31, 18 March 2015; Interview 9, 30 January 2015.

29    Dr John had 'appointed' Salva to succeed him in a public rally in Rumbek prior to his death; Johnson, *Waging Peace in Sudan*, pp. 197–8.

30    This has been confirmed by both 'camps': Interview 47, 25 June 2015; Interview 34, 21 April 2015, Interview 48, 14 February 2015.

31    Nyaba, *South Sudan*, p. 29.

32    As one said, 'I am against the New Sudan; I didn't care what happened in Sudan, as long as we got our independence.' Interview 47, 25 June 2015.

33    Nyaba, *South Sudan*, p. 156; Johnson: *Waging Peace in Sudan*, pp. 203–5. Garang and Ali Osman Taha had a gentleman's agreement that key ministries would be evenly shared between the parties. This did not happen. The NCP got all of them except the Foreign Ministry.

34    They complained that the SPLM was being managed by people who seemed only to want a Southern party, for the referendum only. See Nyaba, *South Sudan*, p. 32; Interview 29, 19 March 2015; Interview 30, 18 March 2015.

35    Including Nhial Deng Nhial, Abdel-Aziz Al-Hilu and Yasir Arman.

36    Interviewees point to the meeting of the SPLM Leadership Council in April 2006 as decisive. Pagan Amum was appointed Secretary General. The leadership resolved again to confront the NCP about implementing the CPA in full. The first sign was a press conference Salva Kiir held not long afterwards, when he publicly criticized the NCP for undermining the CPA. Interview 29, 19 March 2015; Interview 43, 25 April 2015. Interview 30, 18 March 2015.

37    Attempts to get access to the documents leading to their expulsion have been unsuccessful. Most interviewees point to 'aggressive behaviour' and public statements undermining the SPLM as the main issues.

38    The expulsions took place in early 2007. Deng Alor was appointed foreign minister. It has not been possible to get access to the SPLM-documents on the investigations, and accounts differ: Lam Akol was accused of having deviated from SPLM policy as foreign minister. Telar had kept Salva Kiir in the dark about decisions in the Palace where he was state minister, Aleu was accused of implicating the Ugandan government in the death of Dr John Garang, as recounted in Nyaba (a minister in the GoNU at the time), in *South Sudan*, p. 166.

39    Nyaba, *South Sudan*, pp. 140–2.

40    The vice president was a statutory and not an elected position. For the Garang Boys it mattered that Riek Machar had no leadership position at the time of Garang's death. The Leadership Council had been dissolved, and Machar was not guaranteed a leading position.

41    Interview 18, 6 February 2015; Interview 19, 6 February 2015.

42    At this time, Taban Deng Gai had not even been nominated as a delegate to the SPLM Convention. He was a member of the SPLM Political Bureau and was nominated as a delegate by the chairman.

43    Interview with Angelina Teny, Addis Ababa, February 2015, corroborated by other sources.

44    Nyaba, *South Sudan*, pp. 143–5.

45    'Report of the EU Observer Mission'. Available online: http://eeas.europa. eu/eueom/missions/2010/sudan/index_en.htm; 'Report of the Observation Mission of the Carter Center', Atlanta, April 2010. Available online: https:// www.cartercenter.org/resources/pdfs/news/peace_publications/election_ reports/FinalReportSudan-Apr2010.pdf.

46    All political parties participated. Available online: http://www.sudantribune. com/spip.php?article36802.

47    Author's notes on conversations with members of the leadership in 2011 and 2012.

48    Interview 4, 7 January 2015.

49    Interview 31, 18 March 2015; interview 10, 1 February 2015; interview 12, 2 February 2015; author's notes on conversation with member of SPLM leadership, Juba, March 2014.

50    All ministers present have been interviewed and confirmed this account.

51    Sharing this information with potential competitors made some people around Kiir question Alor's motives.

52    Salva later also denied that the conversation had taken place.

53    Available online: http://www.theguardian.com/world/2012/jun/05/south- sudan-president-accuses-officials-stealing.

54    Available online: http://www.ifes.org/~/media/Files/Publications/White% 20PaperReport/2012/South_Sudan_Anniversary_FAQ.pdf.

55    The Convention should take place five years after the previous one in 2008, according to party rules.

56    Multiple interviews; confirmed by Pagan Amum.

57    See footnotes 162 and 163, Chapter 2 and footnote 130, Chapter 3.

58    No arm of government was tasked with monitoring implementation system- atically. The Minister of Cabinet Affairs had some responsibility, but ended up merely preparing cabinet meetings. The presidency had no monitoring capacity. This critical gap was an issue intended for discussion at the retreat.

59    The agenda included the economic crisis, corruption, security sector reform, preparations for the SPLM party process and Convention, and government reform following the GoSS evaluation.

60    On 17 December 2012, the President agreed to hold a SPLM retreat of the five highest-ranking members in mid January; in mid January he agreed to late January, and later suggested mid February. Political Bureau members would be invited to join the second day of deliberations.

61 A surprising choice of contact, and a possible indication that Salva Kiir did not take this process seriously.

62 Meeting in October–November 2012. Riek said he was not planning to contest for the Chairmanship, but could not pre-empt the party; Salva responded that the leadership-question was up to the SPLM. Author's notes from conversations in Juba.

63 The informal group consisted of Taban Deng Gai and Ezekiel Gatkuoth Lul, at Riek's request; and Nhial Deng Nhial on Salva's behalf. James Hoth Mai was less active.

64 They were often joined by James Kok. Also others engaged, often meeting in Deng Alor's house, including John Luk, Oyay Deng, Paul Mayom, Cirino Hiteng and Kosti Manibe.

65 Riek later maintained that he had listed seven points, called 'The Seven Points', while other interviewees (December 2013–June 2015) – and I noted six.

66 Author's notes of conversations with committee members after they met Machar.

67 Interview, James Wani Igga, *The New Nation*, 25 April 2014. Available online: http://www.newnationsouthsudan.com/interviews/you-cannot-force-a-president-to-step-down-at-gunpoint-%E2%80%93-vp.html.

68 According to one of Salva Kiir's closest advisers, who referred to the meeting as 'very bad'. 'After this', he said, 'the President felt that there was lack of respect for his leadership, and he turned to the High Command.'

69 The delegation of powers had been formally anchored in a letter from the President to the Vice President, since Salva Kiir was also First Vice President of Sudan and expected to spend much time in Khartoum. I have not had access to the letter, but the Vice President chaired the most important government clusters (the economic cluster and the governance cluster, among others), and was perceived as the one de facto managing day-to-day affairs of the government. Military and security affairs, as well as foreign affairs, were never delegated.

70 Deng Alor repeatedly asked for a private audience with the President, but this was put on hold for unknown reasons.

71 Four of them were Political Bureau members, but the group had no mandate from the SPLM.

72 These included Deng Alor, James Hoth Mai, Taban Deng, Nhial Deng, James Kok and John Luk, focusing on possible transition arrangements.

73 Presidential decree 03/2013.

74 Interview 47, 25 June 2015.

75 Interview 4, 7 January 2015. Even capacity building funded via Norwegian People's Aid to strengthen the party yielded very limited results.

76 Republican Orders 12/2013 on suspension of the two ministers in accordance with Article 117(3) of the Transitional Constitution of 2011, and 13/2013 on the formation of the Investigations Committee into the case.

77 The report of the Investigations Committee was handed to the President on 5 September 2013. Available online: http://www.sudantribune.com/spip.php?article48210.

78    Kosti Manibe was one of very few ministers generally perceived as uninvolved in serious corruption.

79    Interview in the *Guardian*, 4 July 2013. Available online: http://www. theguardian.com/world/2013/jul/04/riek-machar-south-sudan-ambitions.

80    *Sudan Tribune*, 7 July 2013.

81    The Presidential decree was issued despite the Transitional Constitution, 2011, article 101 (r), which refers to removal of state Governors (only) in 'a crisis in the state that threatens national security and territorial integrity'. Unity State was not in crisis.

82    Available online: http://www.sudantribune.com/spip.php?article47212.

83    Presidential Decree 06/2013, 21 January 2013. He was replaced by Matur Chut Dhuol a retired general expected to improve security. But after a lull, fighting among Dinka clans increased. Yet he remained at his post. Matur proved a hardliner. Chol Tong Mayay was arrested during the 2013 crisis.

84    Taban was also an in-law of Angelina Teny, Riek's wife.

85    Machar's letter to President Kiir, stating that Taban's removal was unconstitutional, 7 July 2013, *Sudan Tribune*, 7 July 2013.

86    BBC 'Focus on Africa', reported in *Sudan Tribune*, 9 July 2013.

87    Thabo Mbeki conveyed to me that Machar had responded that he was willing to reconcile with the President if a win-win solution could be found. Mbeki had also agreed with Salva Kiir that he would participate as observer at the PB-meeting. Author's notes.

88    This was in May, prior to the sacking of Riek Machar.

89    His visit was also prompted by one of the 'friends of South Sudan' who had urged Ethiopian intervention in the leadership crisis. Author's notes.

90    Personal records; interview with Tedros Adhanom, 13 February 2015.

91    Interview with Tedros Adhanom, 13 February 2015.

92    Republican Decree 49/2013, 50/2013 and 51/2013.

93    Chairperson's Order 01/2013.

94    Interview 47, 25 June 2015.

95    Interview 48, 14 February 2015; author's notes on conversations with Sudanese officials August–September 2015. This is confirmed by a document from a national security meeting in Khartoum, received from sources of various states, which includes a statement by President Bashir that 'South Sudan was a great threat to Sudan ... [but] currently, the danger has gone to zero due to the conflict and the balance of power in in [*sic*] their [Sudan's] favor.' The document is 'Ministry of Defense, Chieftancy [*sic*] of Joint Forces, Department of Intelligence and Security, Minutes if [*sic*] the Meeting chaired by Commander-in-Chief, which took place at his office at the Ministry of Defence, 1 July 2014', Attendance: President Bashir, the Minister of Defence Abdurrahim Muhammad Muhammad Hussein, and the Military high command (in English translation from Arabic).

96    Bashir visited Juba *three times* during this period, likely to cement agreements that included the progressive pay-as-you-go disbursement of the $3 billion special compensation fund.

97    Among them were James Hoth Mai, the army's Chief of General Staff,

Major General Mac Paul Kuol, chief of military intelligence, and the acting Secretary General of the SPLM, Anne Itto.

98 Interview 9, 30 January 2015; Interview 10, 1 February 2015; Interview 13, 3 February 2015; Interview 33, 23 March 2015. Those present were reportedly Oyay Deng, Paul Mayom Akec, Madut Bier, Gier Choung Aloung, David Deng Athorbei and possibly Taban Deng Gai. Salva Kiir wanted Pieng Deng to be there, too.

99 Interview 39, 7 March 2014.

100 I had warned the President against this language several times; it was not befitting a head of state, and was noted in Washington DC and at the Security Council.

101 Some versions have 'scratch the faces'. The speech was almost entirely in Dinka, was first reported to me by a source with a transcript (author's notes), and was later confirmed in at least seven interviews.

102 He referred to two particularly bad attacks in 1994 and 1996.

103 Republican Order 17/2013, 7 October 2013.

104 Frequent contact with Riek from my end would be regarded with suspicion, whatever was said. There seemed to be little more I could do to help mend relations.

105 *Sudan Tribune*, 15 November 2013.

106 Media statement, Minister of Information Michael Makuei, 18 November 2013. Available online: http://www.sudantribune.com/spip. php?article48843.

107 Unconfirmed reports that the acting Secretary General of the SPLM had been instructed to prepare for back-to-back meetings of the Political Bureau and the National Leadership Council gave reason to believe that the crisis could still be overcome, influencing the Report of the Secretary General on South Sudan (S/2013/651, 8 November 2013). At the Security Council meeting such an arrangement was less likely, but could not be ruled out.

108 The focus was on what could happen if one side was marginalized in the context of the SPLM Convention in the first quarter of 2014. The process at the NLC was prior to this; there would still be possibilities to mobilize politically before the Convention. Fear of violence was linked to the SPLM Convention itself, to a possible fall-out from the Convention (one side being marginalized, feeling forced to either form their own party, or if this was not seen as viable resorting to arms) or to elections – if the plans for elections in 2015 went ahead.

109 One uncorroborated source indicates that Riek made two statements in Nuer of this nature, one on 2 December 2013 and another later the same week, allegedly saying he would 'fight'.

110 Akol Kuor was Director of internal security (the other Director was responsible for external security), both reporting to the Minister of National Security in the presidency.

111 These included James Hoth Mai, Pieng Deng and, in Paris, *Mac Paul* Kuol. It was through the efforts of all of us that the situation was contained.

112 As the President was abroad when the press conference was held, James Wani Igga later called it the first 'coup attempt'.

113   Rumours had it that Salva Kiir had intended the dissidents' arrest while he was abroad, but that members of his entourage had persuaded him otherwise.

114   Those present included *seven* leading members of the Political Bureau, Riek Machar, former ministers, two sacked governors, the suspended Secretary General of the SPLM and Rebecca Nyandeng de Mabior. Many more had reportedly participated in preparatory meetings, but had pulled out at the last minute.

115   Press Statement, 6 December 2013, in author's possession, does not list the authors; all SPLM-cadres present were co-signatories. Available online: http://www.sudantribune.com/spip.php?article49087.

116   Ibid.

117   Ibid.

118   Øystein Rolandsen, 'Another Civil War in South Sudan: The Failure of Guerilla Government?', *Journal of Eastern African Studies* xli/1 (2015), p. 171.

119   Press Statement, 6 December 2013.

120   Interview 7, 9 December 2014; Interview 8, 29 January 2015; Interview 16, 5 February 2015; Interview 10, 1 February 2015; Interview 30, 18 March 2015; Interview 31, 18 March 2015.

121   Interviewees among the signatories are divided about whether they expected widespread popular support for them or not. The assumption that the President would 'cave in' to pressure was misguided; Salva Kiir characteristically responded to humiliating attacks by digging in his heels.

122   Press conference statement, 8 December 2013, Author's copy.

123   Interview 34, 21 April 2015.

124   According to Pagan Amum, Government security representatives advised him not come, and Pieng Deng, inspector general of police had conveyed the same message to him. Author's notes.

125   They included Archbishop Paulino Lukudo, Archbishop Daniel Deng Bul, Moderator Peter Gai Lual Marrow, Bishop Paride Taban and Imam Juma Said Ali.

126   Minutes from SPLM/A meeting, Rumbek.

127   YouTube. Available online: https://www.youtube.com/watch?v=5y3bp6Oehis.

## Chapter 6: The Nightmare

1   The teleconference in the morning was with Undersecretary General Herve Ladsous, the head of the Department of Peacekeeping Operations.

2   See *Sudan Tribune*, 16 December 2013. Available online: http://www.sudantribune.com/spip.php?article49200.

3   UNMISS Press Statement, 'Ms Hilde Johnson Special Representative of the UN Secretary General for South Sudan Calls for Calm in in [*sic*] Juba', 16 December 2013.

4   Televised statement on 16 December 2013, available on You Tube, www.youtube.com/watch?v=boLU20O5JDI.

5   I knew both leaders also on the Kenyan side, Uhuru Kenyatta and Foreign Minister Amina Mohamed.

6   There were stories about reassignment of Nuer Presidential Guards, who reportedly refused to redeploy without their weapons. Others referred to an order not to give assignments to Nuer officers on 13–14 December 2013. In both versions attempts to take control of the ammunition store at GHQ ensued, with fighting then spreading.

7   See, inter alia, *Sudan Tribune*, 16 December 2013. Available online: http://www.sudantribune.com/spip.php?article49200.

8   SPLA officials denied attempts to disarm soldiers of the Presidential Guard, stating that fighting began after a Nuer Presidential Guard shot and killed a Dinka major, Akuol Reach, and attacked the ammunition store in the GHQ: Human Rights Watch, 'South Sudan's New War: Abuses by Government and Opposition Forces', New York, August 2014.

9   Use of force in a situation of active combat between two belligerent forces would also have presupposed a new mandate from the Security Council.

10  Some 250 Rwandan soldiers protected UN headquarters and the two large bases and another company (150 soldiers) had guard and commando-post functions, transport, logistics and administrative tasks.

11  Adrian Foster from NYHQ remained at the Mission and made three recommendations: (i) political engagement, (ii) documentation of human rights violations, and (iii) protection of people seeking refuge. Our resources were too limited to intervene militarily.

12  The neighbourhoods of New Site, Manga, Mangaten, Mia Saba and Eden were all attacked by government forces: UNMISS, 'UNMISS: Conflict in South Sudan: A Human Rights Report', 8 May 2014; Human Rights Watch, 'South Sudan's New War', August 2014, pp. 24–36.

13  Separate areas were cordoned off within the UNMSS bases, called 'Protection of Civilians' sites' (PoC-sites). It was also within these sites that humanitarian agencies, both UN-agencies and NGOs, would begin operating, delivering food, water, health services, etc.

14  UNMISS, 'Conflict in South Sudan: A Human Rights Report' (Juba, 2014).

15  Human Rights Watch, 'South Sudan's New War' (New York, 2014), p. 37.

16  According to uncorroborated accounts, some forces from National Security opposed forces attacking civilians in an attempt at stopping the violence on 16–17 December.

17  Interview 33, 23 March 2015.

18  Interview 5, 28 January 2015; Interview 33, 23 March 2015.

19  'SRSG Johnson warns against ethnic violence', 17 December 2013.

20  South Sudan Council of Churches, 'Message of Peace and Reconciliation from the Church Leaders', 17 December 2013; Statement by South Sudan Human Rights Commission, 17 December 2013.

21  AU Commission of Inquiry on South Sudan: 'Final Report of the ...', Addis Ababa, 15 October 2014, p. 182.

22  Author's notes of reports from several credible sources.

23  Security Council Presidency Press Statement, 17 December, SC/11221. Available online: http://www.un.org/press/en/2013/sc11221.doc.htm.

24  Transcript of Salva Kiir's press conference, 18 December 2013.

25   Agence France-Presse, 'South Sudan President offers talks with rival accused of coup', 18 December 2013; www.sudantribune.com/spip.php?article49238.

26   'Update 2. Political Background. Juba', 16 December 2013: 'They claimed that the operation was a coordinated 'attempted coup', and stressed that change of leadership in South Sudan would only happen through a democratic process ...'. Nothing else in any way referred to Riek Machar.

27   'South Sudan: Pillay warns against rapidly deteriorating security situation and risk of ethnic clashes,' Geneva, 19 December 2013; the Secretary General's spokesman, and the deputy secretary general, Jan Eliasson, expressed grave concern in New York the same day.

28   Security Council Press Statement on the Situation in South Sudan, 20 December 2013.

29   Security Council Resolution S/RES/2132 (2013), 24 December 2013. The resolution increased UNMISS's mandated force to 12,500 troops.

30   The names of the senior government officials are kept in the author's archives. Should criminal investigations be pursued in this case, the names will be handed over to the relevant authority for further corroboration.

31   Press reports, 17 December 2013, including http://africajournalismtheworld.com/2013/12/17/south-sudan-arrests-followed-failed-coup.

32   This was reported also to the AU Commission, and the fire was returned ('Final Report of the African Union Mission of Inquiry on South Sudan', African Union, Addis Ababa, 15 October 2014, p. 123).

33   For more details see Human Rights Watch, 'South Sudan's New War', pp. 1–44.

34   BBC report at 17.55 hrs 16 December 2015, author's notes. Not available on www.bbc.com.

35   *Sudan Tribune*, 16 December 2013.

36   The others were Gier Choung Aloung, Cirino Hiteng, Majak D'Agoot, Madut Bier, Koul Tong Mayai and Ezekiel Gatkuoth Lul.

37   By then, President Kenyatta and Prime Minister Hailemariam Desalegn had also seen them, as had the American Envoy Donald Booth.

38   Several media outlets, including AFP, available online: http://www.africareview.com/News/Riek-Machar-denies-South-Sudan-coup-attempt/-/979180/2116956/-/8n35tg/-/index.html. Available online: http://www.theguardian.com/world/2013/dec/18/south-sudan-sacked-vp-denies-plotting-coup.

39   In an interview with Radio France International reported by Agence France Press and other media, 19 December 2013.

40   I met Salva Kiir on 18, 23 and 28 December 2013, 2, 9 and 24 January and 11 February. After I reached Riek Machar on 21 December, I called him on the 23rd and 28th, on 2 and 9 January, and later. In February and March, meetings and calls were less frequent, as tensions increased along with accusations of 'support for the rebels'.

41   Al Jazeera, 19 December 2013. Available online: http://www.aljazeera.com/indepth/features/2013/12/south-sudan-machar-speaks-al-jazeera-2013121961331646865.html.

42   According to eye witnesses, local incidents exacerbated the news from Juba: two students from Twic East had been killed, followed by three police officers, which led to fighting between Dinka and Nuer police. Nuer youths then broke into the police armoury, took guns, and engaged in the fighting.

43   According to an eyewitness, the attackers were Dinka prison and police officers.

44   The UN commander at Akobo, with 43 peacekeepers, reported that 32 Dinkas had sought shelter. Six police advisers and two civilian UN staff were also there.

45   The delay was due to the distance, which required a stop in Bor. The late hour meant that evacuation could only be done the following day.

46   Human Rights Watch, 'South Sudan's New War', p. 56.

47   Available online: http://www.sudantribune.com/spip.php?article49541.

48   Small Arms Survey – Timeline, 2014, p. 6.

49   Ibid., pp. 6–7.

50   As a trio of US light aircraft flew in to conduct the evacuation, they were fired upon by Gadet's forces, who assumed a coordinated attack by foreign aircraft. A USAF V-22 Osprey was hit. A communication glitch with our people on the ground led to the very unfortunate injuring of four US Navy Seals.

51   This included the villages of Pariak, Malek and Goy.

52   Human Rights Watch, South Sudan's New War, p. 52.

53   Office of the President, Press Statement, 'President Salva Kiir Mayardit calls for an end to all ethnic violence', 24 December 2014. In possession of the author.

54   Republic of South Sudan, Ministry of Interior, South Sudan National Police Service, Office of the Inspector General, 'Committee to investigate into the allegations labelled as the involvement of some elements of Joint Patrol and other organized forces in human violations and abuses during the failed coup attempt,' including Terms of Reference, 28 December 2013 (Author's copy).

55   SPLA Office of the Chief of General Staff: 'Convening Order forming a Committee to investigate the cause of the shoot out within the Republican Guard Division on 15 December 2013', 31 December 2013 (Author's copy). This Committee was complemented with another focusing on the killings in Juba. Available online: http://eyeradio.org/govt-forms-committees-investigate-reported-targeted-killings/. The police and the SPLA had completed their reports by the time I departed South Sudan, but did not know whether those responsible would face justice; a decision by the President.

56   Small Arms Survey, 'Timeline, 2014', p. 5.

57   UNMISS staff notes of a statement by President Salva Kiir at the National Liberation Council meeting, 23 December 2013.

58   The Bentiu base would eventually hold the highest numbers of IDPs, almost 50,000.

59   Confidential sources; satellite imagery and information gathered through other sources by UNMISS personnel. The number of 25,000 originated from the Minister of Information, Michael Makuei: Available online: http://www.usatoday.com/story/news/world/2013/12/28/south-sudan-white-army-militia/4231213.

60   Interview 5, 29 January 2015; Interview 6, 5 February 2015.

61   These numbers refer to registration conducted in January-February 2014.

62   Available online: http://unmiss.unmissions.org/LinkClick.aspx?fileticket=cbblcMFMNEY%3D&tabid=3465&mid=9396&language=en-US; http://www.un.org/apps/news/story.asp?NewsID=46787#.VZJ-tvmqqko; http://www.un.org/press/en/2013/sc11227.doc.htm.

63   Information from SPLA eyewitnesses, May 2014.

64   Available online: http://www.sudantribune.com/spip.php?article49659.

65   Interview 43, 25 April 2015.

66   In the Al Jazeera interview on 22 January 2014 (www.youtube.com/watch?v=5p4a5MtVV8g), the President repeated other false allegations: 'Rebels ran into UN camps. The UN gave rebels their vehicles. They mounted them with machine guns. The system stayed quiet. Why did they keep quiet? They showed double standards.' On 20 January 2014 I had given Michael Makuei a full set of UNMISS press statements with the facts. The same was given to Ateny Wek Ateny, the Presidential press secretary on the same day. In a press conference on the 22nd, however, Ateny repeated the same accusations, and added (in Arabic), 'we will ask them to leave the country'.

67   Transcript of President Salva Kiir's remarks to the media, 24 January 2014.

68   This issue had been discussed at the High Level Security Committee Meeting of 16 January 2014. On 7 February a 'List of firearms, uniforms, ammunition, [and] traditional weapons stored at UNMISS compounds', as of 4 February, was attached to a letter to Defence Minister Kuol Manyang and copied to other officials. A matrix showed that the amount of firearms held was modest in comparison to speculation.

69   The provisions in the Status of Forces Agreement also provided a legal basis for this view.

70   The Security Council had requested additional resources through 'borrowing' from other UN missions (inter-mission cooperation) and not new deployments. This led to significant delays.

71   The UNMISS transcript of Minister Michael Makuei Lueth's statement at the press gathering on 8 March records that the blame was put not on UNMISS, but on 'the people running it'. Transcript in possession of the author.

72   The Juba demonstration was on 10 March; others took place on 11 and 12 March.

73   See e.g., www.bbc.com/news/world-africa-26520091.

74   One petition handed to UNMISS at Rumbek on 11 March stated: 'Ms Hilde Johnson's role in supporting the rebels is crystal clear ... in harboring rebels in UN compounds, giving UN vehicles to rebels in Bor and Bentiu ... [and] the UN smuggling weapons of destruction ... [T]he irresponsible girl Hilde has meddled herself into our internal affairs in disrepairable [sic] way. We call on the Arab world, the AU, the IGAD and all countries ... to condemn such scandalous action ... and to support our call to immediately dismiss Ms Hilde from South Sudan. This must come to an end or else we the people of this state and indeed of South Sudan are capable of teaching her an unforgettable lesson.'

75   An eyewitness confirms that Michael Makuei persuaded Kiir not to say

anything, despite general support for a statement among senior officials present.

76  The government subsequently released the cargo it had been holding since 8 March.

77  'Facts on UNMISS Related to the December/February Crisis', 3 April 2014, in possession of the author. Available online: www.sudantribune.com/spip.php.?article50528.

78  Media interview with Defence Minister, 14 February 2014. Available online: http://www.sudantribune.com/spip.php?article49963.

79  President Kiir confirmed this to the AU Commission of Inquiry on South Sudan, referring to the assistance of Misseriya and militias from Darfur and thatthey were promised funds per death and per injury. See 'Final Report of the African Union Mission of Inquiry on South Sudan', African Union, Addis Ababa, 15 October 2014, p. 120, para. 394.

80  UNMISS, 'Conflict in South Sudan: A Human Rights Report', 8 May 2014, p. 45.

81  'S Sudan rebel leader rejects massacre claims', Al Jazeera, 22 April 2014. He responded from the first Consultative Conference of the SPLM/IO in Nasir, Upper Nile State, 15–18 April, which passed several resolutions and a Communiqué, but with no commitment to hold their own forces to account.

82  The investigations conducted by UNMISS showed a delayed reaction among some of our troops. This was very regrettable, and led to changes in the UN force to help ensure more robust and decisive action.

83  Available online: http://www.newnationsouthsudan.com/national-news/kiir-condemns-killing-of-58-people-at-un-base-in-bor.html.

84  Both met Riek Machar. The statement by High Commissioner Pillay at a press conference in Juba on 30 April, and that of Special Advisor Adama Dieng, made an impact.

85  This was the second visit of a US secretary of state after independence, as Hilary Clinton visited South Sudan briefly on 3 August 2012, focusing mainly on Sudan–South Sudan challenges.

86  The UNMISS mandate did not provide authority to compel production of evidence, to call and interview witnesses, and to secure or even visit scenes of alleged violations. Nor has any UN Mission ever been provided with a mandate to undertake criminal investigations. For this reason, forensic capacity is normally not available.

87  AU Commission of Inquiry on South Sudan 'Final Report ...', Addis Ababa, 15 October 2014, p. 118.

88  UNMISS, 'Conflict in South Sudan: A Human Rights Report' (Juba, 2014), pp. 56, 60.

89  Available online: http://eyeradio.org/kiir-dissolves-crisis-management-committee.

90  Interview 47, 25 June 2015.

91  Ibid.

92  The figures obtained from several sources were in the order of at least 200–50 million USD, at an exchange rate of 1:3. While the scale has been corroborated, the exact figure has not been verified.

93  *The Sentry*, 'Country Brief South Sudan, Dismantling the Financing of Africa's Deadliest Conflicts,' Washington, July 2015, 4, www.TheSentry.org.

94  Available online: http://eyeradio.org/kiir-dissolves-crisis-management-committee. On 2 May 2014, the presidential press secretary, Ateny Wek Ateny stated on Radio Miraya that there would be an internal audit of the CMC.

95  Author's notes of conversations in Juba, January–July 2014.

96  The land that UNMISS had been allocated in Juba, and in all three states, was swampy during the rainy season. It was very difficult to keep bases operational, even without refugees.

97  The White House, Office of the Press Secretary: 'Executive Order: Blocking property of certain persons with respect to South Sudan', 3 April 2014, evoking relevant acts. On 6 May 2014, two commanders were sanctioned, Peter Gadet, a commander of rebel forces, and Marial Chanuong, commander of the government's Presidential Guard; see online: http://www.theeastafrican.co.ke/news/US-sanctions-two-South-Sudanese-leaders-in-first-step/-/2558/2306772/-/j2b6h5/-/index.html. Others would follow.

98  The EU sanctioned two commanders, Peter Gadet on the opposition side and Santino Deng on the government side on 10 July 2014, 'EU Imposes Sanctions on South Sudanese military leaders', Reuters, 10 July 2014.

99  Stansi Kalyvas, 2006: 5 defines civil war as armed combat within the boundaries of a recognized sovereign entity between parties subject to a common authority at the outset of the hostilities. See also Themnér L. and Wallensteen P., 'Armed conflicts 1946–2013', *Journal of Peace Research* li/4 (2014), pp. 541–54.

## Chapter 7: The Heart of the Matter: Security

1  John Snowden, 'Small Arms Survey, HSBA Working Paper 27', Graduate Institute of International and Development Studies, Geneva 2012, p. 19.

2  Ibid.

3  This included the position of deputy commander-in-chief of the SPLA, a new position.

4  The Eastern Equatorian Defence Force (EDF) was, for example, integrated prior to 2005 (militia groups had also operated both in East and Central Equatoria).

5  Interview 9, 30 January 2015; Interview 30, 18 March 2015; Interview 8, 29 January 2015; Interview 29, 19 March 2015.

6  Many followed: Yohannes Yual, Samuel Both, Saddam Shayot Manyang, Timothy Taban Juuc, and others. Al Fursan and Abdel Bagi forces came in after the Juba Declaration, the former with Peter Gadet. Clement Wani's Mandari militia in Central Equatoria joined at this time, too. See Richard Rands, 'In Need of Review: SPLA Transformation in 2006–10 and Beyond', Small Arms Survey, HBSA paper 23, Geneva, November 2010, pp. 16–18.

7  The source had seen Khartoum's documents on the SSDF, South Sudan Defence Forces, Interview 9, 30 January 2015.

8       Peter Gadet rebelled again in 2010 for six months, was reintegrated again, and defected in December 2013. After the 2010 elections, some who had lost in the nomination process, such as George Athor, or lost the election, such as David Yau Yau and Gwang Roberto rebelled. George Athor was later killed in unknown circumstances, as was James Gatwic Gai, another militia leader.

9       These brought in Gabriel Tanginye (Gabriel Gatwich Chan) and David Yau Yau, as well as the Shilluk militia leader Johnson Olony; and Gordon Kong. During the run-up to independence in 2011, some 18 militia or armed groups had reportedly been integrated into the SPLA. (See Jeremy Astill-Brown, 'South Sudan's Slide into Conflict: Revisiting the Past and Reassessing Partnerships,' Chatham House, Africa Programme, December 2014.)

10      De Waal, 'When kleptocracy becomes insolvent', pp. 113, 358, 452; Interview 8, 29 January 2015.

11      Edward Lino, 'There was no coup in Juba', 9 February 2014. Available online: http://paanluel.com/2014/02/09edward-lino-there-was-no-coup-in-juba/.

12      Interview 32, 21 March 2015; Interview 8, 29 January 2015; Interview 9, 30 January 2015.

13      Interview 32, 21 March 2015; Interview 5, 28 January 2015.

14      According to Interview 9, 31 January 2015, Paul Malong and Salva Mathok in 2005 brought in forces from Aweil and Warrap respectively as the President's bodyguards.

15      From 2006 onwards there were 3,000 Presidential Guards in Juba, of whom at least 1800 were Nuer, the great majority belonging to Paulino Matip. James Wani Igga brought in a few. The rest were from Bahr el Ghazal. Salva Kiir brought in soldiers from Aweil and Gogrial, and made sure that only his own people protected him at the Presidential Residence.

16      Interview 32, 21 March 2015; Interview 9, 30 January 2015.

17      Interview 32, 21 March 2015.

18      E.g. George Athor, Peter Gadet, David Yau Yau and Alfred Ladu Gore.

19      Rands, 'In Need of Review', pp. 33, 38.

20      For a while a unit of 30 or 40 SPLA officers and instructors travelled from unit to unit to conduct training, and after a couple of years an advanced training centre had been built with American funds, but this was far too little too late.

21      Clemence Pinaud, 'South Sudan, civil war, predation and the making of military aristocracy', *African Affairs* cxiii/452 (2014), pp. 192–211.

22      Interview 6, 8 February 2015; Interview 29, 19 March 2015; Interview 9, 31 January 2015.

23      John Snowden, 'Work in Progress: Security Force Development in South Sudan through February 2012', HSBA Working Paper 27, 18, 20. While a number of militia were deployed to JIUs, and constituted an increase in the Army, the SPLA lost the 9th and 10 Divisions located in Sudan and hence, left with the SPLM-N. Still, there was a net increase.

24      Interview 1, 24 October 2014; Interview 2, 5 December 2014; Interview 3, 9 January 2015.

25  We received a total figure of 150,000 from the government, which comprised all security forces, while other sources indicated 120,000, with the SPLA comprising 80,000.

26  Rands, 'In Need of Review'.

27  De Waal, 'When kleptocracy becomes insolvent', p. 361.

28  Mike Lewis, 'Skirting the Law: Sudan's Post-CPA Arms Flows', Small Arms Survey, HSBA Working Paper 18, 2009. Interviewees deny that such deals were made in relation to these particular contracts (Interview 32, 21 March 2015).

29  De Waal, 'When kleptocracy becomes insolvent', p. 356; Lewis, 'Skirting the Law', pp. 39–44; available online: http://paanluelwel.com/2011/09/09/wikileak-cable-on-vp-machar-on-nhial-deng-and-on-cleaning-corruption-in-the-spla/. Interviewees deny that such deals were made in relation to these particular contracts (Interview 32, 21 March 2015).

30  At independence, the SPLA had eight transport helicopters, but it is not clear whether they were all purchased in 2010.

31  Interview 1, 24 October 2014; Interview 2, 5 December 2014; Interview 5, 28 January 2015; Interview 29, 19 March, 2015; Interview 16, 5 February 2015; Interview 17, 11 February 2015; Interview 32, 21 March 2015; Interview 33 23 March 2015.

32  Interview 16, 5 February 2015; Interview 16, 11 February 2015; Interview 32, 21 March 2015; Interview 33, 23 March 2015.

33  Sources say that acquisition of the Air Defence System was primarily motivated by graft: Interview 5, 28 January 2015; Interview 29, 19 March, 2015; Interview 16, 5 February 2015; Interview 17, 11 February 2015; Interview 32, 21 March 2015; Interview 33, 23 March 2015.

34  Parts of the system are still in Uganda, some in Juba: Interview 16, 5 February 2015; Interview 32, 21 March 2015; Interview 5, 28 January 2015; Interview 29, 19 March, 2015; Interview 43, 25 April 2015.

35  Almost no results were achieved despite a large programme under the auspices of UNMIS and the UNDP.

36  'The Report of the Auditor General on the Financial Statements of the Government of Southern Sudan for the Financial Year Ended 31 December 2008 ... June 2012'. Available online: http://www.auditchamber-ss.org/reports/nac-ag-report-financial-statements-2008.pdf.

37  HSBA, 'Small Arms Survey, Issue Brief 22', 2013.

38  Interview 5, 31 January 2015; others confirmed the same: Interview 32, 21 March 2015; Interview 33, 23 March 2015.

39  The SPLA Commandos were multi-ethnic, and efforts were made in some divisions, e.g. Division 4. The plans for mainstreaming this approach faltered, however, as did the efforts to create an integrated multi-ethnic Presidential Guard.

40  Thomas, *South Sudan*, p. 164.

41  Snowden, 'Work in Progress: Security Force Development in South Sudan through February 2012', HSBA Working Paper 27, June 2012, p. 18.

42  Author's notes on conversations with senior officials, January–February 2014.

43    Interview 1, 24 October 2014.

44    Interview 2, 5 December 2014.

45    Rands, 'In Need of Review', p. 33.

46    Ibid., p. 31.

47    Interview 1, 24 October 2014.

48    Sanctions against such support no longer applied after South Sudan's independence.

49    Snowden, 'Work in Progress', p. 23.

50    Author's notes. Conversations with security ministers and leading figures of the SPLA in 2013, as well as assessments by the majority of donors, as reflected in donor meetings in 2012–13.

51    'Objective Force 2017', adopted at the end of 2011; a more detailed defence transformation programme followed (see John Snowden, 'Work in Progress', p. 21).

52    Herbert Wulf, *Security Sector Reform in Developing and Transitional Countries* (Berlin, 2004), p. 5.

53    Snowden, 'Work in Progress', p. 9.

54    Ashraf Ghani and Clare Lockhart, Confidential paper for the SPLM/A Chairman 2005 in possession of the author.

55    South Sudan used a military ranking system in the National Police Service, with the same titles. There were plans to change this to internationally comparable police ranking when the crisis erupted in December 2013.

56    Snowden, 'Work in Progress', p. 28.

57    Ibid.

58    Prior to independence, the name was Southern Sudan Police Service; after independence the name changed to South Sudan National Police Service.

59    Interview 1, 24 October 2014; Interview 2, 5 December 2014.

60    Snowden, 'Work in Progress', p. 27.

61    The UNMIS Human Rights Investigation Report on violations at the Rajaf Police training centre in 2010 was not made public. UN High Commissioner for Human Rights, Navi Pillay, criticized the grave violations in a Press Statement, Juba 7 June 2011.

62    Snowden, 'Work in Progress', p. 27.

63    *The Citizen* (Juba), 27 October 2011.

65    This was the opinion of African Union security experts and UNMISS's National Security Advisor, Kellie Conteh.

66    Interviews with eyewitnesses who visited the training camp; one reviewed the full list of those recruited; Interview 7, 9 December 2014; Interview 8, 29 January 2015; Interview 11, 1 February 2014; Interview 32, 21 March 2014; Interview 34, 15 April 2015.

67    The Dinka name literally means 'a brownish cat that predates on rats'; Latin name not available; Interview 11, 1 February 2014; confirmed by other informants later.

68    Paul Malong was wealthy, not least from the border trade in Northern Bahr el Gahzal state, and reportedly helped fund the forces. Fundraising took place also among business and community leaders from his state and Warrap. But

the forces in Pantiit at times lacked food and basic services (Interview 11, 1 February 2014; confirmed by other informants).

69  Presidential Decree 25/2013. An earlier reshuffle had promoted new officers into senior positions; Available online: http://hornaffairs.com/en/2013/02/26/south-sudan-retires-army-generals.  Available  online: http://www.sudantribune.com/spip.php?article45558.

70  AU Commission of Inquiry on South Sudan: 'Final Report ...', 15 October 2014, p. 10.

71  Interview 32, 21 March 2015; Interview 33, 23 March 2015.

72  Interview 5, 28 January 2015; Interview 6, 8 February 2015; Interview 7, 9 December 2015; Interview 8, 29 January 2015.

73  Interview 5, 28 January 2015; Interview 7, 9 December 2014; Interview 8, 29 January 2015; Interview 11, 1 February 2015; Interview 32, 21 March 2015.

74  Interview 9, 30 January 2015. Recruitment was primarily from Warrap and Gogrial, the President's home state and county, and from Northern Bahr el Ghazal.

75  According to the AU Commission of Inquiry, 'President Kiir confirmed his recruitment of 7500 troops', 'Final Report', Addis Ababa, 15 October 2014, p. 121.

76  Interview 11, 1 February 2015; Interview 7, 9 December 2015.

77  Author's notes on conversations in May–June 2013. This meant approximately 2,250 soldiers. The majority of interviewees estimated the total to be 2,000–3,000 in 2012–13.

78  Interview 22, 21 March 2015: the source says that only some 350 graduated to become Presidential Guards.

79  Interview 47, 24 June 2015. According to the AU Commission of Inquiry, officials reported that between 330 and 700 soldiers were integrated into the Presidential Guard following a commissioning ceremony attended by the President: 'Final Report', p. 22. The total number trained at Luri may still have been larger.

80  A number of forces were allegedly deployed as street cleaners in Juba in December: AU Commission of Inquiry on South Sudan, 'Final Report', p. 22.

81  Interview 1, 24 October 2014; Interview 2, 5 December 2015; Interview 5, 28 January 2015; Interview 11, 1 February 2015; Interview 48, 14 February 2015.

82  The President's National Security spending in 2014 was more than the entire infrastructure budget of South Sudan: available online: http://www.grss-mof.org/wp-content/uploads/2015/01/Q1-Macro-Fiscal-Report.pdf.

83  Interview 5, 28 January 2015; Interview 6, 8 February 2015, claiming that resources were diverted from SPLA Division 5, where funds equal to one month of payroll were transferred to the Pandiit/Luri force. SPLA Division 8 in Bor (Pibor) had salary delayed for the same reason.

84  Interview 30, 18 March 2015.

85  Interview 34, 21 April 2015.

86  Author's notes on conversations with senior security officials in Juba,

October-December 2013;Interview 34, 21 April 2015; Interview 48, 14 February 2015.

87 Interview 5, 28 January 2015; Interview 7, 9 December 2014; Interview 8, 29 January 2015; Interview 11, 1 February 2015; Interview 32, 21 March 2015.

88 Interview 5, 28 January 2015; Interview 11, 1 February 2015.

89 Interview 32, 21 March 2015.

90 According to a well-placed source, the Council consisted of two representatives per county in the Bahr el Gazhal region. Others say it included, or worked with, Aleu Ateny Aleu (interior minister until 2015); Salva Mathok Gengdit (a former deputy chief of staff in the SPLA, and a relative of the President); Bol Akot and Garang Mabil (former generals); and Augustino Atem Kuol Dit (a former SPLA commander and official in the Ministry of Defence), among others. Paul Malong's relations with the Council ran hot and cold, as did those of Major General Marial, commander of the Presidential Guards and Tiger Battalion.

91 Interview 47, 14 February 2015; Interview 5, 28 January 2015; Interview 32, 21 March 2015.

92 Interview 47, 14 February 2015.

93 Interview 3, 9 January 2015; Interview 11, 1 February 2015. Several sources say that the new uniforms came from 'National Security', and the arms and ammunition were 'Galil', from Israel, also through National Security. Others say the supplies came from China.

94 The consignor was NORINCO, China's state-run defence contractor. Some weapons reportedly went also to the Presidential Guards at Luri.

95 Interview 5, 28 January 2015; Interview 7, 9 December 2014; Interview 8, 29 January 2015; Interview 11, 1 February 2015. Witnesses interviewed by the UNMISS Human Rights Section also reported this.

96 Human Rights Watch, 'South Sudan's New War', p. 83; interviews conducted by UNMISS Human Rights Section, December 2013–March 2014.

97 Interview 5, 28 January 2015.

98 Interview 1, 24 October; Interview 2, 5 December 2014; Interview 5, 28 January 2015; Interview 32, 21 March 2015.

99 The information was shared with the author in the first quarter of 2014; the corroborated four names are on the files of the author and will be handed over to the appropriate investigation body, in the event of criminal investigations. Interview 1, 24 October; Interview 5, 28 January 2015; Interview 11, 1 February 2015; Interview 32, 21 March 2015.

100 AU Commission of Inquiry on South Sudan: 'Final Report', p. 225; Interview 21 July 2014.

101 Interview 1, 24 October 2014; Interview 5, 28 January 2015.

102 Interview 5, 28 January 2015; Interview 7, 9 December 2014; Interview 8, 29 January 2015; Interview 11, 1 February 2015; Interview 32, 21 March 2015. The names are on the files of the author and will be handed over to the appropriate investigation body, in the event of criminal investigations.

103 Republican Decree 103/2013; HSBA, 'Small Arms Survey, Timeline of Recent Intra-South Sudan Conflict', Geneva, June 2014, p. 6.

104 Due to insecurity and crime in Juba, the town had a year before been divided

in subsectors, with the establishment of joint operations centres for the SSNPS, the SPLA and National Security combined. This structure therefore was not part of a 'plan', but probably came in handy in December 2013.

105 Interview 9, 31 January 2015. Corroboration with others present was not possible (interviewees not accessible).

106 Interview with Oyay Deng Ajak, January 2015.

107 UNMISS, 'Conflict in South Sudan: A Human Rights Report' (Juba, 2014), p. 4.

108 AU Commission of Inquiry on South Sudan: 'Final Report of the African Union Mission of Inquiry on South Sudan', p. 225.

109 Human Rights Watch, 'South Sudan's New War', p. 83.

110 'Operating' indicates political rallying, but not mobilizing – in more military terms. Author's notes of conversations with senior officials, Juba.

111 Confirmed in interviews with each of those referred to.

112 Author's notes on conversations with senior officials, November–December 2013.

113 Interview 10, 1 February 2015.

114 Interview 37, 8 July 2015; Interview 5, 28 January 2015; Interview 32, 21 March 2015.

115 Interview 16, 5 February 2015; Interview 17, 11 February 2015. Others mention Taban Deng as a frequent visitor to the house of Oyay Deng, the former minister of national security.

116 Interview 16, 5 February 2015; Interview 17, 11 February 2015.

117 Author's notes from conversations with senior Sudanese officials in Juba and Khartoum January and June 2014; Interview 29, 19 March 2015; Interview 43, 25 April 2015.

118 Interview 9, 31 January 2015; Interview 10, 1 February 2015; Interview 16, 5 February 2015; Interview 17, 11 February 2015.

119 Interview 6, 8 February 2015; Interview 47, 25 June 2015.

120 Interview 16, 5 February 2015; Interview 17, 11 February 2015.

121 Interview 5, 29 January 2015.

122 Interview 6, 8 February 2015; Interview 43, 25 April 2015. According to this source, they thought they could control 65 per cent of the force, but miscalculated badly.

123 Interview 4, 7 January 2015.

124 Interview 34, 21 April 2015.

125 Ibid.

126 Interview 5, 28 January 2015; Interview 6, 8 February 2015. Such terminology could easily be meant to signal military resistance.

127 Interview 9, 31 January 2015; Interview 5, 28 January 2015; Interview 33, 23 March 2015. One source heard him say this on the phone several times.

128 Interview 5, 28 January 2015; Interview 6, 8 February 2015, Interview 32, 21 March 2015; Interview 33, 23 March 2015.

129 It is likely that these forces were enforcements coming from the Presidential Guards trained at Luri.

130 Interview 9, 31 January 2015.

131 I have obtained such purported summaries – not transcripts – of phone conversations between Taban and members of the Presidential Guards. While the summaries include references to 'plans', without the audio it is impossible to determine authenticity.

132 AU Commission of Inquiry on South Sudan: 'Final Report', p. 27.

133 Interview 29, 19 March 2015; Interview 33, 23 March 2015.

134 For its part, the AU Commission of Inquiry says: 'We were led to conclude that the initial fighting within the Presidential Guard arose out of disagreement and confusion over the alleged order to disarm Nuer members. The Commission notes further, that there are also suggestions of a mutiny within the Presidential Guards, and the ensuing violence spiralled out of control, spilling out into the general population.' See 'Final Report', 15 October 2014, p. 27.

135 Interview 5, 28 January 2015.

136 Within the Presidential Guards there were soldiers and officers who were loyal to Riek Machar. While remaining in their positions after Machar left office as vice president, he could still instruct them in a situation like this. Interview 9, 31 January 2015; Interview 18, 6 February 2015.

137 At this time, according to this source, in the Giyada barracks of the Presidential Guards there were 1,500 Nuer Guards and 900 Dinka.

138 Interview 5, 28 January 2015; Interview 6, 8 February 2015.

139 Interview 21, 7 February 2015; Interview 22, 7 February 2015; Interview 23, 7 February 2015; Interview 24, 7 February 2015, all commanders of the SPLM/IO. A Dinka eyewitness from Bor, monitoring Peter Gadet's movements and communications during 14–18 December has also provided useful information (Interview 25, 7 February 2015).

140 In December and January the mobile phone network was down in areas of Greater Upper Nile, and it was only later that a number of the commanders could communicate regularly with the leadership.

141 Interview 5, 28 January 2015; Interview 32, 21 March 2015; Interview 33, 23 March 2015, Interview 21, 7 February 2015; Interview 22, 7 February 2015, Interview 23, 7 February 2015, Interview 24, 7 February 2015.

142 Interview 16, 5 February 2015.

143 Interview 49, 31 November 2014; Interview 20, 7 February 2015.

144 Interview 43, 25 April 2015.

145 AU Commission of Inquiry on South Sudan: 'Final Report', p. 229.

146 Available online: http://www.sudantribune.com/spip.php?article50511; Mac Paul said that Taban Deng called him on 13 December about the arrest of a junior officer who had attempted to snatch the keys to the armoury. Available online: http://www.equatoriasun.com/south-sudan-conflict-2/key-witness-declines-to-link-splm-four-to-alleged-coup.

147 HSBA, 'Small Arms Survey – Timeline 2014', 16. Available online: http://www.sudantribune.com/spip.php?article50511.

148 Katsuyoshi Fukui and John Markakis, Introduction, in *Ethnicity and Conflict in the Horn of Africa* (Martlesham, 1994), pp. 4–6.

149 Mats Berdal and David M. Malone, Introduction, in *Greed and Grievances: Economy Agendas in Civil Wars* (Boulder, 2000), pp. 5, 8.

150 Interview 4, 7 January 2015.

151 Barry R. Posen, 'The security dilemma and ethnic conflict', *Survival* xxxv/1 (1993), p. 28.

152 Ibid., pp. 28–43.

153 Interview 8, 29 January 2015.

154 Author's notes.

155 Posen, 'The security dilemma', p. 28.

156 Interview 4, 7 January 2015.

157 Interview 49, 31 November 2014.

158 Interview 1, 24 October 2014, Interview 2, 5 December 2014.

159 Interview 2, 7 December 2014; Interview 49, 31 November 2014; Interview 3, 9 January 2015; Interview 18, 6 February 2015; Interview 19, 6 February 2015.

160 Interview 49, 31 November 2014; Interview 18, 6 February 2015; Interview 19, 6 February 2015.

161 This famous commander had integrated, rebelled, and in 2012 come back to the SPLM/A, allegedly in return for command of the 8 Division at Bor. Uncorroborated rumour also had it that he had been paid a lump sum too, enough to buy a house in Nairobi.

162 Interview 34, 21 April 2015.

163 Ibid.

164 Interview 1, 24 October 2014; Interview 2, 7 December 2014.

165 Interview 2, 7 December 2014. This was public knowledge, both through visible strains in their relationship during 2014–2015, and Machar's dismissal of Gadet in July 2015.

166 Interview 1, 24 October 2014.

167 Interview 6, 8 February 2015.

168 Interview 25, 11 February 2015.

169 Interview 1, 24 October 2014; Interview 2, 5 December 2014; Interview 25, 11 February 2015.

170 Interview 1, 24 October 2014; Interview 2, 5 December 2014; Interview 3, 9 January 2015; Interview 21, 7 February 2015; Interview 22, 7 February 2015; Interview 24, 7 February 2015.

171 Meetings in Addis Ababa, June 2014; Interview 31, 31 November 2014; Interview 20, 7 February 2015; Interview 18, 6 February 2015.

172 Mathiang would later be totally destroyed by opposition forces, and a large number of people killed. Kuol Manyang himself was said to have lost some 20 relatives.

173 Interview 18, 6 February 2015; Interview 19, 6 February 2015; Interview 20, 7 February 2015; Interview 18, 6 February 2015.

174 Interview 48, 14 February 2015. The source added that it was irrelevant whether these atrocities were committed before or after the commanders' meeting took place in late April. Machar publicly declared his leadership over the forces, including the White Army, and must remain responsible for their actions.

175 Interview 49, 31 November 2014; Interview 7, 9 December 2014; Interview 3, January 2015; Interview 20, 7 February 2015.

176 Interview 49, 31 November 2014; Interview 7, 9 December 2014.

177 Telephone conversation with Riek Machar, 28 December 2013 (reported to the Security Council the same evening), confirmed by eyewitness (Interview 49, 31 November 2014).

178 There were significant tensions between Gadet and the White Army.

179 Interview 49, 31 November 2014; Interview 20, 7 February 2015; Interview 3, 9 January 2015.

180 Interview 1, 24 October 2014.

181 Author's notes on telephone conversations with Machar, 21, 23 December 2014.

182 Author's conversations in Juba.

183 Interview 3, 9 January 2015.

184 Available online: http://www.smallarmssurveysudan.org/facts-figures/south-sudan/armed-groups/southern-dissident-militias/ssdma-upper-nile.html.

185 On the government side, 1991 rhetoric dominated, while the SPLM/IO focused on 'tribalization of Government', 'neglect' of the Nuer, etc. (Interview 21, 7 February 2015; Interview 22 7 February 2015; 24, 7 February 2015).

186 Salva Kiir Mayardit's Independence Day speech, 9 July 2011.

187 Figures from the 'Food Security and Livelihoods cluster' under the Humanitarian Coordinator/OCHA in South Sudan, following the Integrated Food Security Phase Classification' (IPC) in 2014.


## Chapter 8: Waging Peace in South Sudan

1 Kofi Annan, Foreword to Johnson, *Waging Peace in Sudan.*

2 Communiqué of the 23rd Extraordinary Session of the IGAD Assembly of Heads of State and Government on the situation in South Sudan, 27 December 2013.

3 As an executive director in the civil service, he had not had any political role. Somehow, he had still been arrested during the turmoil on 16–17 December.

4 Agreement on Cessation of Hostilities between the Government of the Republic of South Sudan (GRSS) and the Sudan People's Liberation Movement/Army (in Opposition) (SPLM/A in Opposition), 23 January 2014.

5 'South Sudan Releases Seven Political Detainees', Available online: http://www.sudantribune.com/spip.php?article49767, 30 January 2014.

6 Communiqué of the 24th Extraordinary Session of the IGAD Assembly of Heads of State and Government on the situation in South Sudan, 31 January 2014.

7 That the parties preferred a delayed mechanism was as expected.

8 IGAD Communiqué of the 25th Extraordinary Session of the IGAD Heads of State and Government on the situation in South Sudan, para. 10–11, 2014.

9 Verified through several sources.

10 Ezekiel Lol Gatkuoth later joined the SPLM/A-IO, making the group G10.

11  Available online: http://www.voanews.com/content/treason-trial-south-sudan-political-detainees/1868977.html.

12  Available online: http://www.equatoriasun.com/south-sudan-conflict-2/key-witness-declines-to-link-splm-four-to-alleged-coup/ 27 March 2014.

13  Agreement to Resolve the Crisis in South Sudan, 9 May 2014: available online: http://southsudan.igad.int/index.php/2014-08-07-10-47-57/249-agreement-to-resolve-the-crisis-in-s-sudan-9-may-14.

14  UNMISS Transcript of President Salva Kiir's speech, 10 May 2014 (author's copy); transcripts of both leaders' speeches are available at *Radio Tamazuj*, 12 May, 2014. Available online: https://radiotamazuj.org/en/article/transcript-kiir-and-machar-speeches-south-sudan-ceasefire-signing. Both statements were seen as undermining what had been agreed between the parties.

15  Communiqué of the 26th Extraordinary Session of the IGAD Assembly of Heads of State and Government on the situation in South Sudan, 10 June 2014.

16  The IGAD Summit took place on 8–9 June, while an inclusive, multi-stakeholder Symposium on 6–7 June in Addis Ababa drew over 200 South Sudanese participants from a broad range of sectors and regions, and provided a platform to engage constructively on key issues toward political transition and peaceful resolution of the crisis.

17  Lucy Poni, 20 June 2014. Available online: http://reliefweb.int/report/south-sudan/south-sudan-peace-process-stalls.

18  IGAD Press Release: 'Multi-stakeholder peace talks adjourn for further consultations', 23 June 2014.

19  IGAD Single Negotiating Text Arising From Draft II Framework for Political and Security Negotiations towards a Resolution of the Crisis in South Sudan.

20  The Security Council Resolution was passed on 29 May 2014, SCRS/RES/2156 (2014).

21  Communiqué of the 27th Extraordinary Session of the IGAD Assembly of Heads of State and Government on the situation in South Sudan, 25 August 2014.

22  IGAD Protocol on Agreed Principles on Transitional Arrangements towards a Resolution of the Crisis, Addis Ababa, 25 August 2014.

23  In early July 2014 Seyoum Mesfin gave a statement to the Security Council, a briefing which created some waves among IGAD member states.

24  Communiqué of the 23rd Extraordinary Session of the IGAD Assembly of Heads of State and Government on the situation in South Sudan, 27 December 2013.

25  Statement by Norwegian Foreign Minister Børge Brende, 'Norway says time for Uganda to reduce troops in South Sudan', Reuters, 29 January 2014.

26  Douglas Johnson, 'Briefing: The crisis in South Sudan', *African Affairs* cxiii/451(2014), p. 309.

27  Meeting on 14 May 2014 with senior official involved in the purchase. Author's notes.

28  At least two shipments of arms from NORINCO, the Chinese defence conglomerate, reached Juba in May–June 2014.

29  *Credible* confidential sources, May–June 2014, September–October 2014 – March 2015.

30  *Credible* confidential sources, September–October 2014, March 2015.

31  Conflict Armament Research, Dispatch from the Field, *Weapons and Ammunition Air-dropped to SPLA-IO Forces in South Sudan: Equipment Captured by the SPLA in Jonglei State, November 2014* (London, 2015).

32  Conflict Armament Research, *The Distribution of Iranian Ammunition in Africa* (London, 2012), pp. 20–1, confirms earlier transfer of Iranian weapons via Sudan to 'rebels' in South Sudan.

33  Minutes from Meeting of the Joint Military and Security Committee held in the National Defense College in Khartoum on 31 August 2014. Chief of Joint General Staff, Lt. Gen Hashim Abdalla Mohammed is quoted as saying: 'We must change the balance of forces in South Sudan. Riak, Taban and Dhieu Mathok came and requested support in the areas of training in MI and especially in tanks and artillery. They requested armament also. They want to be given advanced weapons. Our reply was that we have no objection, provided that we agree on a common objective. Then we train and supply with the required weapons.' The minutes have been provided by *credible* confidential sources.

34  Ibid., Abdel Rahim Mohamed Hussein is quoted as saying: 'I met Riak, Dhieu and Taban and they are regretting the decision to separate the South and we decided to return his house to him. He requested us to assist him and that he has shortage in the MI-personnel, operations command and tank technicians. We must use as many cards we have against the South in order to give them unforgettable lesson.'

35  Interview 27, 16 February 2015; Interview 26, 7 February 2015; Interview 31, 18 March 2015; Interview 30, 18 March 2015.

36  UNHCR statistics, 30 March 2014. Available online: http://data.unhcr.org/SouthSudan/country.php?id=65.

37  Changes along the Ethiopian-South Sudan border were influencing international relations. Ethnic groups previously in the lead now felt marginalized, politically and economically. For the first time, in Gambella State in Ethiopia there was now a Nuer Governor. Ethiopian Nuers were calling for intervention to rescue their brothers in South Sudan, and for a change of government in Juba.

38  *The East African*, 14–20 March 2015.

39  South Sudan's share of total Ugandan exports was 16 per cent in 2012–13, not including the service sector.

40  *BBC Focus on Africa*, 30 September 2014.

41  'Executive Order – Blocking Property of Certain Persons in South Sudan', 3 April 2014. Available online: https://www.whitehouse.gov/the-press-office/2014/04/03/executive-order-blocking-property-certain-persons-respect-south-sudan.

42  UN Security Council Resolution 2206 (2015). Available online: http://www.un.org/press/en/2015/sc11805.doc.htm.

43    Øystein H. Rolandsen, Helene Molteberg Glomnes, et al., 'A year of South Sudan's third civil war', *International Area Studies Review* xviii/1(2015), pp. 87–104. Available online: DOI:10.1177/2233865915573797.

44    Abel Alier's account of Khartoum's policies in *Southern Sudan: Too Many Agreements Dishonoured*, 2nd edn (Exeter, 2003), now seemed to apply to South Sudanese leaders, as well.

45    In the CPA process the Khartoum government and SPLM/A rejected participation by others. Although this likely would have complicated the talks, inclusion could have been arranged sequentially. The IGAD-process faced the same challenge, but also showed the challenges with such an approach.

46    'South Sudan and the Risks of Unrest', *The Sudd Institute Weekly Review*, 3 December 2013, p. 13.

47    Some efforts were made to establish national institutions with an amalgamating perspective, focusing on unity in diversity, with the Ministry of Culture in the lead. In the absence of support from the top, however, they were not given the prominence they deserved, and were not followed up by other unifying initiatives.

48    Transitional Constitution, articles 202 and 203.

49    Zacharia Ding Akol, 'A Nation in Transition: South Sudan's Constitutional Review Process', The Sudd Institute Policy Brief No. 3, 17 February 2013, p. 6.

50    Despite numerous offers of support from international donors and UNMISS, and a framework coordinating the support of all partners, it was not possible to move the process forward. According to the Transitional Constitution, Article 202, sections 6, 7, and 8, national consultations had to be held.

51    Zacharia Ding Akol, 'A Nation in Transition', p. 6.

52    According to IRI polls in 2011 and 2013, 'Survey of South Sudan Public Opinion', IRI 2013, 51–65 and NDI focus group discussions all over the country ('From a Transitional to a Permanent Constitution: Views of Men and Women on Constitutionmaking [sic], NDI, June 2013'), illiterate citizens had clear views on a number of constitutional issues, including the powers of the president and legislature, the role of political parties, freedom of speech, whether elected governors could be dismissed by the president, and the death penalty.

53    The government tended to equate federalism with a weakened role for the President. See Douglas Johnson, 'Federalism in the History of South Sudanese Political Thought', Rift Valley Institute Research Paper 1 (London, 2014), pp. 26ff.

54    Ibid., p. 5.

55    Ibid., p. 27.

56    Ibid., p. 21.

57    In polls conducted in 2011 (Survey of South Sudan Public Opinion, IRI, 2011, p. 68) two-thirds of the population considered themselves as 'only South Sudanese' or 'more South Sudanese than tribe'. A very small minority felt 'more tribe than South Sudanese'. After the current conflict, polls may show different results.

58    *Gurtong*, 12 July 2015.

59    AU Commission of Inquiry on South Sudan calls this 'the official policy of amnesia', see 'Final Report', p. 235.

60   See footnote 154, Chapter 2.

61   In March 2013 the Core Group, an advisory body to UNMISS consisting of religious leaders, civil society leaders, elders from South Sudanese communities, women's groups and youth groups, warned Vice President Riek Machar, as chairman of the National Reconciliation Committee, against a process which was not seen as independent from the government.

62   Jok Madut Jok, 'National Reconciliation in South Sudan: How to Translate Political Settlements into Peace in the Country', Sudd Institute Policy Brief, 31 January 2015, p. 13.

63   Ibid., pp. 13–15.

64   IGAD 'Single Negotiating Text', August 2014.

65   Jok, M. J, 'National Reconciliation in South Sudan', p. 6. HFJ: Jok Madut Jok's surname is Jok, and not Madut Jok.

66   Communiqué of AU Peace and Security Council, 411th meeting, PSC/AHG/COMM1. (CDXI), Rev 1, p. 2, para. 8.

67   African Union, Terms of Reference for the 'African Union Commission of Inquiry on South Sudan', 12 March 2014. Available online: http://www.au.int/en/content/south-sudan-commission-inquiry-sworn.

68   UNMISS, 'Human Rights Investigation Report', 8 May 2014, p. 61.

69   In my discussions with President Salva Kiir, I made sure that the concept of a Special/Hybrid Court was well understood, with South Sudanese and international judicial experts working together.

70   Statement of Secretary General Ban Ki-moon to the 7172nd meeting of the Security Council, 'South Sudan Leaders Must Allow Humanitarian Access, Work Together to Heal Wounds, Secretary General Tells Security Council', SC/11391, 12 May 2014.

## Epilogue

1   These represented 'Faith Based Leaders', 'Civil Society', 'the Women's Bloc' and 'Eminent Personalities'. The representative of 'Other Political Parties', Lam Akol, was prohibited from traveling to Addis Ababa, so no one signed on their behalf.

2   See also 'Report of the Secretary General on South Sudan, covering the period 14 April – 18 August 2015', S/2015/655, 21 August 2015, p. 4, para. 20. Peter Gadet was back as a militia leader, allegedly having received support from both the GRSS and Khartoum, sequentially or simultaneously (Interview 49, 20 November 2015).

3   Republic of South Sudan, 'Establishment Order 26/2015 for the Creation of 28 States in the Decentralized Governance System of the Republic of South Sudan', 2 October 2015. The National Legislative Assembly agreed that the number of states would increase, but did not specify the number. Despite this, the President later proceeded, appointing new Governors for the 28 states on 28 December 2015.

4   'The Report of the Secretary General on South Sudan', the Security Council, S/2015/902, 23 November 2015, p. 10.

5   Decision of the National Liberation Council 16 October 2015, perceived as

a violation of the Arusha Agreement 23 January 2015, see the 'Report of the Secretary General on South Sudan', the Security Council S/2015/902, 23 November 2015, pp. 3, 16.

6  *Radio Tamazuj*, 16 August 2015. Available online: https://radiotamazuj. org/en/article/kiir-sacks-two-equatorian-governors.

7  The 'last' IGAD deadline had been 5 March 2015.

8  Information from a UN colleague.

9  There was speculation that I had been forced to leave. In fact I had remained longer than normal: SRSGs usually serve for two years in the more challenging environments. With the change of mandate on 29 May 2014, through SCRS/RES/2156 (2014), it made sense to pass the torch to a new Head of Mission.

10  UNMISS, 'Statement by SRSG Hilde F. Johnson', Press Conference, 8 July 2014.

11  Security Council Resolution 2206 (2015) of 3 March 2015 laid the groundwork for 'Targeted Sanctions in South Sudan Should a Peace Deal Fail'. On 19 December 2015 the US circulated a resolution proposing an arms embargo against South Sudanese parties. See Al Jazeera, 'US proposes UN arms embargo on South Sudan', 20 August 2015. China joined hands with Russia in opposing sanctions.

12  'Interim Report of the Panel of Experts on South Sudan, established pursuant to SCR 2206 (2015)', S/2015/656, 21 August 2015, p. 10; UNMISS, 'Flash Human Rights Report on the Escalation of Fighting in Greater Upper Nile Region, April/May 2015', 29 June 2015, pp. 3–5; 'Report of the Secretary General on South Sudan, covering the period 14 April – 18 August 2015', S/2015/655, 21 August 2015, pp. 4–5.

13  OCHA Humanitarian Bulletin, Bi-weekly Update on South Sudan (30 June 2015). Available online: https://www.humanitarianresponse.info/en/system/filedocuments/files/ocha_south-Sudan-biweekly_30 _june_2015.pdf.

14  'Final Report of the Panel of Experts on South Sudan, established pursuant to SCR 2206 (2015)', 22 January 2016, p. 37, para. 110.

15  UNMISS, 'Flash Human Rights Report', 15 June 2015, pp. 5–6. The UNMISS site in Bentiu had by the end of June registered and verified over 28,000 arrivals between 29 April and 15 June, chiefly women and children.

16  The United Nations Panel of Experts was established pursuant to SCR 2206 (2015) in support of the Sanctions Committee's work on assessing the need for, inter alia, targeted sanctions, a travel ban and asset freeze.

17  United Nations, 'Interim Report of the Panel of Experts', p. 15, paras 50 and 51. The panel attributed these acts to armed forces aimed at 'depriving SPLM/A in Opposition of a support base at all costs' – in other words indicating government responsibility.

18  UNMISS, 'Flash Human Rights Report', pp. 5–6.

19  Ibid., pp. 7–8; UNICEF, 'Children killed, abducted and raped in South Sudan attacks', 18 May 2015.

20  'The Report of the Secretary General on South Sudan', the Security Council, S/2015/902, 23 November 2015, pp. 9–11.

21    AU Commission of Inquiry on South Sudan: 'Final Report ...', Addis Ababa, 15 October 2014, pp. 21, 194–5, 216.

22    'South Sudan army accused of suffocating 50 civilians', *Al Jazeera*, 4 February 2015, an incident of 22 October 2015, reported by the investigation report of JMEC to the African Union.

23    UNMISS, 'The State of Human Rights in the Protracted Conflict in South Sudan', 4 December 2015, released on 21 January 2016.

24    'Nuer Ethnicity Militarized', p. 6.

25    'Private and Public Interests: informal actors, informal influence and economic order after war', in Mats Berdal and Dominic Zaum, *Political Economy of Statebuilding*, p. 70.

26    Ibid., referring to research by N. L. Carnagey, C. A. Anderson and B. J Bushman, 'The effect of video game violence on physiological desensitization to real-life violence', *Journal of Experimental Social Psychology* xliii/4 (2007), p. 684; L. R. Huesmann, and L. Kirwil, 'Why Observing Violence Increases the Risk of Violent Behavior by the Observer', in D. J. Flannery, A. T Vazsonyi and I. D. Waldman (ed.), *The Cambridge Handbook of Violent Behavior and Aggression* (New York, 2007), pp. 545–70.

27    United Nations, 'Interim Report of the Panel of Experts on South Sudan', p. 15.

28    'Final Report of the Panel of Experts on South Sudan, established pursuant to SCR 2206 (2015)', 22 January 2016, p. 2. Fighting between the SPLA and locally based armed groups, including the Arrow Boys, was spreading to virtually all parts of Western Equatoria State.

29    Pastoral Exhortation from the Catholic Bishops of Sudan and South Sudan, Meeting in Juba, 21–31 January 2014: 'Let us Refound our Nation on a New Convenant', quoting Matthew 7:24–7.

30    'Quote of the Day', *New York Times*, 23 June 2015.

31    On 11 February 2014, the Emergency Relief Coordinator designated South Sudan a 'Level 3' emergency. This is a system-wide classification for the largest-scale emergencies, benefiting from the highest priority by all humanitarian partners worldwide.

32    Integrated Food Security Phase Classification, South Sudan report (IPC), referred to in Report of the Secretary General on South Sudan, the Security Council, S/2015/902, 23 November 2015, pp. 5–6.

33    Integrated Food Security Phase Classification, November 2015, see OCHA South Sudan Humanitarian Bulletin, 6 November 2015. Available online: https://docs.unocha.org/sites/dms/SouthSudan/2015_SouthSudan/OCHA_SouthSudan_HumanitarianBulletin__6_November15.pdf.

34    Available online: http://www.unocha.org/south-sudan, 2 February 2016; http://data.unhcr.org/SouthSudan/regional.php, 4 February 2016.

35    'Report of the Secretary General on South Sudan, the Security Council, S/2015/902', 23 November 2015, pp. 5–6 and 8 says 180,000. The number was reported by UNMISS as 200,000 by end of 2015.

36    From the budgeted price level of $106 per barrel, by the end of the financial year it had almost been halved.

37    'South Sudan's oil revenue only about $10/barrel', *Radio Tamazuj*, 2 April 2015. Available online: https://radiotamazuj/en/article/s-sudan-oil-revenue-only

about-$10barrel; sources in the ministry of finance and economic planning later provided approximately the same figure. It also listed other expenses that South Sudan must carry, estimating the net value of South Sudanese oil revenue at even lower levels.

38    United Nations, 'Interim Report of the Panel of Experts on South Sudan', p. 11.

39    'War-torn South Sudan under economic attack from fall in oil price', *Financial Times*, 21 December 2014, Available online: http://www. ft.com/intl/cms/s/0/6ba9f.528–869c-11e4–8a51–00144f.eabdc0.html; Øystein Rolandsen, 'Dead Economy Walking in South Sudan', 8 May 2015. Available online: http://blogs.prio.org/MonitoringSouthSudan/2015/05/ dead-economy-walking-in-south-sudan.

40    The loans were from 'Qatar Commercial Bank', and the Central Bank of South Sudan had to service the debt at commercial rates: Interview 40, 20 February 2015; Interview 35, 24 April 2015; Interview 46, 22 April 2015. See also United Nations, 'Final Report of the Panel of Experts on South Sudan', p. 15, para. 27.

41    According to sources in the ministry of finance and economic planning, as of May 2015 monthly expenditure for the government payroll was 900 million pounds, and monthly income was 300 million.

42    United Nations, 'Interim Report of the Panel of Experts on South Sudan', pp. 11–12.

43    United Nations, 'Final Report of the Panel of Experts on South Sudan', p. 7.

44    Ibid., p. 3.

45    Exchange restrictions and the dual rate led to large quasi-fiscal losses, as the government had not been servicing its debt to the Central Bank and been building more debt. As of end September 2014, this debt amounted to 4 billion pounds (8.8 per cent of GDP), according to the IMF (IMF Country Report 14/345: 'Republic of South Sudan 2014 Article iv Consultation; Staff report, Staff Statement; and Press Release, December 2014, p. 7. Available online: https://www.imf.org/external/pubs/ft/scr/2014/cr14345.pdf).While the country's total debt was not known, in mid 2014 sources in the ministry of finance and economic planning estimated the total debt at 7 billion pounds.

46    As of June 2015, the official value of the pound against the USD was 11:1, while in December 2015 the official value was 21:1.

47    United Nations, 'Interim Report of the Panel of Experts on South Sudan', p. 11.

48    For dollarization see Christopher Adam and Lee Crawford, 'Exchange Rate Options for South Sudan', 1 May 2012, pp. 8–9.

49    Paul Collier, *The Bottom Billion: Why the Poorest Countries are Failing and What Can Be Done About It* (Oxford, 2008), pp. 38–9.

50    The pound had at times been trading at 18 pounds to the dollar on the black market, with an official exchange rate of 2.95 SSP., 'S Sudan devalues currency after 2 years of war', *New Vision*, 15 December 2015. Available online: http:// www.newvision.co.ug/news/676902-s-sudan-devalues-currency-after-two-years-of-war.html. The pound had at times been trading at 18 pounds to the dollar, with an official exchange rate of 2.95 SSP.

51    The exchange rate at this time, in December 2015, was $1 to 21 SSP.

52    *Sudan Tribune*, 'South Sudan strikes new oil deal with Sudan on oil transit charges', 3 February 2016. Available online: http://www.sudantribune.com/ spip.php?article57895.

53    Ibid.

54    'IGAD Agreement on the Resolution of the Conflict in the Republic of South Sudan', Addis Ababa, Ethiopia 17 August 2015 / Juba, 26 August 2015, pp. 5–14.

55    The power sharing formula gave the government 53 per cent of ministerial seats, South Sudan Armed Opposition 33 percent, and Former Detainees and Other Political Parties 7 per cent each.

56    Elections are stipulated to take place 60 days prior to the end of the transitional period, which was to start 90 days after the signing of the agreement, i.e. 26 November 2015. Elections may therefore be scheduled for the end of March 2018.

57    'The Reservations of the Government of the Republic of South Sudan on the "Compromise Agreement on the Resolution of the Conflict in South Sudan"', Juba 26 August 2015, p. 3. The SPLM/A-IO had been renamed 'South Sudan Armed Opposition', a name not accepted by Riek Machar's group.

58    Apart from references to the SPLM-North, the SPLM/A appears only once, under Riek Machar's signature ('SPLM/SPLA-IO'). In the rest of the agreement, references are made only to the National Defence Forces of South Sudan and the South Sudan Armed Opposition. The correction in handwriting is in the Preamble on p. 1.

59    'Minutes of Permanent Ceasefire and Transitional Security Arrangements workshop' (PCTSA), IGAD, Addis Ababa, 26 October 2015; 'IGAD Outcome of the Principal Signatory Parties to the Agreement on Planning Implementation on the Provisions in Chapter II of the Agreement 21 October–3 November 2015', Addis Ababa, 3 November 2015.

60    The withdrawal from 12 October 2015 was in accordance with Security Council resolution 2241 (2015), 9 October 2015, The Report of the Secretary General on South Sudan, the Security Council, S/2015/902, 23 November 2015, p. 13.

61    AU Commission of Inquiry on South Sudan, 'Final Report of the African Union Mission of Inquiry on South Sudan', African Union, Addis Ababa, 15 October 2014.

62    This included me, as sentences from a background briefing for the AU Commission had been used as an interview, without my knowledge and consent, out of context and given different meaning. Similar things happened to others, who found themselves inaccurately quoted, with their full names, and without their consent (Interview 29, 19 March 2015; Interview 43, 25 April 2015).

63    AU Commission of Inquiry on South Sudan, *Final Report* ... Addis Ababa, 15 October 2014, pp. 297–9.

64    Ibid., pp. 23, 300.

65    'IGAD Agreement on the Resolution of the Conflict in the Republic of

South Sudan', Addis Ababa, Ethiopia 17 August 2015 / Juba, 26 August 2015, pp. 40–6.

66  Ibid., pp. 300–1.

67  UNMISS, 'The State of Human Rights in the Protracted Conflict in South Sudan', 4 December 2015, released on 21 January 2016, p. 4.

68  Ibid., p. 304.

69  'Final Report of the Panel of Experts on South Sudan, established pursuant to SCR 2206 (2015)', 22 January 2016, p. 4.

70  'Statement by SRSG Hilde F. Johnson', 8 July 2014.

71  'Final Report of the Panel of Experts on South Sudan', pp. 9–10, paras 16–17.

72  Sudd Institute, 'Policy Brief', 12 August 2014, p. 1.

73  Fragile States Index (available online: http://library.fundforpeace.org/library/cfsir1423-fragilestatesindex2014-06d.pdf), South Sudan ranked 1st in 2014 and 2015 (available online: http://fsi.fundforpeace.org/rankings-2015); Failed States Index 2014 (available online: http://www.infoplease.com/world/statistics/failed-states-vulnerable-countries.html), although it may appear premature to pass the latter judgement after only three years of independence.

74  IGAD Communique of the 55th extra-ordinary session of the IGAD Council of Ministers, Addis Ababa, Ethiopia, 30–31 January 2016, p. 4, para. 7; AU Peace and Security Council, 571 Meeting at the level of the Heads of State and Government, Communique PSC/AHG/COMM.(DLXXI), Addis Ababa, Ethiopia, 29 January 2016, p. 2, para. 7.

75  'Q&A – The Future of Peace in South Sudan', Al Jazeera, 3 February 2016. Available online: http://www.aljazeera.com/news/2016/02/qa-future-peace-south-sudan-160202104527157.html.

76  In Presidential decree number 59 President Kiir removed James Wani Igga from the position of vice president and reappointed him to the position of (second) vice president, and in Presidential decree number 60, he appointed Riek Machar Teny to the position of first vice president, see 'SPLM-IO welcomes Machar's appointment as South Sudan's first vice president', *Sudan Tribune*, 12 February 2016. Available online: http://www.sudantribune.com/spip.php?article57989.

77  Statement by Ambassador Ezekiel Lol Gatkuoth, Secretary of Foreign Affairs, SPLM-IO, Cairo, February 2016.

78  The Economic and Financial Management Authority had the mandate to 'provide an effective oversight of economic and public financial management, and to ensure transparency and accountability particularly in the oil/petroleum sector', as reflected in section 8.1 of the agreement. The oversight body also had international representation, but it had an unclear mandate and questionable authority.

79  'IGAD Agreement on the Resolution of the Conflict in the Republic of South Sudan', Addis Ababa, 17 August 2015/Juba, 26 August 2015, pp. 48–9.

80  Stina Torjesen, 'Transition from War to Peace: Stratification, Inequality and

Postwar Economic Reconstruction', in Mats Berdal and Dominik Zaum (eds), *Political Economy of Statebuilding*, p. 52.

81    'Final report of the AU ...', 2015, pp. 106–8, referring to an overwhelmed administration appearing to have taken on too much at once, and external support taking on a too technical approach, ignoring political dynamics.

82    Support to reform efforts in the security sector would have to include vetting of personnel in relation to human rights, and for the UN in accordance with the Human Rights Due Diligence policy.

83    Berdal and Zaum, *Political Economy of Statebuilding*, pp. 9–12.

84    Ibid.

85    Torjesen, 'Transition from War to Peace', p. 59.

86    Security Council Resolution, SCR 2252, 15 December 2015, S/RES/2252 (2015).

87    *The Way Forward for the African Union in South Sudan*, Policy Brief, South Sudan Law Society with African colleagues, January 2016 (co-authors: Yasmin Sooka, Arnold Tsunga, David Deng, Betty Kaari Murungi).

88    'Report of the Secretary General on South Sudan', S/2014/537, 25 July 2014, 10; 'Report of the Secretary General on South Sudan', S/2014/708, 30 September 2014, 11; 'Report of the Secretary General on South Sudan', S/2014/821, 18 November 2014, p. 10.

89    'The Way Forward for the African Union in South Sudan', Policy Brief, p. 2.

90    Riek Machar's proposal to create 400 counties, and subsequently 21 states, and Salva Kiir's decision to establish 28 states appear to have strengthening the power base as the primary motivation.

91    'Agreement on the Reunification of the SPLM', Arusha, 21 January 2015.

92    Opening Statement by His Excellency Festus G. Mogae, Chairperson of the Joint Monitoring and Evaluation Commission (JMEC), at the inaugural meeting of JMEC held in Juba, 27 November 2015, p. 8. Available online: http://www.nyamile.com/wp-content/uploads/2015/11/opening-statement-by-festus-mogae-chairman-of-jmec.pdf.

93    The Comprehensive Needs Assessment was presented to the leadership of the SSNPS on 19 August 2013 and to donors on 19 September.

# BIBLIOGRAPHY

Adam, C. and Crawford, L., *Exchange Rate Options for South Sudan* (Oxford, 2012).

African Union, 'Commission of Inquiry on South Sudan: Final Report of the African Union Mission of Inquiry on South Sudan' (Addis Ababa, 2014).

——Terms of Reference for the 'African Union Commission of Inquiry on South Sudan', 12 March 2014. Available online: http://www.au.int/en/content/south-sudan-commission-inquiry-sworn.

Alier, A., *Southern Sudan: Too Many Agreements Dishonoured*, 2nd edn (Exeter, 2003).

Amnesty International, 'South Sudan: Civil Unrest and State Repression, Human Rights Violations in Wau, Western Bahr el Ghazal State', February 2013.

Annan, K., 'Foreword', in H. F. Johnson, *Waging Peace in Sudan: The Inside Story of the Negotiations that Ended Africa's Longest Civil War* (Eastbourne, 2011).

Arensen, J. E., 'Contemporary Issues Facing the Murle', Houghton College research paper, 2012.

——'The History of the Murle Migrations', Houghton College research paper, 2012.

——'Human Ecology of the Murle', Houghton College research paper, 2012.

——'Murle Political Age Sets and Systems', Houghton College research paper, 2012.

Ashworth, J., *The Voice of the Voiceless: The Role of the Church in the Sudanese Civil War, 1983–2005* (Nairobi, 2014).

Astill-Brown, J., 'South Sudan's Slide into Conflict: Revisiting the Past and Reassessing Partnerships', Chatham House, Africa Programme, December 2014.

Audit Chamber, 'The Report of the Auditor General on the Financial Statements of the Government of Southern Sudan for Financial Year Ended 31 December 2005; equivalent – Ended 31 December 2006', equivalent – *Ended 31 December 2007*, equivalent – *Ended 31 December 2008*.

Audit Chamber, 'Presentation of the Report of the Auditor General on the Financial Statements of the Government of the Southern Sudan' (Juba, 2008).

Audit Chamber, 'Presentation of the Auditor General to the South Sudan National Assembly of the Audit Reports on the Accounts of the Government of Southern Sudan for the Years 2005 and 2006' (PAGSSNA), 1 November 2011.

Berdal, M. and Malone, D. M., 'Introduction', in *Greed and Grievances: Economy Agendas in Civil Wars* (Boulder, 2000).

Berdal, M., and Zaum, D. (eds), 'Private and Public Interests: Informal Actors, Informal Influence and Economic Order after War', in Mats Berdal and Dominik Zaum (eds), *Political Economy of Statebuilding* (Abingdon, 2013).

Carnagey, N. L., Anderson, C. A. and Bushman, B. J., 'The effect of video game violence on physiological desensitization to real-life violence', *Journal of Experimental Social Psychology* xliii/4 (2007), pp. 489–96.

Clapham, C., 'From Liberation Movement to Government: Past Legacies and the Challenge of Transition in Africa', The Brenthurst Foundation, Discussion Paper 8/12 (Johannesburg, 2012).

Collier, P., *The Bottom Billion: Why the Poorest Countries are Failing and What Can Be Done About it* (Oxford, 2008).

Commons, John R., *Institutional Economics: Its Place in Political Economy* (New Brunswick, 1990).

Conflict Armament Research, *The Distribution of Iranian Ammunition in Africa* (London, 2012).

Conflict Armament Research, Dispatch from the Field, *Weapons and Ammunition Air-dropped to SPLA-IO Forces in South Sudan; Equipment Captured by the SPLA in Jonglei State, November 2014* (London, 2015).

Cook, T. D. and Moro, L. N., *Governing South Sudan: Opinions of South Sudanese on a Government That Can Meet Citizen Expectations. Findings from Focus Groups with Men and Women in South Sudan* (Juba, 2012). Available online: http://www.ndi.org/files/Focus-group-governing-South-Sudan.pdf (accessed 2 March 2016).

Copnall, J., *A Poisonous Thorn in our Hearts: Sudan and South Sudan's Bitter and Incomplete Divorce* (London, 2014).

Dagne, T., *Sudan: The Crisis in Darfur and the North-South Relationship*, Congressional Research Service, 15 June 2011. Available online: https://www.fas.org/sgp/crs/row/RL33574.pdf (accessed 2 March 2016).

Deng, L. B, *Sudan Tribune*, 'The "curse" of Liberation', 16 February 2013. Available online: http://www.sudantribune.com/spip.php?article45547 (accessed 2 March 2016).

Ding Akol, Z., 'A Nation in Transition: South Sudan's Constitutional Review Process', *The Sudd Institute Policy Brief* 3 (17 February 2013). Available online: http://www.suddinstitute.org/publications/policy-briefs.

Esposito, D. and Crocker, B., *To Guarantee the Peace: An Action Strategy for a Post-Conflict Sudan* (Washington, DC, 2004).

*Financial Times*, 'Fury at unspent funds for Sudan', 16 February 2010.

French, B. and Travis, N., *South Sudan: The Juba Compact*, ODI Budget Strengthening Initiative. Country Learning Notes, July 2012, http://static1.1.sqspcdn.com/static/f/1349767/1924 0936/1342110854410/South+Sudan+The+Juba+Compact.pdf?token=dAwYnGcaoADa VRU7IM7ujl1WJmQ%3D

Fukui, K. and Markakis, J., 'Introduction', in *Ethnicity and Conflict in the Horn of Africa* (Martlesham, 1994).

Gettleman, J., 'Born in Unity, South Sudan is Torn Again', *New York Times*, 12 January 2012. Available online: http://www.nytimes.com/2012/01/13/world/africa/south-sudan-massacres-follow-independence.html (accessed 2 March 2016).

Government of Southern Sudan (GoSS), 'Juba Compact between the Development Partners and the Government of Southern Sudan' (Juba, 30 June 2009).

Government of Southern Sudan (GoSS), MOFEP, 'South Sudan Development Plan 2011–2013'. Available online: www.unicef.org/southsudan/education.html (accessed 2 March 2016).

*Guardian*, 'Omar al-Bashir visits South Sudan ahead of independence vote', 4 January 2011. Available online: http://www.theguardian.com/world/2011/jan/04/bashir-south-sudan-independence-vote (accessed 2 March 2016).

Huesmann, L. R. and Kirwil, L., 'Why Observing Violence Increases the Risk of Violent Behavior by the Observer', in D. J. Flannery, A. T. Vazsonyi and I. D. Waldman (eds), *The Cambridge Handbook of Violent Behavior and Aggression* (New York, 2007).

Human Rights Watch, 'South Sudan's New War: Abuses by Government and Opposition Forces' (New York, 2014). Available online: https://www.hrw.org/sites/default/files/reports/southsudan0814_ForUpload.pdf (accessed 2 March 2016).

Hutchinson, S., 'Nuer ethnicity militarized', *Anthropology Today* xvi/3 (2000), pp. 6–13.

IMF, Country Report 14/345: 'Republic of South Sudan 2014 Staff Report for the Article IV Consultation', December 2014. Available online: https://www.imf.org/external/pubs/ft/scr/2014/cr14345.pdf (accessed 2 March 2016).

International Crisis Group, 'Jonglei's Tribal Conflicts: Countering Insecurity in South Sudan'. 23 December 2009. Available online: http://www.crisisgroup.org/en/regions/africa/horn-of-africa/south-sudan/154-jongleis-tribal-conflicts-countering-insecurity-in-south-sudan.aspx (accessed 2 March 2016).

International Republican Institute (IRI), 'Survey of South Sudan. Public Opinion 6–11 September 2011'. Available online: http://www.iri.org/sites/default/files/2011%20December%20 5%20Survey%20of%20South%20Sudan%20Public%20Opinion,%20September%20 6-27,%202011.pdf (accessed 2 March 2016).

International Republican Institute (IRI), 'Survey of South Sudan. Public Opinion 24 April – 22 May 2013', presented in November 2013. Available online: http://www.iri.org/sites/default/files/2013%20July%2019%20Survey%20of%20South%20Sudan

%20Public%20Opinion,%20April%2024-May%2022,%202013.pdf. (accessed 2 March 2016).

Jobson, Barney, 'Fury at unspent funds for Sudan', *Financial Times*, 16 February 2010.

Johnson, D., 'Note on Panthou/Heglig', 2 May 2012, published on 'Gurtong Net', 5 May 2012. Availableonline:http://www.gurtong.net/ECM/Editorial/tabid/124/ctl/ArticleView/mid/519/articleId/6915/Dr-Douglas-H-Johnson-Note-on-PanthouHeglig.aspx [*Sudan Tribune* 5 May 2012, http://www.sudantribune.com/spip.php?article42499] (accessed 2 March 2016).

——'Briefing: The crisis in South Sudan', *African Affairs* cxiii/451(2014), pp. 300–9.

——*Federalism in the History of South Sudanese Political Thought*, Rift Valley Institute Research Paper 1 (London, 2014).

Johnson, H. F., *Waging Peace in Sudan: The Inside Story of the Negotiations that Ended Africa's Longest Civil War* (Eastbourne, 2011).

Jok, M. J., 'Orphaned: Sudan after John Garang and the Specter of Disintegration', in F. Feng (ed.), *New Sudan in the Making?* (Trenton, 2009).

——'South Sudan and the Risks of Unrest', *Sudd Institute Weekly Review*, 3 December 2013. Available online: http://www.suddinstitute.org/publications/show/south-sudan-and-the-risks-of-unrest (accessed 2 March 2016).

——'South Sudan's Crisis: Weighing the Cost of the Stalemate in the Peace Process', *Sudd Institute Policy Brief*, 12 August 2014. Available online: http://www.suddinstitute.org/publications/policy-briefs (accessed 2 March 2016).

——'National Reconciliation in South Sudan: How to Translate Political Settlements into Peace in the Country', Sudd Institute Policy Brief, 31 January, 2015. Available online: http://www.suddinstitute.org/publications/show/national-reconciliation-in-south-sudan-how-to-translate-political-settlements-into-peace-in-the-coun/ (accessed 2 March 2016).

Leonardi, C., '"Liberation" or capture: Youth in between "Hakuma" and "Home" during civil war and its aftermath in Southern Sudan', *African Affairs* cvi/424 (2007), pp. 391–412.

Lewis, M., 'Skirting the Law: Sudan's Post-CPA Arms Flows', Small Arms Survey, HSBA Working Paper 18, 2009. Available online: http://www.smallarmssurveysudan.org/fileadmin/docs/working-papers/HSBA-WP-17-Beyond-Janjaweed.pdf (accessed 2 March 2016).

Lino, E., 'Edward Lino: There was no Coup in Juba, Part I', *PaanLuel Wel* blog, 9 February 2014. Available online: http://paanluelwel.com/2014/02/09/edward-lino-there-was-no-coup-in-juba/ 2014 (accessed 2 March 2016).

Lugala, V., *Vomiting Stolen Food* (Nairobi, 2010).

National Democratic Institute (NDI), Separate Reports on Findings from Focus Groups with Men and Women in South Sudan, 23 November 2011, 22 March 2012 and June 2013. Accessible on https://www.ndi.org/Focus_Groups_Sudans (accessed 2 march 2016).

*New York Times*, 'Accounts Emerge in South Sudan of 3000 Deaths', 5 January 2012. Available online: http://www.nytimes.com/2012/01/06/world/africa/in-south-sudan-massacre-of-3000-is-reported.html (accessed 2 March 2016).

——'South Sudan Army Faces Accusations of Civilian Abuse', 28 September 2013. Available online: http://www.nytimes.com/2013/09/29/world/africa/south-sudans-army-faces-accusations-of-civilian-abuse.html?_r=0 (accessed 2 March 2016).

Nyaba, P. A., *The Politics of Liberation in South Sudan: An Insider's View* (Nairobi, 1996).

——*South Sudan, The State We Aspire To* (Nairobi, 2011).

Obama, B., President Obama in Ministerial Meeting on Sudan, 'The Fate of Millions', 24 September 2010. Available online: https://www.whitehouse.gov/blog/2010/09/24/president-obama-ministerial-meeting-sudan-fate-millions (accessed 2 March 2016).

OECD, Aid Statistics, Development Cooperation Directorate (DCD-DAC), International Development Statistics (IDS), CRS dataset, Paris, 2014. Available online: www.oecd.org/development/stats/idsonline.htm (accessed 2 March 2016).

Pinaud, C., 'South Sudan, civil war, predation and the making of military aristocracy', *African Affairs* cxiii/452 (2014), pp. 192–211.

Posen, B. R., 'The security dilemma and ethnic conflict', *Survival* xxxv/1 (1993), pp. 27–47.

Prendergast, J., *Frontline Diplomacy: Humanitarian Aid and Conflict in Africa* (Boulder, 1996).

Rands, R., 'In Need of Review: SPLA Transformation in 2006–2010 and Beyond', Small Arms Survey, HBSA Working Paper 23, Geneva, November 2010.

'Report from a Special Mission on the Economic Development of Southern Sudan', IBRD report no. 119a-SU (1 June 1973), http://www.smallarmssurveysudan.org/fileadmin/docs/working-papers/HSBA-WP-23-SPLA-Transformation-2006-10-and-Beyond.pdf

Rolandsen, Ø., *Guerilla Government: Political Changes in Southern Sudan during the 1990s* (Oslo, 2005).

———'Another civil war in South Sudan: The failure of guerrilla government?', *Journal of Eastern African Studies* xi/1 (2015), pp. 163–74.

———'Dead Economy Walking in South Sudan', 8 May 2015. Available online: http://blogs.prio.org/MonitoringSouthSudan/2015/05/dead-economy-walking-in-south-sudan.

Rolandsen, Ø. and Breidlid, I. M., 'What is Youth Violence in Jonglei', PRIO Paper 2013. Available online: http://www.gsdrc.org/document-library/what-is-youth-violence-in-jonglei/ (accessed 2 March 2016).

Rolandsen, Ø. Molteberg Glomnes, H., et al., 'A year of South Sudan's third civil war', *International Area Studies Review* xviii/1(2015). DOI:10.1177/2233865915573797.

The Sentry, 'Country Brief South Sudan, Dismantling the Financing of Africa's Deadliest Conflicts', Washington, July 2015. Available online: https://thesentry.org/country-briefs/south-sudan/ (accessed 2 March 2016).

———*The Nexus of Corruption and Conflict in South Sudan*, Washington, July 2015. Available online: https://thesentry.org/country-briefs/south-sudan/ (accessed 2 March 2016).

Smith, D. (PRIO), 'Towards a Strategic Framework for Peacebuilding: Getting Their Act Together', Overview Report of the Joint *Utstein* Study of Peacebuilding, Evaluation Report 1/2004, Ministry of Foreign Affairs, Oslo, together with the Evaluation departments of UK DFID, the Netherlands and Germany, April 2004. Available online: https://www.regjeringen.no/globalassets/upload/kilde/ud/rap/2004/0044/ddd/pdfv/210673-rapp104.pdf (accessed 2 March 2016).

Snowden, J., 'Work in Progress: Security Force Development in South Sudan through February 2012', HSBA Working Paper 27, June 2012. Available online: http://www.smallarmssurveysudan.org/fileadmin/docs/working-papers/HSBA-WP-27-Security-Force-Development-in-South-Sudan.pdf (accessed 2 March 2016).

Southern Sudan Centre for Census, Statistics and Evaluation, 'Key Indicators for Southern Sudan'. Available online: http://ssnbs.org/storage/key-indicators-for-southern-sudan/Key%20Indicators_A5_final.pdf (accessed 2 March 2016).

SPLM, 'Peace through Development: Perspectives and Prospects in the Sudan', February 2000. Not accessible on line. Available at the SPLM-office, South Sudan.

SPLM, Economic Commission, 'SPLM Strategic Framework: For War-to-Peace Transition', August 2004. Not accessible on line. Available at the SPLM-office, South Sudan.

Ssemwanga, A., 'South Sudanese Pound, Managed under Floating Exchange Rate Regime', in S. S. Wassara and A-T. Zain Al-Abdin (eds), *Post-Referendum Sudan, National and Regional Questions* (Senegal, 2014).

*Sudan Tribune*, 'Text: Minutes of Historical SPLM Meeting in Rumbek 2004', Section: Confidential Report on the Rumbek Meeting 2004, 12 March 2014. Available online: http://sudant-ribune.com/spip.php?article26320 (accessed 2 March 2016).

Themnér L. and Wallensteen P., 'Armed conflicts 1946–2013', *Journal of Peace Research* li/4 (2014), pp. 541–54.

Thomas, E., *South Sudan: A Slow Liberation* (London, 2015).

Torjesen, S., 'Transition from War to Peace', in M. Berdal and D. Zaum (eds), *Political Economy of Statebuilding: Power after Peace* (London, 2013).

Transparency International, Anti-corruption Resource Centre, 'Overview of Corruption and Anti-corruption in South Sudan', U4 Expert Answer 371, 4 March 2013, http://www.transparency.org/files/content/corruptionqas/371_Overview_of_corruption_and_anti-corruption_in_South_Sudan.pdf.

Waal, A. De, 'When kleptocracy becomes insolvent', *African Affairs* cxiii/452 (2014), pp. 347–69.

Willems, R. and Deng, D., 'The Legacy of Kokora in South Sudan', Briefing Paper, Intersections of Truth, Justice and Reconciliation in South Sudan, November 2015. Available online: https://www.google.co.uk/url?sa=t&rct=j&q=&esrc=s&source=web&cd=1&cad=rja &uact=8&ved=0ahUKEwja5aOsp6LLAhUDwxQKHTI4Dg8QFggfMAA&url=http %3A%2F%2Fwww.paxforpeace.nl%2Fmedia%2Ffiles%2Fthe-legacy-of-kokora-in-south-sudan---briefing-paperpdf.pdf&usg=AFQjCNGGD9Uq1MH8qJbJFQ7XfeWzFD4aq Q&sig2=j2ZqBgoP_8mzdsGUQPy3kA (accessed 2 March 2016).

World Bank, 'Sudan – Strengthening Good Governance for Development Outcomes in Southern Sudan: Issues and Options', WB Report No. 48997_SD, April 2010, https:// openknowledge.worldbank.org/bitstream/handle/10986/2854/489970ESW0P1051C0di sclosed051181101.pdf?sequence=1&isAllowed=y

——*Public Expenditures in South Sudan: Are They delivering*? South Sudan Economic Brief, Issue no 2, February 2013, http://documents.worldbank.org/curated/en/2013/02/17682880/ public-expenditures-south-sudan-delivering

——Poverty Reduction and Economic Management Unit, *Sudan Public Expenditure Review*, Synthesis Report No 41840-SD December 2007, Executive Summary, http:// documents.worldbank.org/curated/en/2007/12/8945929/sudan-public-expenditure-review-synthesis-report

Wrong, M., *It's Our Turn to Eat* (London, 2009).

Wulf, H., *Security Sector Reform in Developing and Transitional Countries* (Berlin, 2004).

## UN Documents

'Uniting Our Strengths for Peace, Politics, Partnerships and People'. Report of the High-Level Independent Panel on UN Peace Operations, 16 June 2015. Available online: http://www.un.org/sg/pdf/HIPPO_Report_1_June_2015.pdf (accessed 2 March 2016).

UNMIS, 'Report on the Human Rights Situation during the Violence in Southern Kordofan, Sudan', June 2011.

UNMISS 'Attacks on Civilians in Bentiu and Bor', April 2014, released 30 June 2015.

UNMISS 'Conflict in South Sudan: A Human Rights Report' (Juba, 2014).

UNMISS 'Flash Human Rights Report on the Escalation of Fighting in Greater Upper Nile', April/ May 2015, 29 June 2015.

UNMISS, 'Incidents of Inter-Communal Violence in Jonglei', (June 2012).

UNMISS, 'Interim Report on Human Rights Crisis in South Sudan', Report Coverage 15 December – 31 January 2014, 21 February 2014.

UNMISS 'Report on the 8 February 2013 Attack on Lou Nuer Pastoralists in Akobo West Sub-County', Jonglei State, April 2013.

UNMISS 'The State of Human Rights in the Protracted Conflict in South Sudan', 4 December 2015, released on 21 January 2016.

UN Security Council, Report of the Secretary General on the Sudan, S/2005/57, 31 January 2005. Available online: http://www.un.org/en/peacekeeping/missions/past/unmis/background. shtml (accessed 2 March 2016).

UN Security Council, Report of the Secretary-General on South Sudan, S/2011/678, 2 November 2011.

UN Security Council, Report of the Secretary-General on South Sudan, S/2012/140, 7 March 2012.

UN Security Council Report of the Secretary-General on South Sudan, S/2012/486, 26 June 2012.

UN Security Council Report of the Secretary-General on South Sudan, S/2012/820, 8 November 2012.

UN Security Council Report of the Secretary-General on South Sudan, S/2013/140, 8 November 2013.

UN Security Council Report of the Secretary-General on South Sudan, S/2013/366, 20 June 2013.

UN Security Council Report of the Secretary-General on South Sudan, S/2013/651, 8 November 2013.

UN Security Council Report of the Secretary-General on South Sudan, S/2014/158, 6 March 2014.

UN Security Council Report of the Secretary-General on South Sudan, S/2014/537, 25 July 2014.

UN Security Council Report of the Secretary-General on South Sudan, S/2015/902, 23 November 2015.

UN Security Council Report of the Secretary-General on South Sudan, S/2015/118, 17 February 2015.

UN Security Council Report of the Secretary-General on South Sudan, S/2015/655, 21 August 2015.

UN Security Council Resolution 1996 (2011), Adopted by the Security Council at its 6576th meeting, on 8 July 2011.

UN Security Council Resolution 2046 (2012), Adopted by the Security Council at its 6764th meeting, on 2 May 2012.

UN Security Council Resolution 2132 (2013), Adopted by the Security Council at its 7091st meeting, on 24 December 2013.

UN Security Council Resolution 2155 (2014), Adopted by the Security Council at its 7182nd meeting, on 27 May 2014.

UN Security Council, 'Interim Report of the Panel of Experts, established pursuant to SCR 2206 (2015)' S/2015/656, 2015, United Nations, 21 August 2015.

UN Security Council, 'Final Report of the Panel of Experts on South Sudan, established pursuant to SCR 2206 (2015)', S/2015/656, 22 January 2016.

# INDEX

2013 crisis, 154, 179, 291
  Akobo, 201–3, 208
  arms, 211–13, 250, 261, 273–4, 292, 293
  'attempted coup', 184–6, 195, 197, 198,
    246–50, 253
  Bentiu and Malakal, 203–5, 216, 217, 261
  Bor, 198, 199–200, 202, 206, 218, 258,
    260, 266, 270
  civil war, 214–20, 223, 225, 266
  corruption, 220–2
  detainees, 197–8, 207
  Jonglei, 200–1, 202
  Juba, 205–6, 243, 245, 251, 259–61
  one of the world's biggest humanitarian
    crises, 292
  recommendations for the future, 299–303
  sustainable peace: a longer journey, 280–6
  see also 2013 crisis; Dinka; IGAD peace
    talks; Nuers
2013 crisis, atrocities committed, 187–91,
    193, 196, 202, 204–5, 216, 217, 245,
    266, 285–6, 289–90
  accountability, 285, 286, 291, 294
  AU Commission of Inquiry, 219, 244,
    245–6, 250, 253, 285–6, 294–5
  civilians, targeting of, 187, 188–91, 192–3,
    195, 200, 203, 205, 216, 244, 261
  ethnic violence, 181, 182, 191, 192–3, 195,
    198, 203, 216, 217–18, 250, 251, 256,
    261
  impunity, 279, 286
  massacre in the mosque, 217, 270
  Nuers, targeting and killing of, 183, 186,
    188–91, 195–6, 199, 218, 246, 251–2,
    256
  war crimes and crimes against humanity,
    219–20, 223, 245–6, 256, 295
  see also 2013 crisis and the UN;
    reconciliation; sexual violence
2013 crisis, causes of, 145, 154–5, 169, 178,
    249–50, 253, 263, 295, 296, 302
  corruption, 93, 159
  ethnicity, 251–2, 253, 255, 256–7, 261, 279
  greed for power, 253–4, 278, 288
  kleptocracy, 89

  security dilemma, 253–6
2013 crisis, leaders involved, 244–5, 250, 278,
    288, 295–6
  Kiir, Salva, 181–5, 193–4, 197–8, 203, 204,
    206, 211, 219, 251–2, 255, 278
  Machar, Riek, 181–6, 194, 195–6, 198,
    201, 204, 205–6, 246, 250, 252–3, 255,
    257–9, 278
  see also Deng, Taban; Gadet, Peter; Malong,
    Paul
2013 crisis and the SPLA/security sector,
    182–90 passim, 193, 196, 199, 205,
    223, 225
  implosion of the Army, 251–3
  security dilemma, 253–6
  split along ethnic lines, 199, 201, 202, 204,
    251
  see also Presidential Guards; SPLA;
    SPLM, factionalism and divisions;
    SPLM/A-IO; SSNPS
2013 crisis and the UN
  anti-UN campaign, 207–11, 213–15,
    222–3, 246
  civilians, protection of, 184, 192, 205, 206,
    207–8, 211, 212, 216, 222–3, 292
  UN opens its gates, 183, 186–8, 192, 207
  UN Secretary-General, 209–10, 215, 219
  UN Security Council, 195, 197, 201, 277
  UNMISS, 144, 192, 193, 199, 200, 204,
    205, 211, 260
  UNMISS, attack on, 201, 208, 218, 270
  UNMISS Human Rights Report, 245,
    285–6, 289–90

Abraham, Isaiah (Diing Chan Awuol), 95–6
Abyei, 57, 78, 80–1, 82, 86, 225
  referendum, 88
  SAF, 12, 54, 57, 59–60
  SCR 2046: 79–80
  UNISFA, 59, 86
  see also Heglig/Panthou
accountability, 38, 98, 299, 301, 303
  2013 crisis, atrocities committed, 285, 286,
    291, 294
  lack of, 24, 32, 236, 295

Addis Ababa Peace Agreement (1972), 4
Adhanom, Tedros, 167, 263, 264
Adwok Nyaba, Peter, 25, 155, 197, 266
Agar, Malik, 58, 153
Aguer, Philip, 183
Akol, Jacob J., 282–3
Akol, Lam, 6, 153, 155, 171
Alier, Abel, 3, 9, 156, 164
Alieu, Aleu Ayenyi, 154, 155, 196, 239, 253, 266
All Africa Council of Churches, 3
Alor, Deng, 63, 83, 87, 88, 150, 152, 158–9, 162, 163, 165, 171, 172, 173, 176, 181, 197
Amum, Pagan, 159, 161, 162, 163, 172–3, 176, 197, 264, 269, 287, 298
    border conflict, 80
    oil negotiations, 64, 65, 68–9
    SPLM factionalism, 152, 155, 156, 157
    suspension and removal, 167–8, 185
ANC (African National Congress), 171, 269, 271
Anti-Corruption Commission, 38, 50, 51, 89
Anya-Nya, 3, 5, 6
Appropriations Act (2007), 32, 37
arbitration, 7, 73, 74, 83
Arensen, Jonathan E., 106, 139
Arman, Yasir, 58, 153
arms, 102–3, 106, 107, 112, 200, 243
    2013 crisis, 211–13, 250, 261, 273–4, 292, 293
    corruption, 230–1
    rule by the gun, 296
Ashton, Catherine, 65
Atabani, Ghazi Salahuddin, 71
Athor, George, 107
Atta, Mohammed al-Moula Abbas, 77, 273
AU (African Union), 13, 15, 75–6
    AU Commission of Inquiry, 219, 244, 245–6, 250, 253, 285, 290, 294–5, 300
    AU Peace and Security Council, 78–9, 81, 285, 298, 299
    AUHIP, 57, 60, 64, 65, 76, 78, 80, 82, 83, 274
audit, 28, 32, 35, 36, 89, 92, 230, 231
Audit Chamber, 36–8, 50, 51
austerity, 66, 92, 93, 226
Awet Akot, Daniel, 152, 221
Aziz, Abdel Adam al-Hilu, 58, 153

Balanda, 122
Bank of South Sudan, 51–2
al-Bashir, Omar, 5, 10, 11, 14, 58, 76–7, 85, 93, 273
    border conflict, 80, 81–2

oil negotiations, 59, 61, 68–9, 70, 86
    referendum, 14–15, 46, 59
    visit to Juba, 84, 87–8, 169
Beidas, Sandra, 119–20
Bennett, Richard, 119
Biong Deng, Luka, 20, 88
Blue Nile region, 53–4, 57–8, 59–60, 83, 84, 86, 153
Booth, Donald, 265
border conflict, 69–81, 82–3, 84, 225, 291
    SDBZ, 80, 82
    September Agreements, 81–3, 84, 88
    see also Abyei; border demarcation; Heglig/Panthou; South Sudan/Sudan relationship
border demarcation, 15, 55–6, 57, 68, 82–3
    Permanent Court of Arbitration, 73, 74
    see also Heglig/Panthou
bureaucracy, 29–30, 31, 32–3
Bush, George W., 13, 58

capacity building, 17, 28, 29–30, 32, 44–5, 47, 237
CBTF (Capacity Building Trust Fund), 22, 23
CCM (Chama Cha Mapinduzi-Tanzania), 271
Central Bank, 23, 39, 51, 293
    corruption, 51, 89, 91–2, 221–2
    new currency, 49, 50, 52
centralization, 31–2, 43–4, 95
Cheng, Christine, 290
child, 208, 216
    abduction and killing of, 103, 106–7, 120, 126, 131, 142, 204, 290
    child soldier, 120, 128, 290
China, 79, 243, 277–8
Chol, Lam Tishore, 238
Christianity, 3, 4
    church, 7, 176–7, 191, 192, 216, 261
citizenship, 15, 56, 68–9, 82
civil society, 96, 101, 143, 266, 269, 271
civil war, 2–3, 5–6, 17, 105, 131 see also 2013 crisis
civilians, 101, 105, 236, 261
    protecting themselves, 105–7, 114
    see also 2013 crisis, atrocities committed; protection of civilians; UNMISS; UNMISS in Jonglei
Clapham, Christopher, 19, 30–1
CMC (Crisis Management Committee), 49, 220–2
Collier, Paul, 293
constitution, 281–2, 286, 298
    Transitional Constitution, 38, 95, 151, 164, 268, 281
Copnall, James, 31–2, 36, 39, 86

corruption, 16, 25–6, 27–8, 32, 33, 89, 296
   2013 crisis, 93, 159, 220–2
   bribery, 39, 236
   cash, doling out of, 35–6, 39
   Central Bank, 51, 89, 91–2, 221–2
   CMC, 220–2
   combating corruption, 24, 26–7, 39–40,
      50–1, 52–3, 55, 89–90, 92, 159, 165
   contracts, 33–4, 37–8, 39, 40–1, 90
   currency exchange, 52, 89, 91
   donor and government corruption, 24, 27,
      32, 39, 52, 165
   Garang, John, 24–6
   GoSS, 36–8, 40
   independence of South Sudan, 52, 88–9
   Kiir, Salva, 25–6, 28, 34, 48, 50–1, 52–3,
      89–90, 159, 165, 222
   oil, 24–5, 26–7, 33, 36, 37, 39, 92
   payroll, 36, 37, 55, 237
   the politics of, 90–3
   SPLA, 88, 229–34, 236, 238
   SPLM, 21, 23–8, 33, 34–6, 40–1, 46, 67,
      90–1, 299
   state-building, 48, 51
   Sudan, 27, 46
   *see also* misappropriation/mismanagement
CPA (Comprehensive Peace Agreement),
   7–13, 14, 15, 73, 154
   implementation, 11–12, 14, 47, 59
   local peace process, 7
   'making unity attractive', 13–14, 29, 99
   SPLM/A, 9–10, 14, 18, 225
   *see also* independence of South Sudan
currency, 15
   corruption, 52, 89, 91
   devaluation, 67, 92–3, 293
   new currency, 48–50, 51–2, 54

D'Agoot, Majak, 70, 71, 88, 152, 181, 196,
   246, 269
al-Dabi, Mohammed Ahmed Mustapha, 265
Darfur, 9, 12, 22, 80, 86, 204, 216, 217, 273
DDR (Disarmament, Demobilization and
   Reintegration), *see* disarmament
defence, 147, 294
   budget, 11, 33, 42, 226, 229, 231, 242
   corruption, 34, 231
   reform, 228–9, 233–4, 237, 238
   Strategic Defence and Security Review
     294
   *see also* 2013 crisis and the SPLA/security
     sector; SPLA
demonstration, 76, 83, 96, 210, 211, 213–14,
   218
Deng, David, 171

Deng, Daniel Bul, 108, 115, 164, 284
Deng, Kuol, 86
Deng, Nhial, 150, 152, 154, 162, 171
Deng, Oyay, 119, 152, 197, 239, 245, 269
Deng, Pieng, 88, 152, 197, 238, 245
Deng, Taban, 71, 77, 156, 161, 162, 197,
   245–51 *passim*, 254, 255, 258, 270
   dismissal of, 166
Deng, Telar, 154, 155, 157, 169, 175, 192, 266
Deng, Tor, 157–8, 161
Desalegn, Hailemariam, 81, 265, 267, 268
development, 29, 45
   underdevelopment, 16, 18, 42, 102
Dhieu, Stephen Dau, 63
Dieng, Adama, 219
Diing, Lual, 163
Dim, Dominic, 153–4
dinar, 23, 49 *see also* currency
Dinka, 4, 17, 76, 86, 95, 142, 143, 147–8
   2013 crisis, 182, 186, 188, 190, 191, 199,
     201, 202, 203, 207, 218, 244–5,
     249–50, 252, 255, 256, 278–9
   language, 170, 190, 244
   SPLA, 5, 43, 233, 240–1
   *see also* 2013 crisis
Dinka Council of Elders, 243, 296
diplomacy, 12, 14, 53, 54, 70, 146, 152, 222
disarmament
   civilian disarmament, Jonglei, 102, 114,
     116–17, 118, 120, 121, 132, 143, 249
   DDR, 228, 230, 231, 234, 294
donor, 22, 38, 43, 92, 270, 299
   capacity building, 28, 29, 44–5
   and government corruption, 24, 27, 32, 39,
     52, 165
Duoth, Thomas Guet, 192
Dura Scandal, 37–8, 39, 220
DYY (David Yau Yau), 117, 120–3, 128, 129,
   130, 137, 141, 142

education, 18, 42–3, 46, 92
   illiteracy, 43, 238, 281
Egypt, 2, 68, 145, 276
elections, 13, 103, 156, 157, 158–9, 161, 163,
   166, 167, 237, 245
Ellery, James, 128, 129
Equatorians/Equatorian region, 43, 54, 201,
   214, 232, 233, 282, 283, 291
Ethiopia, 3, 131, 261, 265, 270, 272, 275,
   276, 277
ethnic violence, 44, 94, 95, 102–3, 106–7,
   167, 173 *see also* 2013 crisis,
   atrocities committed; ethnicity; inter-
   communal violence; UNMISS in
   Jonglei

ethnicity, 21, 33, 41, 93–4, 253
  as cause of 2013 crisis, 251–2, 253, 255,
    256–7, 261, 279
  ethnic cleansing, 73, 77, 132, 138, 253
  ethnic diversity, 4, 16, 197
  ethnic divisions, 21, 280, 296
  ethnic identity, 93, 232, 240, 255, 282
  ethnic politics, 94–5, 280, 301
  see also Dinka; ethnic violence; the Murle;
    Nuers
European Union, 233, 277
extrajudicial killing, 130, 188, 195, 266

federalism, 3, 271, 282
Fertit, 122, 283
financial issues, 28, 31, 32, 42
  budget, 28, 42–3, 67, 225, 226, 229, 231
  economic crisis, 59, 65–8, 89, 92, 292–3
  income/expenditure gap, 36, 293
  overspending, 34, 36, 42, 88
  transitional financial arrangements, 15, 27,
    60, 80, 83, 292
  see also corruption; mismanagement;
    MOFEP; oil
food, 25, 46, 292
  famine, 73, 262, 270, 292
Foster, Adrian, 184

Gadet, Peter, 199–202, 249, 257–9, 260,
    264, 287
Gai, Peter Lual Marrow, 164
Garang Boys, 87, 152–3, 155, 156, 157, 158,
    160, 168–70, 171, 173, 197
Garang, John, 10, 32, 174, 146, 177, 226, 282
  corruption, 24–6
  CPA, 8–9, 10
  death, 10, 14, 17–18, 26, 27, 146
  'New Sudan', 5, 10, 146, 154
  SPLM/A, 4–5, 6, 235
  see also SPLM/A
Gatkuoth Lul, Ezekiel, 161, 269
generational issues, 103, 290, 303
Georgieva, Kristilina, 138
Ghani, Ashraf, 235
Githongo, John, 55
Gore, Alfred Lado, 197
GoSS (Government of Southern Sudan), 28,
    30, 32, 42, 45–6
  budget, 28, 42
  corruption, 36–8, 40
  Priority Core Functions, 44
  see also SPLM/A
governance, 20, 21, 33, 41–2, 44, 295
Government of National Unity (Sudan), 10,
    11–12, 23, 25, 34, 155

GRSS (Government of the Republic of South
    Sudan), 54–5, 56, 296
  cabinet, 51, 52, 55, 87, 92, 100, 157–8,
    167–9, 170
  Core Functions, 45, 55
  Jonglei, 105, 108, 110, 114, 125, 128
  restructuring of, 167–9
  see also state

health issues, 43, 46, 92
Heglig/Panthou, 70, 73, 240
  antagonizing the UN, 75–8
  occupation of, 72–5
  SPLA, 70, 72–5, 77
  see also Abyei
High Commissioner for Human Rights (Navi
    Pillay), 143, 195, 219
Hiteng, Cirino, 152, 158, 172
Hoth Mai, James, 138, 161, 244, 246
human-rights, 118, 127, 138, 143 see also 2013
    crisis, atrocities committed; UNMISS
    in Jonglei
Human Rights Watch, 118, 138, 143
humanitarian assistance, 22, 29, 104, 113, 131,
    135, 138–9, 140, 188, 222
Hussein, Abdul Rahman, 71, 72, 76
Hutchinson, Sharon, 106, 290

IDP (Internally Displaced People), 18, 54,
    102, 131, 187, 202–3, 204, 208, 218,
    261, 289
IGAD (Intergovernmental Authority on
    Development), 6, 7–8, 30, 64–5
  IGAD Partners' Forum 6, 7, 146
  see also IGAD peace talks
IGAD peace talks, 150, 171, 263, 264–80, 299
  Cessation of Hostilities Agreement, 267,
    268, 270
  challenges, 265, 266, 272–8
  civil society, 269, 271
  detainees, release of, 263–4, 266, 267–9
  disharmony within IGAD, 272–5, 278
  Kiir, Salva, 266, 268, 270, 278–9, 287–8,
    294
  Machar, Riek, 263–4, 270, 276, 278,
    287–8, 294
  new 28 states, 287, 291, 298
  peace agreement, 287–8, 294, 295, 297,
    299, 300, 302
  reform agenda, 268, 272, 280–1, 296–7
  regional protection force, 269, 272, 276
  transitional government, agreement on,
    271, 272
  UNMISS, 268, 276
  see also Ethiopia; Kenya; Sudan; Uganda

IMF (International Monetary Fund), 23, 27, 49, 52, 66, 91, 92–3
independence of South Sudan, 1, 15, 46–8, 157
  challenging issues, 15, 56, 57
  corruption, 52, 88–9
  Independence Day celebration, 45, 48, 167
  Kiir, Salva, 1–2, 15, 157, 287, 302
  new reform, 50–3, 56
  time for delivery, 44–6
  see also CPA; referendum
insecurity, 46, 56, 124, 134, 188, 213, 292, 297
institution, 17, 29
  institution-building, 16, 17, 35, 42
  weak institution, 17, 18, 32, 33, 39, 89, 160, 224, 240
inter-communal violence, 99, 104–6, 111, 114, 116, 236, 291
  2013 crisis and ethnic violence, 181, 182, 191, 192–3, 195, 198, 203, 216, 217–18, 250, 251, 256, 261
  2013 crisis, ethnicity as cause of 251–2, 253, 255, 256–7, 261, 279
  2013 crisis and SPLA split along ethnic lines, 199, 201, 202, 204, 251
  see also 2013 crisis; ethnic violence; UNMISS in Jonglei
interim period, 10, 11, 14, 17, 28, 31, 88, 226
  audit, 32, 89
  misappropriation, 89, 90, 230
international community, 2, 14, 16–17, 27, 53, 76, 300
IRI (International Republican Institute), 356
Islam, 3, 4, 8, 18, 176
Islamism, 5, 155
Itto, Anne, 160

JEM (Justice and Equality Movement), 72, 77, 78, 85, 87, 204, 273
JIU (Joint Integrated Units), 226
JMEC (Joint Monitoring Evaluation Commission), 299, 300–1
Johnson, Douglas, 73, 282, 283
Jok, Jok Madut, 280, 284, 297
Jonglei, 101–3, 106–7
  2013 crisis, 200–1, 202
  cattle, 102, 106, 112, 115
  see also UNMISS in Jonglei
JPSC (Joint Political and Security Committee), 71
Juba, 2, 17, 43–4, 54, 84, 93
  2006 Juba Declaration, 146, 226, 228, 235, 238
  2013 crisis, 205–6, 243, 245, 251, 259–61

Kamis, John, 291–2

Karti, Ali, 68, 79, 263
Kenya, 43, 152, 265, 272, 275, 276–7
Kenyatta, Uhuru, 185, 263, 265, 267
Kerry, John, 219
Kiir, Salva (Mayardit), 5, 10, 53, 87, 145–9, 158, 159–60
  2015 election, 158–9, 161, 163, 167, 245
  'Big Tent', 11, 146, 226, 232, 252
  border conflict, 74–5, 80, 81, 82–3
  corruption, 25–6, 28, 34, 48, 50–1, 52–3, 89–90, 159, 165, 222
  First Vice President of Sudan, 11
  independence, 1–2, 15, 157, 287, 302
  Jonglei, 118–20, 130
  Machar/Kiir rivalry, 86–7, 96, 145, 150, 156, 161–2, 164–7, 166, 172, 198, 243
  President of GoSS 11, 48
  President of South Sudan, 1, 15, 59, 147–8
  UN, 53, 74
  see also 2013 crisis, leaders involved; IGAD peace talks; SPLM/A
kleptocracy, 41–2, 89
Kok, James, 162
Kuanyin, Kerubino, 5, 73, 153
Kueth Deng, Dak, 108–9, 110, 205
Kuong, John, 200
Kuor, Akol, 173
Kutesa, Sam, 184

Lagu, Joseph, 3, 156
language, 16
  Arabic, 3, 4, 28, 31, 56, 170, 190, 238
  Dinka, 170, 190, 244
  English, 31, 238
  Nuer, 190
Lanzer, Toby, 133, 138, 222
leadership, 302–3
  criticism of, 56, 160, 172, 174, 280, 287, 301
  war crimes and crimes against humanity, 220
  see also 2013 crisis, leaders involved; Garang, John; Kiir, Salva; Machar, Riek
Leonardi, Cherri, 20
Lino, Edward, 40, 88, 227
Local Government Act (2009), 94, 95
Lokuji, Alfred, 28
Lou Nuer see Nuers
Lowilla, Emmanuel, 119
Luk, John, 162, 197
Lukudo, Paulino, 164

Maar, Hussein, 208, 258
Machakos Protocol (2002), 8, 9, 154

Machar, Riek (Teny Dhourgon), 6, 83, 149–52, 242
    2015 election, 163, 166
    dismissal, 164, 167, 168, 246
    establishment of new counties, 94
    Jonglei, 109, 110–11
    Machar/Kiir rivalry, 86–7, 96, 145, 150, 156, 161–2, 164–5, 166, 172, 198, 243
    SPLM/A split, 153
    UNMISS, 100, 151
    Vice President, 45, 62–3, 80, 86–7, 94, 100, 109, 149, 298
    see also 2013 crisis, leaders involved; IGAD peace talks
Magaya, Alison, 238
the Mahdiyya, 2
Makuei, Michael, 197, 208–10, 213
Malong, Paul, 82–3, 152, 240–5 passim, 250, 252, 254
Malwal, Bona, 153–4, 155
Mandela, Nelson, 175, 177
Manibe Ngai, Kosti, 39–40, 49, 62, 63, 152, 158, 162, 165, 197
Manyang Juuk, Kuol, 152, 163, 168, 181, 193, 215
Marial, Barnaba Benjamin, 181, 185, 186, 192, 193, 241, 265, 270
Marona, Joseph, 145
Maror, Akol, 17
massacre, 6, 17, 191, 256, 170, 283
    1991 Bor, 151–2, 177, 256
    see also 2013 crisis, atrocities committed
Mathok, Salva, 154, 241
Matip, Paulino, 11, 226, 228, 241, 249
Mayom, Paul, 158, 162, 171
Mbeki, Thabo, 15, 65, 68, 76, 78, 80, 158, 167, 172
MDTF (Multilateral Donor Trust Fund), 22
media, 95–6, 113, 208, 215
    'Media Case', 217–18
Menkerios, Haile, 15, 49, 57, 68, 70, 71
Mesfin, Seyoum, 265, 272, 277
Mete, Obote Mamur, 152, 175, 181, 193, 239
the military, 21, 41–2
    militarized society, 18, 33, 294, 295
    see also SPLA
militia, 11, 85, 105, 131, 224 see also SPLA
misappropriation/mismanagement, 24, 25, 27, 35, 36–7, 42, 48, 88–9, 90, 93, 94, 220–2, 229 see also corruption
MOFEP (Ministry of Finance and Economic Planning), 31, 37, 39, 49, 51, 61, 220, 293
Monytuiel, Bapiny, 70, 85, 260
Monytuiel, Joseph Nguen, 85, 166, 260

Mozambique, 29
MSF (Doctors Without Borders), 127, 133, 134, 135
the Murle, 102–17 passim, 120–1, 127, 131–2, 142
    the 'disappeared' Murle, 133–6, 138, 139
    see also DYY; UNMISS in Jonglei
Museveni, Yoweri Kaguta, 27, 167, 184, 201
Mustafa, al-Tayyeb, 69
Musyoka, Stephen Kalonzo, 61

nation-building, 16, 280, 281, 296, 297, 298, 301
    lack of strategy for, 263
    UNMISS, 47, 97, 98, 99
National Congress Party, 71, 87
National Legislative Assembly, 36, 50, 63, 69–70, 96, 97, 169, 196
NCP (National Congress Party), 9, 29, 154, 155, 158, 169
NDI (National Democratic Institute), 56
negotiations, see IGAD peace talks; UNMISS in Jonglei
nepotism, 16, 31, 39
New Deal Compact, 92–3
New Sudan Council of Churches, 7
NGO (non-governmental organization), 42, 96, 118, 127, 138, 143
Nimeiri, Jafar Mohamed, 3, 4, 5
NISS (National Intelligence Security Services), 77, 247, 273
NLC (National Liberation Council of SPLM), 69, 70, 160, 171, 172, 175–8, 179, 185, 204, 255, 256
Norway, 24, 150 see also Troika countries
Nuers, 4, 5, 102–17 passim, 127, 136
    2013 crisis, 182, 248–50, 252, 257, 278
    SPLA, 232–3, 240, 248–9
    see also 2013 crisis, atrocities committed; UNMISS in Jonglei; White Army
Nyandeng, Rebecca (de Mabior), 161, 163, 197
Nyuon, William, 5, 153

Obama, Barack, 13, 14, 58, 72, 211, 265
oil, 12, 28, 32, 51, 299
    alternative pipeline, 63, 66
    corruption, 24–5, 26–7, 33, 36, 37, 39, 92
    drop in world price of, 38, 293
    economic crisis, 65–8, 89, 92
    Heglig/Panthou, 73–4
    IGAD summit, 64–5
    income from, 28, 36, 39, 51, 221
    'oil curse', 24, 33, 56, 296
    resumption of oil production, 82, 83–5
    September Agreements, 81–3, 84, 88

shutting down oil production, 61, 62–9, 85–8, 89, 92
Sudan, 14, 15, 60–9, 74, 82, 83, 292
transitional financial arrangements, 60, 83, 292
use of the Sudanese pipeline, 15, 56, 57, 60–1, 82, 83, 292
see also al-Bashir, Omar; South Sudan/ Sudan relationship
Olonyi, Johnson, 260–1, 289

patronage, 21, 28, 31, 41–2, 89, 93, 94–5
Paul, Mac (Kuol Awar) 77, 253, 269
payroll, 28, 55, 230, 231, 238, 239, 252
corruption, 36, 37, 55, 237
massively inflated payroll, 18, 39, 293
mismanagement, 42, 94
peace
-building 45, 55–6, 92, 300
Committee for National Healing, Peace and Reconciliation, 284
sustainable peace: a longer journey, 280–6
UNMISS in Jonglei, peace process, 108–9, 115–16, 140–2
UNMISS peace-building mandate, 47, 97, 98, 99, 100, 104, 112, 186, 239
see also Addis Ababa Peace Agreement; CPA; IGAD peace talks; peacekeeping; UNMISS
peacekeeping, 221
an illusion 122–8
peacekeeping mission 29, 47, 99, 136
peacekeeping operation 228
see also UNMIS; UNMISS
political will, 24, 27, 55, 67, 88, 89, 298
Posen, Barry R., 254
pound see currency
Presidential Guards, 241–4
2013 crisis, 182, 183, 189, 191, 243–4, 249–50, 254–6
see also 2013 crisis and the SPLA/security sector
Prison Service, 201, 235, 237, 239
protection of civilians, 127
2013 crisis and the UN, 184, 192, 205, 206, 207–8, 211, 212, 216, 222–3, 292
2013 crisis, UN opens its gates, 183, 186–8, 192, 207
SPLA, 105, 236, 261
UNMISS, 98–9, 112, 122, 186–7, 271
UNMISS in Jonglei, 101, 104, 109, 110–12, 120, 122, 125–6, 136
see also civilians

Ramciel, 54

reconciliation, 150, 194, 198, 227, 269, 281, 282–6, 294, 297, 301, 302
Committee for National Healing, Peace and Reconciliation, 284
National Commission for Truth, Reconciliation and Healing, 285, 295
National Reconciliation Conference, 164
UNMISS in Jonglei, 105, 108, 113
Red Cross, 193, 197
referendum, 5, 10, 14–15, 46–7, 157
Referendum Act, 12
see also independence of South Sudan
refugee camp, 25, 60, 101
refugee crisis, 275, 292
regime change, 64, 68, 78
Reporters without Borders, 96
Rice, Susan, 13, 60, 79
Rolandsen, Øystein, 20
rule of law, 16, 44, 47, 55, 99, 130, 235, 239
rural area, 21, 42, 94, 94, 131, 238
Russia, 66, 79, 109, 123, 277, 289

SAF (Sudanese Armed Forces), 6
Abyei, 12, 54, 57, 59–60
bombing raids into South Sudan, 60, 70–9 passim, 101
sanction, 79, 80, 223, 233, 277, 289
security sector, 44, 55, 96, 239, 294
budget, 42, 67, 225, 226, 229, 231
control on dissidence, 95–6
misappropriation, 89, 229
see also Prison Service; SPLA; SSNPS; Wildlife Service
self-determination, 2, 3, 4, 5, 7, 8, 9, 14, 27, 33, 97, 154
sexual violence, 117, 191, 202, 204, 205, 216, 266, 290 see also 2013 crisis, atrocities committed
Shilluk, 1, 4, 153, 205, 260, 283
Skadden Arps, 65
Smith, Gayle, 211
SOFA (Status of Forces Agreement), 119, 144
South Sudan/Sudan relationship, 56, 57
challenging issues, 57, 60
secession-related issues, 59
sovereignty, violation of, 60, 72
at war, 53–4, 58, 60, 73–8
see also border conflict; oil
Southern Kordofan, 53–4, 57–8, 59–60, 83, 84, 86, 153
SPDF (Sudan People's Defense Forces/ Democratic Front), 150
SPLA (Sudan People's Liberation Army), 78, 224
audit, 230, 231

'Big Tent' approach, 11, 146, 226, 232, 252
border conflict, 69–78
civilians, protection of, 105, 236, 261
corruption, 88, 229–34, 236, 238
Dinka, 5, 43, 233, 240–1
  ethnic violence within, 236–7
  human rights violations, 116–18, 121–2,
    129–31, 138, 143
Jonglei, 109, 111, 123, 126, 129–33
militia, reintegration of, 226–7, 228,
  232–3, 238, 252
multi-ethnic units and training, 228, 229,
  232–3, 241, 243
National Defence Forces of South Sudan,
  the 294
Nuers, 232–3, 240, 248–9
payroll, 230, 231, 237, 238, 239, 252
reconciliation, 227, 283–4
reform, 228–9, 233–4, 237, 238
salary, 226, 230, 235, 238
split along ethnic lines, 227, 232, 240
transformation into a professional army, 20,
  224–5, 234
see also 2013 crisis and the SPLA/security
  sector; Presidential Guards; Prison
  Service; SSNPS; Wildlife Service
SPLM/A (Sudan People's Liberation
  Movement/Army), 4–5, 19, 46, 224
broken social contract, 42–4
corruption, 21, 23–8, 33, 34–6, 40–1, 46,
  67, 90–1, 299
CPA, 9–10, 14, 18, 225
from liberation movement to government,
  18–20, 56
guerrilla government, 18, 20–3
liberators are not peace-builders, 30–3
Manifesto, 4
SPLM Strategic Framework, 20
transformation into a political party, 57–8,
  159–60, 174
transformation programme, 20, 21–2
see also NLC; SPLA; SPLM, factionalism
  and divisions
SPLM, factionalism and divisions, 4–7, 20, 85,
  87, 93, 145, 171–2, 224
6th December press conference, 172–5,
  176, 177, 196–7, 249, 255
2013 crisis, 20, 154–5, 178, 269–70, 302
dissolution of, 171, 174
Nasir faction, 153, 258
NLC, 175–8, 184, 255
party constitution, 159–60, 178
power struggle, 157–63
reunification process after 2013 crisis,
  269–70, 271, 294, 301–2

Yei faction/crisis, 153–4, 155, 157
see also Kiir, Salva; Machar, Riek
SPLM/A-In Opposition, 149, 253, 267, 270,
  271
2013 crisis, 195–7, 198–206, 216,
  246–8, 251, 253, 258–9, 273–4, 279
South Sudan Armed Opposition, 294
Sudan's support to, 273–4
SPLM/DC (SPLM/Democratic Change), 171
SPLM-N (SPLM-North), 53–4, 57–8, 60,
  80–1, 85
ban on, 58
South Sudan's support to, 58–9, 71–2, 82,
  84, 86, 87
SRSG (Special Representative of the Secretary
  General), 2, 15, 46, 57, 160, 197, 215,
  271
SSDM/A (South Sudan Democratic
  Movement/Army), 260
SSLM/A (South Sudan Liberation Movement/
  Army), 70, 85, 166, 204, 260
SSNPS (South Sudan National Police Service),
  235–7
2013 crisis, 192, 196, 199, 200, 201, 203,
  218, 258
from SSPS to SSNPS, 237–40
see also SPLA
state, 17–23
a country without a state, 47
crisis management, 47, 66, 88, 160, 271
failed/fragile state, 297, 300
'state capture', 20
see also GoSS; GRSS; SPLM; state-building
state-building, 21, 28–9, 47, 56, 88, 89, 92, 97,
  271, 296, 297, 301
building government capacity, 29–30
corruption, 48, 51
international community, 16–17
weak organizational infrastructure, 31–2
see also state
Sudan, 3, 5, 44, 272–3, 274–5
corruption, 27, 46
DYY, 121, 132
economic crisis, 59, 67–8
Sudan Revolutionary Front, 85
Sumbeiywo, Lazarus, 8, 9, 150, 167, 263–4,
  265, 266

Taban, Paride, 141–2
Taha, Ali Osman, 8–9, 11, 14, 81, 226, 274
telecom company, 35–6
Teny, Angelina, 156
Thomas, Edward, 18, 20, 44, 103, 232
Tong, Chol Mayai, 166
transition period, 20, 56, 98

Transitional Constitution, 38, 95, 151, 164, 268, 281
transitional financial arrangements, 15, 27, 60, 80, 83, 292
see also SPLM/A
Transitional Government of National Unity, 294, 297, 298, 299
transparency, 12, 32, 36, 236, 299
Transparency International, 41, 48
Tri-State area, 125, 126, 236
Troika countries, 7–8, 9, 15, 53, 84, 266, 277–8, 289, 300
al-Turabi, Hasan, 5
Tutu, Desmond, 303

Uganda, 41, 131, 184, 201–2, 214, 272–3, 274–7
UPDF, 206, 260, 261, 265–6, 294
UK (United Kingdom), 233, 234, 237 see also Troika countries
UN (United Nations), 2, 22, 75–8, 97–8, 118, 123 see also 2013 crisis and the UN
UN Charter, Chapter VII, 98, 100
UN General Assembly, 14, 53, 54
UN Panel of Experts, 289, 291, 295–6
UN Secretary-General, 53, 74, 77, 79, 97, 195, 209–10, 215
    Annan, Kofi, 263
    Ban Ki-moon, 53, 210, 219, 286
UN Security Council, 9, 13, 60, 75, 79
    2013 crisis, 195, 197, 201, 277
    Abyei, 54, 79–80
UNDP (UN Development Programme), 30, 238
UNHCR (Office of the UN High Commissioner for Refugees), 60
UNICEF (UN Children's Fund), 22, 138, 290
UNMIS (UN Mission in Sudan), 15, 23, 29, 99, 109, 228, 237
UNMISS (UN Mission in South Sudan), 55, 60, 76, 96
    civilians, protection of, 98–9, 112, 122, 186–7, 271
    crisis management, 271
    criticism, 98, 99, 101
    Machar, Riek, 100, 151
    mandate, 47, 98, 100, 104, 112, 186, 239
    new mandate, 271, 301
    peace-building and nation-building, 47, 97, 98, 99
    sovereignty issues, 98–9, 100
    troop deployment, 99, 112, 122, 136, 186, 212
    see also 2013 crisis and the UN; UNMISS in Jonglei
UNMISS in Jonglei, 61, 108–16, 118–20, 130

challenges and shortcomings, 98, 104, 112–13, 122, 124–5, 139
civilians, attacks on, 101, 112–13, 121–2, 126, 130, 142
civilians, protection of, 101, 104, 109, 110–12, 120, 122, 125–6, 136
criticism of UNMISS, 118–20, 127, 132, 133, 137, 142–3
disarmament process, 102, 114, 116–17, 118, 120, 121, 132, 143
ethnic violence, 101, 103–5, 107, 112–13, 114–15, 121–2
GRSS, 105, 108, 110, 114, 125, 128
helicopter incident, 109, 111, 122–5, 132
human-rights issues, 98, 114, 116–19, 121–2, 129–31, 138, 140–4
mobility crisis, 125, 132, 133, 136, 137, 140
peace process, 108–9, 115–16, 140–2
reconciliation, 105, 108, 113
SPLA, 109, 111, 116–18, 121–3, 126, 129–33, 138, 143
success, 126, 138–40
see also DYY; the Murle; Nuers
UNODC (UN Office on Drugs and Crime), 39
UNPOL (UN Police), 236–7, 238
US (United States), 6, 13, 79, 100, 202, 233, 234, 237, 277 see also Troika countries

Waal, Alex de, 41–2, 64, 89, 93, 230
Wani, Clement, 141
Wani Igga, James, 97, 150, 156, 161, 162, 163, 168, 195, 213, 214, 284
    corruption, 26, 220
    Vice President, 169, 174–5, 294
Wau crisis, 96, 122, 128, 187, 188, 291
White Army, 103, 108, 110–12, 136
    2013 crisis, 199, 201, 206, 215, 216, 218, 249, 258, 259, 260, 261
Wildlife Service, 196, 235, 237, 239
women, 46, 106, 208, 216
    abduction of, 103, 104, 120, 142, 290
    killing of, 106–7, 126, 204, 290
    see also sexual violence
Wondu, Stephen, 36–7
World Bank, 22, 23–4, 27, 39, 42, 44, 49, 52, 66, 92
World Food Programme, 42, 208, 229

Yiga, Fred, 238
Yol, Goi, 126, 258
youth, 104, 105–6, 107, 109, 201, 202, 205 see also White Army

Zenawi, Meles, 58, 59, 64, 81, 230
Zenenga, Rai, 329